BARRON'S

THE TRUSTED NAME IN TEST PREP

T0267251

Digital SAT®
Practice Questions

Fourth Edition

Philip Geer, Ed.M.,
and Stephen A. Reiss, M.B.A.

SAT® is a registered trademark of the College Board, which is not affiliated with Barron's and was not involved in the production of, and does not endorse, this product.

Dedication

To my teaching colleagues in the United States, Singapore, Hong Kong, and Australia, particularly Dr. Peter Saunders and Dr. Robert Wilks, with whom I enjoyed many interesting discussions about the English language and other subjects over the years.

And, as always, to my wife Susan for all her help and support.

—Philip Geer

To Iris Lowe-Reiss, my in-home editor and wife-for-life. And thanks to my parents, Elinor and Oscar Reiss, who supported me in all of my endeavors.

To Jennifer Goodenough, my editor, cheerleader, and friend.

—Steve Reiss

SAT® is a registered trademark of the College Board, which is not affiliated with Barron's and was not involved in the production of, and does not endorse, this product.

Copyright © 2025, 2023 by Kaplan North America, LLC, dba Barron's Educational Series
Second edition under *7 SAT Practice Tests* copyright 2016 by Kaplan North America, LLC, dba Barron's Educational Series under the title *6 Practice Tests for the New SAT* and written by Philip Geer and Stephen A. Reiss. First edition © copyright 2012 by Kaplan North America, LLC, dba Barron's Educational Series under the title *6 SAT Practice Tests* and written by Philip Geer and Ira K. Wolf.

All rights reserved.
No part of this publication may be reproduced or distributed in any form or by any means without the written permission of the copyright owner.

Published by Kaplan North America, LLC, dba Barron's Educational Series
1515 W Cypress Creek Road
Fort Lauderdale, FL 33309
www.barronseduc.com

ISBN: 978-1-5062-9644-9

10 9 8 7 6 5 4 3 2 1

Kaplan North America, LLC, dba Barron's Educational Series print books are available at special quantity discounts to use for sales promotions, employee premiums, or educational purposes. For more information or to purchase books, please call the Simon & Schuster special sales department at 866-506-1949.

About the Authors

Philip Geer has taught English language and literature for many years in the United States and abroad. He is the author of a number of textbooks and test preparation books, including the *GRE Verbal Workbook* and *Essential Words for the GRE*, and is the director of Mentaurs Educational Consultants.

Steve Reiss is the founder and owner of the Math Magician and the Reiss SAT Seminars, test preparation centers in San Diego. Jokingly referred to as "San Diego's most boring author," he has authored, co-authored, and edited more than seventy books for the test preparation industry. Reiss is also a member of Mensa, the high IQ society.

Table of Contents

About the Authors iii

Introduction 1

What Is the SAT? How Is It Used? 1
The Digital SAT 1
The SAT Format 2
Your Test Scores 2
Using This Book 3
Reading and Writing 3
Math 6

READING

Reading Practice Questions 11

Words in Context 11
Structure and Purpose 22
Cross-Text Connections 37
Central Ideas and Details 60
Quantitative Evidence 73
Textual Evidence 101
Inferences 114

WRITING

Writing Practice Questions 133

Number and Tense Agreement 133
Punctuation 141
Sentence Structure and Organization 149
Transitions 157
Notes Analysis (Rhetorical Analysis) 165

MATH

Math Practice Questions 189

Algebra 189
Advanced Math 226
Problem Solving and Data Analysis 264
Geometry and Trigonometry 311
Levels of Difficulty 339

Acknowledgments 355

Introduction

What Is the SAT? How Is It Used?

As you probably know, many colleges use the SAT as one of several ways to assess a student's readiness for college-level work. Other important measures used are high school grades and teacher recommendations. Unlike many countries, the United States does not have a common national exam that must be taken by all students to earn a high school diploma. In one sense, therefore, the SAT can be seen as a means to give colleges a common standard by which to assess students' proficiency.

The SAT tests skills in reading, writing, and mathematics, using predominantly multiple-choice questions. (Some of the mathematics questions require you to type in the answers.) Because the test aims to assess readiness for college, the level of the material on it is about the level of work done in the first and second years of college. However, the SAT does not require you to have specialized knowledge of any subject.

The SAT is prepared by the College Board, an organization that promotes college education in the United States. Students can go to the College Board's website at *http://sat.collegeboard.org/home* for detailed information on when the test is given and how to register for it.

Students typically take the SAT in their junior or senior year of high school. They can also retake the test to improve their scores. The College Board has a policy called Score Choice that allows students to have only their best score report sent to colleges to which they have applied for admission. Some colleges accept Score Choice, and others do not. To find out if your selected colleges accept Score Choice and to find further information about how this process works, go to *http://sat.collegeboard.org/register/sat-score-choice*.

The SAT tests the skills that you have developed over the entire course of your education. Whenever you write an essay or solve a mathematics problem, you are developing these skills. However, this does not mean that you should not do additional preparation for this important test. Carefully focused preparation over several weeks (or, even better, a number of months) will almost certainly help you to do better—in many cases, much better. Experts with many years of experience preparing students for the SAT and students who have achieved high scores on the SAT agree that the best way to do well is to practice using well-designed materials that provide full explanations of the answers. This is where this book will help you succeed!

The Digital SAT

The SAT is no longer paper test. The digital SAT continues to test mathematics, reading, and writing. The length of the test is two hours and a calculator use is permitted on all math sections. You may bring your own calculator or use the one that is included in the exam interface. The reading passages will also change, featuring shorter passages and fewer questions. In addition, since the SAT is computer adaptive; i.e., it will increase or decrease the level of difficulty based on the test taker's performance. This book will provide you with the most additional practice with drills on Reading, Writing, and Math questions you will see on test day.

The SAT Format

As mentioned on the previous page, the SAT is a little over two hours and contains two parts: Reading and Writing and Math. Each test contains two modules. The first module is of standard difficulty, while the second module is based on adaptive difficulty, meaning how well you did on the first module for Reading and Writing and Math determines your second module of questions. The Math modules now allow you to use a calculator whenever you need to.

Reading and Writing Modules—32 Minutes, 27 Questions

Reading

Passages are shorter, no longer than 150 words, with just one attached question and the same great variety of genres, including drama and poetry.

Questions are broken down into the following categories:

Words in Context
Structure and Purpose
Central Ideas and Details
Quantitative Evidence
Textual Evidence
Inferences

Writing

Questions are broken down into the following categories:

Number and Tense Agreement
Punctuation
Sentence Structure and Organization
Transitions
Notes Analysis (Rhetorical Analysis)

Math Modules—35 Minutes, 22 Questions

There is a mix of multiple-choice and student-response questions as follows:

Algebra
Problem Solving and Data Analysis
Advanced Math
Geometry and Trigonometry

Your Test Scores

After you take the SAT, you will receive scores that will help you to evaluate your performance and tell you where your strengths and weaknesses lie. These scores usually fall between 200–800 in all Reading and Writing modules as well as the Math modules for a total perfect score of 1600. The SAT can be taken multiple times.

Percentile Scores

You will receive a percentile ranking of 1 to 99 for your total composite score as well as for each of your section scores in Reading and Writing and in Math. The percentiles tell you how well you performed compared with other students taking the test. For example, if you receive a composite percentile ranking of 92%, you have achieved a higher score than 92% of all students taking the test.

Using This Book

The practice questions in this book are modeled after what we expect to see on the digital exam. They closely resemble all question types in Reading, Writing, and Math you will most likely see on test day in format, content, and level of difficulty. If you work diligently on them, you will greatly improve the skills you need to do well.

Work through each section, starting with the area you may need more practice in. When you go over your answers, carefully read the explanation for every question you answered incorrectly so that you fully understand the question and how to better answer it. This will enable you to concentrate on developing the skills needed for each type of module of the test. Good luck!

Reading and Writing

The ability to understand what you read and to put that knowledge to work for you in other applications is an important skill that spans almost every interest, subject, or future dream you have. Consequently, the College Board includes on the SAT a portion that tests your reading and writing skills.

Do you want to earn a high score on the SAT? First, learn to read, and then learn to read well. What does that mean? To answer that question, let's break down the process into a few of its basic parts.

Learn to Read, Part 1: Sight Vocabulary

Learn as many words as you can. Know what each word means and how it's used in sentences. "What words should I learn before the test?" That's the wrong question. No one can predict exactly what unfamiliar words you will encounter on the SAT, in your college classes, or in the career you choose. You can make reasonable assumptions as you prepare, however, and you should do exactly that. A pragmatic approach is to learn as many words as you can using word games and puzzles in as many applications as possible. In other words, make learning new words a way of life.

"How do I answer an SAT Reading question if I don't understand what a word means?" Now, that is a good question! Well, there are tricks to the trade—ways to help you figure out what a word means even if you've never seen it before in your life, which leads us to the next key point. The next part contains one of the best ways to answer vocabulary-based questions correctly.

Learn to Read, Part 2: Context, Context, Context

You have years of reading classes in your rearview mirror, so you probably already know about context clues and how to use them. But be smart. Context can be your best friend when you're taking your reading skills to the next level. Context is so important that about 34% of the reading questions on the digital SAT will be about "words in context."

It's easy to practice. Whatever you're reading—whether it is a textbook, newspaper, novel—when you encounter a word that you don't recognize or know what it means, pause a minute. Don't put the term into your search engine to find the definition—yet. First, use all of those context clue ideas you learned in reading class to figure it out. Then, when you look up the definition, one of two things will happen: either you'll feel really, really good because you got it correct, or if you didn't figure out the meaning, you'll have learned a new word that you will probably never forget. It's a win-win.

Learn to Read Well: Application

Application puts together several important skills that you need for success on the Reading portion of the SAT.

What's the point of reading? Why do we learn to read? Reading is an amazing form of communication. It allows us to learn from others in a tangible form that reaches into the intangible world. Like stepping into a time machine, you can read a written work and discover the thoughts and ideas of people long gone, of different nationalities and cultures, and of almost every field of endeavor ever done by humans. When you know how to read and to read well, you can tap into the thoughts, motives, emotions, and ideas of others.

So what do we get out of reading? Sometimes just pleasure. Becoming part of a story, learning a new skill, and discovering a different way to view something can all be a lot of fun. But reading well is also a survival skill. To know how to read well is to know how to succeed. We live in a world that spins around written words—in print and in digital formats. Inestimable billions and billions of words are generated moment by moment, with a person behind each one of those words. Most writers are trying to get your attention, to have you at least understand what they are communicating, and often those writers are attempting to convince you to agree with them. To read well is to be aware of the aims behind what has been written.

The ability to read well is very powerful. Written words should be handled with care, which is why the application step is so very important. Once you understand how words are defined and used in context, you must decide what the author means by using those words in that way. You can easily see the magnitude of this when you realize that in the digital SAT, about 66% of the reading questions are dedicated to the application step.

Here are the main components of the application step.

Structure and Purpose

In these questions, you must identify the main purpose of the text. Doesn't that make sense? Of course, figuring out why—for what purpose—the author wrote the text will help you better understand what is being said. Sometimes you will be asked to select the function or purpose of an underlined sentence or word(s) within the text, or the question might ask you to select the overall structure of the text. In other words, you need to be able to spot what organizational tools or approaches the writer used to convey ideas.

Cross-Text Connections

Think of all the works that have been written in the last 1,500-plus years in just the various forms of English alone. Could there be very many subjects that have escaped the written word? Consequently, you can expect to find multiple writers who view any given subject from every possible point of view. You name it; you'll find it. Conflict and agreement. Shades of difference and outright hostility. Fence straddling and pushing-the-opponent-into-the-deep-end-of-the-pool-type approaches. The digital SAT Reading portion will include fewer questions of this type on the test. Remember that each question will include two passages, so Cross-Text Connections will still be a significant part of the test.

Cross-Text Connections require you to compare the views, arguments, points of agreement, opinions, and so forth of two different writers, usually on the same topic. This type of question tests your skills on several levels as you evaluate what a given author says and determine how that relates to the writing of the other author. In the twenty-first century, having these skills is essential. Technology has allowed writers to post online opinions, how-to articles, advice, and so forth in forms ranging from blogs to e-books about every subject under the sun. Yet, for the most part, very little of what is posted is fact-checked. You need to develop the ability to spot errors in logic and to identify sound reasoning, to understand conflicting viewpoints, and to compare shades of agreement as well as differences.

The SAT Reading test writers are spot-on and include this question type in the test to motivate you to hone your Cross-Text Connection skills.

Central Ideas and Details

You may be comfortable with the Central Ideas and Details portion of the test because it consists of more traditional types of questions. Of course, you need to recognize the main idea of the text as well as the details that surround that main idea. What point is the writer making? Do be careful, however, not to confuse Central Ideas and Details questions with Structure and Purpose questions. For example, I am writing this paragraph to help you do better on the SAT Reading test (my purpose). My structure includes using a rhetorical question, some cautionary advice, and an example to communicate my purpose. The main idea of this paragraph is that Structure and Purpose questions can be easily confused with Central Ideas and Details questions.

Here's the point: When a question asks you, "Which choice best states the main idea of the text?" be sure your answer choice is the main idea and not the writer's purpose.

Quantitative Evidence and Textual Evidence

Quantitative Evidence and Textual Evidence both center on their common word: evidence. In both types of questions, you will be looking to see what the author of the given text is claiming or what conclusion the author has drawn. Then you will use the available evidence to see if the claim or conclusion has any merit. The questions will ask you to select which answer choice supports, weakens, or illustrates the author's claim. The biggest difference between the two question types is where you will look to find the evidence.

- In the case of Quantitative Evidence, you will be looking at images such as maps, graphs, and charts to find the evidence. So be sure to look at the fine details of whatever graphic accompanies the text in order to recognize the correct answer.
- In Textual Evidence questions, the evidence (to a certain degree) will be found among the answer choices. For example, a researcher claims that yellow jelly beans taste better than red jelly beans based on his observations of children eating only the yellow jelly beans at a party. If the question asks you to find the answer choice that weakens the researcher's claim, you will want to look for that one answer choice that provides the best evidence that yellow jelly beans do not really taste better than red jelly beans. This is an example of a possible correct answer choice: "An independent study of the effects of eating jelly beans on the taste receptor cells found that red jelly beans stimulated more positive gustatory responses than any other color."

Inferences

Inference is a type of logic in which you make an educated guess (using your reasoning powers) based on clues in the text and information based on your own experiences (forms of evidence) in order to determine what the writer is suggesting or implying. Once you have made inferences, you can use them to draw conclusions. Historically, making inferences was called "reading between the lines."

Inference questions are often based on lengthy passages resulting in the reader needing to pull clues from several different places in the selection. On the SAT Reading test, however, you will be given just a few sentences from which to gather the clues. Don't assume that this will make it easier. Because the clues will be more concentrated, your reasoning skills will need to be razor focused as well.

Notes Analysis (Rhetorical Analysis)

The College Board has added a new question type to the SAT Reading and Writing modules that requires you to use your rhetorical synthesis skills.

These questions incorporate a bit of storytelling within the questions themselves. They usually begin with a sentence telling you that a student took some notes while researching a topic. A bulleted list of notes follows. Then they give you more information about the student and what the student wants to do with the notes. Sometimes the student's goal is to prove or disprove a point, suggest a plan of action based on information from the notes, emphasize a conclusion, summarize the information, and so forth. Your job is to decide which of the answer choices supplies the best statement based on the notes that accomplish the student's goal.

Be careful not to get confused by all those notes. Find out what the goal is first, and then read the notes to see which ones are relevant to the student's goal. By establishing that information first, you should be able to eliminate the incorrect answer choices quickly.

The SAT also includes the types of grammar and punctuation questions you have come to expect on a standardized test. These include:

> **TIP**
>
> **Pay close attention to conjunctive adverbs.**

- Number and Tense Agreement (subject/verb agreement, pronoun/antecedent agreement, verb tense agreement, and so forth)
- Punctuation
- Sentence Structure and Organization
- Transitions

Math

There are two Math modules on the digital SAT. The first module will be standard difficulty. The second module will be adaptive, meaning it has a difficulty level based on how you did on the first module. Each module contains 22 questions.

Both multiple-choice and student-response (fill-in) questions will appear in the Math modules. The fill-in questions are sprinkled in about 25% of the exam. They do not appear together the way they did on the paper-based SAT.

The questions will be about 35% Algebra, 35% Advanced Math, 15% Problem-Solving/Data Analysis, and 15% Geometry and Trigonometry. All numbers used in the digital SAT are real numbers. The SAT no longer includes imaginary and complex numbers.

Calculators

Calculators are now permitted on this portion of the SAT. You can bring your own calculator or use the one provided in the program. Also available is a math reference sheet with geometry and trigonometry facts and formulas. Both features can be clicked on right from your computer screen.

- Make sure your calculator has fresh batteries the week of the test.
- Do not purchase a calculator for the test that is more sophisticated than the one you use in school. A graphing calculator may be useful, but most of the graphs can be sketched quickly by hand.

- Try to do as many of the calculations as you can mentally; use your calculator or the one provided by the program to make computations that would waste valuable time if done by hand.

The level of difficulty on the Math section of the digital SAT generally proceeds from easy to medium to hard. The following question is an example of a question that would appear in the difficult section.

Example

$$-16x^2 - 24x + m = 0$$

In the equation above, m is a constant. If the equation has exactly one solution, what is the value of m?

(A) −9
(B) −3
(C) 0
(D) 9

The correct answer is (A). When looking for the number of solutions, use the discriminant. For exactly one solution, the discriminant states:

$$b^2 - 4ac = 0$$
$$-16x^2 - 24x + m = 0$$
$$a = -16 \; b = -24 \; c = m$$
$$(-24)^2 - (4)(-16)(m) = 0$$
$$576 + 64m = 0$$
$$576 = -64m$$
$$m = -9$$

The digital SAT includes negative answers for the first time. Another example of this is below.

Example

What is the *least* value of $\sqrt{(x+2)^2} = \sqrt{4x+13}$?

Square both sides, and solve for x.

$$\left(\sqrt{(x+2)^2}\right)^2 = \left(\sqrt{4x+13}\right)^2$$
$$(x+2)^2 = 4x + 13$$
$$x^2 + 4x + 4 = 4x + 13$$
$$x^2 - 9 = 0$$
$$(x+3)(x-3) = 0$$
$$x = -3 \quad x = 3$$

Check for extraneous solutions.

$$x = -3$$
$$\sqrt{(-3+2)^2} = \sqrt{4x+13}$$
$$1 = 1$$

$$x = 3$$
$$\sqrt{(3+2)^2} = \sqrt{4(3)+13}$$
$$\sqrt{25} = \sqrt{25}$$
$$5 = 5$$

Both 3 and −3 are solutions to the problem. However, the question asks for the *least* value, so enter your −3 on your digital test form.

Reading

Reading Practice Questions

Words in Context

When you are attempting to discover the meanings of words, look for context clues, such as:

- **Definition** (Some older churches contain feretories, shrines used to house relics of saints.)
- **Example** (There are some members of the lily family that we eat every day,—for example, garlic.)
- **Comparison** (An oriel is like a large bay window with attitude.)
- **Contrast** (Unlike the silk flowers in the hall, origami is made of paper.)
- **Restatement** (She realized that her new boss was irascible. In other words, the boss had a quick temper.)
- **Synonym** (He sent in troops to quash, or subdue, the rioting crowd.)
- **Detail** (Frontogenesis occurred over central Texas last night. Cold air from the north collided with warm Gulf air to produce thunderstorms.)

Remember, context clues can lead to the identity of any word you may see in an online article, a book you may be reading, or instructional materials you see in your classroom. The bulleted items mentioned above will be your tools (clues) to do just that!

Try to practice by observing interesting words you may see throughout your busy day that you are not sure the meaning of. Then look for the context clues to help! This is a good exercise for this type of SAT question. It also helps to build your vocabulary.

Practice

Each question has one or more passages. Carefully read each passage and question, and choose the best answer to the question based on the passage(s).

1. This text is from Anne Fadiman, *Ex Libris: Confessions of a Common Reader*, copyright © 1998 by Anne Fadiman.

   I call the "to each his own" quandary the His'er Problem, after a solution originally proposed by Chicago school superintendent Ella Young in 1912: "To each his'er own." I'm sorry. I just can't. My reactionary self has aesthetic as well as grammatical standards, and his'er is hideous. Unlike Ms., his'er could never become reflexive. (I might interject here that when I posed the His'er Problem to my brother, who was raised in the same grammatical hothouse as I, he surprised me by saying, "I won't say his'er. That would be a capitulation to barbarism. But I would be willing to consider a more rhythmically acceptable neologism such as hyr or hes, which would be preferable to having to avoid his by plotting each sentence in advance like a military campaign.")

   As used in the text, what does the word "neologism" most nearly mean?

   (A) New word
   (B) Contraction
   (C) Pronoun
   (D) Correct word

2. The following text is from the beginning of short stories by F. Scott Fitzgerald in *Flappers and Philosophers*, originally published in 1920.

   There he paused for a moment until his eyes became accustomed to the sun, and then seeing the girl under the awning he uttered a long even grunt of disapproval. If he had intended thereby to obtain a rise of any sort he was doomed to disappointment. The girl calmly turned over two pages, turned back one, raised the lemon mechanically to tasting distance, and then very faintly but quite unmistakably yawned.

   As used in the text, what does the word "rise" most nearly mean?

   (A) Increase
   (B) Greeting
   (C) Reaction
   (D) Wave

3. This passage is from Paul Fussell, "Hiroshima: A Soldier's View," copyright © 1981 by *The New Republic.*

   I've already noted what "a few more days" would mean to the luckless troops and sailors on the spot, and as to being thoughtful when "opening up the age of nuclear warfare," of course no one was focusing on anything as portentous as that, which reflects a historian's tidy hindsight. The U.S. government was engaged not in that sort of momentous thing but in ending the war conclusively, as well as irrationally remembering Pearl Harbor with a vengeance.

   As used in the text, what does the word "tidy" most nearly mean?

   (A) Clean
   (B) Orderly
   (C) Substantial
   (D) Satisfactory

4. This passage also is from Paul Fussell, "Hiroshima: A Soldier's View," copyright © 1981 by *The New Republic.*

   Understanding the past requires pretending that you don't know the present. It requires feeling its own pressure on your pulses without any ex post facto* illumination. That's a harder thing to do than Joravsky seems to think.

   As used in the text, what does the word "illumination" most nearly mean?

   (A) Exaggeration
   (B) Intellectual enlightenment
   (C) Pretension to knowledge
   (D) Spiritual enlightenment

*Ex post facto means "after the fact."

5. This passage is from Irving Kristol, *Reflections of a Neoconservative*, copyright © 1983 by Irving Kristol.

   A _______ society, a society whose civilization is shaped by market transactions, is always likely to reflect the appetites and preferences of common men and women. Each may not have much money, but there are so many of them that their tastes are decisive.

   Which choice completes the text with the most logical and precise word or phrase?

   (A) socialistic
   (B) commercial
   (C) philosophic
   (D) philanthropic

6. This passage is from Milton Friend, "Why Bother About Wildlife Disease?" from *U.S. Geological Survey Circular 1401*, 2014.

   Some emerging zoonoses cause major economic impacts for _______ because of their presence in food production species such as poultry (H5N1) and swine (Nipah virus). For example, the highly pathogenic H5N1 avian influenza virus that appeared in Asia during 1997 and reached 51 countries by early 2010 caused billions of dollars in losses for the poultry industries of those countries.

   Which choice completes the text with the most logical and precise word or phrase?

   (A) horticulture
   (B) forestry
   (C) hydroponics
   (D) agriculture

7. The following passage is from Alexis de Tocqueville, *Democracy in America*, translated from French into English by Henry Reeve and originally published in 1835. Alexis de Tocqueville was a French writer and visitor to the United States.

   When I _______ to obey an unjust law, I do not contest the right of the majority to command, but I simply appeal from the sovereignty of the people to the sovereignty of mankind.

   Which choice completes the text with the most logical and precise word or phrase?

   (A) demand
   (B) acquiesce
   (C) refuse
   (D) assent

8. The following passage is from "Sustainability and Renewable Resources" by Steven Hayward, Ph.D., Elizabeth Fowler, and Laura Steadman, copyright © 2000 by the Mackinac Center for Public Policy, Midland, Michigan.

   Renewable resources are subject to a variety of ________, often more powerful than those acting on non-renewables. They are inexhaustible in the sense that they can be continually recycled, but this does not mean they are infinite in amount and does not prevent their degradation.

   Which word choice completes the text with the most logical and precise word or phrase?

   (A) stresses
   (B) conditioned responses
   (C) protections
   (D) refuges

9. The following passage is from OECD/Nuclear Energy Agency (2000), "Nuclear Energy in a Sustainable Development Perspective," *www.oecd-nea.org/sd*.

   Many instances of unsustainable resource use can be attributed not only to a lack of a well-functioning market, but to perverse institutional or legal incentives, such as a lack of property rights to resources, or (especially in underdeveloped nations) a lack of ready resource alternatives.

   As used in the text, what does the word "perverse" most nearly mean?

   (A) Convoluted
   (B) Corrupt
   (C) Caused by selfishness
   (D) Arising from obstinate persistence in an error

10. This passage is from Freeman Dyson, *Disturbing the Universe*, copyright © 1979 by Freeman J. Dyson.

    If a scientist asserts that the stars at these immense distances have a decisive effect on the possibility of human existence, he will be suspected of being a believer in astrology. But it happens to be true that we could not have survived if the average distance between stars were only two million million miles instead of twenty.

    As used in the text, what does the word "decisive" most nearly mean?

    (A) Resolute
    (B) Important
    (C) Extreme
    (D) Conclusive

11. This passage is from Elizabeth Zubritsky, "NASA Finds Friction from Tides Could Help Distant Earths Survive, and Thrive," NASA's Goddard Space Flight Center.

    As anybody who has started a campfire by rubbing sticks knows, friction generates heat. Now, computer modeling by NASA scientists shows that friction could be the key to survival for some distant Earth-sized planets traveling in dangerous orbits.

    As used in the text, what does the word "dangerous" most nearly mean?

    (A) Likely to cause harm
    (B) Threat
    (C) Certain to be destroyed
    (D) Risky

12. This passage is from John L. O'Sullivan, "The Great Nation of Futurity." It was originally published in 1839.

    We have had patriots to defend our homes, our liberties, but no aspirants to crowns or thrones; nor have the American people ever suffered themselves to be led on by wicked ambition to depopulate the land, to spread desolation far and wide, that a human being might be placed on a seat of supremacy.

    As used in the text, what does the word "suffered" most nearly mean?

    (A) Felt guilty
    (B) Endured pain
    (C) Objected to
    (D) Permitted

13. This poem, lines 1–6 are from "The Hurricane" by Philip Freneau, published in 1785.

    Happy the man who, safe on shore,

    Now trims, at home, his evening fire;

    Unmov'd he hears the tempests roar,

    That on the tufted groves expire:

    Alas! On us they doubly fall.

    Our feeble barque must bear them all.

    As used in the text, what does the word "barque" most nearly mean?

    (A) Sailor
    (B) Sailing vessel
    (C) Storm
    (D) Pilot

14. This passage is from Sir Arthur Conan Doyle, *The Great Boer War*, published in 1900.

But it was different with the Dutch. That very rudeness of climate which had so impressed the Portuguese adventurer was the source of their success. Cold and poverty and storm are the nurses of the qualities which make for empire. It is the men from the bleak and barren lands who master the children of the light and the heat. And so the Dutchmen at the Cape prospered and grew stronger in that robust climate.

As used in the text, what does the word "nurses" most nearly mean?

(A) Things that foster certain characteristics in people
(B) Persons trained to look after the sick and injured
(C) Persons who are skilled in conserving precious resources
(D) Foods that are nutritious in a cold, inhospitable climate

15. This passage is from "Scientists Locate Deep Origins of Hawaiian Hotspots," press release 09-232, December 3, 2009, National Science Foundation.

The location of the Hawaiian Islands in the middle of the Pacific Ocean had hampered past efforts to _______ its deep structure. Seismometer deployments limited to land sites on the islands did not provide sufficient coverage for high-resolution imaging, and Hawaii is also far from the most active circum-Pacific zones of earthquakes. Therefore, scientists turned to a more technologically challenging, marine approach by placing temporary instrumentation on the seafloor to record seismic waves.

Which choice completes the text with the most logical and precise word?

(A) transform
(B) exclude
(C) resolve
(D) counteract

16. This passage is from W. E. B. Du Bois, *The Souls of Black Folk*, originally published in 1903.

Being a problem is a strange experience,—peculiar even for one who has never been anything else, save perhaps in babyhood and in Europe. It is in the early days of rollicking boyhood that the revelation first bursts upon one, all in a day, as it were. I remember well when the shadow swept across me. I was a little thing, away up in the hills of New England, where the dark Housatonic winds between Hoosac and Taghkanic to the sea. In a wee wooden schoolhouse, something put it into the boys' and girls' heads to buy gorgeous visiting-cards—ten cents a package—and exchange. The exchange was merry, till one girl, a tall newcomer, refused my card,—refused it peremptorily, with a glance. Then it dawned upon me with a certain suddenness that I was different from the others; or like, mayhap, in heart and life and longing, but shut out from their world by a vast veil.

As used in the text, what does the word "revelation" most nearly mean?

(A) The author's realization that despite their different skin color, whites and blacks are fundamentally the same
(B) The author's realization that blacks are not part of the white people's world
(C) The author's learning that not everyone is kind
(D) The author's realization that he could beat his white classmates at examinations and in a footrace

17. This passage is from W. E. B. Du Bois, *The Souls of Black Folk*, originally published in 1903.

After the Egyptian and Indian, the Greek and Roman, the Teuton and Mongolian, the Negro is a sort of seventh son, born with a veil, and gifted with second-sight in this American world,—a world which yields him no true self-consciousness, but only lets him see himself through the revelation of the other world. It is a peculiar sensation, this double-consciousness, this sense of always looking at one's self through the eyes of others, of measuring one's soul by the tape of a world that looks on in amused contempt and pity.

As used in the text, what does the word "second-sight" most nearly mean?

(A) The unique ability of Negroes to visualize future events
(B) An awareness of the injustice of how the whites treat Negroes
(C) The whites' view of the world
(D) A mystical ability to perceive reality directly

18. This passage is from W. E. B. Du Bois, *The Souls of Black Folk*, originally published in 1903.

This, then is the ___________ of his striving: to be a co-worker in the kingdom of culture, to escape both death and isolation, to husband and use his best powers and his latent genius.

Which choice completes the text with the most logical word or phrase?

(A) estimate
(B) estrangement
(C) end
(D) enhancement

19. This passage is from Joseph Conrad, *Lord Jim*, originally published in 1917.

When a water-clerk who possesses Ability in the abstract has also the advantage of having been brought up to the sea, he is worth to his employer a lot of money and some ___________.

Which choice completes the text with the most logical word or phrase?

(A) chastening
(B) cautious encouragement
(C) audacious criticism
(D) humoring

20. This passage is from Gilbert Highet, *The Art of Teaching*, copyright © 1950 by Gilbert Highet.

His methods were, first, the modest declaration of his own ignorance—which imperceptibly flattered the other man and made him eager to explain to such an intelligent but naive inquirer; second, his adaptability—which showed him the side on which each man could be best approached; and, third, his unfailing good humor—which allowed him always to keep the conversation going and at crises, when the other lost his temper, to dominate it.

As used in the text, what does the word "naive" most nearly mean?

(A) Innocent
(B) Guileless
(C) Uninformed
(D) Credulous

21. This passage is from Charles A. Eastman (Ohiyesa), *The Indian Today: The Past and Future of The First American*, originally published in 1915.

It was not, then, wholly from ignorance or improvidence that he failed to establish permanent towns and to develop a material civilization. To the untutored sage, the concentration of population was the prolific mother of all evils, moral no less than physical. He argued that food is good, while surfeit kills; that love is good, but lust destroys; and not less dreaded than the pestilence following upon crowded and unsanitary dwellings was the loss of spiritual power inseparable from too close contact with one's fellow men.

As used in the text, what does the phrase "untutored sage" most nearly mean?

(A) A wise person who lacks formal education
(B) A wise person who has not received religious instruction from tribal elders
(C) A teacher pretending to be knowledgeable but who, in reality, has little knowledge
(D) A foolish person

22. This passage is from Anne Fadiman, *Ex Libris: Confessions of a Common Reader*, copyright © 1998 by Anne Fadiman.

He replied, "Males. I was thinking about males. I viewed the world of literature— indeed, the entire world of artistic creation—as a world of males, and so did most writers. Any writer of fifty years ago who denies that is lying. Any male writer, I mean."

I believe that although my father and E.B. White were not misogynists, they didn't really see women, and their language reflected and reinforced that blind spot. Our invisibility was brought home to me fifteen years ago, after *Thunder Out of China*, a 1946 best-seller about China's role in the Second World War, was reissued in paperback.

As used in the text, what does the phrase "see women" most nearly mean?

(A) Regard women as human beings
(B) Notice women
(C) Take women seriously
(D) Have women as friends

23. This passage is from Anne Fadiman, *Ex Libris: Confessions of a Common Reader*, copyright © 1998 by Anne Fadiman.

What I am saying here is very simple. Changing our language to make men and women equal has a _______. That doesn't mean it shouldn't be done. High prices are attached to many things that are on the whole worth doing.

Which choice completes the text with the most logical and precise word or phrase?

(A) calling
(B) following
(C) cost
(D) market

24. This passage is from Henry Van Dyke, *The Americanism of Washington*. It was originally published in 1906.

    They were really imprudent, and at heart willing to take all risks of poverty and death in a struggle whose cause was just though its issue was dubious. If it be rashness to commit honor and life and property to a great adventure for the general good, then these men were rash to the verge of reckless.

    As used in the text, what does the word "issue" most nearly mean?

    (A) Offspring
    (B) Moral principle
    (C) Outcome
    (D) Controversial topic

25. This passage is from Henry Van Dyke, *The Americanism of Washington*. It was originally published in 1906.

    He ____________ profitable office and sure preferment under the crown, for hard work, uncertain pay, and certain peril in behalf of the colonies.

    Which choice completes the text with the most logical word or phrase?

    (A) pursued
    (B) garnered
    (C) glorified
    (D) forfeited

Answer Explanations

1. **(C)** The author is discussing new words that have been suggested to replace the word "his" used to refer to both males and females.
2. **(C)** Immediately before the word "rise" is used, the old man is described as grunting: "There he paused ... grunt of disapproval," suggesting that he intended to communicate something to the girl. Thus, in context, "rise" means "reaction."
3. **(B)** In context, the word "tidy" means "orderly." The author is saying that the historian can use hindsight to analyze events of the past in an orderly manner. An example of this is that they know the implications (such as "opening up the age of nuclear warfare") of events, whereas the people involved in them could not know such implications. Thus, the historian, using hindsight, can fit everything into an orderly view of what happened.
4. **(B)** In context, the word "illumination" means "intellectual enlightenment." The author is saying that to understand the past one, must put aside one's knowledge of subsequent events and not consider any intellectual enlightenment that comes with considering these later events.
5. **(B)** The clause that follows the blank defines the correct word choice: "A society whose civilization is shaped by market transactions, ..." Of the choices given, only (B), a commercial society, would be shaped by "market transactions."

6. **(D)** Once again, the correct answer choice has, by definition, a characteristic that is unique in contrast to the other three answer choices. In this case, only agriculture includes domestic farm animals, such as poultry and swine.

7. **(C)** The clue to the correct answer here is in "I do not contest the right of the majority to command. . . ." The subordinate clause that introduces the sentence begins with "when," which means in this context "at the same time." In other words, "At the same time I ________ to obey . . . , I do not contest the right. . . ." To contest something is to oppose it. Logically, then, to oppose obeying an unjust law would mean to refuse to obey it.

8. **(A)** The key point of the excerpt is that just because some resources are renewable does not mean they are infinite in amount. That distinction is significant, and the correct answer will provide a word that correctly labels the "powerful" elements that are working against renewable resources. Of the four choices, only "stresses" is logical in this context.

9. **(D)** In context, "perverse" means "arising from obstinate persistence in an error." The author is saying that often unsustainable resource use is encouraged by policies that continue despite evidence that they do not work.

10. **(D)** The main argument in the passage is that the universe seems designed for life, so it is reasonable that the word "decisive" means "conclusive." The author is saying that without the great distances between stars, life would be impossible.

11. **(A)** In context, "dangerous" means "likely to cause harm." This can be inferred because the sentence in which the word "dangerous" is used is about "the key to survival for some . . . planets." A dangerous orbit is one likely to cause harm to the planet in that orbit.

12. **(D)** From the context, it can be inferred that "suffered" means "permitted." The author is pointing out that Americans never suffered (permitted or allowed) themselves to to be motivated by acquiring crowns or thrones, the symbols of "a seat of supremacy."

13. **(B)** A barque is a sailing vessel. The poem contrasts the man who is safe on shore during the hurricane and those people on whom the storm is falling. In the context of this scene, "Our feeble barque must bear them all" reveals that the barque, the boat, must bear the raging storm and must bear the people seeking survival in it.

14. **(A)** The author says, "Cold and poverty and storm are the nurses of the qualities which make for empire." Clearly, he means that hardships fostered these characteristics in the Boers. The author explains: "It . . . climate" (lines 64–67).

15. **(C)** Context tells us that scientists were having difficulty conducting their studies of the deep structure of the Hawaiian Islands. The text includes such words and phrases as "hampered," "limited," and "not provide sufficient coverage." These words denote negative outcomes. The focus is that "the location . . . hampered past efforts to its deep structure." The word "resolve" implies dealing with difficulties, and one of the synonyms of "to resolve" is "to determine," making (C) the logical choice.

16. **(B)** The author describes how as a child he came to realize that black people are treated differently than white people and are not accepted by them.

17. **(C)** The author says, "The Negro is . . . gifted with second-sight in this American world,—a world which . . . only lets him see himself through the revelation of the other world."

18. **(C)** The word "striving" implies a goal (an end). What is the writer striving for? "To be a co-worker . . . , to escape . . . , to husband and use. . . ."

19. **(D)** Logically, an employer will go to extreme measures to keep an employee who has "Ability in the abstract," meaning one who has knowledge and skill and who instinctively knows how to apply that knowledge and that skill to bring the employer "a lot of money." Chastening and criticism will not make a valuable employee want to remain. Encouragement is a positive; however, "humoring" is the correct choice because to humor is to attempt to please and indulge someone by complying with what the person wants, whether his or her wishes are reasonable or not,—in this case, for the purpose of encouraging the water-clerk to stay.

20. **(C)** In context, "naive" means "uninformed," someone who is intelligent but ignorant concerning a particular subject.

21. **(A)** A "sage" is a "wise person," and "untutored" means "lacking formal education."

22. **(C)** The author quotes her father to illustrate the fact that in the past, men "viewed the world . . . of artistic creation—as a world of males." She says she doesn't believe her father was a misogynist (a man who hates women) but that he and other men in the past didn't "really see women." In context, therefore, "see women" means "take women seriously." Clues to the meaning are "blind spot" and "invisibility."

23. **(C)** "High prices" relate to having a cost (a required payment); a gain in one area results in the loss in another (a cost).

24. **(C)** The author says, "They were . . . willing to take all risks . . . in a struggle whose course was just though its issue was dubious." It makes sense that the word "issue" means "outcome" here because a struggle results in an outcome.

25. **(D)** First, "profitable office" contrasts with "uncertain pay." "Sure preferment" contrasts with "certain peril." Next, add to these contrasts the pivotal conjunction "for," which can mean "in place of" or "instead of." Finally, look in the answer choices for the verb that supports the idea of giving up "profitable office and sure preferment" (the one side of the contrast) for "uncertain pay, and certain peril" (the other side of the contrast). By definition, "forfeited" can mean "to lose or give up."

Structure and Purpose

What should you remember for Structure and Purpose questions on the SAT?

You can remember it this way:

Structure = Purpose

The structure, or how a passage or text is written, helps a reader determine the reason the author wrote the text.

What should you look for?

Keep alert for sequence patterns (such as chronological order) and the use of organizational principles (such as cause and effect relationships). Once you figure out the sequence and organization, you will realize the purpose—the reason behind what is written, a statement of why the author wrote the text.

Practice

Each question has one or more passages. Carefully read each passage and question, and choose the best answer to the question based on the passage(s).

1. This passage is from Paul Fussell, "Hiroshima: A Soldier's View," copyright © 1981 by *The New Republic.*

   In an exchange of views not long ago in *The New York Review of Books,* Joseph Alsop and David Joravsky set forth the by now familiar argument on both sides of the debate about the "ethics" of the bomb. It's not hard to guess which side each chose once you know that Alsop experienced capture by the Japanese at Hong Kong early in 1942, while Joravsky came into no deadly contact with the Japanese: a young, combat-innocent soldier, he was on his way to the Pacific when the war ended. <u>The editors of *The New York Review* gave the debate the tendentious title "Was the Hiroshima Bomb Necessary?" surely an unanswerable question (unlike "Was It Effective?") and one precisely indicating the intellectual difficulties involved in imposing *ex post facto a rational and even a genteel ethics on this event.</u>

   Which choice best describes the function of the underlined sentence in the text as a whole?

   (A) It demonstrates that Americans are still so deeply divided about this event that no definitive answer can yet be given.
   (B) It suggests that the wording of the question is unfair and rhetorically leans toward Joravsky's position on the issue.
   (C) It underscores that ethical issues can never be conclusively decided.
   (D) It implies that questions about the past are meaningless because the past remains the past no matter what is decided about it in retrospect.

*Ex post facto means "after the fact."

2. This passage is from Paul Fussell, "Hiroshima: A Soldier's View," copyright © 1981 by *The New Republic.*

   U.S. government was engaged not in that sort of momentous thing but in ending the war conclusively, as well as irrationally remembering Pearl Harbor with a vengeance. It didn't know then what everyone knows now about leukemia and various kinds of carcinoma and birth defects. Truman was not being sly or coy when he insisted that the bomb was "only another weapon." History, as Eliot's "Gerontion" notes,

   ... has many cunning passages, contrived corridors

   And issues, deceives with whispering ambitions,

   Guides us by vanities ...

   Think

   Neither fear not courage saves us. Unnatural vices

   Are fathered by our heroism. Virtues

   Are forced upon us by our impudent crimes.

   Which choice best describes the function of the underlined quotation in the text as a whole?

   (A) It reminds historians that to understand an event in the past, they must imagine that they are ignorant of what the consequences of the event were.
   (B) It makes the point that a heroic action might result in evil and a cowardly action might result in good.
   (C) It encourages the reader to investigate what great poets have written about both the heroism war inspires and the horrors it entails.
   (D) It reinforces the point that the consequences of an action (for good or ill) are not known by those who decide to take the actions at the time of their decision.

3. This passage is from David Alpaugh, "The Professionalization of Poetry," in *Heavy Lifting,* copyright © 2007 by Alehouse Press.

   Still, the term [prose poem] leads us to expect a combination of and tension between prose and poetic elements. Unfortunately, these expectations aren't always met. Examples abound. Here are two excerpts from "Doubt," by Fanny Howe, which appeared in *The Best American Poetry: 2001*, edited by David Lehman and Robert Hass, both long associated with writing programs:

   Virginia Woolf committed suicide in 1941 when the German bombing campaign against England was at its peak and when she was reading Freud whom she had staved off until then.

   Edith Stein, recently and controversially beatified by the Pope, who had successfully worked to transform an existential vocabulary into a theological one, was taken to Auschwitz in August 1942.

   Which choice best describes the overall structure of the text?

   (A) It provides examples to support the author's contention that many prose poems do not successfully combine prose elements and poetic elements.
   (B) It provides support for the view that prose poetry is a legitimate genre.
   (C) It textually demonstrates that prose poems can make effective use of traditional poetic devices.
   (D) It demonstrates that prose poems are uniquely suited for literary criticism because they combine the analytic precision of prose with the intuitive insight of poetry.

4. This passage is from Paul Fussell, "Hiroshima: A Soldier's View," copyright © 1981 by *The New Republic*.

And in explanation of "the two bombs," Alsop adds: "The true, climactic, and successful effort of the Japanese peace advocates . . . did not begin in deadly earnest until *after* the second bomb had destroyed Nagasaki. The Nagasaki bomb was thus the trigger to all the developments that led to peace."

Which choice best states the main purpose of the italicized word in the text?

(A) It underscores that time was not on the side of the Allied forces at the time the bombs were dropped.
(B) It connects the efforts of the peace advocates to those who were supporting the use of a second bomb.
(C) It argues that the second bomb was not necessary because the peace efforts had already begun.
(D) It emphasizes the significance of sequence to the outcome; consequently, it supports the idea that the second bomb was necessary for peace.

5. This passage is from David Alpaugh, "The Professionalization of Poetry," in *Heavy Lifting*, copyright © 2007 by Alehouse Press.

Most obvious is the "prosification" of poetry—<u>the publication of flat, pedestrian prose with the assurance, explicit or implied, that it is the real thing.</u> The notion that lineation is a magic wand that can turn prose into poetry has been uncritically accepted by too many literary editors. So many poets publish lineated prose today that it would be unfair to single out one or two.

Which choice best describes the function of the underlined phrase in the text as a whole?

(A) It defines "prosification" in a way that commends it to the reader.
(B) It demonstrates the major feature of "prosification."
(C) It serves to define "prosification" by pointing out its major contradictory element.
(D) It analyzes "prosification" in terms of form and structure.

6. This passage is from S. Jeffress Williams, Kurt Dodd, and Kathleen Krafft Gohn, "Coasts in Crisis, Coastal Change," *U.S. Geological Survey Circular 1075*, 1990.

Coastal lands and sediments are constantly in motion. Breaking waves move sand along the coast, eroding sand in one area and depositing it on an adjacent beach. Tidal cycles bring sand onto the beach and carry it back into the surf. Rivers carry sediment to the coast and build deltas into the open water. Storms cause deep erosion in one area and leave thick overwash deposits in another. Plants retain sediment in wetlands and impede movement of coastal dunes. Natural processes that change the water level also affect coastal dynamics. Taken individually, each natural process of coastal transport is complex; taken collectively, they create an intricate system that attempts to achieve a dynamic balance.

What is the main purpose of the text?

(A) It discusses the natural processes of the coastal transport system to demonstrate that they are individually complex and to suggest that the system they collectively create is intricate.
(B) It presents a chronological sequence of tidal effects.
(C) It dynamically balances the effects of coastal tides against the larger system they collectively create.
(D) It provides evidence of the sedentary nature of the coastal transport system, implying that ships would be at the mercy of such an intricate system.

7. This passage is from Dai Sijie, *Balzac and the Little Chinese Seamstress*, copyright © 2001 by Alfred A. Knopf (English translation copyright © 2001 by Ina Rilke).

"What you are about to hear, comrade, is a Mozart sonata," Luo announced, as coolly as before.

I was dumbfounded. Had he gone mad? All music by Mozart or indeed by any other Western composer had been banned years ago. In my sodden shoes my feet turned to ice. I shivered as the cold tightened its grip on me.

"What's a sonata?" the headman asked warily.

"I don't know," I faltered. "It's Western."

"Is it a song?"

"More or less," I replied evasively.

At that instant the glint of the vigilant Communist reappeared in the headman's eyes, and his voice turned hostile.

"What's the name of this song of yours?"

"Well, it's like a song, but actually it's a sonata."

"I'm asking you what it's called!" he snapped, fixing me with his gaze.

"Mozart . . ." I muttered.

"Mozart what?"

"Mozart Is Thinking of Chairman Mao," Luo broke in.

<u>The audacity! But it worked</u>: as if he had heard something miraculous, the headman's menacing look softened. He crinkled up his eyes in a wide, beatific smile.

Which choice best describes the function of the underlined exclamation in the text as a whole?

(A) It establishes a point of contrast in the narrative that leads to character development.
(B) It provides a point of climax to the narrative.
(C) It creates the dramatic setting against which the narrative can continue.
(D) It introduces a new relationship to the narrative.

8. This passage is from Irving Kristol, *Reflections of a Neoconservative*, copyright © 1983 by Irving Kristol.

"Scientific" socialism promised to remove the conflict between actual and potentially ideal human nature by creating an economy of such abundance that appetite as a social force would, as it were, wither away. Behind this promise, of course, was the profound belief that modern science—including the social sciences, and especially including scientific economics—would gradually but ineluctably provide humanity with modes of control over nature (and human nature, too) that would permit the modern world radically to transcend all those limitations of the human condition previously taken to be "natural." The trouble with implementing this belief, however, was that the majority of men and women were no more capable of comprehending a "science of society" than they were of practicing austere self-denial. A socialist elite, therefore, was indispensable to mobilize the masses for their own ultimate self-transformation.

Which choice best states the main purpose of the text?

(A) It summarizes the conflict inherent within human nature and how modern science can provide a cure.
(B) It compares the elite classes with the majority of men and women within a "science of society."
(C) It explains why an "elite" group would be indispensable to the realization of a scientific socialist society.
(D) It links the socialist elite to the limitations of the human condition that most consider to be "natural."

9. This passage is from Milton Friend, "Why Bother About Wildlife Disease?" from *U.S. Geological Survey Circular 1401*, 2014.

<u>What are zoonoses?</u> The common dictionary definition in scientific journals and media coverage of zoonotic disease conveys the limited concept of infectious disease transmissible from animals to humans. However, that perspective is inadequate. Zoonotic disease is multidimensional and ecologically complex, as are many of the pathogens involved. . . . Here, it is sufficient to recognize that zoonoses are infectious diseases transmissible between vertebrate animals and humans and vice versa.

Which choice best states the function of the underlined sentence in the text as a whole?

(A) It sets the tone for the selection.
(B) It introduces the subject of the sentences that follow.
(C) It questions the validity of the definitions currently in place.
(D) It suggests that the definition is not easily deduced from the available scientific journals and media coverage.

10. This passage is from Milton Friend, "Why Bother About Wildlife Disease?" from *U.S. Geological Survey Circular 1401*, 2014.

    Threats from EIDs [Emerging Infectious Diseases] are unlikely to decrease, because the ever-changing relations between humans and the environment are a major factor driving disease emergence. The separation between the relevance of zoonoses to wildlife management and conservation and to public health issues has rigidly existed in the past but has been greatly eroded by the current wave of EIDs, many of which are zoonoses. Further, the great costs of zoonoses for society demand that these diseases be aggressively dealt with. For example, of the 868 zoonoses identified at the start of the 21st century, a review of 56 of them revealed approximately 2.5 billion cases of human illness and 2.7 million human deaths worldwide per year.

    What is the main purpose of the text?

    (A) It argues that zoonoses are real and dangerous.
    (B) It narrates the story behind the rise of EIDs.
    (C) It informs readers of the dangers behind EIDs.
    (D) It attempts to persuade readers that they must demand that zoonoses be dealt with aggressively.

11. The following passage is from Alexis de Tocqueville, *Democracy in America*, translated from French into English by Henry Reeve and originally published in 1835. Alexis de Tocqueville was a French writer and visitor to the United States.

    A general law, which bears the name of justice, has been made and sanctioned, not only by a majority of this or that people, but by a majority of mankind. <u>The rights of every people are therefore confined within the limits of what is just.</u> A nation may be considered as a jury which is empowered to represent society at large and to apply justice, which is its law. Ought such a jury, which represents society, to have more power than the society itself whose laws it executes?

    What is the function of the underlined sentence in the text as a whole?

    (A) It concludes that justice is a law that has universal application.
    (B) It outlines the circumstances in which a representative jury should have more power than society.
    (C) It summarizes the justice-law-jury cycle that leads to empowered representation.
    (D) It analyzes each step of how just laws are made, sanctioned, and represented in a just society.

12. The following passage is from Alexis de Tocqueville, *Democracy in America*, translated from French into English by Henry Reeve and originally published in 1835. Alexis de Tocqueville was a French writer and visitor to the United States.

The main evil of the present democratic institutions of the United States does not arise, as is often asserted in Europe, from their weakness, but from their irresistible strength. I am not so much alarmed at the excessive liberty which reigns in that country as at the inadequate securities which one finds there against tyranny; <u>if an individual or a party is wronged in the United States, to whom can he apply for redress?</u> If to public opinion, public opinion constitutes the majority; if to the legislature, it represents the majority and implicitly obeys it; if to the executive power, it is appointed by the majority and serves as a passive tool in its hands. The public force consists of the majority under arms; the jury is the majority invested with the right of hearing judicial cases; and in certain states even the judges are elected by the majority. However iniquitous or absurd the measure of which you complain, you must submit to it as well as you can.

Which choice best describes the function of the underlined sentence in the text as a whole?

(A) It describes the democratic process in cases of unsubstantiated wrongs.
(B) It rhetorically introduces the writer's argument presented as a series of answers to the question.
(C) It argues that the United States has reached a position of uncontrollable power amid irresistible strength.
(D) It connects the European assertions of America's weakness to the realities of its irresistible strength.

13. This passage is from Sir Arthur Conan Doyle, *The Great Boer War*, published in 1900.

Look at the map of South Africa, and there, in the very center of the British possessions, like the stone in a peach, lies the great stretch of the two republics, a mighty domain for so small a people. How came they there? Who are these Teutonic folk who have burrowed so deeply into Africa? No one can know or appreciate the Boer who does not know his past, for he is what his past has made him. It was in 1652 that the Dutch made their first lodgment at the Cape of Good Hope. The Portuguese had been there before them, but, repelled by the evil weather, and lured forwards by rumors of gold, they had passed the true seat of empire and had voyaged further to settle along the eastern coast. . . .

Which choice best describes the overall structure of the text?

(A) It decries the epicenter position of the Boers in relation to the British Empire.
(B) It explains the geographical existence of the Boers in South Africa by presenting their historical context.
(C) It questions the significance of the Boers as a two-republic domain when their numbers are so small.
(D) It provides a deeper insight into why the British view the Boers as a stone in the center of British possessions.

14. This passage is from David Alpaugh, "What Poets Can Learn from Songwriters," copyright © 2011 by David Alpaugh, copyright © 2011 *Scene4 Magazine.*

    And yet, the line between song and poem is not as firm as Sondheim suggests. William Blake called his greatest books of poetry *Songs of Innocence* and *Songs of Experience.* Walt Whitman called the opening poem of *Leaves of Grass* "Song of Myself." In both cases, their work straddles the line between the genres. Blake's

    Piping down the valleys wild,

    Piping songs of pleasant glee,

    On a cloud I saw a child,

    And he laughing said to me

    practically begs to be set to music, and has been by more than one composer.

    Which choice best describes the function of the underlined sentence in the text as a whole?

    (A) It illustrates how very different a poem is from a lyric.
    (B) It provides an example of a poem that is very much like a lyric.
    (C) It shows that only a simple poem can successfully be set to music.
    (D) It shows that there is no difference between melody in music and repetition in poetry.

15. This passage is from David Alpaugh, "What Poets Can Learn from Songwriters," copyright © 2011 by David Alpaugh, copyright © 2011 *Scene4 Magazine.*

    Whitman's great elegy, beginning

    In the dooryard fronting an old farm-house

    near the white-wash'd palings,

    Stands the lilac-bush tall-growing . . .

    is one of the loveliest "songs" in the Kurt Weill/Langston Hughes musical, *Street Scene.* Perhaps the most significant divergence between these sister arts today is the way in which poets and songwriters imagine their audiences.

    Which choice best describes the function of the underlined phrase in the text as a whole?

    (A) It contrasts the diversity that pervades both poems and songs.
    (B) It suggests that poems and songs are really one and the same.
    (C) It emphasizes the close relationship between poetry and music.
    (D) It conveys a sense of family between songwriters and poets.

16. This passage is from David Alpaugh, "What Poets Can Learn from Songwriters," copyright © 2011 by David Alpaugh, copyright © 2011 *Scene4 Magazine*.

Frost acknowledged poetry's ambition to be heard again and again when he explained that his goal was "to lodge a few poems where they will be hard to get rid of." Too many poets programmatically eschew the memory cues songwriters unabashedly use to accomplish this mission. After talking to writing students, conditioned by their professors to tolerate no rhyme or meter in poetry, James Fenton suggests (in *American Scholar*) that <u>they would "be happier if they accepted that the person who was studying creative writing, with the aim of producing poetry, was the same person who had a car full of country and western tapes, or whatever the music was that delighted them."</u>

Which choice best describes the function of the underlined quotation in the text as a whole?

(A) It gives a reason why more music lovers should enroll in writing courses aimed at producing poets.
(B) It explains why writing students should listen to more music.
(C) It suggests that writing students wanting to become poets should draw on their knowledge and appreciation of music in their attempts to produce poetry.
(D) It argues that writing students are not happy because their professors do not allow them to draw on their knowledge and appreciation of music in their writing of poetry.

17. This passage is from Preston Dyches, "*Cassini* Catches Titan Naked in the Solar Wind," *NASA News and Features*, January 28, 2015.

At Earth, our planet's powerful magnetic field acts as a shield against the solar wind, helping to protect our atmosphere from being stripped away. In the case of Venus, Mars, and comets—none of which is protected by a global magnetic field—the solar wind drapes around the objects themselves, interacting directly with their atmospheres (or in the comet's case, its coma). *Cassini* saw the same thing at Titan. Researchers thought they would have to treat Titan's response to the solar wind with a unique approach because the chemistry of the hazy moon's dense atmosphere is highly complex. But *Cassini's* observations of a naked Titan hinted at a more elegant solution. "This could mean we can use the same tools to study how vastly different worlds, in different parts of the solar system, interact with the wind from the sun," Bertucci said.

Which choice best describes the overall structure of the text?

(A) It describes the relationship of the solar winds to planetary atmospheres.
(B) It suggests that specialized tools are necessary for studying atmospheric conditions on far planets.
(C) It questions the need for specialized tools when existing instruments can be adapted and used.
(D) It narrates the story of how previously used observational tools were found to have universal applications.

18. This passage is from John Okada, *No-No Boy*, published by the University of Washington Press, copyright © 2001. The passage tells about the experiences of people of Japanese heritage living in the United States at the beginning of World War II.

First, the real Japanese-Japanese were rounded up. These real Japanese-Japanese were Japanese nationals who had the misfortune to be diplomats and businessmen and visiting professors. They were put on a boat and sent back to Japan. Then the alien Japanese, the ones who had been in America for two, three, or even four decades, were screened, and those found to be too actively Japanese were transported to the hinterlands and put in a camp. The security screen was sifted once more and, this time, the lesser lights were similarly plucked and deposited. An old man, too old, too feeble, and too scared, was caught in the net.

Which choice best states the main purpose of the text?

(A) It chronologically presents the systematic approach taken to contain those of Japanese lineage living in the United States at the beginning of the Second World War.
(B) It argues the point of the injustices suffered during the last world war.
(C) It legitimizes the need for security screens and illustrates their effective and comprehensive uses, as seen in the containment of those of Japanese lineage living in the United States at the beginning of the Second World War.
(D) It underscores the necessity of an organized home front in the event of war.

19. This passage is from Freeman Dyson, *Disturbing the Universe*, copyright © 1979 by Freeman J. Dyson.

The facts of astronomy include some other numerical accidents that work to our advantage. For example, the universe is built on such a scale that the average distance between stars in an average galaxy like ours is about twenty million million miles—an extravagantly large distance by human standards. <u>If a scientist asserts that the stars at these immense distances have a decisive effect on the possibility of human existence, he will be suspected of being a believer in astrology.</u> But it happens to be true that we could not have survived if the average distance between stars were only two million million miles instead of twenty.

Which choice best describes the function of the underlined sentence in the text as a whole?

(A) It shows that he is familiar with ways of thinking outside of conventional science.
(B) It supports his assertion that stars greatly affect human beings.
(C) It emphasizes how remarkable it is that faraway stars affect life on Earth.
(D) It supports his contention that faraway stars can come near the sun and disrupt Earth's orbit around it.

20. This passage is from Lewis Thomas, *The Medusa and the Snail*, copyright © 1974.

For the real revolution in medicine, which set the stage for antibiotics and whatever else we have in the way of effective therapy today, had already occurred one hundred years before penicillin. It did not begin with the introduction of science into medicine. That came years later. Like a good many revolutions this one began with the destruction of dogma. It was discovered, sometime in the 1830s, that the greater part of medicine was nonsense.

Which choice best states the main purpose of the text?

(A) It reveals penicillin as the precursor to modern medicine.
(B) It demonstrates that the field of medicine was not taken seriously until the 1830s.
(C) It cuts away the false notions of what precipitated the revolution in medicine to highlight the true catalyst.
(D) It compares the elements in place before the real revolution in medicine with those purported to occur after the revolution began.

21. This passage is from Lewis Thomas, *The Medusa and the Snail*, copyright © 1974.

Gradually, over succeeding decades, the traditional therapeutic ritual of medicine was given up, and what came to be called the "art of medicine" emerged to take its place. In retrospect, this art was really the beginning of the science of medicine. It was based on meticulous, objective, even cool observations of sick people. From this endeavor we learned the details of the natural history of illness, so that, for example, it came to be understood that typhoid and typhus were really two entirely separate, unrelated disorders, with quite different causes. Accurate diagnosis became the central purpose and justification for medicine, and as the methods for diagnosis improved, accurate prognosis also became possible.

Which choice best describes the overall structure of the text?

(A) It prioritizes the various levels of medical endeavors throughout history.
(B) It presents examples of what innovations were made in medicine that brought it to the point of being a science.
(C) It outlines the procedures that constitute the science of medicine.
(D) It creatively expresses the various theories behind the beginning of the science of medicine.

22. This passage is from Elizabeth Zubritsky, "NASA Finds Friction from Tides Could Help Distant Earths Survive, and Thrive," NASA's Goddard Space Flight Center.

<u>As anybody who has started a campfire by rubbing sticks knows, friction generates heat.</u> Now, computer modeling by NASA scientists shows that friction could be the key to survival for some distant Earth-sized planets traveling in dangerous orbits.

Which choice best describes the function of the underlined sentence in the text as a whole?

(A) It helps the reader visualize a phenomenon.
(B) It shows that terrestrial and astronomical phenomena are fundamentally different.
(C) It creates humor.
(D) It introduces a mystery that will be explained later in the passage.

23. This passage is from Elizabeth Zubritsky, "NASA Finds Friction from Tides Could Help Distant Earths Survive, and Thrive," NASA's Goddard Space Flight Center.

In this new study Henning and his colleague Terry Hurford explored the effects of tidal stresses on planets that have multiple layers, such as rocky crust, mantle or iron core. One conclusion of the study is that some planets could move into a safer orbit about 10 to 100 times faster than previously expected—in as a little as a few hundred thousand years, instead of the more typical rate of several million years.

Which choice best states the purpose of the text?

(A) It names two remarkable scientists in the field of planetary study and reveals their significant findings.
(B) It compares the findings of Henning to those of Hurford to extrapolate the results.
(C) It explains in detail how planets move into a safer orbit faster than previously expected.
(D) It presents the findings of Henning and Hurford to explain the effects of tidal stress on the orbits of more earthlike planets.

24. This passage is from Elizabeth Zubritsky, "NASA Finds Friction from Tides Could Help Distant Earths Survive, and Thrive," NASA's Goddard Space Flight Center.

<u>Surprisingly</u>, another way for a terrestrial planet to achieve high amounts of heating is to be covered in a very thick ice shell, similar to an extreme "snowball Earth." Although a sheet of ice is a slippery, low-friction surface, an ice layer thousands of miles thick would be very springy. A shell like this would have just the right properties to respond strongly to tidal stress, generating a lot of heat. (The high pressures inside these planets could prevent all but the topmost layers from turning into liquid water.)

Which choice best states the function of the underlined word in the text as a whole?

(A) It suggests, in context, a paradoxical relationship.
(B) It implies that the idea is inexplicable.
(C) It shows that planet heating is actually very simple to explain.
(D) It emphasizes the mysterious elements in planet heating.

25. This passage is from John L. O'Sullivan, "The Great Nation of Futurity," a work originally published in 1839 about the relatively new United States of America.

We have no interest in the scenes of antiquity, only as lessons of avoidance of nearly all their examples. The expansive future is our arena, and for our history. We are entering on its untrodden space, with the truths of God in our minds, beneficent objects in our hearts, and with a clear conscience unsullied by the past. We are the nation of human progress, and who will, what can, set limits to our onward march? Providence is with us, and no earthly power can. We point to the everlasting truth on the first page of our national declaration, and we proclaim to the millions of other lands, that "the gates of hell"—the powers of aristocracy and monarchy—"shall not prevail against it."

Which choice best states the main purpose of the text?

(A) It links the ideas of the present to those of the past in an emerging nation.
(B) It underscores the reason why the United States is "the nation of human progress."
(C) It legitimizes the efforts of the aristocracy and monarchy to stop an emerging nation.
(D) It demonstrates a defiant attitude toward learning from the past.

Answer Explanations

1. **(B)** The author's point is that the question does not fairly and objectively present the crucial issue for debate because it can only be answered "no." A person, such as the author, who on balance favored the use of the atomic bomb, is forced to answer "no" because, strictly speaking, dropping the atomic bomb was not really necessary because the war could have been ended by other means.

2. **(D)** The lines from the poem "Gerontion" suggest that when a person acts, it is difficult for the person to know the consequences of those actions and that acting neither from fear nor from courage ensures that history will judge the person's acts as being virtuous. In the context of the passage, these lines are appropriate because the author is arguing that the people who decided to drop atomic bombs on Japan could not know the full implications of their decision. Perhaps "unnatural vices" (the consequences of the atomic bombings) were "fathered by [their] heroism" in their deciding to drop the bombs, or perhaps their "impudent crimes" (dropping the bombs) resulted in their being considered virtuous.

3. **(A)** The author says that the term "prose poem" leads one to expect a work designated as such to be comprised of "a combination of and tension between prose and poetic elements" but that "these expectations aren't always met." The sentence "Examples abound" signals that the two excerpts from "Doubt" are examples in which prose poetry does not meet these expectations.

4. **(D)** As Alsop directly states, the second bomb was "the trigger to all the developments that led to peace." This is proved by the fact that the peace efforts did not gain momentum until after the Japanese had experienced the dropping of the second bomb.

5. **(C)** The author discusses the phenomenon of poetry becoming more like prose. The "real thing" refers to writing that has not lost the essential character of poetry—that is poetry. The contradiction lies in the idea that "flat, pedestrian prose" can be real poetry, which is set apart by its distinctive meanings, sounds, and rhythms.

6. **(A)** Beginning with the premise that "coastal lands and sediments are constantly in motion," the writer takes each natural process, one by one, and summarizes the motion. The purpose is found in the last sentence. We can expect that when such complex natural processes combine, they will "create an intricate system that attempts to achieve a dynamic balance."

7. **(B)** Luo and the narrator are in obvious danger from the headman. At this point, the dramatic tension is broken because Luo's answer to the headman ("Mozart Is Thinking of Chairman Mao") worked and the headman smiled.

8. **(C)** This selection describes utopian-type promises implicit in the structure of scientific socialism and isolates the main deterrent to its implementation: most people don't understand scientific socialism and can't live the life of self-denial necessitated by it. "A socialist elite, therefore, was indispensable to mobilize the masses for their own ultimate self-transformation." This elite class, then, would tell the masses how to live.

9. **(B)** The writer uses a question to pique the interest of the readers, thus allowing the definition of zoonoses to satisfy the readers' sense of curiosity that was stimulated by his question.

10. **(D)** Argumentative purpose is to convince readers of the truth of a proposition, but in this case the writer uses persuasion (persuasive purpose) to convince readers that "these diseases be aggressively dealt with." In persuasive writing, the purpose is not only to convince readers of the truth of the proposition but also to convince them that some action needs to be taken. Here that means people should "demand" action concerning zoonoses.

11. **(A)** The author is deductively reaching a conclusion that if justice has been made and sanctioned as a law by the majority of mankind, "The rights of every people are therefore confined within the limits of what is just," "—in other words, justice. The clue not to be overlooked in this example is the use of "therefore" in the underlined sentence. It is an adverb that suggests a consequential line of reasoning.

12. **(B)** Immediately after posing the question ("If an individual or a party is wronged in the United States, to whom can he apply for redress?"), the writer answers the question piece by piece by examining established American means of redress, including public opinion, legislature, executive power, and so forth. In each case, the answer logically is the same: the majority is in the power position. The majority rules.

13. **(B)** The text begins with "look at the map." It then poses questions about the Boers: How? Who? At this point, the writer expresses his intent: "No one can know or appreciate the Boer who does not know his past, for he is what his past has made him." We can assume that the next sentence ("It was in 1652 that. . . .") begins the historical synopsis of the Boers' background and will continue until it gives the reader some insight into the answers to the questions posed earlier.

14. **(B)** The author says, "[Blake's] *Songs of Innocence* and *Songs of Experience* . . . [and Whitman's] *Song of Myself* . . . [straddle] the line between genres." He then quotes from *Songs of Innocence* and says the lines "practically [beg] to be set to music."

15. **(C)** An elegy is a serious poem that often contains deep moments of reflection and sometimes laments the dead. Yet, it was turned into a song in *Street Scene*. By calling poetry and music "sister arts," the author is cleverly accenting a relationship that is so close that the one art form (poetry) can be converted into the other (a song). Notice, however, that he does not call them twin arts, only sisters. They are each individuals; hence, as with most sisters, there are some points of "significant divergence."

16. **(C)** Robert Fenton is suggesting that writing students tend to be one "person"—that is, they think in a certain way—when listening to music and another "person" when writing poems, and thus they do not apply what they know about music to their writing of poetry.

17. **(D)** Even in scientific writing, which is so often confined to technical jargon and advanced-level concepts, you will find elements of narrative writing (telling a story). In this case, after learning the background details (the exposition), the story unfolds as researchers face an issue concerning how to study Titan's response to solar winds without developing a "unique" (and we can assume expensive and time-consuming) approach. That is the point of conflict. The main character, *Cassini*, comes to the rescue (the resolution to the conflict) with his observations that "hinted at a more elegant solution." What is the solution? "We can use the same tools to study how vastly different worlds, in different parts of the solar system, interact with the wind from the sun."

18. **(A)** "First, the real Japanese-Japanese were rounded up.... Then the alien Japanese, ... were transported.... The security screen was sifted ... and ... this time the lesser lights were plucked and deposited." The writing is in chronological order, and the approach taken by the government was systematic, meaning that it was intentional and step-by-step.

19. **(C)** Astrology is a form of divination based on the positions of the planets, sun, stars, and moon. As such, it is not given much credence among scientists. Consequently, by saying that a scientist who asserts the effects of stars at great distances on human existence would be accused of believing in astrology serves to emphasize facts that are so amazing they are difficult to believe.

20. **(C)** The author states that the real revolution in medicine was not penicillin or the introduction of science into medicine. He states directly that the revolution began with the discovery that "the greater part of medicine was nonsense."

21. **(B)** The author states, "In retrospect, this art was really the beginning of the science of medicine. It was based on...." At this point, the writer lists examples, such as "observation ... natural history of illness ...," and so on.

22. **(A)** The reference to a common terrestrial experience helps the reader to visualize a process governed by the same fundamental physical laws but on a far larger scale.

23. **(D)** The writer directly names Henning and Hurford in conjunction with a study on tidal stresses on layered planets. We can assume that Earth would fall into this category because Earth has three layers (crust, mantle, and core). The writer then reveals one of their conclusions: tidal stresses can affect a planet's orbit.

24. **(A)** It can be described as paradoxical because a thick covering of something very cold—ice—helps the planet become warmer.

25. **(B)** At the point in history when this work was written, the United States of America had no history as a nation other than its struggles to become a nation. Consequently, the author is underscoring the point that as such, the United States will look not to a past that does not exist, but rather to the future as a history about to be written. The author has confidence in that future being one of progress by writing, "We are the nation of human progress, and who will, what can, set limits to our onward march? Providence is with us, and no earthly power can."

Cross-Text Connections

Cross-text connections are the relationships and commonalities we can find in two different pieces of text. The key word here is "connections." You will know you have come to a Cross-Text Connection question on the exam when you see two small pieces of text labeled "Text 1" and "Text 2." When these questions pop up on the SAT, try to ask yourself the following after reading:

- What do the two texts have in common?
- How do they differ?
- How are they "connected"?

Remember to keep specific to the point of the question being asked. If you need to refer back to each piece of text while answering the question, it is OK.

Practice

Each question has one or more passages. Carefully read each passage and question, and choose the best answer to the question based on the passage(s).

1. Each of the following passages is from the beginning of short stories by F. Scott Fitzgerald in *Flappers and Philosophers*, originally published in 1920.

Text 1

About half-way between the Florida shore and the golden collar a white steam-yacht, very young and graceful, was riding at anchor and under a blue-and-white awning aft a yellow-haired girl reclined in a wicker settee reading *The Revolt of the Angels*, by Anatole France. She was about nineteen, slender and supple, with a spoiled alluring mouth and quick gray eyes full of a radiant curiosity. Her feet, stockingless, and adorned rather than clad in blue-satin slippers which swung nonchalantly from her toes, were perched on the arm of a settee adjoining the one she occupied.

Text 2

Up in her bedroom window Sally Carrol Happer rested her nineteen-year-old chin on a fifty-two-year-old sill and watched Clark Darrow's ancient Ford turn the corner ... Sally Carrol gazed down sleepily. She started to yawn, but finding this quite impossible unless she raised her chin from the windowsill, changed her mind and continued silently to regard the car, whose owner sat brilliantly if perfunctorily at attention as he waited for an answer to his signal. After a moment the whistle once more split the dusty air.

Which of the following words best describes both girls as they are portrayed in Text 1 and Text 2?

(A) Pretty
(B) Relaxed
(C) Intelligent
(D) Indolent

2. Each of the following passages is from the beginning of short stories by F. Scott Fitzgerald in *Flappers and Philosophers*, originally published in 1920.

Text 1

The second half-lemon was well-nigh pulpless and the golden collar had grown astonishing in width, when suddenly the drowsy silence which enveloped the yacht was broken by the sound of heavy footsteps and an elderly man topped with orderly gray hair and clad in a white-flannel suit appeared at the head of the companionway. There he paused for a moment until his eyes became accustomed to the sun, and then seeing the girl under the awning he uttered a long even grunt of disapproval. If he had intended thereby to obtain a rise of any sort he was doomed to disappointment. The girl calmly turned over two pages, turned back one, raised the lemon mechanically to tasting distance, and then very faintly but quite unmistakably yawned.

Text 2

Up in her bedroom window Sally Carrol Happer rested her nineteen-year-old chin on a fifty-two-year-old sill and watched Clark Darrow's ancient Ford turn the corner. The car was hot—being partly metallic it retained all the heat it absorbed or evolved—and Clark Darrow sitting bolt upright at the wheel wore a pained, strained expression as though he considered himself a spare part, and rather likely to break. He laboriously crossed two dust ruts, the wheels squeaking indignantly at the encounter, and then with a terrifying expression he gave the steering-gear a final wrench and deposited self and car approximately in front of the Happer steps. There was a heaving sound, a deathrattle, followed by a short silence; and then the air was rent by a startling whistle.

In both Text 1 and Text 2, the arrival of a male character

(A) primarily helps to create humor.
(B) is followed by a condemnation of self-indulgence.
(C) interrupts a tranquil mood.
(D) establishes a serious atmosphere.

3. Each of the following passages is from the beginning of short stories by F. Scott Fitzgerald in *Flappers and Philosophers*, originally published in 1920.

Text 1

This unlikely story begins on a sea that was a blue dream, as colorful as blue-silk stockings, and beneath a sky as blue as the irises of children's eyes. From the western half of the sky the sun was shying little golden disks at the sea—if you gazed intently enough you could see them skip from wave tip to wave tip until they joined a broad collar of golden coin that was collecting half a mile out and would eventually be a dazzling sunset.

Text 2

The sunlight dripped over the house like golden paint over an art jar, and the freckling shadows here and there only intensified the rigor of the bath of light. The Butterworth and Larkin houses flanking were entrenched behind great stodgy trees; only the Happer house took the full sun, and all day long faced the dusty road-street with a tolerant kindly patience. This was the city of Tarleton in southernmost Georgia, September afternoon.

What do these two narrative texts have in common?

(A) They are both describing places that have an otherworldly atmosphere.
(B) They both provide a setting that focuses on the sun.
(C) They have nothing in common because Text 1 is set at sea and Text 2 is set in Georgia.
(D) They both use personification to describe the sunlight.

4. Text 1 is from Samuel P. Huntington, "The Clash of Civilizations?" copyright © 1993 by the Council on Foreign Relations, Inc. Text 2 is from Albert L. Weeks, "Do Civilizations Hold?" copyright © 1993 by Albert L. Weeks.

Text 1

Civilization identity will be increasingly important in the future, and the world will be shaped in large measure by the interactions among seven or eight major civilizations. These include Western, Confucian, Japanese, Islamic, Hindu, Slavic-Orthodox, Latin American, and possibly African civilization. The most important conflicts of the future will occur along the cultural fault lines separating these civilizations from one another. Why will this be the case?

Text 2

Huntington's classification identifies determinants on a grand scale by "civilizations." His endeavor, however, has its fault lines. The lines are the borders encompassing each distinct nation-state and mercilessly chopping the alleged civilizations into pieces. With the cultural and religious glue of these "civilizations" thin and cracked, with the nation-state's political regime providing the principal bonds, crisscross fracturing and cancellation of Huntington's macro-scale, somewhat anachronistic fault lines are inevitable.

How does the author of Text 2's use of the term "fault lines" differ from that of the author of Text 1?

(A) The author of Text 2 is repeating the term "fault lines" as a play on words, suggesting that the true "fault lines" are elsewhere and that Huntington's theory is faulty.
(B) The author of Text 1 uses the term "fault lines" to become the first to use it in this application; however, the author of Text 2 reuses the term as a means of criticism.
(C) The author of Text 2 takes the term "fault lines" into the areas of geopolitical theory rather than only as a geological feature.
(D) The author of Text 1 displays a sense of candor in directly calling differences in cultures "fault lines" that could end in the earthquakes of war, yet the author of Text 2 is more covert in his rationale, attacking the author of Text 1 rather than directly addressing the issue.

5. Text 1 is from Samuel P. Huntington, "The Clash of Civilizations?" copyright © 1993 by the Council on Foreign Relations, Inc. Text 2 is from Albert L. Weeks, "Do Civilizations Hold?" copyright © 1993 by Albert L. Weeks.

Text 1

First, differences among civilizations are not only real; they are basic. Civilizations are differentiated from each other by history, language, culture, tradition and, most important, religion.... They are far more fundamental than differences among political ideologies and political regimes. Differences do not necessarily mean conflict, and conflict does not necessarily mean violence. Over the centuries, however, differences among civilizations have generated the most prolonged and the most violent conflicts.

Text 2

Huntington's classification identifies determinants on a grand scale by "civilizations." His endeavor, however, has its fault lines. The lines are the borders encompassing each distinct nation-state and mercilessly chopping the alleged civilizations into pieces. With the cultural and religious glue of these "civilizations" thin and cracked, with the nation-state's political regime providing the principal bonds, crisscross fracturing and cancellation of Huntington's macro-scale, somewhat anachronistic fault lines are inevitable.

Based on these two selections, which of the authors would agree with this statement: "Most people in the world identify more strongly with the religion they profess than with the political party to which they belong"?

(A) Both authors
(B) The author of Text 1 only
(C) Neither author
(D) The author of Text 2 only

6. Text 1 is from Samuel P. Huntington, "The Clash of Civilizations?" copyright © 1993 by the Council on Foreign Relations, Inc. Text 2 is from Albert L. Weeks, "Do Civilizations Hold?" copyright © 1993 by Albert L. Weeks.

Text 1

First, differences among civilizations are not only real; they are basic. Civilizations are differentiated from each other by history, language, culture, tradition and, most important, religion. The people of different civilizations have different views on the relations between God and man, the individual and the group, the citizen and the state, parents and children, husband and wife, as well as differing views of the relative importance of rights and responsibilities, liberty and authority, equality and hierarchy. These differences are the product of centuries. They will not soon disappear. They are far more fundamental than differences among political ideologies and political regimes. Differences do not necessarily mean conflict, and conflict does not necessarily mean violence. <u>Over the centuries, however, differences among civilizations have generated the most prolonged and the most violent conflicts.</u>

Text 2

The world remains fractured along political and possibly geopolitical lines; cultural and historical determinants are a great deal less vital and virulent. Politics, regimes, and ideologies are culturally, historically, and "civilizationally" determined to an extent. But it is willful, day-to-day, crisis-to-crisis, war-to-war political decision-making by nation-state units that remains the single most identifiable determinant of events in the international arena. How else can we explain repeated nation-state "defections" from their collective "civilizations"? As Huntington himself points out, in the Persian Gulf War "one Arab state invaded another and then fought a coalition of Arab, Western, and other states."

What would the author of Text 1 most likely consider to be the most significant implication of the underlined statement that places it in direct opposition to the opinions of the author of Text 2?

(A) Differences among civilizations rather than differing political ideologies are likely to cause serious future conflict in the world.
(B) All future conflicts among civilizations will be violent and long-lasting.
(C) Differences among civilizations cause wars of great destruction, but these wars serve, paradoxically, to purify and thus strengthen civilizations.
(D) There will ultimately be a major conflict between all the major civilizations of the world resulting in the destruction of all but one of them.

7. Text 1 is from Samuel P. Huntington, "The Clash of Civilizations?" copyright © 1993 by the Council on Foreign Relations, Inc. Text 2 is from Albert L. Weeks, "Do Civilizations Hold?" copyright © 1993 by Albert L. Weeks.

Text 1

Civilization identity will be increasingly important in the future, and the world will be shaped in large measure by the interactions among seven or eight major civilizations.... The most important conflicts of the future will occur along the cultural fault lines separating these civilizations from one another. Why will this be the case? First, differences among civilizations are not only real; they are basic. Civilizations are differentiated from each other by history, language, culture, tradition and, most important, religion.... Second, the world is becoming a smaller place. The interactions between peoples of different civilizations are increasing; these increasing interactions intensify civilization consciousness and awareness of differences between civilizations and commonalities within civilizations.... Third, the processes of economic modernization and social change throughout the world are separating people from longstanding local identities. They also weaken the nation-state as a source of identity.... Fourth, the growth of civilization-consciousness is enhanced by the dual role of the West. On the one hand, the West is at a peak of power. At the same time, however, and perhaps as a result, a return to the roots phenomenon is occurring among non-Western civilizations.

Text 2

But it is willful, day-to-day, crisis-to-crisis, war-to-war political decision-making by nation-state units that remains the single most identifiable determinant of events in the international arena. How else can we explain repeated nation-state "defections" from their collective "civilizations"? As Huntington himself points out, in the Persian Gulf War "one Arab state invaded another and then fought a coalition of Arab, Western, and other states."

The author of Text 1 would be most likely to respond to the example of the Persian Gulf War cited in Text 2 by saying that

(A) there will continue to be cases in which nation-states act against the interests of the civilization to which they belong, but the more significant trend is for civilizational loyalty to take precedence over loyalty to the nation-state.
(B) most of the Arab states involved in the Persian Gulf War owe their allegiance primarily to the West, not to Islamic civilization.
(C) the Arab states that allied themselves with the West in the Persian Gulf War were forced to do so for larger geopolitical and economic reasons that transcend civilizational concerns.
(D) civilizational loyalty cannot be assessed by the amount of intracivilizational aggression that occurs.

8. Text 1 is from Samuel P. Huntington, "The Clash of Civilizations?" copyright © 1993 by the Council on Foreign Relations, Inc. Text 2 is from Albert L. Weeks, "Do Civilizations Hold?" copyright © 1993 by Albert L. Weeks.

Text 1

Civilization identity will be increasingly important in the future, and the world be shaped in large measure by the interactions among seven or eight major civilizations.

Text 2

Huntington's classification identifies determinants on a grand scale by "civilizations." His endeavor, however, has its fault lines. The lines are the borders encompassing each distinct nation-state and mercilessly chopping the alleged civilizations into pieces.

The author of Text 2 most likely put quotation marks around the word *civilizations* to

(A) suggest that it is very possible that what Huntington defines as civilizations are not in actuality civilizations.
(B) make it clear that his definition of civilization is not the same as Huntington's.
(C) suggest the term "civilization" has no meaning.
(D) express his scorn for scholars who use important terms carelessly.

9. Text 1 is from "Sustainability and Renewable Resources" by Steven Hayward, Ph.D., Elizabeth Fowler, and Laura Steadman, copyright © 2000 by the Mackinac Center for Public Policy, Midland, Michigan. Text 2 is from OECD/Nuclear Energy Agency (2000), "Nuclear Energy in a Sustainable Development Perspective," *www.oecd-nea.org/sd.*

Text 1

[A] river system can be dedicated to a variety of purposes: power generation, drinking water, irrigation, industrial use, sport and commercial fishing, recreation in various forms such as rafting and canoeing, swimming, sailing or motor-boating on lakes and reservoirs, scenery for hikers and campers, sites for resorts or cottages, or pure wilderness. Once dedicated, it cannot be used again without disturbing the constituencies that use its features and whose property values depend on them. Some of these uses may degrade the quality of the water, or spoil it for other uses. In some cases, so much water is withdrawn for various uses that not much reaches the sea or ocean—the Nile and the Colorado are in this condition at times. This in turn can have an impact on coastal currents and water quality, salinity of water in the delta, etc.

Text 2

Groundwater resources in the U.S., for instance, are often overused because of subsidies, a lack of tradable rights to water ("use it or lose it"), and a lack of clear property rights to water tables. Overfishing in the oceans provides a better example. It is easy to imagine that cattle might be scarce, just as buffalo became scarce, if they were owned in common and were taken from one vast domain, rather than being privately owned on separate ranches. While the exact analogue to barbed wire for fishing grounds in the ocean may be hard to conceive, assigning ownership rights to the ocean should not be much more difficult than assigning ownership rights to the radio frequency spectrum, as is currently being done throughout the world.

Text 1 and Text 2 are similar in that they both

(A) center on the significance of water resources as the primary agenda in renewable resource conservation.
(B) point out areas in which the current efforts at regulating the use of renewable resources are failing.
(C) fear for the future of renewable resources as they relate to private ownership.
(D) resist the efforts made by governmental agencies, no matter how well-meaning, to interfere with the free-market system of environmental resource management,

10. Text 1 is from "Sustainability and Renewable Resources" by Steven Hayward, Ph.D., Elizabeth Fowler, and Laura Steadman, copyright © 2000 by the Mackinac Center for Public Policy, Midland, Michigan. Text 2 is from OECD/Nuclear Energy Agency (2000), "Nuclear Energy in a Sustainable Development Perspective," *www.oecd-nea.org/sd.*

Text 1

Renewable resources, including air, water, and land, are subject to pressures for different uses, which may be incompatible. Air and water are particularly susceptible to pollutants because of the ease with which they can be used as open-access resources for receiving and disseminating waste. Habitat for plant and animal species may be very sensitive to environmental impacts, and easily destroyed. For example, a river system can be dedicated to a variety of purposes: power generation, drinking water, irrigation, industrial use, sport and commercial fishing, recreation in various forms such as rafting and canoeing, swimming, sailing or motorboating on lakes and reservoirs, scenery for hikers and campers, sites for resorts or cottages, or pure wilderness. Once dedicated, it cannot be used again without disturbing the constituencies that use its features and whose property values depend on them. Some of these uses may degrade the quality of the water or spoil it for other uses.

Text 2

It is easy to imagine that cattle might be scarce, just as buffalo became scarce, if they were owned in common and were taken from one vast domain, rather than being privately owned on separate ranches. While the exact analogue to barbed wire for fishing grounds in the ocean may be hard to conceive, assigning ownership rights to the ocean should not be much more difficult than assigning ownership rights to the radio frequency spectrum, as is currently being done throughout the world.

What comment would the author of Text 1 most likely make about the suggestion in Text 2 that ownership rights to the ocean could be assigned?

(A) It might have some merit, but the results would have to be closely monitored because habitats could be destroyed and what is done by one owner could have a great effect on the areas of the ocean owned by others.
(B) It has some merit, but ownership rights to the ocean should be given only for fishing.
(C) It would be an excellent idea both for fostering economic activity and for environmental conservation.
(D) It is a good idea if owners are prohibited from oil exploration and promise to provide scientists with information on the effects of their commercial activities on the ecosystem.

11. Text 1 is from "Sustainability and Renewable Resources" by Steven Hayward, Ph.D., Elizabeth Fowler, and Laura Steadman, copyright © 2000 by the Mackinac Center for Public Policy, Midland, Michigan. Text 2 is from OECD/Nuclear Energy Agency (2000), "Nuclear Energy in a Sustainable Development Perspective," *www.oecd-nea.org/sd.*

Text 1

Habitat for plant and animal species may be very sensitive to environmental impacts, and easily destroyed. Thus renewable resources should be seen as finite and vulnerable to pressures.... Policy for renewable resources, including pricing policy, should reflect their scarcity value, multiple uses, and susceptibility to degradation or irreversible loss.

Text 2

There is much enthusiasm for "getting the incentives right." This produces nods of agreement on the general level, and furious disagreement about its specific application. "Getting the incentives right" should mean chiefly assigning property rights to environmental goods, rather than using government power to set the "correct price" for the use of a commonly held environmental good. Any so-called "market-based incentive" policy that involves government setting the "correct price" to establish a "level playing field" is inherently flawed, because it misunderstands the nature of markets and prices. The government will always lack the necessary knowledge to set the "right" price, and such policies will usually introduce new distortions into the marketplace that will likely be counterproductive and wasteful of resources.

Which of the following best describes a fundamental difference of opinion between the two authors?

(A) The role of capitalism in government policy making
(B) The significance of the global market to commonly held environmental goods
(C) Renewable resource conservationist versus entrepreneur
(D) The appropriate role of government policy for renewable resources

12. Text 1 is from "Hotspots: Mantle Thermal Plumes" in *This Dynamic Earth: The Story of Plate Tectonics* by Jacqueline Kious and Robert I. Tilling, U.S. Geological Survey, 1996. Text 2 is from "Scientists Locate Deep Origins of Hawaiian Hotspots," press release 09-232, December 3, 2009, National Science Foundation.

Text 1

The vast majority of earthquakes and volcanic eruptions occur near tectonic plate boundaries, but there are some exceptions. For example, the Hawaiian Islands, which are entirely of volcanic origin, have formed in the middle of the Pacific Ocean more than 3,200 km from the nearest plate boundary. How do the Hawaiian Islands and other volcanoes that form in the interior of plates fit into the plate-tectonics picture? In 1963, J. Tuzo Wilson came up with an ingenious idea that became known as the "hotspot" theory. Wilson noted that in certain locations around the world, such as Hawaii, volcanism has been active for very long periods of time. This could only happen, he reasoned, if relatively small, long-lasting, and exceptionally hot regions—called hotspots—existed below the plates that would provide localized sources of high heat energy (thermal plumes) to sustain volcanism.

Text 2

The Hawaiian Islands are one of the outstanding volcanic features on Earth, but their origins have been shrouded in mystery. Still in debate has been a theory proposed 40 years ago, which states that mid-tectonic plate hotspots such as Hawaii are generated by upwelling plumes of lava from the base of Earth's lower mantle. A team of scientists put the theory to the test. They deployed a large network of sea-floor seismometers in Hawaii, through an expedition called the Plume-Lithosphere Undersea Melt Experiment (PLUME), opening up a window into the Earth. PLUME allowed scientists to obtain the best picture yet of a mantle plume originating from the lower mantle and revealed Hawaii's deep roots.

Which best describes the relationship between Text 1 and Text 2?

(A) Text 1 describes a theory in detail and provides some evidence for it; Text 2 describes two experiments that have been done to test the theory described in Text 1.
(B) Text 1 describes two competing theories and the evidence for one of them; Text 2 evaluates the two theories described in Text 1 and reaches a conclusion about which one is better supported by the evidence.
(C) Text 1 describes the main geological processes involved in creating the Hawaiian Islands; Text 2 describes an experiment done to gather information about these processes.
(D) Text 1 introduces readers to the hotspot theory; Text 2 describes an experiment that produced evidence supporting the theory described in Text 1.

13. Text 1 is from "Hotspots: Mantle Thermal Plumes" in *This Dynamic Earth: The Story of Plate Tectonics* by Jacqueline Kious and Robert I. Tilling, U.S. Geological Survey, 1996. Text 2 is from "Scientists Locate Deep Origins of Hawaiian Hotspots," press release 09-232, December 3, 2009, National Science Foundation.

Text 1

Wilson hypothesized that the distinctive linear shape of the Hawaiian Island-Emperor Seamounts chain resulted from the Pacific Plate moving over a deep, stationary hotspot in the mantle, located beneath the present-day position of the Island of Hawaii. Heat from this hotspot produced a persistent source of magma by partly melting the overriding Pacific Plate. The magma, which is lighter than the surrounding solid rock, then rises through the mantle and crust to erupt onto the seafloor, forming an active seamount. Over time, countless eruptions cause the seamount to grow until it finally emerges above sea level to form an island volcano.

Text 2

Combining the timing measurements from earthquakes recorded on many seismometers allowed scientists to construct a sophisticated 3-dimensional image of the Hawaiian mantle. In the upper mantle, the Hawaiian Islands are underlain by low shear-wave velocities, linked with hotter-than-average material from an upwelling plume. Low velocities continue down into the Earth's transition zone, at 410 to 660 km depth, and extend even deeper into the Earth's lower mantle down to at least 1,500 km depth.

Why would a three-dimensional image of the Hawaiian mantle in Text 2 be of significance to Wilson's hypothesis about the Hawaiian Islands in Text 1?

(A) There is no correlative significance between the two.
(B) The three-dimensional image would most likely prove Wilson's hypothesis to be incorrect because "the Hawaiian Islands are underlain by low shear-wave velocities."
(C) The three-dimensional image and Wilson's hypothesis both involve the mantle below the Hawaiian Islands.
(D) The presence of magma contradicts the idea of hotter-than-average material from the plume.

14. Text 1 is from David Alpaugh, "The Professionalization of Poetry," in *Heavy Lifting*, copyright © 2007 by Alehouse Press. Text 2 is from David Alpaugh, "What Poets Can Learn from Songwriters," copyright © by 2011 David Alpaugh, copyright © 2011 *Scene4 Magazine*.

Text 1

Examples abound.... These excerpts [from "Doubt" by Fanny Howe] are part of a "prose poem" that goes on for four pages. Howe offers interesting insights in a style appropriate for a scholarly or critical journal. But it's hard to find any definition from Aristotle to the present that would admit such writing as poetry, certainly not under the term free verse or open form; for it has been the concern of responsible poets in those movements to find nontraditional, personalized strategies for making poetry musical. "Poetry atrophies, when it gets too far from music," Ezra Pound observes in his *ABC of Reading*.

Text 2

In *Finishing the Hat*, Stephen Sondheim zeroes in on the essential difference between the art of the lyricist and that of the poet: "Poetry doesn't need music," he writes, "lyrics do." Poetry is the art of "concision," written to stand on its own; lyrics, the art of "expansion," written to accommodate music.

As defined by these two texts, what is the difference between a prose poem and a lyric in relationship to poetry?

(A) Concise prose versus expanded rhythms
(B) The degree of musical elements incorporated into the work
(C) Lyric poetry's expansive response to the independence of the stand-alone poem form
(D) The degree to which the poem is open verse, determining its classification

15. Text 1 is from David Alpaugh, "The Professionalization of Poetry," in *Heavy Lifting*, copyright © 2007 by Alehouse Press. Text 2 is from David Alpaugh, "What Poets Can Learn from Songwriters," copyright © 2011 by David Alpaugh, copyright © 2011*Scene4 Magazine.*

Text 1

The current popularity of the genre is attested to by Peter Johnson, editor of *The Best of the Prose Poem: An International Journal*. "I have read so many prose poems," he complains, "that I feel as if a large gray eraser is squatting in the hollow of my head. I am not even sure what my criteria are, anymore."

Text 2

Poets who want to achieve wider readership might consider the qualities that attract millions of intelligent men and women to their sister art [lyrics]. First in importance, the primary mission of the poem should be the same as the primary mission of the song: to make the listener want to hear the song again and again.

Based on the "primary mission" expressed in Text 2, Peter Johnson would probably agree with which of the following statements?

(A) The primary mission of lyric poetry is to become divorced from its musical elements to become more adept at conversational components.

(B) The primary mission of all forms of poetry should be to take each form to its most prose-like function.

(C) The primary mission of poets should be to incorporate as much lyricism in their poetry as possible and shun elements of prose.

(D) The primary mission of the prose poem sometimes becomes lost in its radical departure from the lyric elements of traditional poetry.

16. Text 1 is from David Alpaugh, "The Professionalization of Poetry," in *Heavy Lifting*, copyright © 2007 by Alehouse Press. Text 2 is from David Alpaugh, "What Poets Can Learn from Songwriters," copyright © 2011 by David Alpaugh, copyright © 2011 *Scene4 Magazine.*

Text 1

The ever-increasing prosification of poetry assures prospective students that they needn't employ meter or rhyme or cadence or figurative language, or any of the devices, for that matter, in a standard poet's dictionary; that the drabbest encyclopedia prose, even technical jargon, can be hailed as "poetry" of the highest order. It's the profession's way of redefining the art downward to accommodate its talent pool.

Text 2

Whereas poetry is aimed almost exclusively at a limited number of fellow poets, hundreds of millions of men and women listen to songs on power of advertising, remind us that our desire for repetition is based on pulse and heartbeat and the nature of the human brain. It's suicidal for poets to reject their own biology!

What point is being made in both Text 1 and Text 2?

(A) The rejection of the lyric elements of poetry is an error that reveals inadequacies within the poet.
(B) Both prose and poetry are being burdened with such boring and unresponsive elements as technical jargon.
(C) The prose poet's talent pool and the poet's brain are calling for more lyrical elements to be included in their works of art.
(D) Rejection of prose poetry is due to a low talent pool, but the acceptance of lyric poetry is due to advertising.

17. Text 1 and Text 2 are from Milton Friend, "Why Bother About Wildlife Disease?" from *U.S. Geological Survey Circular 1401*, 2014.

Text 1

Here, it is sufficient to recognize that zoonoses are infectious diseases transmissible between vertebrate animals and humans and vice versa. In addition, the animal component has an essential role in maintaining the pathogen in nature for diseases transmitted to humans, for example, foxes and rabies. Humans serve that same role for diseases being transmitted to lower vertebrates, for example, measles and great apes. These revelations have direct ramifications for wildlife conservation.

Text 2

This interfacing of previously disparate cohorts of the same and other wildlife species provides fresh opportunities for pathogen transfers resulting in disease events. Furthermore, the infection of transient cohorts by their resident urban cohorts can facilitate disease transfer to other areas as those migrants continue their journey.

A key player in Text 1 that is not included in Text 2 includes

(A) pathogens.
(B) transient cohorts.
(C) humans.
(D) vertebrate animals.

18. Text 1 and Text 2 are from Milton Friend, "Why Bother About Wildlife Disease?" from *U.S. Geological Survey Circular 1401*, 2014.

Text 1

Globally, an estimated 200–500 million people were sickened during the 1917–19 H1N1 influenza virus "Spanish flu" pandemic, more than 20 million of whom died. The specter of that pandemic contributed greatly to the unprecedented global response following the 1997 diagnoses of highly pathogenic H5N1 avian influenza virus in Asia and the subsequent spread of that virus throughout much of Asia and Europe.

Text 2

Urban waterfowl commonly litter park areas and golf courses with their feces. That type of contamination periodically results in public health agencies closing public swimming areas because of *E. coli* from waterfowl feces. An extremely hazardous feces shed parasite is *Echinococcus multilocularis*, a tapeworm of foxes. People who accidentally ingest the eggs of this parasite may develop alveolar hydatid disease. Because dogs and cats can also become infected and serve as definitive hosts, usually by feeding on infected small rodents (intermediate hosts), they can bring the parasite to one's home as well as to public areas where companion animals are walked or allowed to roam.

How does the scope of governmental response to outbreaks of disease caused by interaction with wildlife in Text 1 differ from that in Text 2?

(A) Text 1: Asia and Europe; Text 2: the United States
(B) Text 1: quarantine; Text 2: animal containment
(C) Text 1: H1N1; Text 2: *E. coli*
(D) Text 1: global; Text 2: local

19. Text 1 and Text 2 are from Milton Friend, "Why Bother About Wildlife Disease?" from *U.S. Geological Survey Circular 1401*, 2014.

Text 1

The emergence of highly pathogenic H5N1 is just one of a number of recent Emerging Infectious Diseases (EIDs) that have wildlife roots, including numerous diseases that have caused epizootics of great concern for society. The World Health Organization reported that in 2006, 39.5 million people were currently infected with HIV/AIDS worldwide and that for the next year alone (2007), 18 billion dollars would be needed to prevent future HIV transmission and provide care for those already infected. A myriad of other emerging zoonoses followed HIV/AIDS to the headlines of major newspapers as well as serving as subject matter for major media venues of all types. These diseases have also become a major focus for scientific investigations and the development of specialized programs and facilities to address them.

Text 2

Duck plague first appeared in North America in 1967 as the cause for a major epizootic* in the Long Island, New York white Pekin duck industry. The subsequent eradication of duck plague from the commercial duck industry of the United States has been followed by numerous duck plague epizootics in urban, migratory, and other waterfowl flocks across the nation.

*a disease that appears as new cases in a given animal population, during a given period, at a rate that substantially exceeds what is expected based on recent experience

In addition, there have been two large-scale epizootics involving migratory waterfowl. Aggressive actions taken to combat urban waterfowl duck plague epizootics may have contributed to the rare documentation of duck plague in migratory waterfowl populations despite recurring outbreaks in a variety of urban and suburban captive and free ranging wildlife populations.

Which of the following best describes the major similarity and the corresponding difference between the two texts?

(A) Both texts are about epizootics, but Text 1 departs from that topic to address the HIV epidemic. Text 2, on the other hand, stays on topic.
(B) Both texts are about infectious diseases involving animals. Text 1 focuses on the impact on people of such diseases, and Text 2 highlights the eradication measures taken to combat disease.
(C) Both texts are about infectious diseases involving animals, but Text 1 addresses the topic from a more political perspective than Text 2.
(D) There are no major similarities between the two texts because Text 1 is mainly about the HIV epidemic and Text 2 is about diseases in ducks.

20. Text 1 and Text 2 are from Milton Friend, "Why Bother About Wildlife Disease?" from *U.S. Geological Survey Circular 1401*, 2014.

Text 1

A recent major rabies epizootic that occurred among raccoons in the mid-Atlantic and northeastern United States illustrates that even a zoonosis of antiquity can reassert its prominence in the modern era as a challenge for humans and wildlife alike. Throughout history, zoonoses also have been the cause of humanity at local, regional, and global level.

Text 2

The establishment of parvovirus and heartworm infections in wolves and parvovirus and heartworm infections in wolves in the United States are examples of disease transfers from infected dogs to wild mammals. Pathogen-laden feces are a common means for disease transmission. Infection of the southern sea otter with toxoplasmosis is an example of the transfer of an infectious pathogen from the domestic cat to a marine mammal (via runoff into the nearshore environment with contaminated cat feces). In addition, during 2008 an *Escherichia coli* outbreak among a cluster of children was traced to elk droppings on football fields near Denver, Colorado and resulted in a decision to cancel football games on fields close to where elk graze.

Text 1 states that "throughout history, zoonoses also have been the cause of humanity at local, regional, and global level." Which of the following events mentioned in Text 2 would probably illustrate that statement?

(A) Parvovirus and heartworm infections in wolves
(B) Wildlife rabies from infected dogs
(C) The *Escherichia coli* outbreak from elk droppings in 2008
(D) Infection of the southern sea otter with toxoplasmosis

21. Text 1 is from Peter Matthiessen, *Indian Country*, copyright © 1984 by Peter Matthiessen. Text 2 is from Charles A. Eastman (Ohiyesa), *The Indian Today: The Past and Future of the First American*, originally published in 1915.

Text 1

The Hopi chairman's brother, Wayne, a prosperous Mormon, proprietor of a thriving Hopi craft shop, with holdings in the family ranch and a construction company, complains in his progressive newspaper, *Qua Toqti*, of the poor attitude of the traditionals toward "their fellow tribesmen in business," and criticizes white supporters of the traditionals for "wanting to keep us in our 'primitive' state." He has declared, "We will never go back to our cornfields and orchards unless we are forced to." In another column in the newspaper, Wayne Sekaquaptewa inquires, "When will someone come along to convince us that we are squabbling like untrained children over everything in the name of our useless religion?" (Sekaquaptewa believes that the true story of the Hopi may be found in the *Book of Mormon.*) Not surprisingly, *Qua Toqti* vociferously supports the eviction of the "enemy Navajo" from Hopi land.

Text 2

The native American has been generally despised by his white conquerors for his poverty and simplicity. They forget, perhaps, that his religion forbade the accumulation of wealth and the enjoyment of luxury. To him, as to other single-minded men in every age and race, from Diogenes to the brothers of Saint Francis, the love of possessions has appeared a snare, and the burdens of a complex society a source of needless peril and temptation. Furthermore, it was the rule of his life to share the fruits of his skill and success with his less fortunate brothers. Thus he kept his spirit free from the clog of pride, cupidity, or envy, and carried out, as he believed, the divine decree—a matter profoundly important to him.

What is the relationship of Text 2 to Text 1?

(A) Text 2 probably describes some of the beliefs held by the traditionals that are held in derision by Wayne in Text 1.
(B) Text 1 represents a better and more progressive lifestyle, and Text 2 describes a lifestyle of backward notions without any ideals or goals.
(C) Text 2 probably describes the belief system of the enemy Navajo, and Text 1 provides the reasons why the Hopi have not forced them from their lands.
(D) Text 1 presents the views of Diogenes, but Text 2 is more closely aligned with the *Qua Toqti.*

22. Text 1 is from Peter Matthiessen, *Indian Country*, copyright © 1984 by Peter Matthiessen. Text 2 is from Charles A. Eastman (Ohiyesa), *The Indian Today: The Past and Future of the First American*, originally published in 1915.

Text 1

The traditionals have always been wary of the white man's consumer mentality, and now they were worried about what could happen when the Black Mesa mine was dead, when a dependent and poverty stricken people, having been left with waste and desecration where a sacred mountain had once stood, found themselves forced to accept more leases and more desolation. This threat was increased by the prospect of legal "termination," or dissolution of a people as a cultural unit, with which Indians are threatened every other year.

Text 2

All who have lived much out of doors know that there is a magnetic and nervous force that accumulates in solitude and that is quickly dissipated by life in a crowd; and even his enemies have recognized the fact that for a certain innate power and self-poise, wholly independent of circumstances, the American Indian is unsurpassed among men.

Which of the following statements best describes the relationship of Text 1 to Text 2?

(A) There is no relationship between Text 1 and Text 2 except as a continuance of the narrative.
(B) It can be inferred that the living conditions described in Text 1 would have resulted in the loss of the Native American's innate power described in Text 2.
(C) The two texts provide a comparison and contrast of two different indigenous groups of people, one living in submission and one living in freedom.
(D) Because the force described in Text 2 "is quickly dissipated by life in a crowd," the Native American people have little choice but to succumb to the powers that want to subject them to "dissolution ... as a cultural unit."

23. Text 1 and Text 2 are taken from "Man-Woman" (ca. 1855) by Lydia H. Sigourney.

Text 1

Man's home is everywhere. On ocean's flood,

Where the strong ship with storm-defying tether

Doth link in stormy brotherhood

Earth's utmost zones together,

Where'er the red gold glows, the spice-trees wave,

Where the rich diamond ripens, mid the flame

Of vertic suns that ope the stranger's grace,

He with bronzed check and daring step doth rove;

He with short pang and slight....

Text 2

It is not thus with Woman. The far halls

Though ruinous and lone,

Where first her pleased ear drank a nursing mother's tone';

Where breathed a parent's prayer around her bed;

The valley where, with playmates true,

She culled the strawberry, bright with dew;

The bower where Love her timid footsteps led;

The hearthstone where her children grew; . . .

Which of the following works best reflects the central contrast between Text 1 and Text 2?

(A) *Women: The Misunderstood Majority*—an examination of myths about women
(B) *Men Are from Mars, Women Are from Venus*—an exploration of gender-based differences
(C) *The Husband's Message and The Wife's Lament*—two Old English poems calling for reunion with a missing spouse
(D) *Gone With the Wind*—a woman determined to restore her home

24. Text 1 is from *The Importance of Being Earnest* is, a play by Oscar Wilde. Text 2 is from Louisa May Alcott's Work: *A Story of Experience.*

Text 1

[In this scene, Algernon has told Lady Bracknell that his friend (Mr. Bunbury) will not be coming to Lady Bracknell's dinner party that evening.]

Algernon. Yes; poor Bunbury is a dreadful invalid.

Lady Bracknell. Well, I must say, Algernon, that I think it is high time that Mr. Bunbury made up his mind whether he was going to live or to die. This shilly-shallying with the question is absurd. Nor do I in any way approve of the modern sympathy with invalids. . . . I should be much obliged if you would ask Mr. Bunbury, from me, to be kind enough not to have a relapse on Saturday, for I rely on you to arrange my music for me. It is my last reception, and one wants something that will encourage conversation, particularly at the end of the season when everyone has practically said whatever they had to say, which, in most cases, was probably not much.

Text 2

Madame was intent on a water-color copy of Turner's "Rain, Wind, and Hail," that pleasing work which was sold upside down and no one found it out. Motioning Christie to a seat she finished some delicate sloppy process before speaking. In that little pause Christie examined her, and the impression then received was afterward confirmed. Mrs. Stuart possessed some beauty and chose to think herself a queen of society. She assumed majestic manners in public and could not entirely divest herself of them in private, which often produced comic effects.

In what way is the description of Lady Bracknell in Text 1 and that of Mrs. Stuart in Text 2 similar?

(A) The descriptions suggest that both women are sincere and gracious hostesses.
(B) The descriptions present both women as thoughtful and caring of others.
(C) The descriptions reveal that both women are self-deprecatory in their attitudes.
(D) The descriptions imply that both women are self-delusional, producing a comic effect.

25. Text 1 is from John L. O'Sullivan, "The Great Nation of Futurity." It was originally published in 1839.

Text 2 comes from George Washington's "Farewell Address" in 1796.

Text 1

What philanthropist can contemplate the oppressions, the cruelties, and injustice inflicted by them [monarchies and aristocracies of antiquity] on the masses of mankind, and not turn with moral horror from the retrospect? America is destined for better deeds.... We have had patriots to defend our homes, our liberties, but no aspirants to crowns or thrones; nor have the American people ever suffered themselves to be led on by wicked ambition to depopulate the land, to spread desolation far and wide, that a human being might be placed on a seat of supremacy. We have no interest in the scenes of antiquity, only as lessons of avoidance of nearly all their examples.

Text 2

The unity of government which constitutes you one people is also now dear to you. It is justly so, for it is a main pillar in the edifice of your real independence.... But as it is easy to foresee that from different causes and from different quarters much pains will be taken, many artifices employed, to weaken in your minds the conviction of this truth, as this is the point in your political fortress against which the batteries of internal and external enemies will be most constantly and actively (although often covertly and insidiously) directed, it is of infinite moment that you should properly estimate the immense value of your national union to your collective and individual happiness....

Which of the following pairs of words best expresses the difference of Text 1 and the message of the author of Text 2 toward the future of the United States of America?

(A) Text 1: pride; Text 2: shame
(B) Text 1: retaliation; Text 2: caution
(C) Text 1: enthusiasm; Text 2: vigilance
(D) Text 1: encouragement; Text 2: paranoia

Answer Explanations

1. **(B)** Both of the girls are depicted as being relaxed. The girl in Text 1 is sitting in a wicker settee, very relaxed, and reading a book. Sally Happer in Text 2 is resting her chin on a windowsill, gazing down sleepily at the car. Choice (A) is not correct because, although there is some suggestion that the girl in Text 1 is pretty ("Slender and supple ... alluring mouth"), nothing is suggested about Sally Happer's appearance. There is a suggestion that the girl in Text 1 is intelligent ("Quick gray eyes full of a radiant curiosity"), but there is nothing to suggest that Sally is intelligent. Neither girl can be described as indolent (habitually lazy) because not enough information is provided to show whether they are frequently lazy.

2. **(C)** In Text 1 "the drowsy silence" is broken by the "heavy footsteps" of the elderly man. In Text 2, Sally Happer looks down sleepily at Clark Darrow's noisy arrival in his old Ford. In Text 1, the arrival of the elderly man does not mainly create humor. In Text 2, there is a stronger suggestion than in Text 1 that the arrival of the male character is intended, at least in part, to be humorous. However, in neither passage does the male character's arrival mainly serve to create humor. It is possible that the elderly man grunts because he condemns the girl's self-indulgence, but there is nothing to suggest a condemnation of self-indulgence in Text 2. In Text 1, the elderly man interrupts the mood briefly, but this does not really change the atmosphere; the girl ignores him and continues reading and eating a lemon. In Text 2, Clark Darrow's arrival does not create a serious atmosphere. On the contrary, it creates a somewhat comical atmosphere.

3. **(B)** Obviously, these two texts are both introductions to stories and are both providing the reader with the settings. The sun plays a prominent role in both texts. In Text 1, "the sun was shying little golden disks at the sea—if you gazed intently enough you could see them skip from wave tip to wave tip until they joined a broad collar of golden coin that was collecting half a mile out and would eventually be a dazzling sunset." Text 2 includes simile as the "sunlight dripped over the house like golden paint over an art jar."

4. **(A)** Huntington's social theory is that "The most important conflicts of the future will occur along the cultural fault lines separating these civilizations from one another,"; in other words, future conflicts will be between civilizations. Weeks takes exception to this idea by taking Huntington's concept of "fault lines" and redefining it on two levels (using the term as a play on words). First, he says that Huntington's "endeavor ... has its fault lines," suggesting weak spots in his rationale. Second, Weeks says that the real "fault lines" are the "borders encompassing each distinct nation-state and mercilessly chopping the alleged civilizations into pieces." Of interest is Weeks's use of the word "alleged" in describing "civilizations," as this term suggests that he would even differ with Huntington on what constitutes a civilization.

5. **(B)** The author of Text 1 writes, "Civilizations are differentiated from each other by history, language, culture, tradition and, most important, religion" and "[These differences] are far more fundamental than differences among political ideologies." We can infer from this that the author believes that most people identify more strongly with their religion than with their political party. The author of Text 2, on the other hand, sees "the religious glue" as "thin and cracked."

6. **(A)** The author of Text 1 is arguing that what he considers the most fundamental differences among civilizations ("Civilizations are differentiated ... equality and hierarchy") have "over the centuries ... generated the most prolonged and the most violent conflicts." It is reasonable to suppose that the author would consider the most important implication of the statement to be that differences among civilizations rather than differing political ideologies will cause serious future conflict in the world.

7. **(A)** The author of Text 1 does not argue that all conflict is at present caused by conflicts among civilizations or that this will be true in the future. He argues that "the world will be shaped in large measure by the interactions among seven or eight major civilizations" and that "the most important conflicts of the future will occur along the cultural fault lines separating these civilizations from one another." Thus, he would be likely to say that the Persian Gulf War is an example of nation-states putting their interests ahead of the interests of the civilization to which they belong. However, this one example does not invalidate his four-point argument that civilizational loyalty is becoming more important than loyalty to the nation-state in causing conflict in the world.

8. **(A)** After describing Huntington's classification as "[identifying] determinants [of international events] on a grand scale by 'civilizations,'" the author of Text 2 describes what he sees as the difficulties with Huntington's classification: "His endeavor, however, has its own fault lines. The lines are the borders encompassing each distinct nation-state and mercilessly chopping the alleged civilizations into pieces." From this we can infer that the author of Text 2 has serious doubts about whether the term "civilization" can be applied to the entities described as such by Huntington.

9. **(B)** Text 1 blames the overuse and degradation of river systems dedicated to commercial purposes on the fact that such water sources cannot be changed because of the impact on property values of constituencies. Text 2 blames overuse of groundwater resources on "a lack of tradable rights to water ..., and a lack of clear property rights to water tables."

10. **(A)** The author of Text 1 says, "Air and water are particularly susceptible to pollutants because of the ease with which they can be used as open-access resources for receiving and disseminating waste." Thus, he would probably argue for close monitoring of the results of assigning ownership rights. In his discussion of the example of a river system, the author stresses that the various uses it is put to can have a great effect on other uses it has on the system itself and on things outside the system related to it. Thus, it is likely he would be concerned about the effects of the activity of one owner on the parts of the ocean owned by others.

11. **(D)** The author of Text 2 sees unsound government policies, particularly in pricing, as an unsuccessful means to protect natural resources from destruction, whereas the author of Text 1 suggests that we look to creating policy, including pricing, for renewable resources to protect them.

12. **(D)** Text 1 poses a question: "How do the Hawaiian Islands and other volcanoes that form in the interior of plates fit into the plate-tectonics picture?" The answer to that question introduces the reader to the hotspot theory, which says that hotspots exist "below the plates that would provide localized sources of high heat energy (thermal plumes) to sustain volcanism." Text 2 not only tells us that an experiment (called PLUME) was conducted to "put the [hotspot] theory to the test," but also claims that the outcome of the experiment "obtain[ed] the best picture yet of a mantle plume originating from the lower mantle," suggesting that they did find evidence supporting the theory.

13. **(C)** A data-producing three-dimensional image of the upper mantle, transition zone, and lower mantle under the Hawaiian Islands would enable researchers to pinpoint the areas that Wilson claims are instrumental in the formation of the island, including the "deep, stationary hotspot in the mantle," "the melting [of] the overriding Pacific Plate," as well as the formation of the seamount and eventual volcanic mountain.

14. **(B)** This is a matter of opposing extremes: the prose poem sometimes lacks the musical elements of poetry; the lyric can be so musical it is no longer concise as is a poem.

15. **(D)** Johnson "complains" about reading so many prose poems that we can assume that he does not want to read or listen to very many of them "over and over again," as one would want to read or listen to a poem that, like a song, incorporates lyric elements.

16. **(A)** "It's the profession's way of redefining the art downward to accommodate its talent pool" in Text 1 implies that the writers of prose poems that are completely devoid of the traditional elements of poetry, which would include lyrical components, are incapable of writing true poetry. Text 2 continues the critique of poets by stating, "It's suicidal for poets to reject their own biology!" This statement suggests that the poet's own body is calling for lyric elements to be part of the poem.

17. **(C)** Text 2 focuses on transient cohorts/groups of wildlife that transfer disease to other wildlife as they migrate through an area; Text 1 is primarily concerned with disease transfer not just among wildlife but also between wildlife and humans.

18. **(D)** Text 1 tells us that H5N1 sparked an "unprecedented global response." In Text 2 we can assume, because of the action taken (public health agencies closing public swimming areas), that the response was on a more localized level. Text 2 never reveals in what country or area the public swimming areas were closed.

19. **(B)** Text 1 is about the "Emerging Infectious Diseases (EIDs) that have wildlife roots, including numerous diseases that have caused epizootics of great concern for society." Text 2 likewise discusses epizootics, specifically duck plague. In contrast, however, the effects on people are the main area of concern in Text 1, citing the almost 40 million people with HIV/AIDS in 2006, the costs of combating the disease in people, and the investigations and programs the disease has spurred. Text 2 deals very little with the impact on humans and instead talks mostly about ramifications of duck plague from various perspectives.

20. **(C)** The *Escherichia coli* outbreak of 2008 involved contraction of the disease by children, a circumstance that we can reasonably assume would become a major cause of humanity at every level.

21. **(A)** We can infer that the religion that Wayne considers "useless" in Text 1 is that of the "traditionals." Consequently, when Text 2 describes the Native American religion as one that "forbade the accumulation of wealth and the enjoyment of luxury," the clash between Wayne, who is described as prosperous with many holdings, and the religion of the traditionals becomes easy to understand.

22. **(B)** Text 2 states "that for an innate power and self-poise, wholly independent of circumstances, the American Indian is unsurpassed among men." That "innate power" was the result of "a magnetic and nervous force" acquired from living outdoors. However, the Native Americans described in Text 1 are no longer living outdoors but, rather, are living in fear, dependence, and poverty.

23. **(B)** "*Man's home is everywhere*" in Text 1 but "*It is not thus with Woman*" in Text 2 immediately tells you that these texts are providing a contrast between man and woman. The fact that the poet italicized these lines indicates intent. Only choice (B) provides a title that correlates to the idea that "home" means something different for man than it does for woman.

24. **(D)** Lady Bracknell in Text 1 has the idea that she can tell an ill man "not to have a relapse on Saturday, for I rely on you to arrange my music for me." Likewise in Text 2, Mrs. Steward "chose to think herself a queen of society," but the author tells us that her manners were "assumed" to the point that she even acted that way in private, implying that she was deluding herself.

25. **(C)** The enthusiasm of the author of Text 1 is evident when he says, "America is destined for better deeds." He does not entertain even the possibility of the American government at some future point repeating any of the sins of other nations. Although Washington does express enthusiasm as well when he speaks of the value of the "unity of government" that the nation was enjoying at that point in time, he goes into detail warning the listeners against covert and insidious efforts on the part of enemies to destroy America's unity in the future. The implication of this warning is the need for an increased sense of vigilance against such attacks.

Central Ideas and Details

Remember that the central or main idea is a statement of the writer's point. Try not to confuse it with the author's purpose. The central idea always comes with supporting details found in the text or passage. You want to look at the following:

- Who?
- What?
- Where?
- When?
- How?

After reading the entire passage, reread it first to identify the topic and then to see what the author is saying about the topic. Keep in mind that it is OK if you need to read the short passage a few times to find the correct details. Some are harder to see than others.

Practice

Each question has one or more passages. Carefully read each passage and question, and choose the best answer to the question based on the passage(s).

1. This passage is from John Okada, *No-No Boy*, published by the University of Washington Press, copyright © 2001.

   The lieutenant who operated the radar-detection equipment was a blond giant from Nebraska. The lieutenant from Nebraska said: "Where you from?" The Japanese-American who was an American soldier answered: "No place in particular." "You got folks?" "Yeah, I got folks." "Where at?" "Wyoming, out in the desert." "Farmers, huh?" "Not quite." "What's that mean?" "Well, it's this way. . . . ." And then the Japanese-American whose folks were still Japanese-Japanese, or else they would not be in a camp with barbed wire and watchtowers with soldiers holding rifles, told the blond giant from Nebraska about the removal of the Japanese from the Coast, which was called the evacuation, and about the concentration camps, which were called relocation centers.

   According to the text, at the time of this account the narrator's parents are

   (A) living on their farm in Wyoming.
   (B) living in Japan.
   (C) living in a relocation camp in Wyoming.
   (D) deceased.

2. This passage is from Freeman Dyson, *Disturbing the Universe*, copyright © 1979 by Freeman J. Dyson.

There are some striking examples in the laws of nuclear physics of numerical accidents that seem to conspire to make the universe habitable. The strength of the attractive nuclear force is just sufficient to overcome the electrical repulsion between the positive charges in the nuclei of ordinary atoms such as oxygen or iron. But the nuclear forces are not quite strong enough to bind together two protons (hydrogen nuclei) into a bound system which would be called a diproton if it existed. If the nuclear forces had been slightly stronger than they are, the diproton would exist and almost all the hydrogen in the universe would have been combined into diprotons and heavier nuclei. Hydrogen would be a rare element, and stars like the sun, which live for a long time by the slow burning of hydrogen in their cores, could not exist. On the other hand, if the nuclear forces had been substantially weaker than they are, hydrogen could not burn at all and there would be no heavy elements.

According to the text, if the nuclear forces in atoms had been slightly stronger than they are,

(A) there would be many more stars like the sun than there are.
(B) the universe would be made up of over 99% hydrogen.
(C) most of the hydrogen in the universe would have burned up.
(D) stars like the sun would not exist.

3. This passage is from Lewis Thomas, *The Medusa and the Snail*, copyright © 1974.

It is customary to place the date for the beginnings of modern medicine somewhere in the mid-1930s, with the entry of sulfonamides and penicillin into the pharmacopoeia, and it is usual to ascribe to these events the force of a revolution in medical practice. This is what things seemed like at the time. Medicine was upheaved, revolutionized indeed. Therapy had been discovered for great numbers of patients whose illnesses had previously been untreatable. Cures were now available. It seemed a totally new world. Doctors could now cure disease, and this was astonishing, most of all to the doctors themselves.

Why, according to the text, were doctors astonished around the mid-1930s?

(A) They were amazed that drugs were able to cure diseases.
(B) Cures were becoming available for some illnesses, whereas before these doctors had little capacity to cure illnesses.
(C) The practice of medicine was being revolutionized by a bold young breed of doctors.
(D) They were surprised that people still had so much respect for doctors and medicine.

4. This passage is from Irving Kristol, *Reflections of a Neoconservative*, copyright © 1983 by Irving Kristol.

   Throughout history, artists and writers have been candidly contemptuous of commercial activity between consenting adults, regarding it as an activity that tends to coarsen and trivialize the human spirit. And since bourgeois society was above all else a commercial society—the first in all of recorded history in which the commercial ethos was sovereign over all others—their exasperation was bound to be all the more acute. Later on, the term "philistinism" would emerge to encapsulate this sentiment.

   According to the text, the term "philistinism" arose because

   (A) artists and writers became aware that they would increasingly have to participate in commercial activities.
   (B) artists and writers became increasingly frustrated and annoyed as society became more commercial and bourgeois.
   (C) a new word had to be found to refer to the new commercial ethos that was emerging in the eighteenth century.
   (D) artists and writers needed a word to conveniently describe their changing role in bourgeois society.

5. This passage is from Milton Friend, "Why Bother About Wildlife Disease?" from *U.S. Geological Survey Circular 1401*, 2014.

   The general importance of zoonoses for humanity has waxed and waned over time in concert with changing conditions including changes in the number of human cases and (or) exposures associated with enzootic areas, such as chronic disease presence and activity levels, for specific zoonoses. The occurrence of major epizootics or epidemics involving the expansion of established geographic range for specific diseases and (or) the appearance of "new" zoonoses within a geographic area is also of great concern.

   According to the text,

   (A) the effects of zoonoses on human beings have remained relatively consistent through human history.
   (B) zoonoses have had little effect on human activities.
   (C) zoonoses have often been the decisive factor in the extinction of civilizations.
   (D) the effects of zoonoses on human beings have varied considerably through human history.

6. This passage is from Milton Friend, "Why Bother About Wildlife Disease?" from *U.S. Geological Survey Circular 1401*, 2014.

   Rabies is a well-established zoonosis and, except for anthrax, perhaps the next earliest zoonosis to confront humans. The first recorded description of canine rabies dates back to about 500 B.C. Rabies is an important zoonosis in much of the world, because death is the outcome once clinical signs appear. Human deaths from rabies are rare in the United States, but the disease is diagnosed annually in wildlife and other animals where it continues to cause periodic epizootics.

   According to the text, rabies

   (A) is maintained in nature by animals.
   (B) affects only domesticated animals.
   (C) is no longer a threat to human life.
   (D) cannot be transmitted from an animal to a human.

7. The following passage is from Alexis de Tocqueville, *Democracy in America*, translated from French into English by Henry Reeve and originally published in 1835. Alexis de Tocqueville was a French writer and visitor to the United States.

   A majority taken collectively is only an individual, whose opinions, and frequently whose interests, are opposed to those of another individual, who is styled a minority. If it be admitted that a man possessing absolute power may misuse that power by wronging his adversaries, why should not a majority be liable to the same reproach?

   According to the text,

   (A) it is possible for a majority to establish an unjust law.
   (B) what is decided by a majority in a society is always just.
   (C) what is just cannot be decided by human beings.
   (D) what is just can be decided only by the members of that society for that society.

8. The following passage is from Alexis de Tocqueville, *Democracy in America*, translated from French into English by Henry Reeve and originally published in 1835. Alexis de Tocqueville was a French writer and visitor to the United States.

   I am therefore of the opinion that social power superior to all others must always be placed somewhere; but I think that liberty is endangered when this power finds no obstacle which can retard its course and give it time to moderate its own vehemence.

   According to the text,

   (A) once superior power is placed into the hands of a single group, nothing will be able to limit its power.
   (B) to preserve freedom, it is necessary for there to be some opposition to the dominant power group in a society.
   (C) individual liberty is not possible when a society is dominated by a single principle.
   (D) individual liberty is possible only when society is dominated by a powerful minority.

9. This passage is from Peter Matthiessen, *Indian Country*, copyright © 1984 by Peter Matthiessen.

   By eliminating an Indian nation termination quiets Indian claims to tribal lands that were never ceded to the U.S. government by treaty, which happens to describe almost all the "federal" land in the Far West; instead, the people must accept whatever monetary settlement has been bestowed upon them by the Court of Claims, which was set up not to administer justice but to expedite adjudication of land titles and head off any future claims that Indians might make on lands already coveted by the white economy.

   According to the text, the Court of Claims

   (A) adjudicates cases fairly.
   (B) almost always favors Indian claims to land over white claims to land.
   (C) has little real effect on Indian affairs.
   (D) is biased toward white people in its judgments.

10. This passage is from Henry Van Dyke, *The Americanism of Washington*. It was originally published in 1906.

    I see Benjamin Franklin, in the Congress of 1776, already past his seventieth year, prosperous, famous, by far the most celebrated man in America, accepting without demur the difficult and dangerous mission to France, and whispering to his friend, Dr. Rush, "I am old and good for nothing, but as the store-keepers say of their remnants of cloth, 'I am but a fag-end, and you may have me for what you please.'"

    According to the text, which of the following is not true about Benjamin Franklin?

    (A) He was wise.
    (B) He believed deeply in natural rights and liberty.
    (C) He never went to Europe.
    (D) He was widely admired in his country.

11. This passage is from Henry Van Dyke, *The Americanism of Washington*. It was originally published in 1906.

    He made no extravagant claims for his own motives, and some of his ways were not distinctly ideal. He was full of prudential proverbs and claimed to be a follower of the theory of enlightened self-interest. But there was not a faculty of his wise old head which he did not put at the service of his country, nor was there a pulse of his slow and steady heart which did not beat loyal to the cause of freedom.

    According to the text, Benjamin Franklin said that he was

    (A) motivated by what would benefit him.
    (B) motivated to action by the highest ideals.
    (C) chivalrous.
    (D) the most useful person that his country could send on a mission to France.

12. This passage is from Suparna Choudhury, "Culturing the Adolescent Brain: What Can Neuroscience Learn from Anthropology?" in *Social Cognitive and Affective Neuroscience*, 2010.

All of these factors were thought to make Samoan adolescence relatively tranquil and enjoyable and led to Mead's assertion of the primacy of nurture over nature.

According to the text, from her observation that adolescence in Samoa is different from adolescence in America, Margaret Mead argued that

(A) Samoan culture is different from American culture.
(B) culture has a larger part in shaping human behavior than does genetics.
(C) girls are treated better in Samoa than they are in America.
(D) people go through the same basic life experiences in all societies but do so at different times in their lives.

13. This passage is from Suparna Choudhury, "Culturing the Adolescent Brain: What Can Neuroscience Learn from Anthropology?" in *Social Cognitive and Affective Neuroscience*, 2010.

Schlegel and Barry's cross-cultural study of adolescents in tribal and traditional societies using data collected from over 175 societies around the world demonstrated that adolescence as a distinctive, socially marked stage of life is ubiquitous. These researchers put forward a biosocial theory, arguing that the social stage of adolescence is a response to the development of the reproductive capacity.

According to the text, Schlegel and Barry's cross-cultural study of adolescents in tribal and traditional societies showed that

(A) the phenomenon of adolescence is found everywhere.
(B) adolescence is a time of great conflict in every society.
(C) antisocial behavior always increases during adolescence.
(D) adolescent boys become aggressive in every society.

14. This passage is from Gilbert Highet, *The Art of Teaching*, copyright © 1950 by Gilbert Highet.

In that, perhaps, they are the ancestors of the modern journalists who have the knack of turning out a bright and interesting article on any new subject, without using special or expert information. The sophists dazzled everyone without convincing anyone of anything positive. They argued unsystematically and unfairly, but painted over the gaps in their reasoning with glossy rhetoric. They had few constructive ideas, and won most applause by taking traditional notions and showing they were based on convention rather than logic. They demonstrated that almost anything could be proved by a fast talker—sometimes they made a powerful speech on one side of a question in the morning and an equally powerful speech on the opposite side in the afternoon.

According to the text, what is not true about the sophists?

(A) They used superficial elements of the art of persuasion in their arguments.
(B) They were fast talkers.
(C) Some of them were very effective at proving their points.
(D) They were always scrupulously fair in arguments.

15. This passage is from Milton Friend, "Why Bother About Wildlife Disease?" from *U.S. Geological Survey Circular 1401*, 2014.

However, in some instances the culling of urban waterfowl collections infected by duck plague has been vigorously opposed by various segments of society. That opposition highlights one of the difficulties associated with wildlife disease management within urban environments; companion animal status conferred upon these waterfowl by segments of the public may interfere with needed disease control actions and facilitate disease establishment and spread when eradication was possible.

According to the text, a difficulty faced by authorities in charge of wildlife management in urban areas is that

(A) people in urban areas often have little interest in wildlife.
(B) many people in urban areas take action to destroy nonindigenous wildlife.
(C) quite a few people can become quite emotionally attached to animals and seek to protect them despite the need for disease control measures.
(D) the interests of fishermen, hunters, and wildlife conservationists seldom coincide.

16. This passage is from Milton Friend, "Why Bother About Wildlife Disease?" from *U.S. Geological Survey Circular 1401*, 2014.

Another disease dynamic of increased importance within urban environments is the transfer of pathogens between wildlife and companion animals (dogs and cats). A recent study of urban areas in California has disclosed that domestic cats, wild bobcats and mountain lions that live in the same area share the same diseases. The passage of those pathogens from wildlife to domestic cats provides a vehicle for bringing those diseases into the home, thereby bridging an "infection gap" between people and wildlife. Rabies, plague, and tularemia are among the diseases of wildlife that cats and dogs have brought into the home. There is also potential for companion animals to transmit their pathogens to free-ranging wildlife.

According to the text, pet dogs and cats in urban areas

(A) are immune to the diseases of wildlife in their area.
(B) are rapidly beginning to share the characteristics of wildlife in their area.
(C) frequently bring disease-causing agents from wildlife into homes but never bring disease-causing agents to wildlife.
(D) sometimes bring diseases into homes and can also bring their disease-causing agents to wildlife.

17. This selection is taken from *The Trained Memory*, Vol. 4 of *Applications of Psychology to the Problems of Personal and Business Efficiency* by Warren Hilton (1920).

If you find it difficult to remember a fact or a name, do not waste your energies in "willing" it to return. Try to recall some other fact or name associated with the first in time or place or otherwise, and lo! When you least expect it, it will pop into your thought.

According to the author, when you apply the principle of association to recall information that you are struggling to remember, the result will be

(A) instantaneous recall.
(B) willful recall.
(C) delayed recall.
(D) unassociated recall.

18. This passage is from Joseph Conrad, *Lord Jim*, originally published in 1917.

He was an inch, perhaps two, under six feet, powerfully built, and he advanced straight at you with a slight stoop of the shoulders, head forward, and a fixed from-under stare which made you think of a charging bull. His voice was deep, loud, and his manner displayed a kind of dogged self-assertion which had nothing aggressive in it. It seemed a necessity, and it was directed apparently as much at himself as at anybody else. He was spotlessly neat, appareled in immaculate white from shoes to hat, and in the various Eastern ports where he got his living as a ship-chandler's water-clerk he was very popular.

According to the text, Jim is

(A) effeminate and extremely neat in appearance.
(B) lonely and aggressive.
(C) powerfully built and popular.
(D) academically gifted, especially in abstract subjects.

19. This passage is from W. E. B. Du Bois, *The Souls of Black Folk*, originally published in 1903.

In a wee wooden schoolhouse, something put it into the boys' and girls' heads to buy gorgeous visiting-cards—ten cents a package—and exchange. The exchange was merry, till one girl, a tall newcomer, refused my card,—refused it peremptorily, with a glance. Then it dawned upon me with a certain suddenness that I was different from the others; or like, mayhap, in heart and life and longing, but shut out from their world by a vast veil. I had thereafter no desire to tear down that veil, to creep through; I held all beyond it in common contempt, and lived above it in a region of blue sky and great wandering shadows. That sky was bluest when I could beat my mates at examination-time, or beat them at a foot-race, or even beat their stringy heads.

According to the text, what is true about the lesson the narrator learns from his experience with the visiting-cards?

(A) As a black man, he is fundamentally different from white people.
(B) White people accept all blacks except him.
(C) He is fundamentally the same as white people but separated from them by their attitudes toward blacks.
(D) White boys but not white girls accept him.

20. This passage is from Simon Singh, *Fermat's Enigma*, copyright © 1997 by Simon Singh.

One theory suggests that the cicada has a parasite that also goes through a lengthy life cycle and that the cicada is trying to avoid. If the parasite has a life cycle of, say, 2 years then the cicada wants to avoid a life cycle that is divisible by 2, otherwise the parasite and the cicada will regularly coincide. Similarly, if the parasite has a life cycle of 3 years then the cicada wants to avoid a life cycle that is divisible by 3, otherwise the parasite and the cicada will once again regularly coincide. Ultimately, to avoid meeting its parasite the cicadas' best strategy is to have a long life cycle lasting a prime number of years. Because nothing will divide into 17, *Magicicada septendecim* will rarely meet its parasite. If the parasite has a 2-year life cycle they will meet only every 34 years, and if it has a longer life cycle, say 16 years, then they will meet only every 272 (16 × 17) years.

According to the text, why (theoretically) do cicadas have a 17-year life cycle?

(A) Seventeen years is the optimum length of time for cicadas to most efficiently use available food and other resources in order to reproduce.
(B) No parasite species can survive 17 years without reproducing.
(C) It evolved as the most advantageous way for cicadas to coexist with a parasite that has now become extinct.
(D) It evolved as a successful defense against a parasite.

21. The following poem was written in the late 1870s by Alfred, Lord Tennyson.

Popular, Popular, Unpopular!

'You're no Poet'—the critics cried!

'Why?' said the Poet. 'You're unpopular!'

Then they cried at the turn of the tide—

'You're no Poet' 'Why?'—"'You're Popular!'

Pop-gun, Popular and Unpopular!

Which choice states the main idea of the poem?

(A) Critics, influenced by perceptions of popularity, are like children playing with toys.
(B) The poet is criticized for not being popular, despite his attempts.
(C) Critics are defined by implication as those who analyze and review literary poetry.
(D) Popularity and unpopularity both convey a sense of danger to the poet.

22. This selection is taken from a speech by Abbey Kelly Foster (1851).

My friends, I feel that in throwing out this idea, I have done what was left for me to do. But I did not rise to make a speech—my life has been my speech. For fourteen years I have advocated this cause by my daily life. Bloody feet, sisters, have worn smooth the path by which you have come up hither. You will not need to speak when you speak by your everyday life. Oh, how truly does Webster say, action, action is eloquence! Let us, then when we go home, go not to complain, but to work. Do not go home to complain of the men, but go and make greater exertions than ever to discharge your everyday duties.

Which choice best states the main idea of the text?

(A) Put your money where your mouth is.
(B) The early bird catches the worm.
(C) A picture is worth a thousand words.
(D) Don't just talk the talk, but walk the walk.

23. This selection is taken from Samuel Johnson's *The Rambler, No. 4* (1750).

I remember a remark made by Scaliger upon Pontanus, that all his writings are filled with the same images; and that is you take from him his lilies and his roses, his satyrs and his dryads, he will have nothing left that can be called poetry. In like manner also most all the fictions of the last age will vanish. If you deprive them of a hermit and a wood, a battle and a shipwreck.

Which choice best states the main idea of the text?

(A) The writings of Scaliger are critical.
(B) The errors of Pontanus include overuse of certain images.
(C) Fictions of the last age are difficult to understand.
(D) Past writers have overused conventional characters and images.

24. The following selection is from Maria Edgeworth's *Letters for Literary Ladies* (1795).

Even if literature were of no other use to the fair sex than to supply them with employment, I should think the time dedicated to the cultivation of their minds well bestowed: they are surely better occupied when they are reading or writing than when coquetting or gaming, losing their fortunes or their characters. You despise the writing of women—you think that they have made at least as good a use of it as learned men did of the needle some centuries ago, when they set themselves to determine how many spirits could stand upon its point, and were ready to tear one another to pieces in the discussion of this sublime question.

Which choice best states the main idea of the text?

(A) Despite the opinions of critics, women should engage in reading and writing.
(B) Criticisms of women's writing efforts are justified.
(C) Women waste their time and destroy their characters by coquetting or gaming.
(D) Women should stop and learn to sew with divine needles, as learned men did years ago.

25. The following lines come from John Dryden's "The Art of Poetry" (circa 1680).

A poem, where we all perfections find,
Is not the work of a fantastic mind;
There must be care, and time, and skill, and pains:
Not the first heat of inexperienced brains.
Yet sometimes artless poets, when the rage
Of a warm fancy does their minds engage,
Puffed with vain pride, presume they understand,
And boldly take the trumpet in their hand:
Their fustian muse each accident confounds;
Nor can she fly, but rise by leaps and bounds,
Till, their small stock of learning quickly spent,
Their poem dies for want of nourishment.

Which choice best states the main idea of the poem?

(A) The best poems are the product of "a fantastic mind."
(B) For poems to be perfect, they must engage the fustian muse.
(C) A poem written by an artless poet dies from the poet's lack of knowledge.
(D) Most poetry has a basis in emotional presumptions on the part of the poet.

Answer Explanations

1. **(C)** Although he directly tells the blond lieutenant that his parents are in the Wyoming desert (A), the correct and most complete answer is inferred from the details of his explanation in answer to the blond lieutenant's question about what he means when saying that his folks were "not quite" farmers. He answers with the account of how his parents were removed from the Coast and placed in concentration camps/relocation centers.
2. **(D)** The author directly states, "If the nuclear forces had been slightly stronger than they are . . . hydrogen would be a rare element, and stars like the sun . . . could not exist."
3. **(B)** The correct answer combines what the author says about new cures ("Therapy [new and effective drugs] had been discovered for great numbers of patients whose illnesses had previously been untreatable") and about the reactions of the doctors to these new cures ("Doctors could now cure disease, and this was astonishing, most of all to the doctors themselves.").
4. **(B)** The phrase "this sentiment" refers to the "exasperation" of artists and writers with highly commercial society. Philistinism—an attitude of smug ignorance and conventionalism toward artistic and cultural values—neatly describes the attitude that artists and writers found exasperating.
5. **(D)** The author directly states, "The general importance of zoonoses for humanity has waxed and waned over time in concert with changing conditions. . . ."

6. **(D)** The author directly states that rabies "is diagnosed annually in wildlife and other animals where it continues to cause periodic epizootics."

7. **(A)** The author asks, "If it be admitted that a man possessing absolute power may misuse that power by wronging his adversaries, why should not a majority be liable to the same reproach?" This rhetorical question makes the point that the majority can take actions, such as passing laws, that wrong people. Along this line of reasoning, such laws would be unjust.

8. **(B)** The author directly states the correct answer: "... liberty is endangered when this power [the dominant social power] finds no obstacle which can retard it course...."

9. **(D)** When the author states that "the Court of Claims ... was set up not to administer justice but to ... head off any future claims that Indians might make on lands coveted by the white economy," he is saying that the Court of Claims is biased toward white people.

10. **(C)** Franklin's acceptance of the "dangerous mission to France" contradicts the claim that he never went to Europe.

11. **(A)** According to his claim, Benjamin Franklin was a follower of the "theory of enlightened self-interest." Logically, then, he would seek what was in his self-interest (what would benefit him).

12. **(B)** "Nurture" refers to cultural influences, and "nature," in context, refers to the influence of a person's genetic makeup.

13. **(A)** In this context, "ubiquitous" means "existing everywhere," making choice (A) the only logical choice.

14. **(D)** The author directly states that they "argued unsystematically and unfairly," the exact opposite of being "scrupulously fair." That they used superficial elements in the art of persuasion (A) is seen in "painted over the gaps in their reasoning with glossy rhetoric." For rhetoric (the art of persuasion) to be "glossy" means that it includes elements that are superficial. Both (B) and (C) are clearly stated.

15. **(C)** The author states that some people living in urban areas regard resident waterfowl as companions ("companion animal status [is] conferred"). We can infer from this that many of these people would actively oppose the culling of resident waterfowl because of their emotional attachment to these animals, making wildlife management and disease control difficult.

16. **(D)** The author lists "Rabies, plague, and tularemia" as examples of wildlife diseases brought into homes. Also, the reciprocal relationship is stated directly: "There is also potential for companion animals to transmit their pathogens to free-ranging wildlife."

17. **(C)** The writer suggests to readers that "willing" (B) lost information to return is a waste of energy. Recalling facts or information associated with the lost information, on the other hand, results in recall. "When you least expect it" implies that you may not immediately remember (A). This statement further implies that your mind has moved on to other thoughts—making the "lo!" moment delayed.

18. **(C)** Jim is directly described as "powerfully built" and "very popular."

19. **(C)** The lesson he learned is best summarized in choice (C), based on the context of the narrative. A girl refused his card. "Then it dawned upon me . . . that I was different from the others; or like, mayhap, in heart and life and longing, but shut out from their world by a vast veil."

20. **(D)** The theory suggests that "to avoid meeting its parasite the cicadas' best strategy is to have a long life cycle lasting a prime number of years."

21. **(A)** That the poet is between a rock and a hard place is easy to see. He is the target for critics whether his works are popular or unpopular. But in the last line, we see a clue to his attitude toward all the negative reviews made by the critics. "Pop-gun, Popular and Unpopular!" A pop-gun is a children's toy that that uses air to blow harmless corks or pellets. By using this comparison, the poet is telling us that the erratic behavior of the critics is childish and lacks any real impact on their target (the poet).

22. **(D)** "You will not need to speak when you speak by your everyday life." Money (A), time (B), and visuals (C) are not the central idea here. If "action is eloquence," then to walk is the only "action" or choice.

23. **(D)** Conventional characters and images, such as those mentioned in the selection, are those that recur in various literary forms. Even if you do not know what a satyr or dryad might be, you can tell his point from "his lilies and his roses." The overuse of them can make the character or image become expected and stereotypical. Although choices (A) and (B) are in the passage, these statements are too narrow for the main idea or theme. The speaker generalizes to say that past writers (represented by Pontanus and those of the "last age") filled their poetry and fictions with conventional characters (represented by hermits) and images (represented by lilies and roses).

24. **(A)** This selection defends women who read and write by pointing out that these activities are less self-destructive than coquetting or gaming and that their literary efforts (plays, and poetry, and romances) are of as much value as that of some of the "learned men."

25. **(C)** "A poem, where we all perfections find," —in other words, a really well-written poem— is the product of "care, and time, and skill, and pains." This observation sets the standard against which poetry is to be judged and brings the poet to his main point: the poems of artless poets written with pride and accident from a "small stock of learning" die "for want of nourishment."

Quantitative Evidence

For these questions, you will be using a graphic, such as a chart, map, or graph, to evaluate the writer's claim, whether it is supported, not supported, or illustrated by the evidence. You will then choose which answer choice "effectively" uses the data you see in order to complete the statement.

Practice

Each question has one or more passages. Carefully read each passage and question, and choose the best answer to the question based on the passage(s).

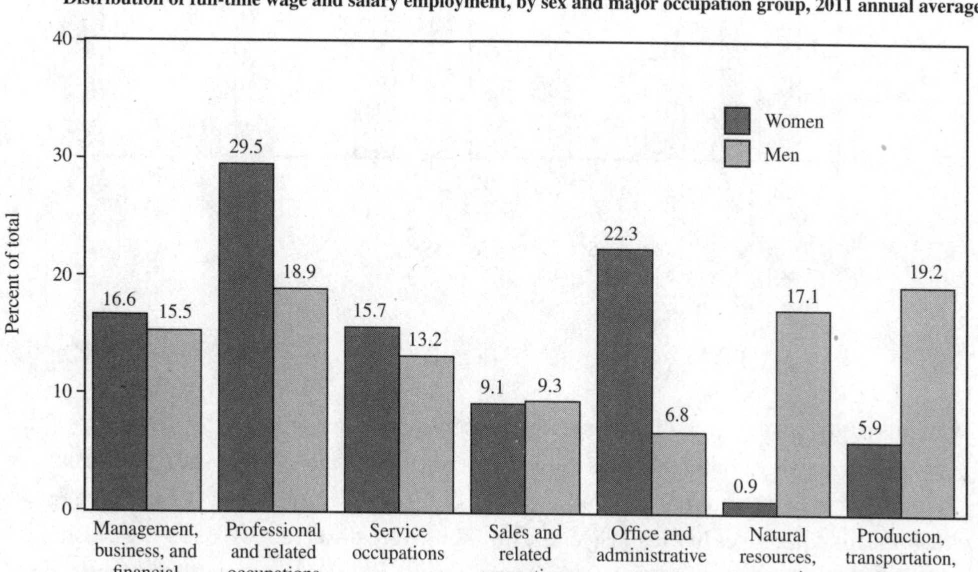

1. The occupational distributions of female and male full-time workers differ significantly. Compared with men, relatively few women work in construction, production, or transportation occupations, and women are far more concentrated in ________.

   Which choice most effectively uses information from the graph to complete the statement?

   (A) natural resources
   (B) sales and related occupations
   (C) office and administrative support occupations
   (D) management, business, and financial operations occupations

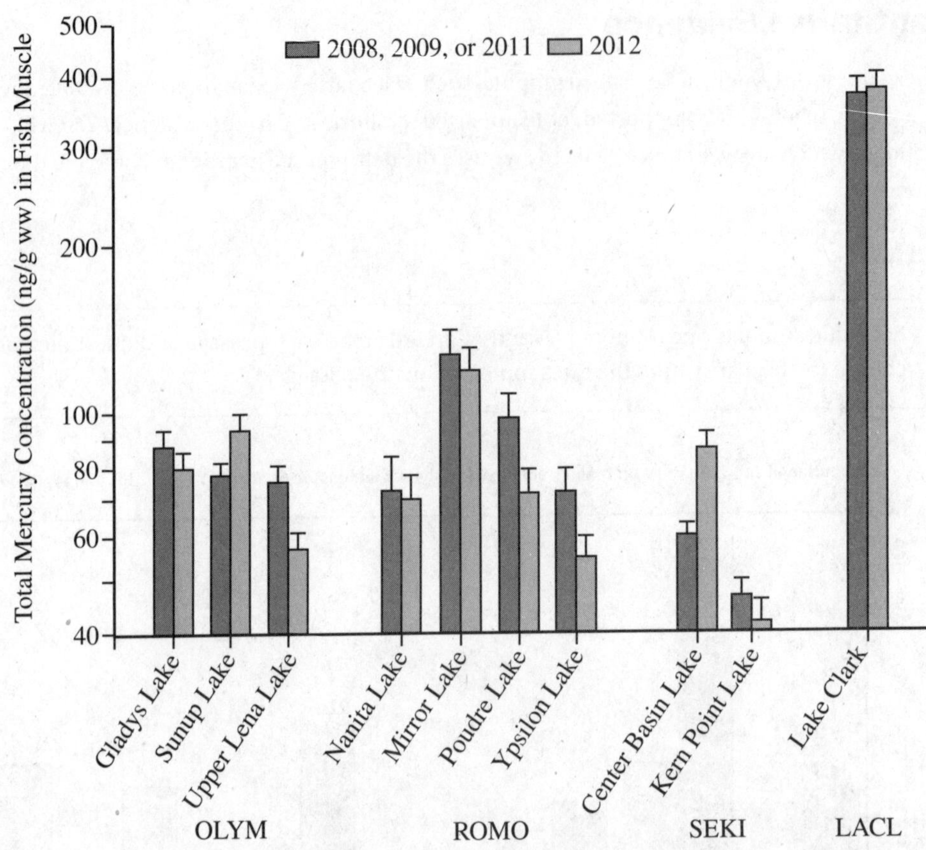

2. In this study, we examined mercury (Hg) concentrations in nonmigratory freshwater fish in 86 sites across 21 national parks in the western United States. There were no consistent patterns in interannual variability across the 10 sites sampled over separate years. Significant differences in mean Hg concentrations were observed at 5 of 10 sites. Fish total Hg (THg) concentrations increased significantly from the first sampling to the second at two sites: Sunup Lake and Center Basin Lake. Conversely, fish THg concentrations decreased significantly from the first sampling event to the second in three sites: ________________________.

Which choice most effectively uses information from the graph to complete the statement?

(A) Lake Clark, Mirror Lake, and Ypsilon Lake
(B) Lake Clark, Poudre Lake, and Ypsilon Lake
(C) Upper Lena Lake, Poudre Lake, and Ypsilon Lake
(D) Upper Lena Lake, Mirror Lake, and Lake Clark

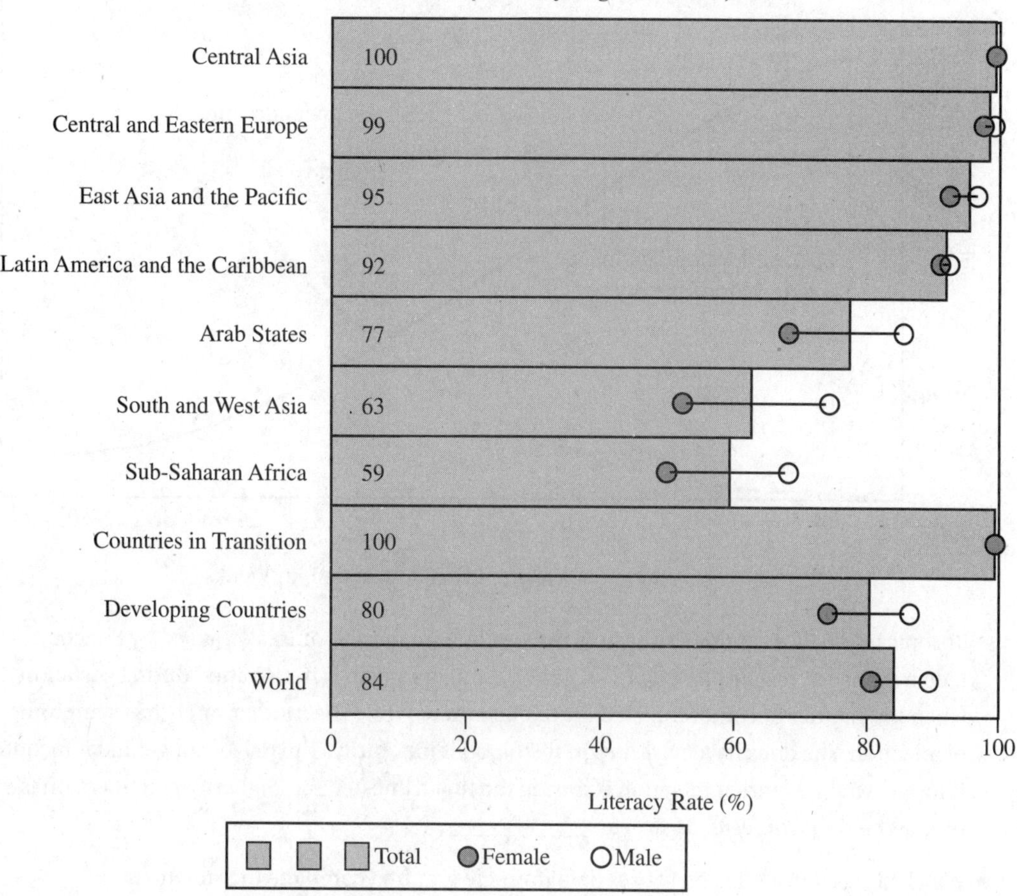

Note: 2011 data refer to the period 2005–2011.
Source: UNESCO Institute for Statistics, May 2013.

3. In 2011, the global adult literacy rate for the population aged 15 and older was 84%. Regional averages of the adult literacy rate in 2011 were calculated for 151 countries and territories from eight regions except ____________ due to the limited number of countries in the regions that report literacy rates.

   Which choice most effectively uses information based on the graph to complete the statement?

   (A) North America and Western Europe
   (B) East Asia and the Pacific
   (C) Sub-Saharan Africa and the World
   (D) South and West Asia

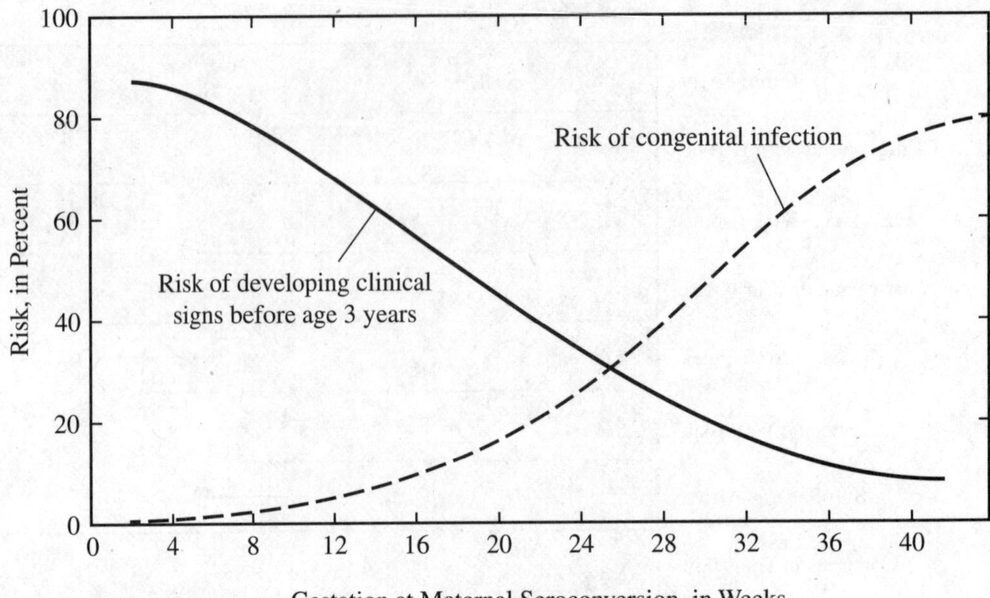

4. Toxoplasmosis is a zoonotic protozoal disease of humans and animals caused by the coccidian parasite *Toxoplasma gondii* (*T. gondii*). The organism is transmitted during gestation when the mother becomes infected for the first time. While the mother rarely has symptoms of infection, she does have parasites in the blood temporarily. The risk of congenital infection is lowest when maternal infection is during the first trimester and highest when infection is during the third trimester. However, ______________.

Which choice most effectively uses data from the graph to complete the statement?

(A) the risk of developing clinical signs before age 3 years is lower when congenital infection occurs during the first trimester than it is when the infection occurs during the third trimester.

(B) the risk of developing clinical signs before age 3 years is higher when congenital infection occurs during the first trimester than it is when the infection occurs during the third trimester.

(C) the risk of developing clinical signs before age 3 years increases when congenital infection occurs in the second or third trimester instead of the first trimester.

(D) the risk of developing clinical signs before age 3 is the same whether congenital infection occurs during the first, second, or third trimester.

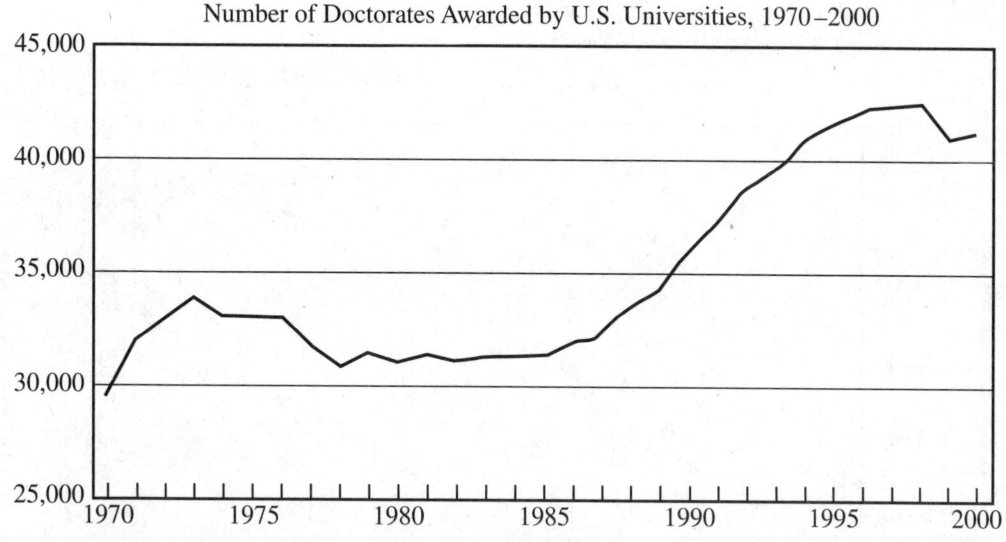

Source: National Science Foundation/SRS, Survey of Earned Doctorates

5. The Survey of Earned Doctorates shows that in 2000, more than half of all Ph.D. recipients held a bachelor's degree in the same subject as that of their doctoral study—and nearly three-fourths held a master's. According to the same survey, the total number of new research doctorates awarded each year in the late 1970s ________. After rising steadily from the late 1980s, the total number of degrees awarded reached a high point in about 1998.

   Which choice most effectively uses data from the graph to complete the statement?

   (A) remained constantly higher than in previous years
   (B) remained constantly higher than the following years
   (C) dipped slightly from previous years
   (D) dipped significantly lower than those awarded in 1970

Total Nonfarm Employment and Healthcare and Related Employment, January 2004–14 (in Thousands)

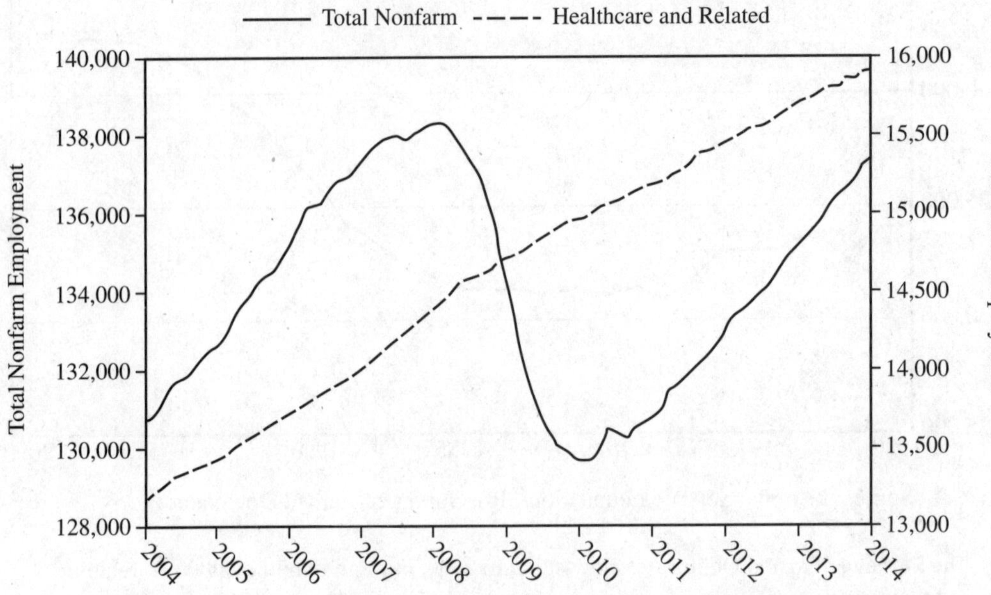

Note: Healthcare and related include series CEU6562000101, CEU9091622001, CEU9092262201, and CEU9093262201; January 2014 data are preliminary.
Source: U.S. Bureau of Labor Statistics, Current Employment Statistics (wage and salary employment, seasonally adjusted).

6. Employment in the healthcare industry has been growing steadily for years, U.S. Bureau of Labor Statistics data show. This growth is due, in part, to people depending on health services no matter what the economic climate. Even when total U.S. employment fell during the 2007–2009 recession, for example, healthcare employment __________. And because healthcare-related jobs often require personal interaction, they are difficult to outsource or replace with automation, as happens in some other industries.

Which choice most effectively uses data from the graph to complete the statement?

(A) had only a slight fall
(B) remained stable
(C) continued to rise
(D) experienced a lull

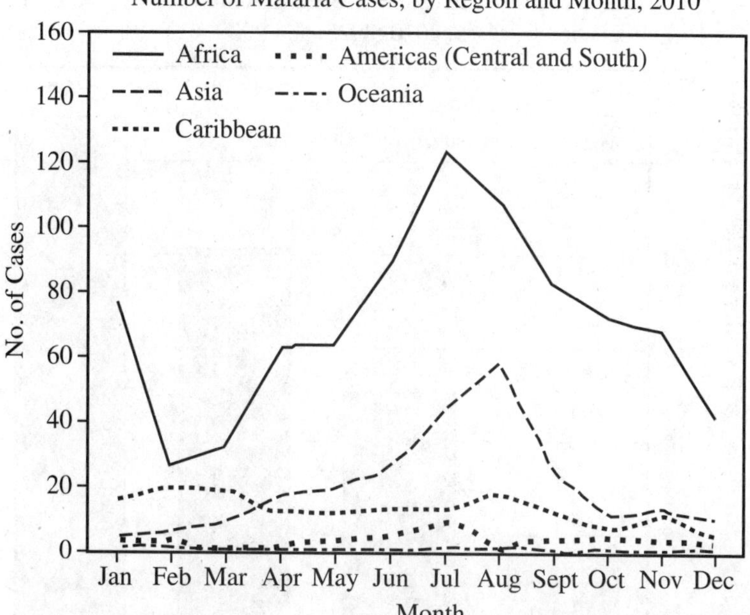

7. Most cases of malaria reported in the United States among persons who indicated travel to Africa peaked in January and July. These peaks likely correlated with peak travel times to African destinations related to winter and early-summer holidays. The majority of cases reported in the United States among those who indicated travel to Asia (most of whom had traveled to India) peaked in August, followed by a smaller peak in _______.

   Which choice most effectively uses data from the table to complete the statement?

   (A) December
   (B) October
   (C) November
   (D) February

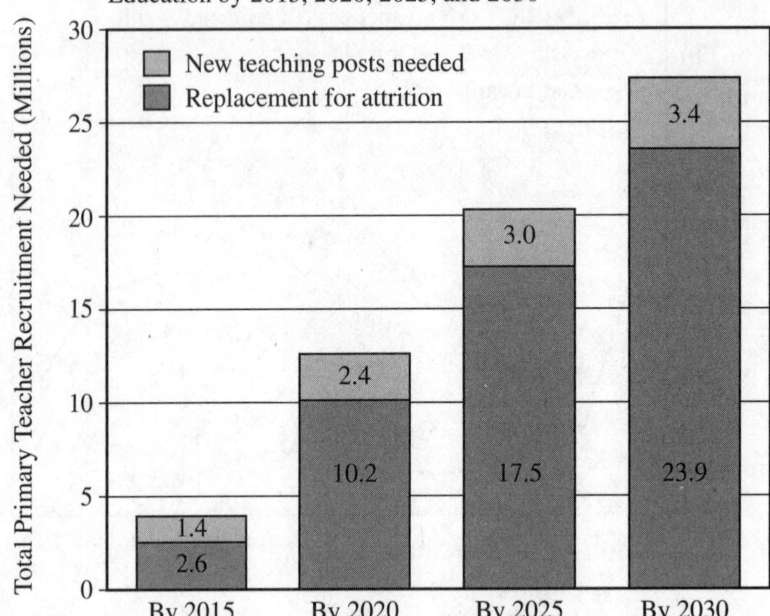

Source: UNESCO Institute for Statistics database

8. Universal primary education (UPE) will not be achieved by 2015, as 58 million children are still out of school. For this reason, the analysis presented determines how many teachers would be needed if the goal of achieving UPE was shifted to 2020 or 2040. To achieve UPE by 2020, for example, countries will need to recruit a total of 12.6 million primary teachers. This includes the creation of about 2.4 million new teaching positions and the replacement of 10.2 million teachers expected to leave the profession due to attrition. By 2030, the total demand for teachers would rise to ______________ million to compensate for attrition.

Which choice most effectively uses data from the table to complete the statement?

(A) 27.3 million, with about 23.9 million new posts needed for UPE and the remaining 3.4 million
(B) 27.3 million, with about 3.4 million new posts needed for UPE and the remaining 23.9
(C) 12 million, with about 3.4 million new posts needed for UPE and the remaining 23.9
(D) 20 million, with about 23.9 million new posts needed for UPE and the remaining 3.4

	Live births				Marriages		Deaths		Infant deaths	
			Rate per 1,000 women aged 15–44 years							
Period	Number	Rate per 1,000 population	Unadjusted	Seasonally adjusted[1]	Number	Rate per 1,000 population[2]	Number	Rate per 1,000 population	Number	Rate per 1,000 live births
2003:										
January	330,000	13.4	62.5	65.3	141,000	5.7	224,000	9.1	2,400	7.1
February	307,000	13.8	64.5	65.6	146,000	6.6	200,000	9.0	2,100	6.9
March	337,000	13.7	63.9	65.4	150,000	6.1	212,000	8.6	2,300	6.9
April	330,000	13.8	64.7	65.5	168,000	7.0	194,000	8.1	2,200	6.7
May	346,000	14.0	65.6	66.0	179,000	7.2	197,000	8.0	2,300	6.8
June	338,000	14.1	66.1	65.3	229,000	9.6	193,000	8.1	2,300	7.0
July	365,000	14.7	69.1	66.1	221,000	8.9	192,000	7.7	2,400	6.6
August	361,000	14.6	68.3	65.8	215,000	8.7	188,000	7.6	2,300	6.4
September	360,000	15.0	70.3	66.5	217,000	9.0	192,000	8.0	2,300	6.6
October	354,000	14.3	66.9	67.5	207,000	8.4	204,000	8.2	2,400	6.8
November	322,000	13.4	62.8	65.2	156,000	6.5	197,000	8.2	2,200	6.7
December	342,000	13.8	64.7	65.3	158,000	6.3	230,000	9.3	2,300	6.6
2004:										
January	331,000	13.4	63.0	65.9	146,000	5.9	234,000	9.5	2,400	7.0
February	316,000	13.6	64.2	65.3	137,000	5.9	200,000	8.6	2,100	6.6

[1]The method of seasonal adjustment, developed by the U.S. Census Bureau, is described in *The X-11 Variant of the Census Method II Seasonal Adjustment Program*, Technical Paper No. 15 (1967 revision).

[2]Marriage rates may be underestimated due to incomplete reporting in Oklahoma; see "Technical Notes."

NOTES: Figures include all revisions received from the States and, therefore, may differ from those previously published. National data are based on events occurring in the United States, regardless of place of residence; see "Technical Notes."

9. Marketing groups often review vital statistics gathered annually to watch for peak periods of activity and seasonal trends. Once pinpointed, this information can be used to develop products and provide services at optimum times; for example, __________.

   Which choice most effectively uses data from the chart to complete the example?

   (A) spring weddings are both traditional and popular at outdoor venues
   (B) clothing designs generally focus on wedding gowns aimed at Christmas weddings
   (C) knowing that most weddings occur during April and May allows bakers to anticipate inventory needs for wedding cakes
   (D) wedding planners would benefit by knowing that most weddings occur during summer and early fall months

Percent Change in Grades K–12 Enrollment in Public Schools, by State: Fall 2001 to Fall 2013

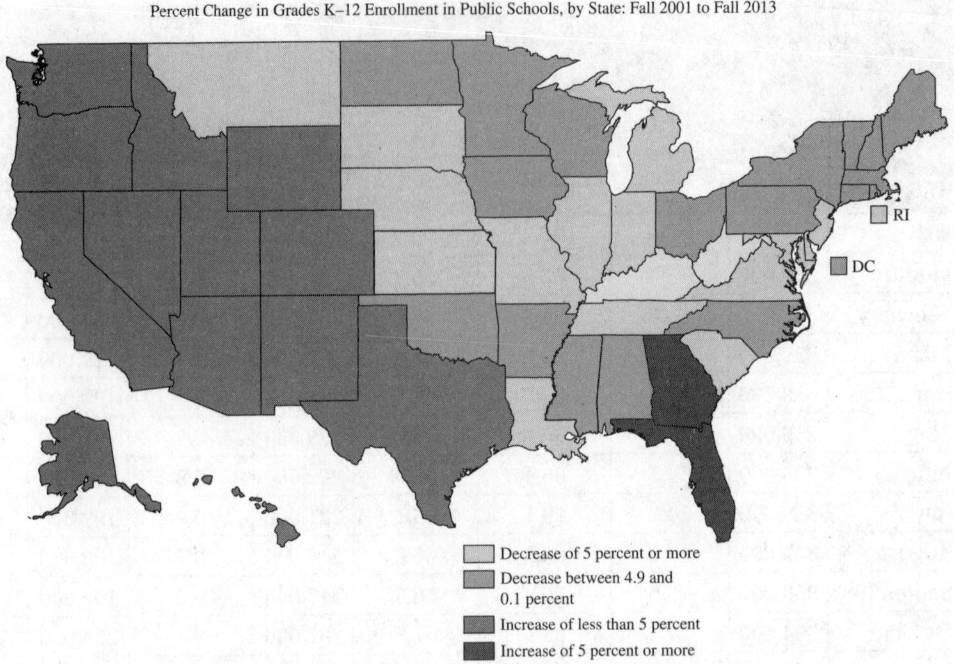

Source: Table 5, *Projections of Education Statistics to 2013*, based on U.S. Department of Education, National Center for Education Statistics, Common Core of Data Surveys; and State Public Elementary and Secondary Enrollment Model.

10. A student was given this map of the United States that depicts projected changes in the enrollment of elementary and secondary students during a twelve-year period. The student, who was assigned to develop an application for the information, concluded that the projections indicate a significant migration of young families within the United States from the Eastern Seaboard and Midwest primarily to states in the West. As a result, such migration would create an urgency to shift federal funds to those states for infrastructure improvement within the next ten years. A fellow student cited a flaw in the application because the state projections of increased school enrollment do not specify the causes of the increases, such as migration, new births, and immigration from other countries. The instructor, however, accepted the student's application of the information presented for several reasons, such as __________.

Which choice most effectively uses data from the graph to complete the example?

(A) a larger number of states are projected to increase than the two states that decrease
(B) the instructor was incorrect to accept the application because there are no indications that increase is due to migration
(C) the declining percentages in the central and eastern states are suggestive of a population shift to some extent is possible
(D) the large bubble of uncertainty exists in those states in which the numbers declined

National Population and Labor Force
(Millions)

	Canada			Mexico			United States		
	1990	1995	1996	1990	1995	1997	1990	1995	1996
National population, total	**27.8**	**29.6**	**30.0**	**81.2**	**91.2**	**93.7**	**248.7**	**262.9**	**265.3**
Females	14.0	14.9	15.1	41.3	46.3	48.0	127.5	134.3	135.5
Males	13.8	14.7	14.9	39.9	44.9	45.7	121.2	128.5	129.8
Age structure									
Ages 14 and under	5.8	6.0	6.0	31.1	32.3	32.7	53.5	57.2	57.7
Percent of total population	20.9	20.3	20.0	38.3	35.4	34.9	21.5	21.8	21.8
Ages 15–34	9.2	8.9	8.9	29.3	33.7	33.6	80.0	77.6	76.6
Percent of total population	33.1	30.1	29.7	36.1	37.0	35.9	32.2	29.5	28.9
Ages 35–64	9.7	11.1	11.5	16.9	20.9	22.8	83.9	94.7	97.1
Percent of total population	34.9	37.5	38.3	20.8	22.9	24.3	33.7	36.0	36.6
Ages 65+	3.1	3.6	3.6	3.9	4.3	4.6	31.2	33.4	33.8
Percent of total population	11.1	12.1	12.0	4.8	4.7	4.9	12.6	12.7	12.7
Urban population									
Percent of urban population	N	N	77.9	71.3	73.5	74.0	79.7	79.8^{e}	79.8^{e}
Population density									
Number of people (per square kilometer)	3	3	3	41	46	48	27	29	29
Labor force, total	**14.3**	**14.9**	**15.1**	**31.2**	**35.6**	**36.6**	**125.8**	**132.3**	**133.9**
Percent of total population	51.4	50.3	50.3	37.5	39.0	39.6	50.6	50.3	50.5

KEY: e = Data are estimated. N = Data are nonexistent.

11. Historical changes in the North American population and labor force numbers toward the end of the last century are being examined in detail to determine at what point current trends began to identify future variable factors. Take, for example, the years 1990, 1995, and 1996. Some analysts argue that because all three major North American countries saw increases in their general populations, every economic and social sector should plan for continued growth through the next fifty years.

    Which choice best describes data from the table that would weaken the analysts' conclusion?

    (A) Decreases in the 15–34 age populations in Canada and the United States
    (B) The growing numbers of people ages 65+
    (C) Canada's lack of data in 1990 and 1995 in urban populations
    (D) Canada's stabilized population density

Dairy Products: Production by Product, United States, January, 1999–2000

Product	Jan 1999	Dec 1999[1]	Jan 2000	Change From Jan 1999	Change From Dec 1999
	1,000 Pounds	*1,000 Pounds*	*1,000 Pounds*	*Percent*	*Percent*
Butter	123,336	117,151	140,566	14.0	20.0
Cheese					
American Types[2]	289,680	307,391	312,672	7.9	1.7
Cheddar	233,772	241,399	246,642	5.5	2.2
Swiss	18,650	16,262	15,946	−14.5	−1.9
Brick and Muenster	7,301	7,594	7,490	2.6	−1.4
Cream and Neufchatel	44,425	61,565	44,689	0.6	−27.4
Blue	4,386	4,270	6,964	58.8	63.1
Hispanic	6,162	6,939	6,489	5.3	−6.5
Mozzarella	203,828	219,079	214,539	5.3	−2.1
Other Italian Types	55,206	58,934	62,508	13.2	6.1
Total Italian Types	259,034	278,013	277,047	7.0	−0.3
All Other Types	9,089	10,588	8,956	−2.4	−15.4
Total	638,727	692,622	680,253	6.5	−1.8
Cottage Cheese, Curd[3]	34,769	34,696	34,985	0.6	0.8
Cottage Cheese, Cream[4]	26,028	26,679	26,699	2.6	0.1
Cottage Cheese, Lowfat[5]	26,586	25,894	27,213	2.4	5.1
Canned Evaporated and Condensed Whole Milk	29,142	39,820	33,910	16.4	−14.8
Dry Whole Milk	10,957	9,902	8,755	−20.1	−11.6
Nonfat Dry Milk, Human	120,027	129,297	131,086	9.2	1.4
Dry Skim Milk, Animal	400	480	439	9.8	−8.5
Dry Buttermilk	6,274	4,700	5,806	−7.5	23.5
Yogurt, Plain & Flavored	126,445	141,990	136,328	7.8	−4.0
	1,000 Gallons	*1,000 Gallons*	*1,000 Gallons*	*Percent*	*Percent*
Frozen Products					
Ice Cream, Hard	57,387	55,759	61,696	7.5	10.6
Ice Cream, Lowfat, Hard	6,777	6,245	6,154	−9.2	−1.5
Ice Cream, Lowfat, Soft	13,560	15,209	14,261	5.2	−6.2
Ice Cream, Lowfat, Total	20,337	21,454	20,415	0.4	−4.8
Ice Cream, Nonfat, Hard	2,167	2,382	2,400	10.8	0.8
Sherbet, Hard	3,170	3,180	3,217	1.5	1.2
Water and Juice Ices	4,162	3,315	4,271	2.6	28.8
Frozen Yogurt, Total	5,946	4,772	5,448	−8.4	14.2
Regular & Lowfat, Hard	2,231	1,966	2,167	−2.9	10.2
Nonfat, Hard	1,545	1,130	1,111	−28.1	−1.7
Other Frozen Dairy Products	874	979	865	−1.0	−11.6
Mix for Frozen Products					
Ice Cream Mix	31,453	30,252	34,002	8.1	12.4
Ice Cream, Lowfat, Mix	12,607	13,426	12,746	1.1	−5.1
Ice Cream, Nonfat, Mix	1,283	1,371	1,553	21.0	13.3
Sherbet Mix	2,248	2,181	2,472	10.0	13.3
Yogurt Mix	3,763	3,020	3,448	−8.4	14.2

[1] Revised.

[2] Includes Cheddar, Colby, and Monterey Jack.

[3] Mostly used for processing into cream or lowfat cottage cheese.

[4] Fat content 4 percent or more.

[5] Fat content less than 4 percent.

12. The year prior to the turn of the twenty-first century, the USDA Agricultural Statistics Board collected data concerning American dairy production. Using these statistics to build a business plan, a group of young entrepreneurs decided to venture into retail sales of dairy-based treats, specializing in lowfat ice cream as the best choice.

    Which choice best describes data from the graph that would discourage investors from supporting the entrepreneurs' new business?

    (A) An increase in production of nonfat dairy ice cream
    (B) A drop in production of lowfat dairy ice cream
    (C) The large competitive jump in production of water and juice ices
    (D) The combined availability of hard ice cream and hard frozen yogurt

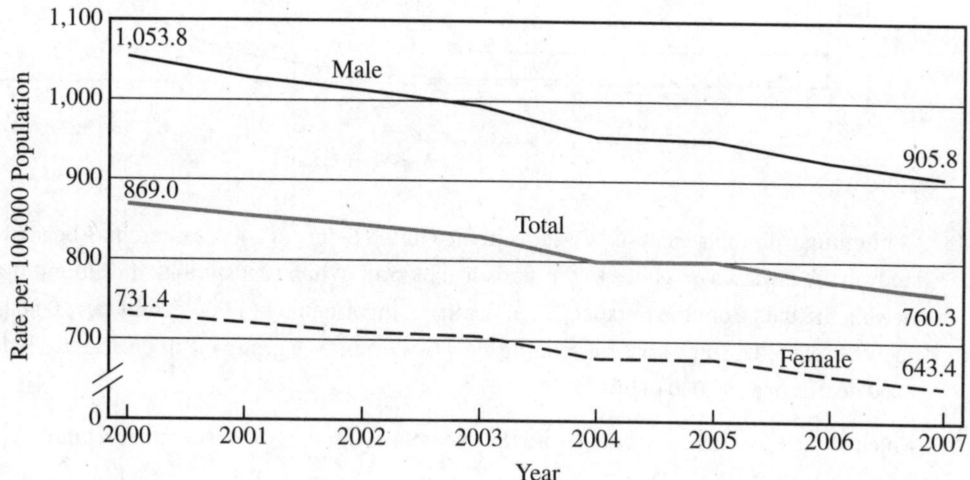

13. A 2007 analysis of deaths in the United States concludes that almost 2,500,000 people, regardless of gender, died in that year. However, that women traditionally outlive men has been well-known for generations. To provide context, researchers decided to compare graphically the number of deaths of men to those of women between the years 2000 and 2007. They concluded that the gap between gender-based deaths narrowed somewhat during those years.

    Which choice best describes data from the graph that supports the researchers' conclusion?

    (A) The rate of decline in deaths among the general population was greater than the rate of decline among women.
    (B) The rate of deaths per 100,000 among women saw a greater decline than among men.
    (C) The rate of deaths per 100,000 among men saw a greater decline than among women.
    (D) The rate of decline in deaths among men was greater than the rate of decline in the next generation.

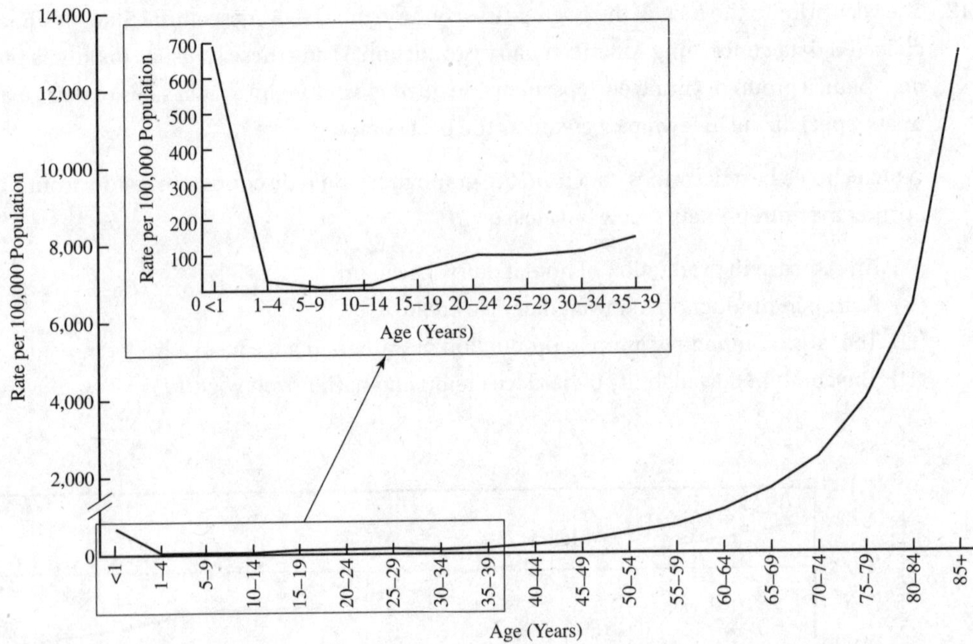

14. Continuing with their analysis of deaths in the United States in 2007, researchers began to study in what ways age relates to the statistical picture. When first studied, they found that viewing the data from the perspective of deaths in increments of 1,000 deaths per 100,000 people provided a somewhat misleading view for certain age groups with death rates below 1,000 deaths per 100,000 people.

Which choice best describes data from the chart that supports the researchers' claim?

(A) The highest death rate is in the 1–4 group.
(B) The highest death rate is in the 5–9 group.
(C) The lowest death rate is in the 1–4 group.
(D) The lowest death rate is in the 5–9 group.

Age-adjusted death rates, by state and the District of Columbia: United States, preliminary 2007

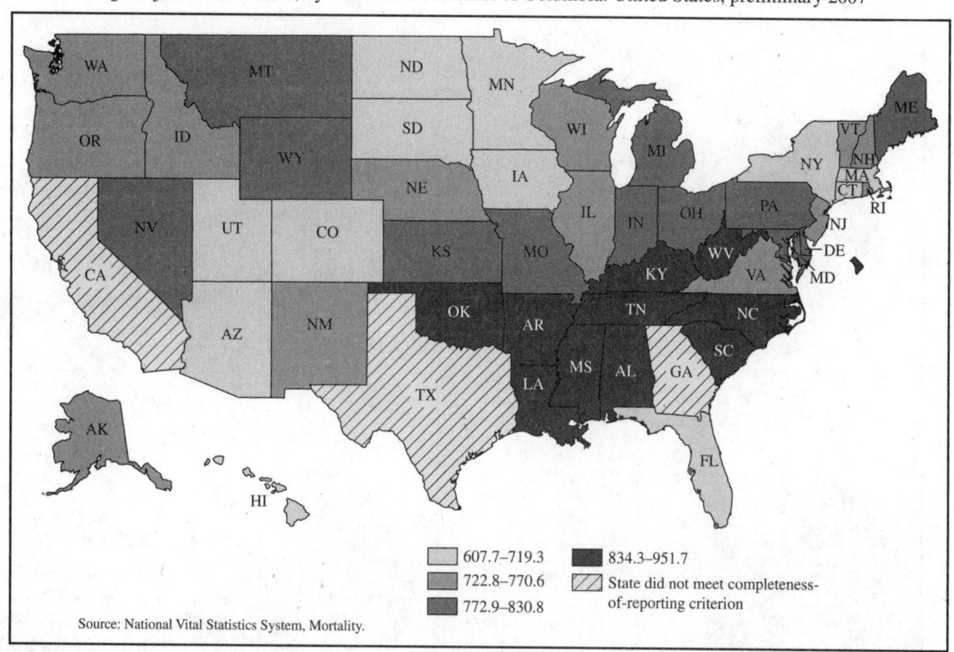

15. The risk of dying each year can increase by geographic location. The 2007 figures were used by researchers to determine age-adjusted death rates on a state-by-state basis. Not only do death rates vary by state, researchers also found that certain regions shared a mortality pattern.

    Which choice best describes data from the graph that would weaken the writer's conclusion?

    (A) Age-adjusted death rates in the Four Corners states
    (B) Age-adjusted death rates in the New England states
    (C) Age-adjusted death rates in the Pacific Northwest states
    (D) Age-adjusted death rates in the Southeast Mississippi Delta states

Percent distribution of five leading causes of death, by age group: United States, preliminary 2007

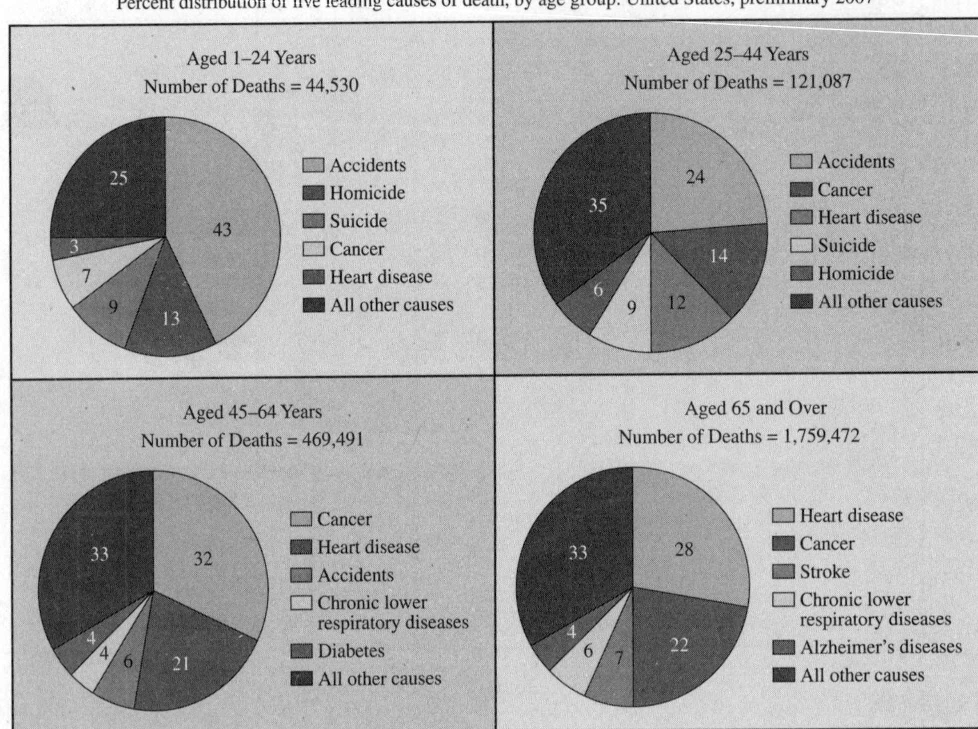

Source: National Vital Statistics System Mortality.

16. The three most prevalent causes of death in the United States in 2007 were found to be heart disease, cancer, and stroke. Despite increased longevity noted by statisticians since 1980 through the first decade of the twenty-first century, cancer persists as a growing concern. Researchers also believe that age is a significant factor in the death-by-cancer risk, particularly at midlife ages.

Which choice best describes data from the graphs that would support the writer's argument?

(A) Cancer is the second-highest cause of death between the ages of 25 and 44.
(B) Cancer is the second-highest cause of death for people over the age of 65.
(C) Cancer is the leading cause of death for people between the ages of 46 and 64.
(D) Accidents, homicides, and suicides are more common causes of death for those under 25.

Elementary and Secondary School Enrollment (in Thousands), by Control and Grade Level of School, with Projections: Fall 1970–2008

	Public schools			Private schools[1]		
Year/period	Grades PreK–12	Grades PreK–8	Grades 9–12	Grades PreK–12	Grades PreK–8	Grades 9–12
1970	45,894	32,558	13,336	5,363	4,052	1,311
1988	40,189	28,501	11,687	5,241	4,036	1,206
1998	46,792	33,522	13,270	5,927	4,588	1,339
	Projected[2]			Projected[2]		
2008	48,201	33,455	14,746	6,067	4,579	1,488
	Percentage change			Percentage change		
1970–88	−12.4	−12.5	−12.4	−2.3	−0.4	−8.0
	Projected percentage change			Projected percentage change		
1988–98	16.4	17.6	13.5	13.1	13.7	11.0
1998–2008	3.0	−0.2	11.1	2.4	−0.2	11.1

[1] Beginning in fall 1980, data include estimates for the expanded universe of private schools.

[2] Enrollment includes students in kindergarten through grade 12 and some nursery school students.

NOTE: Details may not add to totals due to rounding.

SOURCE: U.S. Department of Education, National Center for Education Statistics, *Digest of Education Statistics 1998* (based on Common Core of Data) and *Projections of Education Statistics to 2008*, 1998.

17. In preparing a degree program thesis, a graduate student in the field of social sciences decided to investigate data to suggest that in the late-twentieth century, perceptions were beginning to form that many couples were choosing to postpone having children until later in life. The student concludes that using school enrollment statistics and projections collected during the focus years would supply circumstantial evidence to introduce the topic of the thesis. An example includes ____________________.

    Which choice most effectively uses data from the chart to complete the example?

    (A) a −12.5 percent enrollment change between 1970 and 1988 in grades PreK-8 in public schools
    (B) a projected 17.6 percent enrollment change between 1988 and 1998 in grades PreK-8 in public schools
    (C) a projected 3 percent enrollment change between 1998 and 2008 in grades PreK-12 in public schools
    (D) a percentage change of −1.4 between 1970 and 1988 in grades PreK-8 in private schools

Projected Percentage Change in Public Elementary and Secondary School Enrollment, by Region: Fall 1988–2008

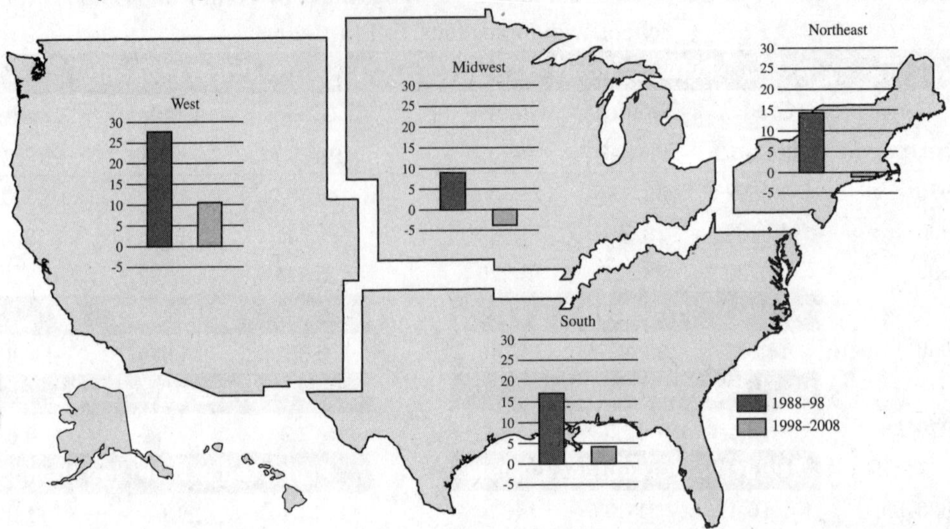

18. Most people agree that education is a valuable asset. Acquiring a high school diploma is a significant first step toward a higher-paying and more satisfying career. Consequently, much time, money, and effort are expended on determining how best to help students visualize and achieve their academic goals. One government official proposed that additional funds be allocated and educator training programs be implemented to facilitate student success on an individual regional basis. He speculates that an emphasis should be placed on students being attracted to being in school with aggressively promoted after-school programs to draw students into a sense of school community and equally aggressively promoted economic programs to attract parents of school-age children to the target region to ensure success.

Which choice describes the region on the map that supports the government official's conclusion?

(A) West
(B) Midwest
(C) South
(D) Northeast

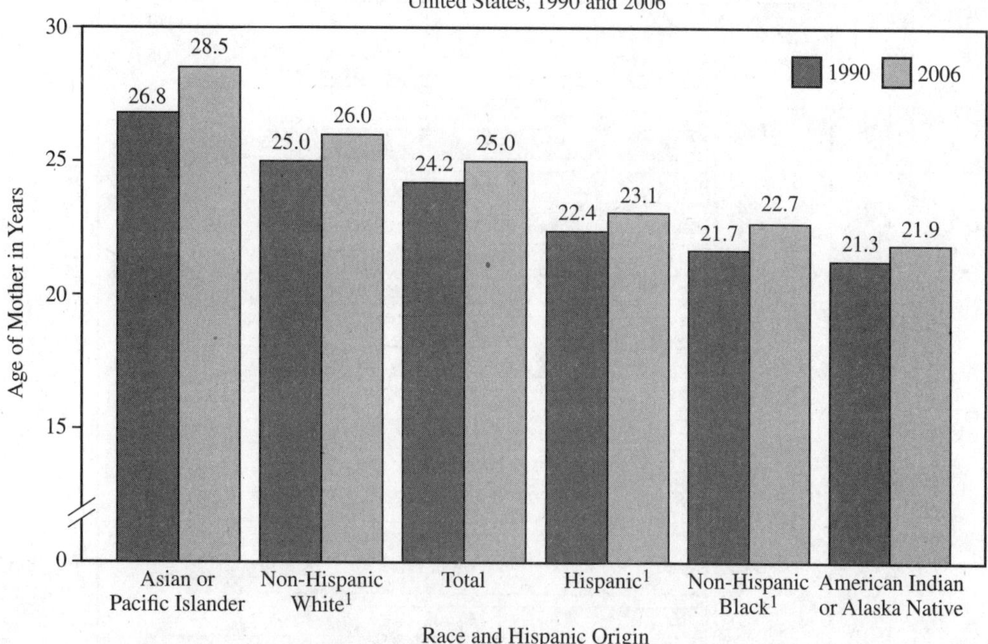

[1]For 1990, excludes data for New Hampshire and Oklahoma, which did not report Hispanic origin.
Source: CDC/NCHS, National Vital Statistics System.

19. Delayed childbearing is a significant factor to consider when attempting to determine population projections of a country. Also, the resulting consequences of women waiting longer to have children will determine a country's needs on many different levels. A researcher became interested in the public image being projected by women in the media. They frequently expressed the desire to be more career oriented and, once established as independent women, then consider giving birth and raising children. The researcher decided to explore the subject by investigating studies done on the ages of women when they gave birth for the first time. The researcher speculated that the shift in thinking was limited on an ethnic or racial basis.

    Which choice best describes data from the graph that would weaken the researcher's conclusion?

    (A) Birth rates were already low in Hispanic, non-Hispanic black, and American Indian or Alaska Native populations.
    (B) The numbers suggest a cultural shift concerning women becoming first-time mothers within the Asian or Pacific Islander population.
    (C) The total numbers reflect a higher age for first-time mothers.
    (D) Every ethnic group studied experienced an increase in the age of women giving birth for the first time.

Average Age of Mother at First Birth: Selected Countries, 1970 And 2006

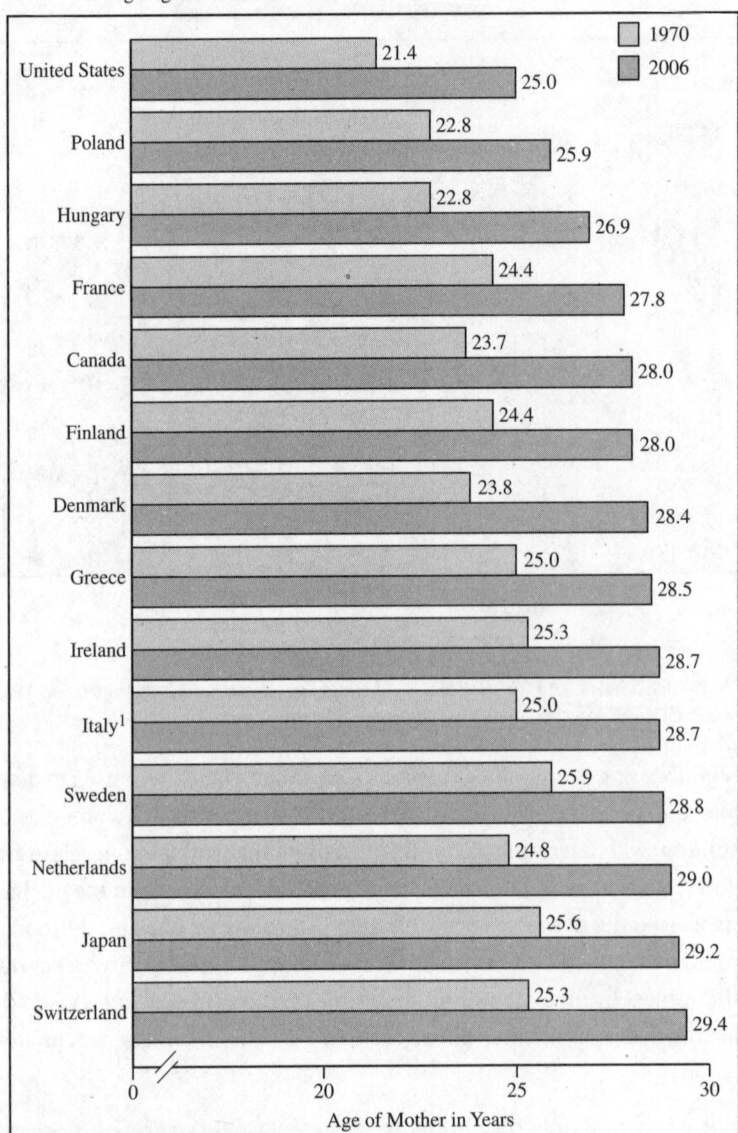

[1]Latest data are for 2005.
Sources: CDC/NCHS, National Vital Statistics System, Council of Europe, Vienna Institute of Demography, Statistics Canada, and Japanese Ministry of Health, Labour and Welfare.

20. The researcher gathered international reports taken in 1970 and 2006 documenting the average ages of women giving birth for the first time in 14 developed nations, including the United States. The average ages of the women at the time of their first births in 2006 increased from the ages reported in 1970. Despite the magnitude of the global impact of this worldwide trend, the United States did stand out from the rest of the nations because ____________.

Which choice most effectively uses data from the graph to complete the example?

(A) Switzerland's age of first birth in 1970 was higher than that of the United States in 2006
(B) The United States jumped ahead of Poland by almost one year
(C) The average age at first birth in the United States was the youngest in both 1970 and 2006
(D) The representation of the United States on the graph does not reflect younger women's ages before their first birth

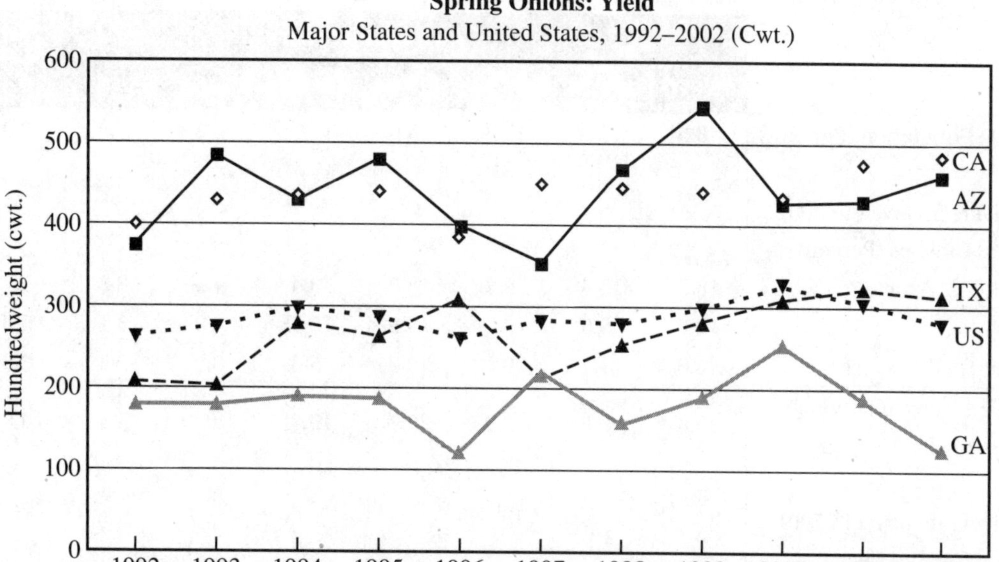

21. The quality and yield of onion crops are affected by a myriad of factors, such as air and soil temperatures, rain and irrigation amounts, planting times, and fungal diseases such as *Stemphylium* fungus. Agriculturalists look for patterns from one year to the next to anticipate what challenges are ahead. Several states over the ten years represented by the graph routinely experienced major production fluctuations, with only one state escaping dramatic losses, that being __________.

    Which choice most efficiently uses data from the graph to complete the example?

    (A) Arizona
    (B) Texas
    (C) Georgia
    (D) California

Drivers Involved in Fatal Crashes and Driver Involvement Rates by Age Group, 2002

	Age Group (Years)							
	15–20	21–24	25–34	35–44	45–54	55–64	65–69	70+
2002 Population (Percent)	8.5	5.6	13.8	15.6	13.9	9.2	3.3	9.0
Drivers Involved in 2002 Fatal Crashes (Percent)								
Single-Vehicle	18.5	13.5	20.7	18.0	13.4	7.4	2.3	5.7
Multi-Vehicle	12.2	9.6	19.7	19.9	15.9	9.8	3.1	9.8
All Fatal Crashes	14.6	11.1	20.1	19.2	15.0	8.9	2.8	8.2
2001 Licensed Drivers* (Percent)	6.6	6.8	18.9	21.7	19.3	12.3	4.4	10.0
Drivers Involved in 2001 Fatal Crashes per 100,000 Licensed Drivers	64.8	46.2	32.1	27.1	22.6	20.0	19.3	25.2

* 2002 data not available.

22. Fatal traffic crashes and the number of drivers involved for the most part are increasing. Many conclude that with more drivers on the road, issues such as texting, drinking, road rage, climate change affecting road conditions, and inadequate roadways and bridges to handle the numbers of vehicles are inevitably going to affect driver safety and road safety. Age of the driver as it relates to fatal crashes has been studied for decades. A study in 2002 examined percentages of drivers involved in fatal crashes. This study would suggest that the age of the driver may be a factor in driving safely. One age group, however, stands out as being involved in significantly fewer fatal crashes: ___________________________.

    Which choice most effectively uses data from the graph to complete the example?

    (A) 15-20
    (B) 21-24
    (C) 65-69
    (D) 70+

Children Under Age 18 and Adults Ages 65 and Over as a Percentage of the Total U.S. Population: 1950–2001 and Projected, 2010 and 2020

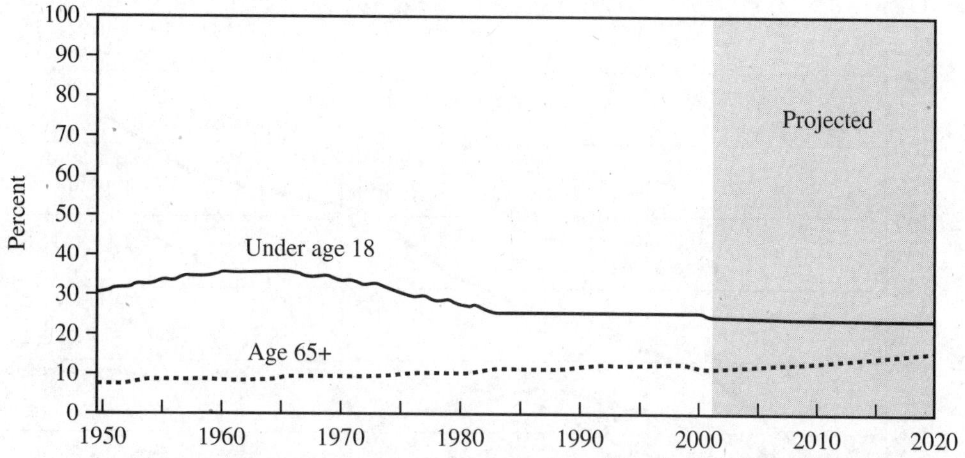

Sources: U.S. Census Bureau (2003). National Population Estimates, Characteristics. [On-line]. Available: http://eire.census.gov/popest/data/national/tables/asro/US-EST2001-ASRO-01.php; U.S. Census Bureau. (2002). *Statistical Abstract of the United States,* 2001; U.S. Census Bureau. (1996). *Current Population Reports,* P25-1130; U.S. Census Bureau. (1982). *Current Population Reports,* P25-917; U.S. Census Bureau. (1974). *Current Population Reports,* P25-519; U.S. Census Bureau. (1965). *Current Population Reports,* P25-311.

23. Historically, children under the age of 17 and adults over the age of 65 are considered to comprise part of the population called "dependents." Of course, variables exist at both ends of the spectrum. Some 16-year-olds are earning a living to support their families and at the same time are working toward graduation. On the other hand, senior citizens seem to be "getting younger," with 70 being seen as the "new 60." Even the Social Security Administration and the Internal Revenue Service are viewing the old as young as retirement age is going higher. Regardless, both groups have been seen as "dependents" because of their age and how that age affects their ability to be economically active. What's interesting is the contrasting nature of their populations over the last 70 years: ________________.

Which choice most effectively uses data from the graph to complete the example?

(A) the older generation is growing in numbers and will soon outnumber the under-17 group
(B) the elderly population has grown, but the younger age group has declined and stabilized
(C) although the younger population outnumbers the elderly, the number of younger ones is still growing
(D) the combined numbers of the over-65 population and those under 17 constitute a new workforce for America

Labor Productivity of For-Hire Transportation Industries: 1990–2000

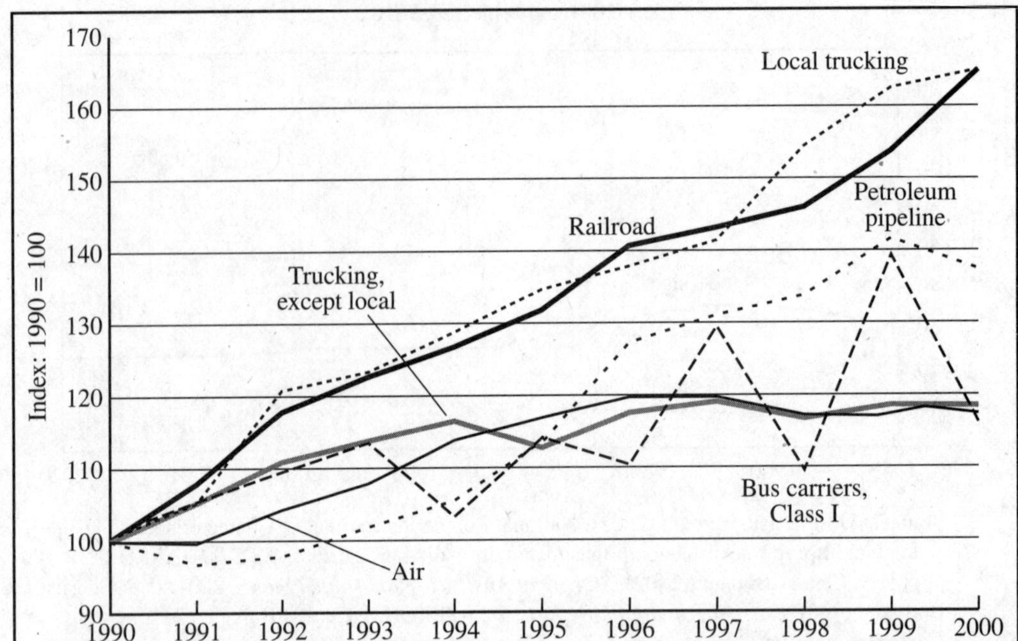

24. According to the Bureau of Labor Statistics, when you compare output with how much labor was needed to produce the output, the result is a measure of economic performance called labor productivity. This idea leads into higher wages and, we can reasonably assume, better working conditions. For example, if you decide to make and sell bead necklaces to earn some spending money, you need to determine your labor productivity as a step toward deciding whether the venture will be profitable. If you spend 2 hours a day, 6 days per week making the necklaces (12 hours/week) and you produce 24 necklaces per week, your productivity is 2 necklaces per hour. On the other hand, using data about ________ to determine labor productivity in for-hire transportation is sometimes less stable, as you can see from the graph.

Which choice best illustrates data from the graph that would support the writer's conclusion?

(A) bus carriers, class 1
(B) trucking, except local
(C) railroad
(D) local trucking

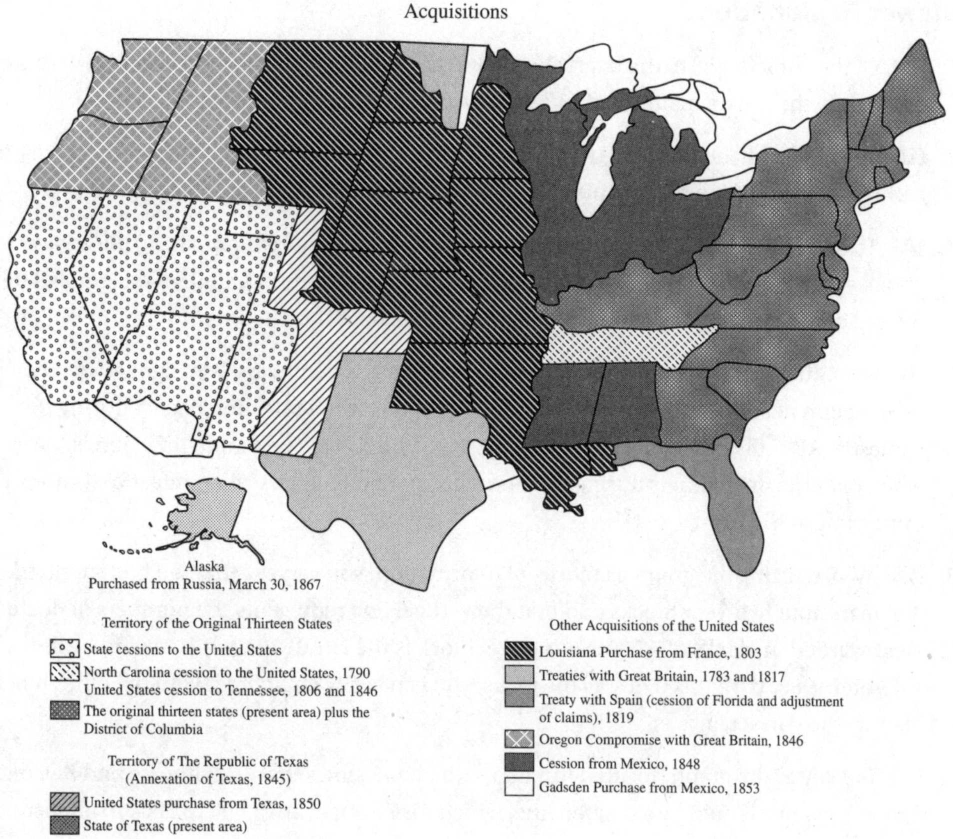

25. Much of the land acquired by the United States between 1781 and 1867 was purchased with monies going to Louisiana, Spain, Russia, Mexico, France, and some of the states themselves. These purchases brought billions of acres of undeveloped lands into the public domain of the United States. One of the notable purchases made by the United States included ____________________.

Which choice most effectively uses data from the map to complete the example?

(A) the original thirteen colonies because of the French and Indian War
(B) parts of New Mexico, Oklahoma, Colorado, Wyoming, and Kansas from the Republic of Texas
(C) the Louisiana Purchase from Great Britain
(D) the Pacific Northwest from Russia

Answer Explanations

1. **(C)** Of the choices given, the chart shows that women are far more concentrated in this category than the others mentioned.

2. **(C)** The lighter shaded bars are much shorter than the darker bars for these three lakes, indicating a decrease from the samples taken in earlier years.

3. **(A)** To determine the correct answer in to this question requires comparing the answer choices with the figure to determine which regions are not represented on the graph. Only the regions in choice (A) do not have representative data shown.

4. **(B)** From the graph, the risk of developing clinical signs before age 3 is higher when congenital infection occurs during the first trimester than it is when infection occurs during the third trimester. Also, the preceding sentence says that "the risk of congenital infection is lowest when maternal infection is during the first trimester and highest when infection is during the third trimester."

5. **(C)** By visualizing the graph as blocks of information, you can see that the bottom horizontal line marks out five-year blocks and that the vertical line represents the numbers of doctorates awarded in blocks of 5,000. Your target block is the late 1970s, which would be between 1975 and 1980. With this block as the focus, you can easily compare it with the other blocks to identify the correct answer.

6. **(C)** The key to the graph (located just above the box) shows that "Healthcare and Related" figures are represented by a dashed line, which rose from over 13,000 in 2004 to almost 16,000 in 2014.

7. **(C)** Cases peaked in August, declined, and then reached a much smaller peak in July.

8. **(B)** Reading and understanding the keys (in this case, the use of shading) and the labels identifying the vertical and horizontal lines that make up the blocks of information will help you answer these types of questions. The years are on the horizontal plane. By going over to the "By 2030" bar, you can move up to find the figures you need. Finally, apply the key or legend to determine which number refers to new teaching posts and which one refers to attrition.

9. **(D)** Under the number column in the marriage section of the chart, you will find that at the traditional beginning of summer vacation season (June), marriages jump from 179,000 in the previous month to 229,000 and remain above 200,000 until the end of October.

10. **(C)** Although the graphic does not specify the cause(s) of the 5+% increase of school enrollment in over one dozen states with lesser amounts of increase in over a dozen more, it is reasonable to assume that some of the increase can be attributed to migration from those states experiencing decline. Regardless, the student's call for the need for more infrastructure is logical given that over 25 states would have increased school-age populations and an almost equal number of states would have declining populations and need fewer resources.

11. **(A)** Only Mexico grew from 29.3 to 33.6 million in the 15-34 population. The Canadian and American declines in these numbers, which represent the beginning workforce and young-family years, would negatively affect the numbers of entry-level jobs needed and the educational resources required to address the declining numbers.

12. **(B)** We can assume that many factors would contribute to the substantial drop in production of lowfat dairy ice cream; however, regardless of the cause, a decreasing inventory would logically result in increasing prices and supply-demand issues. Such factors as these would most likely cause the investors to hesitate.

13. **(C)** The graph shows that 1,053.8 men died per 100,000 in 2000; only 905.8 men died per 100,000 in 2007. According to the graph, only 731.4 women per 100,000 died in 2000; however, 643.4 women died per 100,000 in 2007, representing a lower rate of decline than that of men.

14. **(D)** At first glance, the main (larger) chart shows groups 1–4, 5–9, 10–14, and even 15–19 at the same level. The graph that projects a telescopic view of these groups (based on a 100 scale rather than on a 1,000 scale) does show that the 5–9 group has the lowest death rate with the 1–4 group higher to the left and the 10–14 group higher to the right.

15. **(B)** Only New Mexico in the Four Corners states has rates one step above the other three states. Both Pacific Northwest states (Washington and Oregon) and the Southeast Mississippi Delta region appear to be among the highest in the nation. Only the cluster of New England states reflects a diversity of age-adjusted death rates that range from the very lowest to the very highest.

16. **(C)** Cancer ranks fourth place among those below the age of 25. It falls just below accidents as the leading cause of death in the 25–44 age group but rises to first place among those ages 45–64 before falling to second place again for those in retirement age.

17. **(A)** Many different factors could and probably did influence the actual data and the projections made in the late-twentieth century. However, it would be reasonable to assume that young couples in the 1960s postponing beginning their families (which would affect school enrollment in the 1970s and 1980s) could be one contributing element. Because the negative numbers indicate decreases in enrollment, the most pronounced example is the actual figure (not projected) of a −12.5% (indicating decline) in enrollment in grades PreK–8 in public schools. The private school enrollment of −0.4% also suggests a decline but to a lesser degree.

18. **(B)** When taken as a whole, every region shown on the map was projected to experience falling school enrollment and, consequently, supports the overall premise of the official. However, implied in his plan is to identify the region in greatest need of such efforts. Although enrollment in the Midwest and Northeast are projected to fall substantially, enrollment in the Midwest and Northeast are both projected to fall to deficit numbers. Of the two, the Midwest began at a lower starting point, making it the potential "poster child" of the government official's proposal.

19. **(D)** The ages of women giving birth for the first time went up significantly among Asian or Pacific Islander women and also went up (although more modestly) among non-Hispanic whites, Hispanics, non-Hispanic blacks, and American Indian or Alaska Native women. The data give support to the idea that this trend is possibly part of a cultural shift based on gender rather than race.

20. **(C)** In the larger picture, the United States impressively jumped from 21.4 to 25 for the ages of first births; however, these are both younger ages than in any other nation.

21. **(D)** California's worst year was 1996 when its production fell just slightly below 400.

22. **(C)** The 65–69 age group comprises only 3.3% of the 2002 population, and these individuals were involved in only 2.85% of the fatal crashes that year.

23. **(B)** As shown in the graph, the under-17 group at one time was around 35% of the general population but has dropped by around 10%. Senior citizens, in contrast, have grown from under 10 percent to around 15 percent.

24. **(A)** Most of the for-hire transportation data on the graph show reasonably stable rises or status quo conditions. Data for bus carriers, class 1, however, suggest a less predictable labor productivity with frequent rises and falls.

25. **(B)** The only answer that is supported by the map is choice (B). Because the map does not identify the names of the states, having a basic knowledge of American geography is helpful.

Textual Evidence

You will again be evaluating a writer's claim, but this time you will be determining whether it is supported, not supported, or illustrated by evidence presented in the answer choices. You may need to read and reread the text, and that's OK. Take your time, be a digital SAT sleuth, and find your evidence!

Practice

Each question has one or more passages. Carefully read each passage and question, and choose the best answer to the question based on the passage.

1. A noted historian wrote several in-depth scholarly articles centering on the generational contexts of the Women's Movement, from its inception over one hundred years ago to today. Part of his studies focused on discriminatory ordinances and laws in both the public and private sectors. He claims that these instruments of discrimination have shifted from being reflections of the prevailing attitudes (of both males and females) dictating the roles women can and should take in our day-to-day lives to such ordinances and laws now being viewed as repugnant, resulting in a call to action for their overthrow or repeal.

   Which recent actions, if true, would most directly undermine the historian's claim?

   (A) Voters overwhelmingly supporting a law allowing women to be drafted
   (B) A state law still on the books, although overlooked in practice, making it illegal for a woman to cut her hair without her husband's consent
   (C) A local news report that male and female employees of a local corporation walked off their jobs in response to accusations that the women are being paid substantially less than the men
   (D) Title VII of the Civil Rights Act being enacted to prohibit an employer from treating a woman differently from a man

2. "The Parting" is a poem written around 1900 by Michael Drayton about a romance that is ending. The poem directly addresses the lover who is leaving and reveals the pain that the speaker is experiencing, but it also reaches out with an expression of hope of reconciliation: __________

   Which quotation from "The Parting" most effectively illustrates the claim that the speaker is still seeking reconciliation with the lover?

   (A) Since there is no help, come let us kiss and part— / Nay, I have done, you get no more of me;
   (B) And I am glad, yea, glad with all my heart, / That thus so cleanly I myself can free.
   (C) Now at the last gasp of Love's latest breath, / When, his pulse failing, Passion speechless lies,
   (D) Now if thou would'st, when all have given him over, / From death to life thou might'st him yet recover.

3. In the late-twentieth century, a clinical professor of family studies suggested that American teens in the 1980s were adopting an ethic of self-indulgence because they personally had never experienced an international war and growing up had all their needs met, giving them a sense of confidence in their futures. At the same time, however, she observed that the constant threat of nuclear war, reinforced by the Cuban Missile Crisis and the Cold War, brought out in the same generation feelings that they should make the most of life now because tomorrow may never come. She concludes, then, that although the causal factors are in direct opposition, the results are the same.

   Which of the following, if true, would support the professor's claim?

   (A) An international study in 1988 found that young people in Europe were more likely to fear nuclear conflict than their American counterparts.
   (B) A randomized survey of adults with teenaged children in 1982 found that 34% felt the children in their community were self-indulgent, but only 21% believed that their own children were fearful of a nuclear confrontation.
   (C) A survey in 1995 found that 42% of Americans (ages 25–40) in major debt reported that they did not know how to create a budget and never felt the need to save, and another 37% of those surveyed felt, while growing up, that being financially responsible had no real future value.
   (D) A statistical increase in blue-collar workers was reported among the workforce between the years 1980 and 2000.

4. A scientist in the field of ethology (the study of the behavior of animals) applies for a research grant to conduct a study of the communication between horses and humans as demonstrated in "horse whispering." Horse whispering is a technique in which the horse trainer becomes aware of the horse's nonverbal communications and responds sympathetically, attempting to meet the needs of the animal as part of the training experience. The scientist includes in the grant application a claim that observing, isolating, studying, and applying the different components of horse whispering would result in a paradigm that could be incorporated into animal-training programs for equine therapy animals.

   Which finding, if true, would most directly support the researcher's claim?

   (A) A study of the interaction between 12 horses at a horseback riding venue and special-needs children between the ages of 10 and 15 who were introduced to the horses as part of their therapy program revealed that 11 of the 12 horses exhibited physical movements indicating recognition when the children came into view after only one visit.
   (B) The 1995 novel *The Horse Whisperer* by Nickolas Evans was made into a movie.
   (C) A report issued by a leading equine publication points out that despite the consistent use of natural horsemanship, many trainers schooled in the techniques of horse whispering found that the horses often acquired bad habits.
   (D) A growing trend among horse trainers is to market their skills based on the degree of gentleness found in their training techniques.

5. "The Flower" is a poem written about 1830 by Alfred, Lord Tennyson to address those who criticize his poetry. The speaker throws down a seed (representing his poetry) that takes root and grows. The people call it a weed until it grew to be a tall and beautiful flower. Thieves stole it, and it was sown everywhere (other poets copying his style and so forth), until it became common, with some flowers that were pretty and some that were poor, at which point the people once again called it a weed. The speaker claims that this story is a fable, meaning it contains a moral or lesson.

   Which quotation from "The Flower" most effectively illustrates the claim?

   (A) Up there came a flower, / The people said, a weed.
   (B) Till all the people cried, / 'Splendid is the flower.
   (C) Most can raise the flowers now, / For all have got the seed.
   (D) And now again the people / Call it but a weed.

6. Rabbit hemorrhagic disease virus 2 (RHDV2) is threatening both the wild and domestic populations of rabbits in the continental United States. It is transmitted by contact with infected rabbits, of course, but it is so contagious that it can also be spread by just about anything from clothing and equipment to water and insects. The talons of birds of prey have been reported to spread the disease from one area to another. One researcher claims that many owners of domestic rabbits may be unaware of the magnitude of the ecological disaster ahead if the progress of this disease is not stopped. She proposes that a massive educational campaign be funded by state governments to make people more aware of the serious nature of the situation and to give them the knowledge and resources they need to stop its spread.

   Which finding, if true, would most directly support the researcher's claim?

   (A) RHDV2 has been found in jackrabbit populations in California.
   (B) A statistical report from April 2022 reveals that RHDV2 was found in both the wild and domestic rabbit populations of 11 states. In addition, only the domestic rabbits were infected in an additional nine states.
   (C) Vets in Texas have been given authorization to import RHDV2 vaccine from Europe to treat domestic rabbits; however, the vaccine only helps rabbits survive and does not protect against contracting the disease.
   (D) RHDV2 can be contracted only by rabbits; humans and domestic animals, such as dogs, cats, cows, and birds, are unaffected.

7. A writer has been collecting anecdotal evidence about the relationship human health has to pet ownership. He has been talking to friends, family, and coworkers about their pets and their health and has plans to publish their stories in an e-book format. Based on these interviews, he is convinced that people who have pets are healthier and live longer lives than those who do not have pets.

   Which finding, if true, would most directly undermine the writer's claim?

   (A) A 12-year study published in *Circulation: Cardiovascular Quality and Outcomes* leads researchers to believe that people with heart conditions can reduce their risk of death by as much as 21% by owning a dog.
   (B) Based on a 2005 study, researchers speculate that dogs may transmit bacteria that can cause halitosis in their owners.
   (C) A study recently found that suicide rates are lower among those who own dogs. Follow-up studies reveal that dog ownership gives people a sense of purpose.
   (D) The University of Michigan conducted a study that suggests that owning a dog/pet can improve memory.

8. Soil biodiversity is an increasingly debated topic in the global conversation about how to meet the challenges of climate change and food shortages. For soil to be healthy, it must contain many diverse organisms that can function in an interdependent relationship with vegetation, called nutrient cycling. Soil scientists claim that fungi can actually help regulate our climate through nutrient cycling.

   Which finding, if true, would most directly support the scientists' claim?

   (A) A study revealed that edible fungi, mushrooms, are an important source of micro- and macro-nutrients.
   (B) Researchers discovered that many edible mushrooms (up to 6 percent) are also medicinal.
   (C) A study found that fungi join with plants in a soil-food web, allowing them to capture literally tons of carbon from the atmosphere to store it harmlessly in the soil.
   (D) Based on the science, a movement has begun to protect soil fungi by limiting the conversion of raw land to traditional agricultural activities and tightening regulations against deforestation.

9. Canadian poet Emily Pauline Johnson (Tekahionwake) was the daughter of a Mohawk chief and an English woman. In the "Author's Forward" to her volume of collected verse, Johnson tells us that she titled the collection *Flint and Feather* because both "flint and feather bear the hallmark of my Mohawk blood."

   Which quotation from the "Author's Forward" of *Flint and Feather* most effectively supports her claim?

   (A) "Flint . . . is the arrow tip, the heart quality of mine own people; . . . Indian life and love . . . And yet that feather may be the eagle plume that crests the head of a warrior chief."
   (B) "This collection of verse I have named *Flint and Feather* because of the association of ideas."
   (C) "Flint suggests the Red Man's weapons of war."
   (D) "Skyward floating feather, / Sailing on summer air."

10. *She Stoops to Conquer* is a play by Oliver Goldsmith written in 1773. Critics claim that the play is a satire focused on the landed gentry and their unwillingness or inability to change in a changing eighteenth-century world.

    Which quotation from *She Stoops to Conquer* most effectively illustrates the claim?

    (A) "I vow, Mr. Hardcastle, you're very particular."
    (B) "I wonder why London cannot keep its own fools at home."
    (C) "I love everything that's old: . . ."
    (D) ". . . you'll own I have been pretty fond of an old wife."

11. Frances Willard gave a speech in 1876 in which she advocates for women's suffrage. She claims that men should be instrumental in facilitating the efforts to make it legal for women to vote because men bear the responsibility of suppressing women's suffrage.

    Which quotation from Willard's speech most effectively illustrates the claim?

    (A) "I wonder if poor, rum-cursed Wisconsin will ever get a law like that!"
    (B) "Yes, Josiah, there'll be such a law all over the land someday, when women vote."
    (C) "And pray, how will you arrange it so that women shall vote?"
    (D) "Well, I say to you, as the Apostle Paul said to his jailor: 'You have put us into prison, we being Romans, and you must come and take us out.'"

12. The Tiny House Movement is a trend that promises a life that is simpler and more sustainable by downsizing to a home generally under 400 square feet and built on wheels as compared to the average American home of 2,500 square feet on a solid foundation. Advocates of tiny homes point out that they are more economical to build, reduce living expenses, and are environmentally friendly.

    Which finding in a recent study, if true, would most directly undermine the claims of the Tiny House Movement?

    (A) Although utilities are lower, specialty construction costs and hidden costs such as special permits and land rental are making the cost of tiny houses comparable to larger homes.
    (B) There is very little privacy in a little house.
    (C) Tiny homes often have inadequate storage.
    (D) Many owners of tiny homes report feeling lonely or isolated.

13. As one would expect, dancing has many physical benefits, including improving heart and lung health. Social scientists, however, now believe there are correlations between dancing and brain function, particularly to lessen forms of dementia such as Alzheimer's disease.

    Which of the following, if true, would best support this claim?

    (A) A Swedish study concluded that female dancers experience decreased levels of anxiety and stress during periods of actively dancing.
    (B) Seven out of 10 amateur dancers report improved flexibility as a result of dancing.
    (C) The *Almanac of Developing and Physical Life* reports that seniors experience improved balance by dancing the tango.
    (D) A report published in the *New England Journal of Medicine* reports that working on multiple crossword puzzles each week reduced the risk of dementia by 47% but frequent dancing reduces the risk by 76%.

14. *Bretziella fagacearum* is the fungus that causes oak wilt, usually killing an infected oak tree by growing into and blocking the tree's water-conducting system. It is found largely in the central United States. This invasive disease is known regionally to cost landowners millions of dollars in dead tree removal and in property value losses as it spreads from property to property though its root systems underground and sap beetle migrations. A study reports that as a result of climate change, the southern Ontario, Canada, region may soon experience a costly and destructive invasion of this fungus.

    Which of the following, if true, would most directly support the claim?

    (A) Development of a fungicide to treat oak wilt is showing promising results.
    (B) Insects carrying the oak wilt environmental DNA were found near the border between the United States and Canada.
    (C) Cutting down healthy trees that surround those with oak wilt is found to stall its spread.
    (D) Canadian law does not allow firewood to be brought into Canada to prevent pests from entering the country.

15. A literary historian writes an article for publication about the events leading to the first example of completed English prose, called "Handbook" (A.D. 887) under the leadership of King Alfred. In her article, she claims that these events,—for example, putting English into written form so that everyone could gain an English education,—served to save the English individualized kingdoms from falling into the hands of the Danes; and they gave the English people a sense of national pride and unity that significantly contributed to England becoming one nation.

    Which finding, if true, would most directly undermine the historian's claim?

    (A) King Alfred consolidated the people on the basis of their "Englishness" by emphasizing the English language they all spoke, collecting it and putting English into writing.
    (B) An English educational system was developed exclusively for children of nobility.
    (C) Latin books were translated into English, allowing English-speaking people to read them.
    (D) English chronicles were written to give the people a sense of national history.

16. The French author Alexis de Tocqueville, in *Democracy in America* (translated from French into English by Henry Reeve and originally published in 1835), discusses his views on laws and social power as they were emerging in the democratic institutions of the United States. In his discussion, he claims that he is not alarmed by America's excessive liberty but is concerned about the "inadequate securities which one finds there against tyranny."

    Which quotation from *Democracy in America* most effectively illustrates the claim?

    (A) "If an individual or a party is wronged in the United States, to whom can he apply for redress? If to public opinion, public opinion constitutes the majority . . . legislature represents the majority . . . the executive power is appointed by the majority. . . ."
    (B) "I do not think that, for the sake of preserving liberty, it is possible to combine several principles in the same government so as really to oppose them to one another."
    (C) "Men do not change their characters by uniting with one another. . . ."
    (D) "England in the eighteenth century . . . was essentially an aristocratic state, . . ."

17. Anthropologists have been studying "Melungeon," a triracial people first identified living near Newman's Ridge in Hancock/Hawkins County, Tennessee, around the turn of the nineteenth century. They are the subject of many mysterious Appalachian legends, and their true origins have been difficult to determine. Some researchers claim that the term "Melungeon" has been overused, and its use should be limited to those who lived on Newman's Ridge for half a century before 1844.

    Which finding, if true, would directly undermine the researchers' claim?

    (A) Several mixed-race groups have been found along the Atlantic coast; however, their DNA provides no connection to the Melungeons of Tennessee.
    (B) An internet craze in the 1990s had amateur family historians attempting to identify their own families as Melungeon with little, if any, proof other than surnames sometimes associated the Melungeon culture.
    (C) Records were found that showed some of the Newman's Ridge Melungeons migrated away to other areas after 1944.
    (D) The term "Melungeon" was used politically to insult members of the opposition party during the post–Civil War years.

18. In a book written in 1968, the authors describe the Yahgans, who once lived in the regions of Cape Horn and lived mostly from food caught or hunted in the waters of Tierra del Fuego. The area is very cold, and their work put them out in the frigid Antarctic winds; however, they generally were naked or half-clothed and lived in noninsulated shelters of skins or branches. After western civilization reached the Yahgans, their tribal numbers began to diminish from 3,000 in 1832 to 40 in 1933. The authors claim that the extinction of this tribe by the middle of the twentieth century is due in part to clothing. Because the western culture values clothing as a societal norm, the tribe began wearing clothing to work in the cold waters. The clothing would get wet, and the fires they kept on their canoes were inadequate to dry their clothing. By wearing wet clothing in the cold Antarctic winds, they fell victim to such respiratory diseases as influenza and pneumonia brought to them by the explorers.

    Which finding, if true, would most directly support the claim of the authors?

    (A) Soaking your feet in hot water containing Epsom salt at the end of the day has been found to mitigate the effects of cold exposure during extreme work hours.
    (B) A 2021 study found that cold-air exposure improved the driving performance of drivers who were sleepy due to extreme sleep deprivation.
    (C) In a research study conducted in 2022, scientists discovered that sustained exposure to cold weather increases the likelihood of contracting viruses because extreme cold temperatures can dry out our mucous membranes and allow influenza type A virus penetration.
    (D) Twenty-first century scientists studying human longevity discovered that exposure to extreme temperatures, such as in a cold shower or a sauna, act as stressors that can help the body develop healthy resilience by reducing inflammation and stress resistance.

19. As toll roads continue to be built to ease traffic congestion in urban areas and to facilitate mass transit options, controversies arise over what speed limits should be enforced on toll roads. Some states have allowed speeds of 80 miles per hour, considered by many to be too fast. Opponents to high speed limits claim that this trend may cost more lives.

    Which finding, if true, would most directly support the opponents' claim?

    (A) Proponents of high speeds on toll roads maintain that when all drivers are collectively driving at the same speed, accidents are avoided.
    (B) Statistics have shown that driving at high speeds increases the amount of time needed to slow down for road hazards and that high-speed accidents result in greater injuries.
    (C) Some drivers think that it is permissible to drive a little over the posted speed limit.
    (D) People who drive on toll roads are advised to keep their vehicles in top performance condition.

20. The United States Senate has approved a bill that, if enacted, will make Daylight Savings Time (DST) permanent on November 20, 2023. This measure has met with much debate. The supporters of DST point out that it benefits us in the areas of public safety, the general economy, and healthy lifestyle choices. Wait just a minute, counter the opponents to this governmental move. DST has some serious downsides, such as it is bad for our health and it causes workers to be sleep-deprived.

    Which finding, if true, would most directly undermine the objections of the opponents to DST becoming permanent?

    (A) Heart attack numbers reportedly increase by 10% on the Monday and Tuesday following a change to DST.
    (B) A study found that an additional 3% of the general population moved away from their television sets and began participating in outdoor activities as a result of DST.
    (C) A study found that DST causes disruption of the human body's circadian clock, making people tired and less productive.
    (D) In 2007, the Air Transport Association cited a cost of almost 150 million U.S. dollars to the industry because of conflicting time schedules with countries that do not adhere to DST.

21. With 2,340 passengers onboard the *Titanic* on its maiden voyage, why the ship's captain did not reduce speed to more safely navigate the icy waters or change course to the south to avoid any possible icebergs are questions that have hovered over the story for years. Some historians believe that the blame should be placed on the faulty idea that the ship was unsinkable, meaning that collisions would pose little threat.

    Which finding, if true, would most directly support this claim?

    (A) Captain Edward Smith, with 40 years of experience, was also captain of the *Titanic's* sister ship, the *Olympic*, which had collided with a warship but was able to sail home to port safely.
    (B) The crew of the *Titanic* was known to be inexperienced and consequently did not perform any safety drills.
    (C) The emphasis, historians came to conclude, was not on the voyage such as is the case on luxury ships today but rather on the ship being a means of speedy transportation, with emphasis on getting to the destination.
    (D) The cabins were sealed shut with steel doors that prevented hundreds of people from escaping the ship.

22. The first automatic transmission was invented in 1921 by a Canadian. This early transmission system required air pressure rather than hydraulic fluid and had no reverse. But once automatic transmissions became available to the general public, there was no reversing drivers' addiction to the sheer convenience they offer. However, there are those who maintain that the old stick shifts simply make a car more fun to drive. That conclusion, of course, rests with the individual driver. Yet there are claims being made that stick shifts provide better fuel economy and are even safer due to allowing for more control of the vehicle.

    Which finding, if true, would most directly undermine the claim?

    (A) Research shows that a stick shift improves gas mileage by as much as 5 miles per gallon over automatics.
    (B) A survey of car dealerships found that vehicles with stick shifts on average cost up to 1,000 dollars less than vehicles with automatic transmissions.
    (C) Because of their lack of popularity, vehicles with stick shifts are not produced in large numbers and varieties, meaning sometimes they are less comfortable than those with manual transmissions.
    (D) The Governors Highway Safety Association (GHSA) has issued a statement that encourages first-time drivers to emphasize safety by postponing the complexities of learning stick shift driving until they have mastered automatics.

23. In the late 1700s, Franz Joseph Gall attempted to make a correlation between brain function and the cranial bumps on the head. He was joined by J. G. Spurzheim, and the two anatomists began emphasizing the significance of the areas of the brain, especially the cortex, in relation to mental functions. They believed that the larger the cranial bump, the better the brain functions, and that the brain is not a single mass that lacks form as believed by scientists of the era, but rather it consists of different locations for different functions. This field of study became known as "phrenology" and was largely discounted many years ago as what many scientists would call nonsense. However, in the late 1990s, brain researchers, in efforts to study relationships between the brain and the mind, have seen some of Gall's work as foundational to what is known today.

    Which finding, if true, would most directly support this claim?

    (A) Modern brain researchers have found that where Gall thought the brain center for parental love is located is actually part of our visual functions.
    (B) In mapping out the bump-brain correlations, Gall's assigned brain functions have been found to be arbitrarily designated.
    (C) In a written treatise, Gall states that if a part of the brain is not used, it will shrink and the cranial bump will flatten.
    (D) Modern brain researchers identify the cerebral cortex as being instrumental in high-level function, such as memory, reason, and language, for example.

24. An atmospheric water generator (AWG) is a machine that can pull potable water from the air. These machines, according to the Environmental Protection Agency, work along the same lines as a home air conditioner. They form water through a condensation process using coils and fans. Concerns were expressed by some scientists that although an AWG creates clean water, the system may have the potential for microbial contamination from air contaminates as well as the possibility of mold growth in the condensation unit itself, especially when being used as an emergency water source in unfavorable conditions. To evaluate whether these concerns were justified, researchers conducted a three-month test, running an AWG continuously without any sterilization procedures in place.

    Which finding from the test, if true, most directly supports the basis of the researchers' concerns?

    (A) High microbial numbers were detected by heterotrophic plate counts.
    (B) No *Legionella* or *Mycobacterium* were found.
    (C) No fecal contamination was present in the test samples.
    (D) All other tests indicated that the water was potable.

25. Studies have shown that a vegetarian diet has many benefits to overall health; however, some studies suggest that a totally vegetarian diet can cause certain nutritional deficits if not carefully planned. Most of the diets associated with Blue Zone areas (places where people live healthy lives to 100 years old and sometimes beyond) are for the most part a variation of vegetarianism. A school district health counselor has proposed to change the district's school lunch program diet to be a plant-forward omnivorous whole-foods diet (consisting of such unprocessed foods as whole grains, fresh fruits and vegetables, modest portions of lean, pasture-raised organic meats, eggs, unsweetened dairy products, and wild-caught seafood) and is collecting data to present to the school board and parents.

    Which finding, if true, would most directly support the counselor's efforts to initiate this dietary change into the school district's lunch program?

    (A) A Gallop poll found that 5% of Americans were vegetarian in 2019.
    (B) Many studies suggest that vegetarianism decreases an individual's chances of having cardiovascular disease, obesity, Type 2 diabetes, and some forms of cancer, as well as some forms of dementia, and results in a lower risk of all-cause mortality.
    (C) *Progress in Cardiovascular Diseases* published a review of existing studies emphasizing that vegans are at risk for nutritional deficiencies and that a diet that combines foods found in a healthy vegan diet with healthy animal foods is the more balanced approach for meeting nutritional needs.
    (D) *Psychology Today* reported studies conducted in 2018 that found not only are vegetarian men more depressed than meat eaters, but also vegetarians in general suffer more bad moods and have less meaning in life, compounded by lower self-esteem.

Answer Explanations

1. **(B)** Part of the historian's claim is that discriminatory laws and regulations in recent times result in a call to action for their overthrow or repeal. Choice (B) reveals that this clearly discriminatory law is being tolerated ("overlooked in practice"), with no mention of efforts to take it off the books.

2. **(D)** Choices (A) and (B) reveal the "see if I care" response of the speaker to cover obviously hurt feelings. Although "Love" is dying in choice (C), the speaker reveals in choice (D) that his lover can, at will, bring Love from death to life again, logically resulting in a reconciliation.

3. **(C)** The claim is that young Americans in the 1980s who lived for the moment did so because they had never experienced hardships and assumed the good life would never end or, in contrast, because they believed tomorrow would never come. The 1995 statistics, taken when the young people in question would be adults, support this idea because people who believe prosperity is endless would not strive to save for hard times and those who believe the world will end during their lifetimes would see no future value in saving money.

4. **(A)** The claim is that the physical communication of horses toward people can be observed, isolated, studied, and then applied to training the horses to be therapy animals. The observation that the horses used physical movements indicating that they recognized special-needs children would illustrate that the first step toward developing such a program is possible.

5. **(D)** The lesson is found in the full-circle moment at which the speaker points out that the weed that turned into a flower and was coveted by the people became so common that they once again viewed it as a weed. In the speaker's view, his style of poetry, original for the time, was criticized until it bloomed in full expression of his art, and then became the target of thieves whose attempts at his poetic style made it so common that it no longer had the attractive beauty of a rare flower.

6. **(B)** The claim is that owners of domestic rabbits may be unaware of how serious the threat of RHDV2 is and the importance of stopping its spread. The fact that it is spreading at a faster rate among domestic rabbits than it is spreading in the wild supports this idea.

7. **(B)** The claim is that owning a dog increases health and longevity. Bacterial halitosis is not a sign of good health.

8. **(C)** The claim is that fungi can help mitigate climate change. A key element of climate change is the large amounts of CO_2 released into the atmosphere. Consequently, the ability of the soil-food web to sequester large-scale amounts of CO_2 would help effect change.

9. **(A)** The poet's claim is that flint and feathers are hallmarks of Mohawk ancestry. A hallmark is a distinguishing characteristic or trait. Flint is often associated with the Native American arrowhead, a weapon of war. Feathers are generally thought to be soft and easily blown away by the wind. Johnson cleverly combines these two hallmarks by pointing out the contrasting elements of each within the Mohawk culture. The tip of a flint arrowhead represents Indian life and love; the feather rests upon the head of a warrior.

10. **(C)** The claim is that the play focuses on the resistance of landed gentry to the changes happening in a changing world. Loving everything that is old usually is an antithesis of the desired change, whereas dissatisfaction with the old often is the catalyst for change.

11. **(D)** This statement supports the claim by shifting the responsibility for securing voting rights for women to being the responsibility of the men who were denying women the means to accomplish this goal. Her biblical allusion in choice (D) likens women to the Apostle Paul and compares men to the jailor who took away his freedoms.

12. **(A)** The claim is that tiny homes provide a life that is simpler, more sustainable, economical, and environmentally conscious. No claims are made in this selection concerning privacy issues, storage availability, or psychological impacts of the lifestyle of living in a tiny home.

13. **(D)** The claim is based on a correlation between dancing and brain health. Only choice (D) addresses both dancing and dementia (brain illness).

14. **(B)** The claim is that Canada may soon experience the devastating destruction of oak wilt disease because the effects of climate change may bring oak wilt further north. Finding evidence that the insects that carry the oak wilt environmental DNA (possibly sap beetles) have migrated near the Canadian border would suggest that the disease could, indeed, be at Canada's doorstep.

15. **(B)** The claim includes that the events leading to completed English prose made the English language a unifying force instrumental in defeating the Danes and establishing England as one nation rather than many independent kingdoms. Allowing only the noble classes to be educated would serve to divide, not unify, the people.

16. **(A)** The claim is that America's democratic system provides no checks and balances against potential tyranny. Tyranny is governmental rule that is cruel and/or oppressive, often with power used in an unreasonable or arbitrary manner. We can infer by his reasoning that the speaker views the majority rule concept in America as an opportunity for tyranny because if someone is mistreated there is no one to plead his or her cause against the majority.

17. **(C)** The claim is that the term "Melungeon" has been overused (implying that the term has been applied to and/or claimed by people with no real connections to this group) and only the people living in a specified area before 1944 can truly be called "Melungeon." Choices (A), (B), and (D) support this idea by emphasizing the uniqueness of the Newman's Ridge group and how the name has been misused over the years. Choice (C), however, by inference suggests that because they migrated from their Tennessee homes after 1844, their descendants, who would also be of Melungeon lineage, would be entitled to the name.

18. **(C)** The claim is that prolonged exposure in wet clothing to cold weather conditions allowed the people to contract deadly viruses. Choices (A) and (B) are off topic. Choice (D) provides a possible explanation for why these people were able to survive with little clothing before the arrival of the western culture, presumably a period in which they were not exposed to viruses. However, choice (C) directly addresses the claim.

19. **(B)** Choices (A) and (D) relate to allowing high speeds on toll roads. Choice (C) is more germane to law enforcement issues; however, choice (B) addresses the logic of allowing speeds that can result in greater injuries than slower speeds.

20. **(B)** Both choices (A) and (C) would support objections to moving to DST based on health reasons. Choice (D) is a reasonable objection; however, it is not based on health reasons. Only choice (B) addresses health: we can infer that outdoor activities are healthier than watching television.

21. **(A)** Given that the two ships were "sisters," meaning that they were of the same class and almost identical in design, the captain—who was able to bring the *Olympic* safely home after a collision—might have logically assumed that the *Titanic* would also be as sturdy against collisions and be "unsinkable."

22. **(D)** The claim is that vehicles with stick shifts provide better fuel economy and are even safer than automatics. The GHSA's suggestion implies that for a select group (namely, first-time drivers) a stick shift might be a safety issue until they learn the basics of driving.

23. **(D)** The claim is that some of Gall's ideas are turning out to be correct. The descriptive highlights of some of his ideas include that "the two anatomists began emphasizing the significance of the areas of the brain, especially the cortex, in relation to mental functions."

24. **(A)** The AWG produces clean (potable) drinking water. However, the potential exists for the machine to capture and grow contaminates, making the water unsafe. Although seriously egregious contaminates were not found during the test, the fact of high microbial numbers (A) present does support the concerns that the potential for the water to be unsafe is there.

25. **(C)** The counselor wants the school's diet to combine both whole healthy plant foods with whole healthy animal foods. Choices (A) and (B) address only vegetarianism. Choice (D) undermines vegetarianism. Only choice (C) directly supports the key elements of a plant-forward omnivorous whole-foods diet.

Inferences

In these questions you will be combining clues in the text with your own sense of logic and reason to "read between the lines" of what the author is saying. You should look for implications and suggestive statements that point to what the writer is really saying.

Practice

Each question has one or more passages. Carefully read each passage and question, and choose the best answer to the question based on the passage.

1. This passage is from OECD/Nuclear Energy Agency (2000), "Nuclear Energy in a Sustainable Development Perspective," *www.oecd-nea.org/sd.*

   "Groundwater resources in the U.S., for instance, are often overused because of subsidies, a lack of tradable rights to water ('use it or lose it'), and a lack of clear property rights to water tables. Overfishing in the oceans provides a better example. It is easy to imagine that cattle might be scarce, just as buffalo became scarce, if they were owned in common and were taken from one vast domain, rather than being privately owned on separate ranches. While the exact analogue to barbed wire for fishing grounds in the ocean may be hard to conceive, assigning ownership rights to the ocean should not be much more difficult than assigning ownership rights to the radio frequency spectrum, as is currently being done throughout the world." The implication is clear: ____________________.

   Which choice most logically completes the text?

   (A) people have little incentive to conserve cattle.
   (B) cattle are much easier to kill than buffalo.
   (C) public or common ownership is better than private ownership.
   (D) private ownership is better than public or common ownership.

2. This passage is from OECD/Nuclear Energy Agency (2000), "Nuclear Energy in a Sustainable Development Perspective," *www.oecd-nea.org/sd.*

   "There is much enthusiasm for 'getting the incentives right.' This produces nods of agreement on the general level, and furious disagreement about its specific application. 'Getting the incentives right' should mean chiefly assigning property rights to environmental goods, rather than using government power to set the 'correct price' for the use of a commonly held environmental good. Any so-called 'market-based incentive' policy that involves government setting the 'correct price' to establish a 'level playing field' is inherently flawed, because it misunderstands the nature of markets and prices. The government will always lack the necessary knowledge to set the 'right' price, and such policies will usually introduce new distortions into the marketplace that will likely be counterproductive and wasteful of resources." Consequently, ______________________________.

   Which choice most logically completes the text?

   (A) one of the most important roles of government in the conservation of unsustainable resources is to assign property rights to environmental goods
   (B) if property rights are assigned to environmental goods, there will be no more instances of unsustainable resource use
   (C) the private market has no role in the conservation of unsustainable resources
   (D) only government has the expertise, access to information, and manpower to set the price of a commonly held economic good

3. This passage is from Preston Dyches, "*Cassini* Catches Titan Naked in the Solar Wind," *NASA News and Features*, January 28, 2015.

   "Titan spends about 95 percent of the time within Saturn's magnetosphere. But during a *Cassini* flyby on Dec. 1, 2013, the giant moon happened to be on the sunward side of Saturn when a powerful outburst of solar activity reached the planet. The strong surge in the solar wind so compressed the sun-facing side of Saturn's magnetosphere that the bubble's outer edge was pushed inside the orbit of Titan. This left the moon exposed to, and unprotected from, the raging stream of energetic solar particles." These observations lead us to believe that ______.

   Which choice most logically completes the text?

   (A) the strength of the solar wind varies
   (B) the solar wind does not affect the atmosphere of planets in orbit around the sun
   (C) the solar wind is stronger at Saturn than at Earth
   (D) no known force can affect the solar wind

4. This passage is from Preston Dyches, "*Cassini* Catches Titan Naked in the Solar Wind," *NASA News and Features*, January 28, 2015.

   "Using its magnetometer instrument, which is akin to an exquisitely sensitive compass, *Cassini* has observed Titan (Saturn's largest moon) many times during the mission's decade in the Saturn system, but always within Saturn's magnetosphere. The spacecraft has not been able to detect a magnetic field coming from Titan itself. In its usual state, Titan is cloaked in Saturn's magnetic field." This circumstance therefore implies that ______.

   Which choice most logically completes the text?

   (A) Titan may have a magnetic field that is difficult to detect because of Saturn's powerful magnetic field
   (B) Titan definitely does not have its own magnetic field
   (C) Titan definitely has its own magnetic field
   (D) scientists will never be able to determine if Titan has its own magnetic field

5. In *No-No Boy*, published by the University of Washington Press, copyright © 2001, John Okada describes the effects of World War II on the people of Japanese and Chinese heritage living in the United States during those years.

   "First, the real Japanese-Japanese were rounded up.... Then the alien Japanese, the ones who had been in America for two, three, or even four decades.... And so, a few months after the seventh day of December of the year nineteen forty-one, the only Japanese left on the west coast of the United States was Matsusaburo Inabukuro who, while it has been forgotten whether he was Japanese-American or American-Japanese, picked up an 'I am Chinese'—not American or American-Chinese or Chinese-American but 'I am Chinese'—button and got a job in a California shipyard." The implications here are that wearing the button ____________.

   Which choice most logically completes the text?

   (A) helped him get the job because people believed that he wasn't Japanese
   (B) had no effect on his job application because people thought he was a Japanese person trying to make people believe he was a Chinese person
   (C) helped him get the job because people believed that a Chinese person in America was likely to be an American citizen
   (D) may have helped him in the short term but ultimately would end in his dismissal

6. This passage is from Lewis Thomas, *The Medusa and the Snail*, copyright ©1974. In it, he chronicles the advent of what many consider "modern medicine."

   "Then, sometime in the early nineteenth century, it was realized by a few of the leading figures in medicine that almost all of the complicated treatments then available for disease did not really work, and the suggestion was made by several courageous physicians that most of them actually did more harm than good. Simultaneously, the surprising discovery was made that certain diseases were self-limited, got better by themselves, possessed a 'natural history.'" The inference of calling the physicians "courageous" is that the author believes that it took courage for physicians to ____________________.

   Which choice most logically completes the text?

   (A) risk injuring their own health by administering new drugs to patients
   (B) suggest that the methods used in their profession were almost completely wrong since doing so would make them unpopular with other members of the profession and possibly endanger their standing in the medical profession
   (C) suggest that the profession should try new methods of treating patients
   (D) admit to their fellow professionals that they had been wrong in their criticism of accepted medical practice

7. In *No-No Boy*, published by the University of Washington Press, copyright © 2001, John Okada describes the effects of World War II on the people of Japanese and Chinese heritage living in the United States during those years.

   "By now, the snowball was big enough to wipe out the rising sun. The big rising sun would take a little more time, but the little rising sun which was the Japanese in countless Japanese communities in the coastal states of Washington, Oregon, and California presented no problem. The whisking and transporting of Japanese and the construction of camps with barbed wire and ominous towers supporting fully armed soldiers in places like Idaho and Wyoming and Arizona, places which even Hollywood scorned for background, had become skills which demanded the utmost of America's great organizing ability." This "snowball" likely refers to ____________________________.

   Which choice most logically completes the text?

   (A) the accumulating tears of Japanese family members who have seen their relatives moved to relocation camps
   (B) the steadily increasing, accumulating efforts of Americans to defeat the Japanese
   (C) the steadily growing efforts of Americans to relocate Japanese aliens living in America
   (D) the steadily accumulating efforts of Japanese aliens living in America to return to Japan to fight for their country

8. This passage is from Elizabeth Zubritsky, "NASA Finds Friction from Tides Could Help Distant Earths Survive, and Thrive," NASA's Goddard Space Flight Center.

   "As anybody who has started a campfire by rubbing sticks knows, friction generates heat. Now, computer modeling by NASA scientists shows that friction could be the key to survival for some distant Earth-sized planets traveling in dangerous orbits.

   "The findings are consistent with observations that Earth-sized planets appear to be very common in other star systems. . . .

   "Simulations of young planetary systems indicate that giant planets often upset the orbits of smaller inner worlds. Even if those interactions aren't immediately catastrophic, they can leave a planet in a treacherous eccentric orbit—a very elliptical course that raises the odds of crossing paths with another body, being absorbed by the host star, or getting ejected from the system."

   The author goes on to describe research centered on tidal stresses (producing friction and heat) on planets that can move some planets into safer (round) orbits. The implication of this research is that ____________________________.

   Which choice most logically completes the text?

   (A) nearly all the Earth-size planets in a typical star system are in a circular orbit
   (B) Earth-size planets are rare
   (C) all of the Earth-size planets that exist in other star systems were once in elliptical orbits around their host star
   (D) some of the Earth-like planets in other star systems have always been in a circular orbit, while others were previously in elliptical orbits

9. This passage is from Suparna Choudhury, "Culturing the Adolescent Brain: What Can Neuroscience Learn from Anthropology?" in *Social Cognitive and Affective Neuroscience*, 2010.

In this article, the author says, "If we assume that a transitional period of the life cycle, akin to adolescence, organized around puberty and of variable length, exists almost universally, the next question is what forms it takes and whether its features, too, are universal. Ethnographic research in Samoa conducted by anthropologist Margaret Mead brought the issue of cultural difference in the experience of adolescence to the fore." After examining some of Mead's work as well as studies by others, she concludes that "in summary, adolescence conceptualized as a prolonged period of identity development linked to increased autonomy, intergenerational conflict, peer-relatedness and social psychological anxieties, is not the norm across cultures. Indeed, these features seem to depend on degrees of individualism, social/economic role expectations, gender and class. A historical appreciation of adolescence as a category of science as well as cross-cultural investigations of the experience of adolescence demonstrates that characteristics associated with this developmental stage may not only have biological bases but also social and cultural origins." These comments imply that the author believes that ______________________________.

Which choice most logically completes the text?

(A) one of the main features of adolescence everywhere is rebellion by young people against parental authority
(B) adolescence as a distinct period of life is unique to industrialized societies
(C) adolescence occurs in every culture (or at least nearly every culture), but the form that it takes varies from culture to culture
(D) adolescence as a distinct period of life occurs only in "individualistic" societies

10. This selection is from John L. O'Sullivan, "The Great Nation of Futurity." It was originally published in 1839.

Speaking of America, O'Sullivan wrote: "... our national birth was the beginning of a new history, the formation and progress of an untried political system, which separates us from the past and connects us with the future only; and so far as regards the entire development of the natural rights of man, in moral, political, and national life, we may confidently assume that our country is destined to be the great nation of futurity. It is so destined because the principle upon which a nation is organized fixes its destiny, and that of equality is perfect, is universal. It presides in all the operations of the physical world, and it is also the conscious law of the soul—the self-evident dictates of morality, which accurately defines the duty of man to man, and consequently man's rights as man. Besides, the truthful annals of any nation furnish abundant evidence that its happiness, its greatness, its duration, were always proportionate to the democratic equality in its system of government." The author's position on the future of America implies that ______________________________.

Which choice most logically completes the text?

(A) democracy is the best form of government
(B) war is never justified
(C) nothing can be learned from history
(D) religious ideals have no place in a nation's politics

11. This passage is from Gilbert Highet, *The Art of Teaching*, copyright © 1950 by Gilbert Highet.

"The innovations Socrates made were to use ordinary conversation as a method of teaching, and to act on one society only, ... And he made the other fellow do most of the talking. He merely asked questions. But anyone who has watched a cross-examination in court knows that this is more difficult than making a prepared speech. Socrates questioned all sorts, from schoolboys to elderly capitalists, ... average Athenians and famous visitors. It was incredibly difficult for him to adapt himself to so many different characters and outlooks, and yet we know that he did. Socrates looked ugly. He had good manners, but no aristocratic polish. Yet he was able to talk to the cleverest and the toughest minds of this age and to convince them that they knew no more than he did. His methods were, first, the modest declaration of his own ignorance—which imperceptibly flattered the other man and made him eager to explain to such an intelligent but naïve inquirer; second, his adaptability—which showed him the side of which each man could be best approached. . . ." Based on this description of Socrates, we can assume that, although not mentioned directly, he also had ________.

Which choice most logically completes the text?

(A) the ability to write entertaining dramatic literature
(B) an excellent understanding of human nature
(C) an ability to charm women
(D) great legal acumen

12. This passage is from Henry Van Dyke, *The Americanism of Washington*. It was originally published in 1906.

"I hear John Dickinson saying: 'It is not our duty to leave wealth to our children, but it is our duty to leave liberty to them. We have counted the cost of this contest, and we find nothing so dreadful as voluntary slavery.' I see Samuel Adams, impoverished, living upon a pittance, hardly able to provide a decent coat for his back, rejecting with scorn the offer of a profitable office, wealth, a title even, to win him from his allegiance to the cause of America. I see Robert Morris, the wealthy merchant, opening his purse and pledging his credit to support the Revolution, and later devoting all his fortune and his energy to restore and establish the financial honor of the Republic, with the memorable words, 'The United States may command all that I have, except my integrity.'" The inclusion of this quote from Robert Morris suggests that the author thinks Morris ________________.

Which choice most logically completes the text?

(A) had no integrity
(B) was not loyal to the United States
(C) was a person of both great integrity and great patriotism
(D) was not completely reliable

13. This selection is from Suparna Choudhury, "Culturing the Adolescent Brain: What Can Neuroscience Learn from Anthropology?" in *Social Cognitive and Affective Neuroscience*, 2010.

"Cross-cultural researchers stress that the meanings of developmental tasks associated with adolescence such as the establishment of independence or autonomy may differ according to culture, and may be subject to change over time. For example, developing independence in some cultures may mean taking on duties to care for siblings or elders, and not necessarily separating from adults and orienting towards peers. Based on a study comparing five cultures that could be contrasted as 'traditional' and 'modern' or 'collectivistic' and 'individualistic,' Trommsdorff suggested that 'turbulent' features such as intergenerational conflict stem from the focus on attaining independence from parents during this period and are linked to cultural values of individualism in Western societies." Based on this premise, we can conclude that Trommsdorff would most likely agree that ________________.

Which choice most logically completes the text?

(A) modern cultures are "collectivistic"
(B) individualistic cultures are "traditional" cultures
(C) adolescents in "collectivistic" cultures do not argue with their parents as much as adolescents in "individualistic" cultures do
(D) adolescents in "collectivistic" societies never become fully adult because they never achieve independence from their parents

14. This passage is from Milton Friend, "Why Bother About Wildlife Disease?" from *U.S. Geological Survey Circular 1401*, 2014.

In his article, Friend discusses the various challenges that arise from growing urban environments as they relate to the fauna and related diseases. He says, "Urban environments are important wildlife habitats and need to be managed in ways that benefit free-ranging wildlife. Furthermore, human attitudes towards wildlife will increasingly be shaped by human experiences in urban environments, because this is where most within urbanized society now interface with wildlife. Thus, it is imperative that wildlife disease be adequately addressed in these environments so that wildlife continue to be cherished." Consequently, we can conclude that he would likely agree that ________________.

Which choice most logically completes the text?

(A) based on past experience in urban areas, there is little that wildlife managers and public health officials can do to stop the spread of disease between animals and humans
(B) as the world becomes more urbanized, it is important for wildlife managers and public health professionals to work closely together to monitor and control human and animal disease
(C) zoos must be abolished to reduce the spread of disease from captive animals to wild animals
(D) the health of resident wildlife in urban environments has little to do with the health of free-ranging wildlife

15. This selection is taken from "Scientists Locate Deep Origins of Hawaiian Hotspots," press release 09-232, December 3, 2009, National Science Foundation.

    "The seismometers were used to record the timing of seismic shear waves from large earthquakes around the world. This information was used to determine whether seismic waves travel more slowly through hot rock as they pass beneath Hawaii. Combining the timing measurements from earthquakes recorded on many seismometers allowed scientists to construct a sophisticated 3-dimensional image of the Hawaiian mantle. In the upper mantle, the Hawaiian Islands are underlain by low shear-wave velocities, linked with hotter-than-average material from an upwelling plume. Low velocities continue down into the Earth's transition zone, at 410 to 660 km depth, and extend even deeper into the Earth's lower mantle down to at least 1,500 km depth." These earthquakes probably ______________________________.

    Which choice most logically completes the text?

    (A) were caused by the eruption of volcanoes in the Hawaiian Islands
    (B) were caused by midtectonic hotspots
    (C) were largely or entirely unrelated to geological activity on or near the Hawaiian Islands
    (D) occurred simultaneously

16. "Hotspots: Mantle Thermal Plumes" in *This Dynamic Earth: The Story of Plate Tectonics* by Jacqueline Kious and Robert I. Tilling, U.S. Geological Survey, 1996, provides the next selection.

    "In 1963, J. Tuzo Wilson came up with an ingenious idea that became known as the "hotspot" theory. Wilson noted that in certain locations around the world, such as Hawaii, volcanism has been active for very long period of time. This could only happen, he reasoned, if relatively small, long-lasting, and exceptionally hot regions—called hotspots—existed below the plates that would provide localized sources of high heat energy (thermal plumes) to sustain volcanism. Wilson hypothesized that the distinctive linear shape of the Hawaiian Island-Emperor Seamounts chain resulted from the Pacific Plate moving over a deep, stationary hotspot in the mantle, located beneath the present-day position of the Island of Hawaii." Chronologically, the narrative of how Wilson most likely came up with the "hotspot theory" implies first his use of ______________________________.

    Which choice most logically completes the text?

    (A) observation, then deduction, and finally formation of hypothesis
    (B) observation, then induction, and finally formation of hypothesis
    (C) observation, then formation of hypothesis, and finally testing of hypothesis
    (D) formation of hypothesis, then deduction, and finally observation

17. This passage is from Joseph Conrad, *Lord Jim*, originally published in 1917.

    "Jim had always good wages and as much humoring as would have bought the fidelity of a fiend. Nevertheless, with black ingratitude he would throw up the job suddenly and depart. To his employers the reasons he gave were obviously inadequate. They said 'Confounded fool!' as soon as his back was turned. This was their criticism on his exquisite sensibility. To the white men in the waterside business and to the captains of ships he was just Jim—nothing more. He had, of course, another name, but he was anxious that it should not be pronounced. His incognito, which had as many holes as a sieve, was not meant to hide a personality but a fact. When the fact broke through the incognito he would leave suddenly the seaport where he happened to be at the time and go to another—generally farther east. He kept to seaports because he was a seaman in exile from the sea, and had Ability in the abstract, which is good for no other work but that of a water-clerk. He retreated in good order towards the rising sun, and the fact followed him casually but inevitably." This narrative implies that Jim regularly gives up the job he has in a particular port and moves to another port to take up a similar position because ______________________.

    Which choice most logically completes the text?

    (A) he becomes tired of living under a false name
    (B) a secret about him becomes known in the area
    (C) he wants to advance his career
    (D) when his real identity becomes known, people shower him with honors which he finds so embarrassing that he has to leave

18. This selection is from the beginning of a short story by F. Scott Fitzgerald in *Flappers and Philosophers*, originally published in 1920.

    "The second half-lemon was well-nigh pulpless and the golden collar had grown astonishing in width, when suddenly the drowsy silence which enveloped the yacht was broken by the sound of heavy footsteps and an elderly man topped with orderly gray hair and clad in a white-flannel suit appeared at the head of the companionway. There he paused for a moment until his eyes became accustomed to the sun, and then seeing the girl under the awning he uttered a long even grunt of disapproval. If he had intended thereby to obtain a rise of any sort he was doomed to disappointment. The girl calmly turned over two pages, turned back one, raised the lemon mechanically to tasting distance, and then very faintly but quite unmistakably yawned." This narrative would lead the reader to believe that the man ______________________.

    Which choice most logically completes the text?

    (A) is the girl's grandfather
    (B) does not enjoy being on a yacht
    (C) does not often come on deck because his illness confines him to bed below deck
    (D) does not approve of the girl spending so much of her time reading

19. The following passage is from the beginning of a short story by F. Scott Fitzgerald in *Flappers and Philosophers*, originally published in 1920.

    "Up in her bedroom window Sally Carrol Happer rested her nineteen-year-old chin on a fifty-two-year-old sill and watched Clark Darrow's ancient Ford turn the corner. The car was hot—being partly metallic it retained all the heat it absorbed or evolved—and Clark Darrow sitting bolt upright at the wheel wore a pained, strained expression as though he considered himself a spare part, and rather likely to break. He laboriously crossed two dust ruts, the wheels squeaking indignantly at the encounter, and then with a terrifying expression he gave the steering-gear a final wrench and deposited self and car approximately in front of the Happer steps. There was a heaving sound, a death rattle, followed by a short silence; and then the air was rent by a startling whistle. Sally Carrol gazed down sleepily. She started to yawn, but finding this quite impossible unless she raised her chin from the window-sill, changed her mind and continued silently to regard the car, whose owner sat brilliantly if perfunctorily at attention as he waited for an answer to his signal. After a moment the whistle once more split the dusty air." One can easily infer that the words "sat brilliantly if perfunctorily at attention" suggest that Clark Darrow regards his visit to the Happer house largely as ________________________.

    Which choice most logically completes the text?

    (A) a dramatic way to demonstrate his romantic interest in Sally Happer
    (B) a great honor
    (C) an uninteresting routine duty to be performed, albeit in a somewhat showy manner
    (D) an exciting change from his regular activities

20. This passage is from Paul Fussell, "Hiroshima: A Soldier's View," copyright © 1981 by *The New Republic*.

    "In arguing the acceptability of the bomb, Alsop focuses on the power and fanaticism of War Minister Anami, who insisted that Japan fight to the bitter end, defending the main islands with the same techniques and tenacity employed at Iwo Jima and Okinawa. Alsop concludes: 'Japanese surrender could never have been obtained, at any rate without the honor-satisfying bloodbath envisioned by . . . Anami, if the hideous destruction of Hiroshima and Nagasaki had not finally galvanized the peace advocates into tearing up the entire Japanese book of rules.'" The implications behind a "Japanese book of rules" can be understood as ________________________.

    Which choice most logically completes the text?

    (A) the guidelines Japanese peace advocates had been following before the destruction of Hiroshima and Nagasaki
    (B) the deeply held values governing Japanese conduct, especially regarding national pride, individual honor, and conduct in war
    (C) the plan devised at the highest levels of Japanese government to defend the homeland against invasion at all costs
    (D) the code of conduct of Japanese soldiers

21. This passage is from David Alpaugh, "The Professionalization of Poetry," *in Heavy Lifting*, copyright © 2007 by Alehouse Press.

"As colleges and universities increasingly make the education, publication, sustenance, and honoring of American poets their business, writing program professionals have assumed a number of nonpoetic responsibilities. It has become part of their business to attract students and sponsor an ever-growing body of work produced by graduates and colleagues. Such practical concerns have led professionals to tolerate aesthetic trends designed not so much to make poetry better as to make it easier to produce and publish." With these statements, the author implies that ______________________________.

Which choice most logically completes the text?

(A) quite a few people involved in teaching the writing of poetry at American colleges and universities care more about furthering their careers than encouraging the writing and publication of good poetry
(B) most of the people involved in teaching the writing of poetry in American colleges and universities care more about maintaining a high standard of poetry than they do about encouraging the production of poetry, regardless of its quality
(C) many of those who teach the writing of poetry in American colleges and universities do so because they are unable to write good poetry themselves
(D) most teachers of the writing of poetry in American colleges and universities are, as a rule, unable to distinguish good poetry from bad poetry

22. This passage is from David Alpaugh, "The Professionalization of Poetry," in *Heavy Lifting*, copyright © 2007 by Alehouse Press.

"If the profusion of prose made to look like poetry is disconcerting, it is equally annoying when similar fare is dished up under the faddish moniker 'prose poem,' a form in which text is set like prose in ragged or justified type, line breaks thereby losing significance. The "poem" part of the equation promises greater density and compression than we normally expect from prose, achieved through poetic devices such as rhythm, imagery, metaphor, simile, and figures of speech." For a prose poem to have an "equation" suggests it involves __________.

Which choice most logically completes the text?

(A) the combination of poetic elements with elements from prose to create prose poetry
(B) the use of poetic devices in prose to create poetic prose
(C) the poetic elements in prose poetry that can be quantified
(D) the widespread but incorrect belief that the production of good poetry (of any sort) is, like everything, governed by precise, definable law

23. This passage is from David Alpaugh, "The Professionalization of Poetry," in *Heavy Lifting*, copyright © 2007 by Alehouse Press.

"The current popularity of the genre is attested to by Peter Johnson, editor of *The Best of the Prose Poem: An International Journal*. 'I have read so many prose poems,' he complains, 'that I feel as if a large gray eraser is squatting in the hollow of my head. I am not even sure what my criteria are, anymore.' At least one prestigious graduate writing program understands the genre well enough to offer students an entire course in 'The Prose Poem.' The jury is still out on definitions. Some critics deny that the term has any meaning at all. Others concede that the term is muddied, since it is difficult to define the genre without opening the door to the heightened prose of many a novelist and short story writer." The author's comment that "at least one prestigious graduate writing program understands the genre . . ." implies a tone that is ________________.

Which choice most logically completes the text?

(A) ironic
(B) sarcastic
(C) self-deprecating
(D) ambivalent

24. This passage is from S. Jeffress Williams, Kurt Dodd, and Kathleen Krafft Gohn, "Coasts in Crisis, Coastal Change," *U.S. Geological Survey Circular 1075*, 1990.

"Winds create waves that ripple across the surface of lakes and seas until they break on the shallowing bottom and crash into the shore. In many areas, prevailing winds produce waves that consistently approach the coast at oblique angles. Even the slightest angle between the land and the waves will create currents that transport sediment along the shore. These longshore currents are a primary agent of coastal movement; they are a major cause of sand migration along barrier and mainland beaches." This cause and effect relationship suggests that if waves hit a shore so that there is no angle between the land and the waves, ________________________________.

What choice most logically completes the text?

(A) an undertow will be created
(B) sediment will be deposited along the shore as a result
(C) sediment will not be moved along the shore as a result
(D) currents will be created along the shore

25. This passage is from Dai Sijie, *Balzac and the Little Chinese Seamstress*, copyright © 2001 by Alfred A. Knopf (English translation copyright © 2001 by Ina Rilke).

This is the story of two teenagers in China who are in a confrontational situation during the Cultural Revolution. At this point, the village headman (who had been threatening the boys) has softened his attitude because of the quick thinking of Luo; and the narrator is about to play his violin for the villagers. "As soon as I had tightened my bow there was a burst of applause, but I was still nervous. However, as I ran my swollen fingers over the strings, Mozart's phrases came flooding back to me like so many faithful friends. The peasants' faces, so grim a moment before, softened under the influence of Mozart's limpid music like parched earth under a shower, and then, in the dancing light of the oil lamp, they blurred into one. I played for some time, Luo lit a cigarette and smoked quietly, like a man. This was our first taste of re-education. Luo was eighteen years old. I was seventeen." That Luo "smoked quietly, like a man" implies that ______________.

Which choice most logically completes the text?

(A) he is worried about what will happen when the narrator stops playing the Mozart sonata
(B) he is planning another way to fool the gullible headman
(C) he is justifiably satisfied with himself for orchestrating a daring and successful plan to gain the favor of the villagers
(D) he realizes that he has been accepted as a full-fledged adult member of the village

Answer Explanations

1. **(D)** The author cites the example of cattle to illustrate the principle that private ownership often results in more effective conservation of resources than public ownership. We can infer that the author believes that cattle might become scarce if they were owned in common because individuals would have little incentive to care for cattle and limit the number of cattle they consume. (In fact, the author might argue that people would have an incentive to kill as many cattle as they can before others do.)

2. **(A)** The author argues throughout the passage that, in many cases, assigning ownership rights is the most effective way to conserve unsustainable resources. By inference, "getting the incentives right" should mean, according to the author, chiefly assigning property rights to environmental goods.

3. **(A)** The author mentions "a powerful outburst of solar activity," from which we can infer that the strength of the solar wind varies. He also mentions "the strong surge in the solar winds."

4. **(A)** We can infer that Titan may have a magnetic field because the author says *Cassini* has only observed Titan when it was within Saturn's powerful magnetosphere. The fact that a magnetic field coming from Titan has not been found does not mean it does not exist. Titan may have a magnetic field that is relatively weak and thus difficult to detect due to interference from Saturn's powerful magnetic field. The author does not mention whether *Cassini* looked for a magnetic field coming from Titan when Titan was outside Saturn's magnetic field, but presumably the intense solar wind that existed at this time would have made the detection of a weak magnetic field difficult.

5. **(A)** The inference (the conclusion to be drawn) is that the "I am Chinese" button gained him the job because America was at war with Japan and it is reasonable to think that some people would hire a person who they believed was Chinese but not a person they believed to be Japanese.

6. **(B)** It makes sense that the author believes it took courage for physicians to suggest that their profession was using faulty methods because members of a field who criticize their profession would likely be regarded as disloyal by other members of the field.

7. **(B)** Presumably, the image of the snowball was used by the author in an earlier part of the book from which this passage was taken. However, it can be inferred that the "snowball" refers to the accumulating efforts of Americans to destroy the Japanese because the author is describing the steps taken by Americans to prevent Japanese nationals, Japanese aliens, and Japanese-Americans in America from aiding Japan in the war against America. He says, "The snowball was big enough to wipe out the rising sun," suggesting that these efforts had stopped the Japanese threat on American soil. This question illustrates how even without background knowledge you can reasonably deduce the correct answer by just using the contextual clues present.

8. **(D)** The author says that "Earth-sized planets appear to be very common in other star systems" and that "simulations of young planetary systems indicate that giant planets often upset the orbits of smaller inner worlds." She then goes on to describe a theory that explains how tidal friction may help some Earth-sized planets in elliptical orbits return to circular orbits. We can infer from this information that since their creation, some Earth-sized planets have always been in a circular orbit, others have always been in an elliptical orbit, some were once in a circular orbit but are now in an elliptical orbit, and still others once were in an elliptical orbit but have since returned to a circular orbit.

9. **(C)** The author says, "If we assume that a transitional period of the life cycle, akin to adolescence, organized around puberty and of variable length, exists almost universally. . . ." She also says, "Adolescence conceptualized as a prolonged period of identity development linked to increased autonomy, intergenerational conflict, peer-relatedness and social psychological anxieties, is not the norm across cultures."

10. **(A)** The author says that the more "democratic equality" a country has, the greater it is. We can infer from this that he believes that democracy is the best form of government.

11. **(B)** The author says that "Socrates questioned all sorts" of people and that he adapted to them. He also says that Socrates's "adaptability . . . showed him the side on which each man could be best approached." We can infer from this information about Socrates that he had an excellent understanding of human nature because it would have been difficult for him to adapt to so many people without it.

12. **(C)** It can be inferred that the author quotes these words to show that Robert Morris had great integrity and patriotism because Morris said he will do anything asked of him by his country unless it would mean a loss of his integrity.

13. **(C)** According to the author, based on a study, "Trommsdorff suggested that 'turbulent' features such as intergenerational conflict stem from the focus on attaining independence from parents during this period and are linked to cultural values of individualism in Western societies."

14. **(B)** The author would agree with this statement because he stresses the importance of managing wildlife in urban areas. We can therefore infer that he would agree that increased urbanization requires effective cooperation between wildlife managers and public health officials.

15. **(C)** It can be inferred that the earthquakes around the world were largely or entirely unrelated to geological activity on or near the Hawaiian Islands. The purpose of recording the seismic waves from the earthquakes was to "determine whether seismic waves travel more slowly through hot rock as they pass beneath Hawaii."

16. **(A)** This is the best choice because the passage says that Wilson first "noted that in certain locations . . . volcanism has been active for very long periods of time." Wilson then "reasoned [that] if . . . hotspots . . . existed below the plates that would provide . . . energy . . . to sustain volcanism." Finally, he "hypothesized" about how volcanism occurred in a specific area, creating an island volcano, and about how plate movement affects this process. Note that the process of reasoning Wilson used was deduction—reasoning that infers something from a general principle.

17. **(B)** This can be inferred from information provided in the passage: "Nevertheless . . . he would throw up the job suddenly and depart"; "His incognito, which . . . go to another. . . ."; "He retreated in . . . casually but inevitably." We can infer that the "fact" mentioned refers to a secret about Jim.

18. **(D)** The elderly man is described as "utter[ing] a long even grunt of disapproval" when he sees the girl sitting and reading a book. It cannot be conclusively inferred that he is disapproving of her reading a novel, but the fact that the grunt is described as one of "disapproval" means that he does not approve of something. There is some evidence for (A), (B), and (C), but none of it is as strong as the evidence for (D). Thus, (D) is the best choice.

19. **(C)** Choice (C) is the best answer because perfunctorily means "done routinely and with little interest." The fact that Clark Darrow is sitting in this way suggests that visiting the Happer house is probably part of his routine. "Sat brilliantly . . . at attention" suggests that he regards the visit as something to be done in a somewhat showy manner. Choice (A) is incorrect because although "sat brilliantly . . . at attention" suggests that Clark Darrow regards the visit as something to be done dramatically, the word "perfunctorily" suggests that he regards the visit as something done as a duty and that he has little interest in. If Clark Darrow were visiting the Happer house to show his romantic interest in Sally, he would probably not be sitting perfunctorily. Choice (B) is incorrect because, although the words "sat brilliantly . . . at attention" suggest that he could regard his visit as an honor, one would not typically respond to a great honor by sitting perfunctorily (in a manner suggesting that one regards it as a duty). Choice (D) is incorrect because the fact that Clark Darrow sits perfunctorily shows that he regards the visit as a routine duty, not as an exciting change from his regular activities.

20. **(B)** Choice (B) is the best answer because the passage helps explain how the Japanese, as part of their culture and according to their book of law, would fight until the end to defend their culture and their mainland. They deeply held values of national pride and honor, and they had a specific way of conducting themselves during an act of war.

21. **(A)** The author says that writing professionals have made it their business to attract students to their poetry writing programs and that in so doing have assessed the value of poetry more on the basis of "practical concerns" than on its aesthetic merit. It is reasonable to infer from this that quite a few of these writing program professionals care more about their careers than they do about encouraging the production of good poetry.

22. **(A)** The author refers to the "'poem' part of the equation." From this we can infer that in order to create a prose poem it is necessary to add poetic elements to prose elements. (Prose elements + poetic elements = prose poem.)

23. **(B)** The author makes the comment immediately after citing Peter Johnson, who says, "I am not even sure what my criteria [for deciding what a prose poem is] are, anymore." Thus, we can infer that the author is being sarcastic in saying that one graduate writing program understands the genre well enough to offer an entire course in it. Also, in the paragraph after this comment, the author says that the definition of the genre of prose poetry is still very controversial.

24. **(C)** The author says even a slight angle between the land and waves "will create currents that transport sediment along the shore." From this we can infer that if there is no angle, sediment will not be moved along the shore.

25. **(C)** The narrator says that Luo was only eighteen years old when the events recounted in the passage occurred. It can be inferred that when Luo lights a cigarette and smokes it while the narrator plays the violin for the villagers, he is feeling satisfied with the successful outcome of his daring plan. The fact that the narrator describes Luo as smoking "quietly, like a man" suggests that he has just undergone an experience that made him more mature and that he is aware that he has become more mature.

Writing

Writing Practice Questions

Number and Tense Agreement

What to Remember

Number

- Collective nouns that are treated as one unit:
  "A flock of birds is approaching."
- Being able to identify the real subject for the verb to see if it is singular or plural:
  "One in seven cars is a small number."
  "The ribbon that is wrapped around those three apple boxes is loose."
- Words that are singular in meaning but look plural and take the plural verb:
  "The scissors are on the sewing table."
- Neither/either/nor/or constructions:
  "Neither (one) is coming with us."
  "Neither the student nor the teacher is able to attend."

Tense

- Consistent usage:
  "When we stayed behind, we were happy." (both past tense)
- Except in special circumstances:
  "I will stay behind when you agree to stay as well."
  (future tense in the main clause and present tense in the subordinate clause)

Practice

> **DIRECTIONS:** For each set of practice questions in this entire section of the practice book, you will be tested on a variety of important writing skills. Carefully read each question and set of answer choices, and then choose the best answer.

1. Sometimes the ceiling _______ to open and let down a second course of meats, with showers of flowers and perfumed waters, while ropedancers performed over the heads of the company.

   Which choice completes the text so that it conforms to conventions of standard English?

   (A) was contriving
   (B) was contrived
   (C) contrived
   (D) had contrived

2. One of the greatest minds of the century ______ a ray of light on this gloomy picture by tracing the origin of woman's slavery to the same principle of selfishness and love of power in man that has thus dominated all weaker nations and classes.

   Which choice completes the text so that it conforms to conventions of standard English?

   (A) thrown
   (B) throwing
   (C) has thrown
   (D) being thrown

3. The slavish instinct of an oppressed class has led it to toil patiently through the ages, ______ all and asking little, cheerfully sharing with man all perils and privations by land and sea that husband and sons might attain.

   Which choice completes the text so that it conforms to the conventions of standard English?

   (A) given
   (B) give
   (C) giving
   (D) gave

4. It is so often asserted that as woman has always been man's slave—subject—inferior—dependent, under all forms of government and religion, slavery must be her normal condition. This might have some weight ______ the vast majority of men also been enslaved for centuries to kings and popes, and orders of nobility, who, in the progress of civilization, have reached complete equality.

   Which choice completes the text so that it conforms to the conventions of standard English?

   (A) if not
   (B) were it not
   (C) was it not
   (D) had not

5. How significant are the levels of THg in the fish populations of our national parks? In a recent study, variations in site-specific fish THg concentrations within each park ______ that more intensive sampling will be required in some parks to characterize more accurately THg contamination levels.

   Which choice completes the text so that it conforms to the conventions of standard English?

   (A) suggest
   (B) suggests
   (C) suggesting
   (D) having suggested

6. In addition to educating people through writing about birds, ornithologists share their knowledge by teaching college courses. But education is not limited to teaching college students. Outreach activities _______ giving talks and making presentations to various groups and organizations.

   Which choice completes the text so that it conforms to the conventions of standard English?

   (A) did include
   (B) might include
   (C) including
   (D) included

7. Those tribes or nations having a well-developed social order, with government, laws, and other fixed social customs are said to be civilized, while those peoples without these characters are assumed to be uncivilized. It may also be considered in a somewhat different sense, when the arts, industries, sciences, and habits of life are stimulated civilization _______ determined by the degree in which these are developed.

   Which choice completes the text so that it conforms to the conventions of standard English?

   (A) was
   (B) being
   (C) is being
   (D) has been

8. The art masters of ancient Egypt never troubled themselves to tabulate the proportions of the human body or _______ them to a system.

   Which choice completes the text so that it conforms to the conventions of standard English?

   (A) reducing
   (B) to reduce
   (C) having reduced
   (D) have to reduce

9. Nothing in what remains to us of Egyptian works _______ the belief that they ever possessed a canon based on the length of the human finger or foot.

   Which choice completes the text so that it conforms to the conventions of standard English?

   (A) justify
   (B) justifies
   (C) justified
   (D) justifying

10. Theirs was a teaching of routine and not of theory. Models executed by the master _______ over and over again by his pupils until they could reproduce them with absolute exactness.

    Which choice completes the text so that it conforms to the conventions of standard English?

    (A) copied
    (B) copy
    (C) to copy
    (D) were copied

11. "It may seem like I'm asking a bunch of unrelated questions," he says, "but I'm trying to find the nature of the complaint." Based on information gathered from the form and the interview, Jon _______ treatment.

Which choice completes the text so that it conforms to the conventions of standard English?

(A) has recommended
(B) is recommending
(C) had recommended
(D) recommends

12. When the window is finished, these pieces are put together like a puzzle and joined by grooved strips of lead soldered at the joints, just as any lattice window is put together; but before this _______ done, the details of the design—features, folds of drapery, patterns, and so on—are painted on the glass in an opaque brownish enamel make of iron oxide.

Which choice completes the text so that it conforms to the conventions of standard English?

(A) is
(B) has
(C) is being
(D) had been

13. North America and western Europe _______ near universal literacy rates.

Which choice completes the text so that it conforms to the conventions of standard English?

(A) assumes
(B) being assumed
(C) is assuming
(D) are assumed to have

14. The socioeconomic impact of toxoplasmosis on human suffering and the cost of care of sick children, especially those with intellectual disability and blindness, _______ enormous in these countries today.

Which choice completes the text so that it conforms to the conventions of standard English?

(A) are
(B) is
(C) were
(D) was

15. Prior to embarking on doctoral studies, many students already _______ several years of formal study in their chosen field.

Which choice completes the text so that it conforms to the conventions of standard English?

(A) has completed
(B) have completed
(C) completes
(D) is completing

16. Generally, fields with the greatest increases in the numbers of doctoral degrees ________ also had the most job growth.

Which choice completes the text so that it conforms to the conventions of standard English?

(A) awarding
(B) award
(C) awarded
(D) awards

17. Computer science _______ similar increases today, having demonstrated particularly strong growth from 1980 to 1990.

Which choice completes the text so that it conforms to the conventions of standard English?

(A) showing
(B) shows
(C) having been shown
(D) are showing

18. Home health care services _______ the fastest growing detailed industry in the economy, with employment projected to increase substantially as we approach the mid-21st century.

Which choice completes the text so that it conforms to the conventions of standard English?

(A) are expected to be
(B) is expected to be
(C) were expected to be
(D) was expected to be

19. For a similar space of time, too, the delusion that Cuba was a part of the continent generally prevailed. It is true that on a map of Juan de la Cosa's, to which the date of 1500 _______, Cuba is indicated to be an island.

Which choice completes the text so that it conforms to the conventions of standard English?

(A) attributed
(B) is attributed
(C) attributes
(D) was attributing

20. Coastal areas around Aceh, southern Java, the north coast of Sulawesi, and East Nusa Tenggara ________ a number of typhoons every year.

Which choice completes the text so that it conforms to the conventions of standard English?

(A) have an experience with
(B) had experienced
(C) have the experience of
(D) experience

21. Columbus _______ in authority in Hispaniola by Francisco de Bobadilla, and the latter in turn had in 1501 given way to Nicholas de Ovando. It does not appear that Ovando sought to colonize Cuba.

    Which choice completes the text so that it conforms to the conventions of standard English?

    (A) had succeeded
    (B) succeeded
    (C) had been succeeded
    (D) had been succeeding

22. Malaria in humans is caused by infection with one or more of several species of *Plasmodium*. The infection is transmitted by the bite of an infective female *Anopheles* mosquito. *P. falciparum* and *P. vivax* species _______ the most infections worldwide.

    Which choice completes the text so that it conforms to the conventions of standard English?

    (A) cause
    (B) causes
    (C) causing
    (D) being causes of

23. It is our duty now to begin to lay the plans and determine the strategy for the winning of a lasting peace and the establishment of an American standard of living higher than ever before known. We cannot be content, no matter how high that general standard of living _______, if some fraction of our people—whether it be one-third or one-fifth or one-tenth —is ill-fed, ill-clothed, ill housed, and insecure.

    Which choice completes the text so that it conforms to the conventions of standard English?

    (A) was
    (B) may be
    (C) were
    (D) had been

24. In our day these economic truths have become accepted as self-evident. We have accepted, so to speak, a second Bill of Rights under which a new basis of security and prosperity _______ for all regardless of station, race, or creed.

    Which choice completes the text so that it conforms to the conventions of standard English?

    (A) can establish
    (B) will establish
    (C) can be established
    (D) established

25. America's own rightful place in the world depends in large part upon how fully these and similar rights _______ into practice for our citizens.

    Which choice completes the text so that it conforms to the conventions of standard English?

    (A) is carrying
    (B) will carry
    (C) have been carried
    (D) had been carried

26. The doctor took us on Sunday afternoon to his club—whose name I think means the perfume of the maple—to see and to listen to some Japanese plays that are given in the club theater _______ for the purpose.

    Which choice completes the text so that it conforms to the conventions of standard English?

    (A) building
    (B) had been built
    (C) built
    (D) having built

27. We walked in with careful attention to make no noise, _______ that in our stocking feet we could have made none had we wished, and we found the doctor's place in a box reserved for him and us, and marked with his name, written large.

    Which choice completes the text so that it conforms to the conventions of standard English?

    (A) we forgot
    (B) we had forgot
    (C) forgotten
    (D) forgetting

Answer Explanations

1. **(B)** The ceiling is the subject that requires the passive form of the verb.
2. **(C)** Choice (A) is not grammatical. Choice (C) casts the verb "throw" in the present perfect tense and makes good sense because the writer's actions ("throwing a ray of light") began in the past and is continuing at present.
3. **(C)** One of the uses of the present progressive is to emphasize that action is continuing over a period of time. Clues to the answer are the verbs "asking" and "sharing."
4. **(D)** Answer choice (D) is both grammatical and makes good sense. It creates an adverb clause of condition (beginning with "had" and ending with "equality") modifying the verb "might have."
5. **(A)** The subject of the verb is "variations," requiring the plural form of the verb "suggest."
6. **(B)** Eliminating the obviously incorrect answers, combined with context, highlights the correct answer choice. The introductory sentences place the activities in the present tense, eliminating choices (A) and (D).
7. **(B)** This is the only choice that is grammatical. It changes the verb "was" to the present participle of "be," creating a participial phrase modifying the noun "civilization."
8. **(B)** The coordinating conjunction "or" creates a compound object of the verb "troubled," requiring equal constructions: "to tabulate . . . or to reduce. . . ."
9. **(B)** The subject of the verb is "nothing," not "works," and requires the singular, present tense.
10. **(D)** The correct verb choice must be in the past tense to agree with the context of the sentence and must agree with the subject "models" in number.
11. **(D)** The main text is in the present tense, "he says." Answer (D), "Jon recommends treatment," maintains the present tense.

12. **(A)** The present tense is correct in context because a statement of fact is being made.

13. **(D)** The compound subject requires the plural form of the verb.

14. **(A)** The compound subject ("impact . . . and . . . cost") requires the plural verb. The clue to tense is "today."

15. **(B)** The plural subject ("students") requires the plural form of the verb.

16. **(C)** The participial phrase modifies the noun "degrees," telling us what type of degrees they are.

17. **(B)** Answer choice (B) provides subject-verb agreement with "science."

18. **(B)** Note that the phrase "home health care services" is singular because in the context of the passage, it is a singular "industry" category within the economy.

19. **(B)** The linking verb "is" is necessary to create a grammatical sentence.

20. **(D)** Choice (B) is incorrect because it is in the past tense. In this context, the past tense is not suitable because a statement of fact is being made, which requires the present tense. Choices (A) and (C) are grammatical but not idiomatic.

21. **(C)** The prepositional phrase "by Francisco de Bobadilla" tells you that the verb must be in the passive voice, incorporating "been" (the past participle of "to be"). Only answer choices (C) and (D) are in the passive voice. Answer choice (D) does not make sense.

22. **(A)** Choices (C) and (D) do not create grammatical sentences. Choice (B) does not agree in number with the plural subject, "species."

23. **(B)** The modal verb may be used here to express a certain measure of likelihood that the "general standard of living" will be high in the future. Although answer choices (A) and (D) are grammatically correct, they do not make good sense in context.

24. **(C)** Use of the modal verb phrase "can be" indicates possibility, which fits the context of the passage.

25. **(C)** Choices (A) and (B) are grammatically incorrect. The present perfect tense is appropriate in context. The sentence suggests that the action started in the past (rights being put into practice) is continuing in the present.

26. **(C)** This is the correct choice because it creates a sentence in which the participial phrase "built for the purpose" modifies the noun "theater."

27. **(D)** Choices (A) and (B) create run-on sentences. Choice (D) is correct because "forgetting" is the present participle of "forget." This creates a participial phrase beginning with "forgetting" and ending with "wished," which is grammatical.

Punctuation

What to Remember

Watch out for the following examples of punctuation errors by reviewing punctuation rules in an English textbook:

- Commas in the wrong place or missing
- Using a colon or semicolon in the wrong place
- Confusing "its" with "it's"; "whose" with "who's"
- Using an apostrophe where it does not belong, such as "your's" or "her's"
- Comma splices

Practice

1. Another writer asserts that the tyranny of man over woman has its roots, after all, in his nobler __________ to protect woman in the barbarous periods of pillage, lust, and war.

   Which choice completes the text so that it conforms to the conventions of standard English?

   (A) feelings; his love, his chivalry, and his desire
   (B) feelings his love, his chivalry, and his desire
   (C) feelings: his love, his chivalry, and his desire
   (D) feelings; his love, his chivalry and his desire

2. Sixty-eight percent of fish sampled were above exposure levels recommended by the Great Lakes Advisory Group (50 ng/g ww) for unlimited consumption by ______ the fish assessed for risk to human consumers (that is, species that are large enough to be consumed by recreational or subsistence anglers), only one individual fish had a muscle Hg concentration exceeding the benchmark.

   Which choice completes the text so that it conforms to the conventions of standard English?

   (A) humans—of
   (B) humans; of
   (C) humans, of
   (D) humans. Of

3. Zion, Capital Reef, Wrangell-St. Elias, and Lake Clark National Parks all contained sites in which most fish exceeded benchmarks for the protection ______.

   Which choice completes the text so that it conforms to the conventions of standard English?

   (A) of human and wildlife health
   (B) of human, and, wildlife health
   (C) of: human and wildlife health
   (D) of human and wildlife, health

4. Ornithologists and their students have done fieldwork in locations as remote as the Andes Mountains in South America and as nearby as the forests of southern Ohio and the ______ usually involves surveying, or counting, birds and monitoring their nests.

   Which choice completes the text so that it conforms to the conventions of standard English?

   (A) Midwest: fieldwork
   (B) Midwest, fieldwork
   (C) Midwest. Fieldwork
   (D) Midwest; fieldwork

5. As soon as people began to cooperate with one another in obtaining food, when building houses, or for protection against wild animals and wild ____________ were becoming civilized.

   Which choice completes the text so that it conforms to the conventions of standard English?

   (A) men, that is when they began to treat each other civilly, they
   (B) men, that is, when they began to treat each other civilly, they
   (C) men—that is, when they began to treat each other civilly—they
   (D) men that is when they began to treat each other civilly, they

6. The palette was of thin wood, in shape a rectangular oblong, with a groove in which to lay the brush at the lower end. At the upper end were two or more cuplike hollows, each fitted with a cake of ______ being the colors most in use.

   Which choice completes the text so that it conforms to the conventions of standard English?

   (A) ink; black and red
   (B) ink black and red
   (C) ink—black and red
   (D) ink (black and red)

7. It's a complex approach to well-being, he says, not a quick fix: "Acupuncture is more than just sticking needles in somebody's ______ a whole system of healing."

   Which choice completes the text so that it conforms to the conventions of standard English?

   (A) body, its
   (B) body. Its
   (C) body its
   (D) body. It's

8. The most common acupuncture treatment is ______ inserting and manipulating thin, solid needles at specific points along the skin.

   Which choice completes the text so that it conforms to the conventions of standard English?

   (A) needling strategically
   (B) needling: strategically
   (C) needling; strategically
   (D) needling. Strategically

9. A new patient begins the first visit to Jon's New York City office by completing a form to describe his or her ________________ on specific symptoms.

   Which choice completes the text so that it conforms to the conventions of standard English?

   (A) condition, Jon reviews the form and then in an interview with the patient focuses
   (B) condition. Jon reviews the form and then, in an interview with the patient, focuses
   (C) condition, Jon reviewing the form and then in an interview with the patient focusing
   (D) condition. Jon, reviewing the form, and then in an interview with the patient, focuses

10. ______ effect, in the hand of an artist, is to decorate and enrich what would otherwise be somewhat crude and papery in effect.

    Which choice completes the text so that it conforms to the conventions of standard English?

    (A) Its'
    (B) It's
    (C) Its
    (D) It is

11. Central and eastern Europe, Central Asia, and East Asia and the Pacific are projected to __________ one percentage point of the 2015 target.

    Which choice completes the text so that it conforms to the conventions of standard English?

    (A) reach, or come within
    (B) reach or come within
    (C) reach or come, within
    (D) reach; or come within

12. I should say the greatest obstacles that writers today have to get over ______ the dazzling journalistic successes of twenty years ago.

    Which choice completes the text so that it conforms to the conventions of standard English?

    (A) are:
    (B) are;
    (C) ,are
    (D) are

13. One of the areas most affected by the sea level rise is the north coast of Central __________ the impacts of sea level rise also observed in several coastal villages in East Nusa Temggara.

    Which choice completes the text so that it conforms to the conventions of standard English?

    (A) Java: with
    (B) Java, with
    (C) Java; with
    (D) Java. With

14. Bedono Village, located on the north coast of Central Java Province, is an example that illustrates the vulnerability of coastal communities to hydrometeorological hazards and the impacts of climate ___________ people in this village cultivated rice on paddy fields.

Which choice completes the text so that it conforms to the conventions of standard English?

(A) change before 1995, Most
(B) change: before 1995, most
(C) change. Before 1995, most
(D) change; before 1995, most

15. These early painters achieved three-dimensional volume using delicate contrasts of light and dark and created drama by using ___________ lines between light and dark.

Which choice completes the text so that it conforms to the conventions of standard English?

(A) strong, definitive
(B) strong definitive
(C) strong—definitive
(D) strong; definitive

16. A careful study of shadows and shadowing techniques traditionally used by _______ will set the groundwork.

Which choice completes the text so that it conforms to the conventions of standard English?

(A) artists,
(B) artists
(C) artists:
(D) artists;

17. According to Arlene Dohm, a supervisory economist in the Office of Occupational Statistics and Employment ___________ 21st century farmers are a more diversified group than ever.

Which choice completes the text so that it conforms to the conventions of standard English?

(A) Projections,
(B) Projections
(C) Projections—
(D) Projections;

18. Like many World War II veterans, Gerald never tired of telling stories about the time he spent in _______ where he had many adventures that make for great storytelling.

Which choice completes the text so that it conforms to the conventions of standard English?

(A) Japan,
(B) Japan
(C) Japan;
(D) Japan, and

19. He was a sergeant in the Army Corps of ____________ serving in one of the first units to enter Hiroshima and Nagasaki after the atomic bombs destroyed those two cities.

 Which choice completes the text so that it conforms to the conventions of standard English?

 (A) Engineers. He was
 (B) Engineers; he was
 (C) Engineers,
 (D) Engineers—

20. Fifteen minutes after eating several _______ lips and tongue began to itch and swell.

 Which choice completes the text so that it conforms to the conventions of standard English?

 (A) grapes. My
 (B) grapes my
 (C) grapes, my
 (D) grapes—

21. Wild plants can be contaminated with pesticides or, according to the staff at Decoding _______ they can harbor such parasites as intestinal protozoa.

 Which choice completes the text so that it conforms to the conventions of standard English?

 (A) Science
 (B) Science,
 (C) Science—
 (D) Science;

22. The orange *Amanita caesarea* is _______ but *Amanita frostiana* is poisonous.

 Which choice completes the text so that it conforms to the conventions of standard English?

 (A) edible,
 (B) edible
 (C) edible;
 (D) edible:

23. My older poodle has become a wonderful watchdog when strangers come into the yard. However, his __________________ I should be alerted to trespassing butterflies.

 Which choice completes the text so that it conforms to the conventions of standard English?

 (A) companion who is a puppy thinks
 (B) companion, who is a puppy thinks
 (C) companion, who is a puppy, thinks
 (D) companion who is a puppy, thinks

24. When people retire to Texas, they are often looking for the images they have come to associate with the Lone Star ________ steer, and bluebonnets.

    Which choice completes the text so that it conforms to the conventions of standard English?

    (A) State, armadillos, cowboys, long-horned
    (B) State: armadillos, cowboys long-horned
    (C) State—armadillos, cowboys, long-horned
    (D) State; armadillos, cowboys, long-horned

25. She believes that the entire collection is ______ however, she has no bill of sale to prove her claim.

    Which choice completes the text so that it conforms to the conventions of standard English?

    (A) her's;
    (B) hers:
    (C) hers;
    (D) her's:

26. I made stuffed dates by mixing cream cheese with a little powdered sugar and a hint of vanilla. They are very fattening. The ________ is delicious.

    Which choice completes the text so that it conforms to the conventions of standard English?

    (A) taste however
    (B) taste, however,
    (C) taste; however,
    (D) taste: however,

27. Across the region, more than 7 in 10 countries are faced with an acute shortage of teachers. The situation in many countries may deteriorate as governments struggle with overcrowded classrooms and the rising demand for education from growing school-age ________ for every 100 children in 2012, there will be 147 primary school-age children in 2030.

    Which choice completes the text so that it conforms to the conventions of standard English?

    (A) populations:
    (B) populations,
    (C) populations;
    (D) populations

Answer Explanations

1. **(C)** The colon is often used to introduce several ideas. In this instance, "love," "chivalry," and "desire to protect women" all tell what man's "nobler feelings" are.
2. **(D)** This is the best choice because it creates two sentences, each giving information about a related but different topic.
3. **(A)** No punctuation is necessary because "of human and wildlife" is a prepositional phrase that directly modifies "health."

4. **(C)** Choice (C) creates two clear and grammatical sentences. Choice (A) is incorrect because the information given after the colon does not relate directly to the information given before the colon. Choice (B) creates a run-on sentence. Choice (D) could work but is not as good a choice as (C) because a semicolon is typically used to create a sentence containing two independent clauses containing closely related information. In this case, two quite separate points are made.

5. **(C)** The adverb clause "when they began to treat each other civilly," together with the phrase "that is," is set off by dashes. The material set off by dashes amplifies what has just been said. Note that this use of dashes is often effective, but dashes should be used sparingly in formal writing.

6. **(C)** Choice (A) is incorrect because a semicolon can only join two independent clauses, and in this case the part of the sentence after the semicolon is not an independent clause. Choice (B) is not grammatical. Choice (C) is correct because a dash can be used to introduce additional information about a topic, which in this case is "ink." Note that the words after the dash do not have to create an independent clause as they must after a semicolon.

7. **(D)** Answer choice (D) corrects the run-on sentence by creating a new sentence. Note that "it's" is the contraction of "it is."

8. **(B)** This choice creates an effective sentence in which the practice of needling is clearly explained. The colon is used appropriately to set off the explanation of an important procedure.

9. **(B)** Answer choices (A) and (C) create run-on sentences. Choice (D) is not grammatical.

10. **(C)** Context requires the possessive form of the personal pronoun "it."

11. **(B)** In this sentence, "or" serves as a coordinating conjunction that connects two infinitives ("to reach" or "(to) come") and requires no punctuation.

12. **(D)** The clause following the linking verb "are" cannot stand alone as a sentence. Consequently, it does not require connective punctuation.

13. **(B)** The portion of the sentence following "Java" cannot stand alone as a sentence; however, it serves as a dependent clause that provides details in support of the main sentence.

14. **(C)** Because the sentence beginning with "Before" introduces a new idea rather than one closely related to the previous sentence, it makes sense to use punctuation and capitalization to create a new sentence.

15. **(A)** In answer choice (A), the comma is correctly used in this phrase, serving as a substitute for the conjunction "and."

16. **(B)** Punctuation usually does not separate the complete subject (even if it is lengthy) from the verb.

17. **(A)** A comma is used after an introductory clause or phrase. In this case, it also ends the nonrestrictive appositive noun phrase that renames "Arlene Dohm."

18. **(A)** A comma is used because the concluding relative clause is not essential to the meaning of the sentence.

19. **(C)** Choices (A) and (B) repeat the subject and verb of the first sentence ("he was"), an avoidable redundancy. Answer (C) logically combines the two sentences, providing the who, what, and where of a narrative.

20. **(C)** By joining the fragment sentence to the next sentence, the fragment becomes an introductory phrase requiring a comma.

21. **(B)** The parenthetical phrase ("according . . . Science") should be set off with commas. The dash in choice (C) could have been used if the phrase had been introduced with a dash. However, the phrase begins with a comma, requiring that it end with a comma.

22. **(A)** Two independent clauses joined by a coordinating conjunction ("but") requires a comma before the conjunction.

23. **(A)** The point centers on the comparison of an obviously mature dog to a puppy. Because the description is essential to pointing out this difference, there is no need for it to be set off by commas.

24. **(C)** To be correct, choice (A) would need a transition into the list ("Lone Star State, such as, armadillos . . ."). Choice (B) is missing a comma between list items, and a semicolon is not used to introduce a list as is shown in choice (D). The dash in choice (C) indicates a pause before the list begins.

25. **(C)** Possessive pronouns by definition already show ownership. They do not need the apostrophe and "s" to be possessive. Use of the conjunction "however" to combine two independent sentences requires the semicolon before "however."

26. **(B)** In this case, "however" is not being used to combine two independent sentences. Instead, it is being used to emphasize a contrast between "fattening" and "delicious." When used in this context (emphasis), "however" is nonessential to the meaning of the sentence and should be set off with commas.

27. **(A)** This is the correct choice because the information given after the colon gives detailed information about the problem that will be caused by "growing school-age populations" mentioned in the independent clause before the colon.

Sentence Structure and Organization

What to Remember

- Remember what you have learned for parts of speech and how to use them correctly.
- Watch out for errors, such as sentence fragments, run-on sentences, dangling modifiers, double negatives, and errors in pronoun reference.

Practice

1. In 1979, the first year for which ______ earning data are available, women earned 62 percent of what men earned.

   Which choice completes the text so that it conforms to the conventions of standard English?

   (A) comparing
   (B) comparison
   (C) comparable
   (D) comparability

2. ______ full-time in management, business, and financial operations jobs had median weekly earnings of $977 in 2011, which is more than women earned in any other major occupational category.

   Which choice completes the text so that it conforms to the conventions of standard English?

   (A) Women working
   (B) Women worked
   (C) Women have worked
   (D) Women, those working

3. Women are more likely than men to work in professional and related ______ the proportion of women employed in the higher-paying job groups is much smaller than the proportion of men employed in them.

   Which choice completes the text so that it conforms to the conventions of standard English?

   (A) occupations. Being within this category, though,
   (B) occupations. Within this category, though,
   (C) occupations. Looking at those which are within this category, though,
   (D) occupations which are within this category. Though

4. In 2011, 8 percent of female professionals were employed in ______ computer and engineering fields, compared with 44 percent of male professionals.

   Which choice completes the text so that it conforms to the conventions of standard English?

   (A) the relative high-paying
   (B) relating to
   (C) relation to the high-paying
   (D) the relatively high-paying

5. Professional women were more likely to work in education and healthcare occupations, in which the pay is generally lower ______ computer and engineering jobs.

   Which choice completes the text so that it conforms to the conventions of standard English?

   (A) than
   (B) than that which would be earned in
   (C) than it is in
   (D) than what employees get paid in

6. Median weekly earnings for female part-timers were $235 in 2011, ______ the $226 median for their male counterparts.

   Which choice completes the text so that it conforms to the conventions of standard English?

   (A) a little different than
   (B) with little difference than
   (C) little different from
   (D) and this is a little different than

7. The Arctic is a gigantic "natural laboratory" of surprising ______ that offers exciting research possibilities in almost every branch of science.

   Which choice completes the text so that it conforms to the conventions of standard English?

   (A) divergence
   (B) diversity
   (C) discrepancy
   (D) incongruity

8. This means that charged particles from the sun enter Earth's atmosphere in these regions, producing ______ effects such as the aurora, magnetic storms, and ionospheric disturbances, which may black out radio communication.

   Which choice completes the text so that it conforms to the conventions of standard English?

   (A) ostentatious
   (B) glaring
   (C) conspicuous
   (D) protrusive

9. Lower in the atmosphere, the high-velocity westerly jet stream is affected by processes of energy exchange at Earth's surface in the Arctic—by sea ice distribution and ocean and land temperatures—and ______ the weather and climate of the entire hemisphere of even the whole Earth.

   Which choice completes the text so that it conforms to the conventions of standard English?

   (A) in turn effects
   (B) in turn affects
   (C) in turn effect
   (D) in turn affect

10. Within its boundary, Alaska encloses _______ associated with a deep ocean trench, 40 active volcanoes, and heavy earthquake activity.

Which choice completes the text so that it conforms to the conventions of standard English?

(A) a long island, the arc associated
(B) a long island of arc
(C) a long island arc
(D) a long island for an arc

11. In their rooms, their couches, and all the furniture of their entertainments, ___________ to their highest point.

Which choice completes the text so that it conforms to the conventions of standard English?

(A) this was where magnificence and extravagance were carried
(B) it was magnificence and extravagance that were carried
(C) this was where they carried magnificence and extravagance
(D) magnificence and extravagance were carried

12. The decorations of the rest of the room were noble and yet ______ the destination; garlands, entwined with ivy and vine branches, divided the walls into compartments bordered with fanciful ornaments.

Which choice completes the text so that it conforms to the conventions of standard English?

(A) owing to
(B) appropriate to
(C) surprising for
(D) foreign to

13. Writers on the question of the origin of woman's subjection to man differ as to the cause of the universal ______ of woman in all periods and nations.

Which choice completes the text so that it conforms to the conventions of standard English?

(A) corruption
(B) criticism
(C) knowledge
(D) fear

14. Woman's steady march onward, and her growing desire for a broader outlook, prove that she has not reached her normal condition and that society has not yet _______ all that is necessary for its attainment.

Which choice completes the text so that it conforms to the conventions of standard English?

(A) acquiesced
(B) conceded
(C) assented
(D) complied

15. The national park network in the United States __________ some of the most pristine and sensitive wilderness in North America.

Which choice completes the text so that it conforms to the conventions of standard English?

(A) is comprising
(B) is comprised of
(C) is being comprised of
(D) comprised of

16. For example, __________ during fieldwork are analyzed in the lab for a variety of purposes, including genetic mapping.

Which choice completes the text so that it conforms to the conventions of standard English?

(A) feather collecting
(B) collections of feathers
(C) feathers collected
(D) feathers, having been collected

17. Ornithologists often write reports about their research or publish articles in scientific journals focused on biology, ecology, conservation, or __________.

Which choice completes the text so that it conforms to the conventions of standard English?

(A) managing wildlife
(B) wildlife management
(C) wildlife being managed
(D) managed wildlife

18. Those who want to develop their own research projects, work in high-level management positions, or teach at a university usually need a Ph.D. in ______ related to their work.

Which choice completes the text so that it conforms to the conventions of standard English?

(A) a regimen
(B) an instruction
(C) a discipline
(D) a preparation

19. That the students also studied from life is shown by the facility with which they seized a likeness or ______ the characteristics and movements of different kinds of animals.

Which choice completes the text so that it conforms to the conventions of standard English?

(A) converted
(B) yielded
(C) rendered
(D) furnished

20. He uses needles, herbs, and other devices to treat ailments such as headaches, back problems, and foot pain. Through his work, Jon _______ Oriental medicine's centuries-old precept that the body is interconnected—head to toe and everything in between.

Which choice completes the text so that it conforms to the conventions of standard English?

(A) alleges
(B) pleads
(C) advocates
(D) bears

21. It must be clearly understood then that the color effects that are the glory of the art are not directly produced by painting at all but by the window's being built up of a multitude of small pieces of white and colored glass—glass, that is, colored in the making and of which the artist must choose the exact shades he needs, cut them out to shape, and ____________ to form his design, using a separate piece for every color or shade of color.

Which choice completes the text so that it conforms to the conventions of standard English?

(A) fitting themselves together
(B) having been fit together
(C) he fits them together
(D) fit them together

22. Adult literacy rates were below the global average in South and West Asia (63%) and sub-Saharan Africa (59%), where more than one-third of adults could not read and write. However, the average for Latin America and the Caribbean _______ lower literacy rates in the Caribbean, where the adult literacy rate was only 69% in 2011.

Which choice completes the text so that it conforms to the conventions of standard English?

(A) evades
(B) harbors
(C) conceals
(D) curbs

23. In career news, healthcare is everywhere. _______ the healthcare industry is projected to add more jobs—and grow more than 13%—than any other industry between 2022 and 2032, according to the U.S. Bureau of Labor Statistics (BLS).

Which choice completes the text so that it conforms to the conventions of standard English?

(A) Because
(B) That's because
(C) The cause of this is that
(D) This is caused by the fact that

24. Hospitals _______ the largest number of jobs in healthcare, about 39 percent of total healthcare employment.

Which choice completes the text so that it conforms to the conventions of standard English?

(A) purported
(B) explained
(C) accounted for
(D) professed

25. "__________ is one of the best parts about any healthcare career," says pharmacist Jennifer Adams, a senior director at the American Association of Colleges of Pharmacy.

Which choice completes the text so that it conforms to the conventions of standard English?

(A) Jobs being stable
(B) That jobs have stability
(C) That the jobs are stable
(D) Job stability

26. Ohiyesa's new home was a pioneer log cabin on a farm at Flandreau, Dakota Territory, where a small group of progressive Native Americans had taken up homesteads like white men __________ an independent livelihood.

Which choice completes the text so that it conforms to the conventions of standard English?

(A) and had earnings of
(B) whose earning were
(C) and were earning
(D) so that they earned

27. His long hair was cropped. He was put into a suit of citizen's clothing and sent off to a mission day school. __________, he soon became interested; two years later, he voluntarily walked 150 miles to attend a larger and better school at Santee, Nebraska.

Which choice completes the text so that it conforms to the conventions of standard English?

(A) First, he was reluctant
(B) Being that he was first reluctant,
(C) At first reluctant
(D) Reluctant first

Answer Explanations

1. **(C)** The adjective "comparable" (admitting of comparison) is the best choice. Comparable data would be needed to allow an accurate comparison of women's earnings in different years.

2. **(A)** The participial phrase beginning with the word "working" modifies the noun "women," which is the subject of the sentence.

3. **(B)** This choice divides the text into two complete, meaningful sentences. Use of the preposition "within" concisely introduces the parameters of the sentence's purpose: to compare the two groups that comprise the professional category.

4. **(D)** The adjective "relative" makes little sense in context. The adverb "relatively" is correct because it is saying that these fields are high paying in comparison with other fields.
5. **(C)** The given sentence has an error in parallelism because it compares "pay" and "jobs," which are not comparable. This choice corrects the error so that pay in two occupational categories is compared.
6. **(C)** Although choice (A) is grammatically correct, standard usage is "little different from." Choice (A) would be correct if it read "which is little different than."
7. **(B)** Context provides a clue: "offers exciting research possibilities in almost every branch of science." A diverse "laboratory" would allow many types of research.
8. **(C)** "Conspicuous" (attracting attention) makes good sense because the atmospheric effect described would attract attention.
9. **(B)** This choice makes good sense. The jet stream is "affected by" (influenced by) processes of heat exchange and then ("in turn") affects the Earth's weather and climate. Note that the verb "affects" (influences) is correct in context. Choice (A) "in turn effects" is incorrect because the verb "effect" means "to bring about."
10. **(C)** The adjectives "long" and "island" modify the noun "arc," which is the direct object of the verb "encloses." The other choices are not grammatical.
11. **(D)** In choice (A), the prepositional phrase in the first part of the sentence, beginning with "in" and ending with "entertainments," refers to "magnificence and extravagance," which should come immediately after the prepositional phrase. Choice (D) corrects this error.
12. **(B)** The decorations were "noble," so it would have been easy for them to be inappropriate to the destination, "yet" they were not.
13. **(A)** An enlarged vocabulary will help identify the correct answer in this type of question. In context, "corruption" means "change from original state."
14. **(B)** "Conceded" (granted) makes good sense in the context that woman has not yet attained equality ("her normal condition") because society has not granted her everything necessary for her to achieve it. Choice (A) would be correct if it were "acquiesced to."
15. **(B)** Only answer choice (B) supplies the correct form and tense of the verb to create a complete sentence.
16. **(C)** The correct answer needs to provide a subject for the verb "are analyzed," which eliminates choice (A). Choice (B) does not make sense with "during fieldwork." Finally, choice (C) is the most concise and appropriate answer.
17. **(B)** The answer is one of four in a series of topics. To maintain parallelism, standard usage requires that all the nouns be in the same form.
18. **(C)** Context requires a word meaning a "field of knowledge." A Ph.D. in a relevant discipline is required for certain occupations related to ornithology.
19. **(C)** "Rendered" means "represented in drawing." This makes sense because this sentence is describing how the students improved their ability to depict things.
20. **(C)** Jon "advocates" (supports) that the body is interconnected by his selection of treatments.

21. **(D)** Parallelism requires that the verb "fit" be in the present tense. This can be seen by looking at the two preceding verbs in the series: "the artist must choose . . . [and] cut."

22. **(C)** Only one literacy rate is given for the category "Latin America and the Caribbean," so there is no way to determine the literacy rate in each separate area.

23. **(B)** Answer choice (A) does not create a complete sentence. Of the remaining options, choice (B) is the most clear and concise.

24. **(C)** "Accounted for," by definition, means "gave an explanation or a reason for something."

25. **(D)** Answer choices (A), (B), and (C) are grammatically correct; however, choice (D) is the best because it is clear and concise.

26. **(C)** The past progressive tense indicates that the group of Native Americans were earning their living over a period of time.

27. **(C)** "At first reluctant" is a standard phrase meaning "although he was reluctant at first." The sentence goes on to say that "he soon became interested."

Transitions

What to Remember

- Some transition words may have similar meanings but meanings that do differ slightly.
- Reviewing these words by typing "transition words" in your search engine to find lists of transition words, their meanings, and often example sentences is helpful.

Practice

1. Women who worked part-time made up 26 percent of all female wage and salary workers in 2011. _______ 13 percent of men in wage and salary jobs worked part-time.

   Which choice completes the text with the most logical transition?

   (A) Similarly,
   (B) In contrast,
   (C) Consequently,
   (D) Notwithstanding this,

2. If we consider that civilization involves the whole process of human achievement, it must admit of a great variety of qualities and degrees of development; ___________ it appears to be a relative term applied to the variation of human life.

   Which choice completes the text with the most logical transition?

   (A) hence
   (B) furthermore
   (C) likewise
   (D) finally

3. In 2010, the Centers for Disease Control and Prevention received 1,691 reports of malaria among persons in the United States, representing a 14% increase from the 1,484 cases reported with onset of symptoms in 2009. ___________, the number of cases reported in 2010 are the largest number of malaria cases that have been reported in the United States since 1980.

   Which choice completes the text with the most logical transition?

   (A) Both
   (B) Besides
   (C) Additionally
   (D) Such as

4. The "poem" part of the equation promises greater density and compression than we typically expect from prose, achieved through poetic devices _______ rhythm, imagery, metaphor, simile, and figures of speech.

   Which choice completes the text with the most logical transition?

   (A) furthermore
   (B) above all
   (C) perhaps even
   (D) such as

5. Somewhat more significant is ______ Peter Martyr spoke of Cuba as an island and said that some sailors pretended to have circumnavigated it.

   Which choice completes the text with the most logical transition?

   (A) whereas
   (B) while
   (C) despite
   (D) the fact that

6. England in the eighteenth century, which has been especially cited as an example of this sort of government, was essentially an aristocratic state, ______ it comprised some great elements of democracy; for the laws and customs of the country were such that the aristocracy could not but preponderate in the long run and direct public affairs according to its own will.

   Which choice completes the text with the most logical transition?

   (A) although
   (B) regardless of
   (C) or at least
   (D) in other words

7. Researchers studying data from NASA's *Cassini* mission have observed that Saturn's largest moon, Titan, behaves much like Venus, Mars, or a comet when exposed to the raw power of the solar wind. The observations suggest that unmagnetized bodies like Titan might interact with the solar wind in the same basic ways, ____________ their nature or distance from the sun.

   Which choice completes the text with the most logical transition?

   (A) or perhaps even
   (B) nevertheless
   (C) regardless of
   (D) when in fact

8. He replied, "Males. I was thinking about males. I viewed the world of literature—______, the entire world of artistic creation—as a world of males, and so did most writers."

   Which choice completes the text with the most logical transition?

   (A) at least
   (B) indeed
   (C) and yet
   (D) conversely

9. A study in the November 1998 *Journal of the American Medical Association* reports that between 1990 and 1997, patient visits to practitioners of alternative medicine increased about 47 percent. In a survey published in the January 2001 *American Demographics*, 70 percent of respondents had tried ______ 1 of 8 selected forms of alternative medicine, including acupuncture.

   Which choice completes the text with the most logical transition?

   (A) in spite of
   (B) at least
   (C) instead
   (D) nevertheless

10. Tides help determine where the waves break—low on the beach at low tide, high on the beach at high tide—and, ___________ where sand is deposited and removed.

    Which choice completes the text with the most logical transition?

    (A) therefore,
    (B) in the case that,
    (C) so as to
    (D) to ensure that

11. The traditionals know that those who follow the lead of the progressives will be assimilated—that is, swept away into a competitive economy for which they have no training. ___________ the Hopi hold their land, those still able to make corn grow in the slow, patient techniques of dry farming will survive even when all help has been taken away, . . .

    Which choice completes the text with the most logical transition?

    (A) With this in mind,
    (B) Accordingly,
    (C) Lest
    (D) So long as

12. Delirium tremens, a disorder long believed to be fatal in all cases _______ subjected to constant and aggressive medical intervention, was observed to subside by itself more readily in patients left untreated, with a substantially improved rate of survival.

    What choice completes the text with the most logical transition?

    (A) unless
    (B) last but not least
    (C) to return
    (D) at any rate

13. If I'm satisfied with listening to a song once, the song is a failure! Yet, how many times have I heard poets introduce their poems with words like these: "I think I may have read this poem here before. ___________ I hope you'll bear with me. Hopefully there are others here who haven't heard it, . . .

    Which choice completes the text with the most logical transition?

    (A) If so,
    (B) Moreover,
    (C) Furthermore,
    (D) To summarize,

14. Oxides of iron, other metals, and ground soft glass are mixed with oil or gum and water ______ apply it, and then the glass is placed into a kiln and "fired" until the enamel is fused on and, if well fired, becomes part of the glass itself, . . .

    Which choice completes the text with the most logical transition?

    (A) Nevertheless
    (B) In order to
    (C) Moreover
    (D) In the hope that

15. Take this formidable people and train them for seven generations in constant warfare against savage men and ferocious beasts, in circumstances under which no weakling could survive, place them __________ they acquire exceptional skill with weapons and in horsemanship, and give them a country that is eminently suited to the tactics of the huntsman, the marksman, and the rider.

Which choice completes the text with the most logical transition?

(A) centrally
(B) only if
(C) so that
(D) accordingly

16. __________, the infection of transient cohorts by their resident urban cohorts can facilitate disease transfer to other areas as those migrants continue their journey.

Which choice completes the text with the most logical transition?

(A) Although
(B) Despite
(C) Immediately
(D) Furthermore

17. __________ arriving at the entrance to the cave, the spelunkers were told to check their head lanterns and leave behind any unnecessary gear that might slow their progress through the dark and winding underground tunnels.

Which choice completes the text with the most logical transition?

(A) Last but not least
(B) Immediately upon
(C) At the final point
(D) To summarize

18. Resplendent blooms were cascading across the outreaches of the jetty. Jasmine was not impressed. She did not want flowers or moonlight or island breezes. She wanted freedom, __________ the same freedoms her brother enjoyed.

Which choice completes the text with the most logical transition?

(A) moreover
(B) for example
(C) particularly
(D) in contrast to

19. __________ she looked up and inspected the girl as if a new servant were no more than a new bonnet, a necessary article to be ordered home for examination. Christie presented her recommendation, made her modest little speech, and awaited her doom.

Which choice completes the text with the most logical transition?

(A) Presently
(B) Across
(C) To illustrate
(D) On the other hand

20. In me thou see'st the twilight of such day

 ____________ sunset fadeth in the west; . . .

 Which choice completes the text with the most logical transition?

 (A) Worst of all
 (B) Because
 (C) As after
 (D) Namely

21. The name of American, which belongs to you in your national capacity, must always exalt the just pride of patriotism ____________ any appellation derived from local discriminations.

 Which choice completes the text with the most logical transition?

 (A) since
 (B) understandably
 (C) more than
 (D) thus

22. Assonance occurs when the same (or similar) vowel sounds are repeated in nearby words, usually in stressed syllables. ____________ rhyme, which has similarity of both vowel and final consonant sounds, assonance repeats only the vowel sounds and ends with different consonant sounds.

 Which choice completes the text with the most logical transition?

 (A) Of course
 (B) Unlike
 (C) Likewise
 (D) That is

23. "Can you authenticate that this is a genuine Monet?" Andre paused, waiting for Joseph to answer. __________, he repeated the question, sounding out each syllable of "authenticate" as if Joseph might not understand the meaning of the word.

 Which choice completes the text with the most logical transition?

 (A) In conclusion
 (B) Finally
 (C) Specifically
 (D) On the other hand

24. We stood between his troopers and my warriors. We placed a large stone on the blanket before us. Our treaty was made by this stone, _______ it was to last until the stone should crumble to dust.

 Which choice completes the text with the most logical transition?

 (A) besides
 (B) obviously
 (C) moreover
 (D) as

25. The mistake I made was in driving the mules after the "norther" commenced. Had I gone immediately into camp, before they became heated and wearied, they would probably have eaten the grass, and this, I have no doubt, would have saved them; but, ___________, their blood became heated from overwork, and the sudden chill brought on a reaction that proved fatal.

    Which choice completes the text with the most logical transition?

    (A) because
    (B) since
    (C) as it was
    (D) in other words

26. When she could fly with them, circle in the air, float upon the water, dive for little fish, and be happy and gay—then indeed she was one of them and they loved her. ___________ she had broken her wing, it was different. The little Chinese seabird shook her little head mournfully.

    Which choice completes the text with the most logical transition?

    (A) But since
    (B) Despite the fact
    (C) For that reason
    (D) Best of all

27. ___________ the door was unlocked on the inside and flung violently open. Miss Sally dived into her own bedroom; Mr. Brass, who was not remarkable for personal courage, ran into the next street.

    Which choice completes the text with the most logical transition?

    (A) Since
    (B) Suddenly
    (C) As a result
    (D) Near

Answer Explanations

1. **(B)** This is the best choice because it makes a contrast between men and women who work part-time.

2. **(A)** What comes after the word "hence" is a consequence of what comes before the word "hence."

3. **(C)** "Additionally" introduces new information to an already established subject.

4. **(D)** Choice (D) "such as" introduces the series of nouns that are examples of poetic devices.

5. **(D)** Only choice (D) creates a complete sentence.

6. **(A)** "Although" generally means "regardless of the fact," which makes it a transition word flagging some type of contrast or conflict of ideas. In this case, the contrast is ironic: an aristocratic state containing elements of democracy.

7. **(C)** The only answer that makes sense with the context is "regardless of," a transition that suggests concession.

8. **(B)** "Indeed" is a transitional word that results in placing emphasis on a point being made. Sometimes the statement expands the point, as in this case.

9. **(B)** The first sentence provides the context: an increase in the number of patients seeking alternative medicine. In such a case, the writer's emphasis is on proving the point by showing that a large percentage of respondents (70%) tried at least one form of alternative medicine, with the implication that some would have tried even more.

10. **(A)** By using "therefore" in this context, a cause and effect relationship is established between tides and the locations of sand deposits.

11. **(D)** What do the "traditionals" know? First, the idea that "progressives" will not survive because they are not trained for a competitive society is implied. Second, traditionals know that some Hopi will survive, but this is a conditional prediction. To survive they must hold the land and grow corn using dry farming methods. The correct transition word must convey this conditional relationship. "So long as" means "providing that" and conveys the idea that conditions must be met for the Hopi to survive.

12. **(A)** This is another example in which establishing conditional circumstances is key. The central contrast is between medical intervention and patients being left untreated. This contrast is made possible by the transition word "unless," meaning what would be expected to happen if something else did not happen or were not true. Patients were expected to die if they did not receive medical intervention.

13. **(A)** "If so" means "if that is the case," a transition that obviously expresses the speaker's meaning.

14. **(B)** When used with the infinitive form of the verb, "in order to" is a transition word that conveys the purpose of something, in this case, the purpose of mixing with "oil or gum and water."

15. **(C)** The transition "so that" suggests a consequence or result, in this case, acquiring exceptional skill.

16. **(D)** Choices (A) and (B) create sentences that do not make sense. "Immediately" is not supported by context because the disease is spread through migration, which is not an immediate means of transfer. "Furthermore," however, means "in addition to what precedes."

17. **(B)** The spelunkers are not "at the final point" because they are entering the cave to go through the tunnels. "Immediately upon" tells the reader that there was no delay when they arrived at the entrance.

18. **(C)** The context provides a helpful clue: She wanted the "same freedoms." As a transition word, "particularly" means "especially" and connotes an emphasis on "same."

19. **(A)** This excerpt is clearly a narrative in which the element of time would be a factor.

20. **(C)** The correct answer choice is (C) because the poet is comparing himself to the twilight, which comes after sunset.

21. **(C)** Choice (C) provides a logical transition between the idea of the pride of patriotism and whatever feelings might result from a name "derived from local discriminations." Context does not reveal whether such an appellation is negative or positive; however, for the pride of patriotism to be exalted suggests that it must be "more than."

22. **(B)** The correct answer introduces a sentence that points out the difference between assonance and rhyme.

23. **(B)** As is common in narrative texts, transition words are used to convey the passage of time. "Finally" can refer to a final point, or it can mean "after a long delay."

24. **(D)** "As" can have several meanings. In this context, it means "in other words" and is used to point to the idea that the stone represented the treaty.

25. **(C)** First, the speaker is speculating on what might have happened if he had taken different actions. Then he narrates what actually did happen, using the transition "as it was" to signal to his readers that he is about to depart from speculation to reality.

26. **(A)** Identifying the main contrast found within this little narrative is important. The bird was happy and gay but now is mournful. The transition that suggests contrast and makes sense in the context is "but since."

27. **(B)** Context describes a quickly unfolding chain of events that suggests the door was unlocked and opened suddenly.

Notes Analysis (Rhetorical Analysis)

What to Remember

These questions require you to focus on a goal without getting distracted. Remember to do the following:

- Watch out for the bulleted lists so that they don't confuse you.
- Determine the general subject of the notes and go to the stated goal.
- Be sure you understand what the goal is and eliminate wrong answers until you can identify the one correct answer that accomplishes the stated goal.

Practice

1. While researching a topic, a student has taken the following notes:

   - A large variety of symbols are seen in different cultures around the world.
   - Many symbols are repeated in cultures that are geographically far apart.
   - Some are repeated because members of the same race have migrated and carried the symbols with them.
   - Some shared symbols are due to elements of the human mind.
   - Some are repeated because of amalgamation, when two cultures blend together, and assimilation, when one culture mixes itself into another.
   - Some are the result of the elements common to humans, such as a round ball as the symbol for the sun and moon.

   The student wants to emphasize that many shared symbols across the world have explainable causes. Which choice most effectively uses relevant information from the notes to accomplish this goal?

   (A) Our brains interact with our surroundings and our social environment to create a system of symbols that can be shared cross-culturally.
   (B) The reasons for the cross-cultural appearance of some symbols can be readily understood within the realm of rational explanations, such as migration, amalgamation, assimilation, and experiences common to most humans.
   (C) The advances in technology in our global economy have facilitated the proliferation of cross-cultural symbols.
   (D) Symbols seen in different cultures reflect the belief systems of those peoples; however, often these beliefs and their corresponding symbols are borrowed by other cultures.

2. While researching a topic, a student has taken the following notes:

- Abbreviations, first used on ancient stone monuments and coins, are used to save space.
- Roughly 60 percent of English is based on Latin and includes many Latin abbreviations.
- Abbreviations are found in scientific names of organizations, the structural elements of books (such as in footnotes, indexes, and bibliographies), college degrees, etc.
- Some professions have specialized abbreviations unique to their field, such as librarians.
- The United States Postal Service adopted a two-letter abbreviation system for the names of the states.
- Digital communications, such as text messaging, include many abbreviations that change over time.

The student wants to emphasize the prevalence of abbreviations in written communication. Which choice most effectively uses relevant information from the notes to accomplish this goal?

(A) Abbreviations are a resourceful means to save space when writing for books, scientific journals, and government publications.
(B) From the earliest-known stone monuments to the latest electronic messaging of the twenty-first century, abbreviations in almost every field have been used to save space in written communications.
(C) When written communications were started, abbreviations in Latin were included to save space and to communicate more effectively.
(D) Regardless of the time and place, abbreviations in English and Latin have been used in both graphic representations and verbal communications.

3. While researching a topic, a student has taken the following notes:

- Yeti is a name given to a legendary creature reported by natives to live in the Himalayas.
- Yeti, also called the Abominable Snowman, is apelike with human facial features.
- It walks upright, and it is said that it leaves giant footprints (first seen in the 1890s) in the mountain snow.
- It has a reputation among the natives for being violent and dangerous.
- Several expeditions have searched without success for signs of Yeti.
- No proven evidence has been found to confirm its existence.
- Scientists suggest that the large snow prints that have been attributed to the Abominable Snowman may instead be normal-sized bear prints that have enlarged in the warm sun.

The student wants to present a nonbiased perspective on whether Yeti is real or not. Which choice most effectively uses relevant information from the notes to accomplish this goal?

(A) The legend of Yeti is unverified and based only on the claims of witnesses.
(B) Science has yet to prove the existence of the Abominable Snowman, even though many have seen it.
(C) Despite mounting circumstantial evidence of Yeti's existence, scientists have failed to find the proof needed.
(D) Verifiable evidence has never been found to prove the existence of Yeti; however, natives living in the Himalayas report that it is real and dangerous.

4. While researching a topic, a student has taken the following notes:

- Acerola is a native fruit grown in the warm climate of Mexico, the West Indies, Central America, and northern South America.
- Acerola fruit are small, red, and tart and contain extremely high levels of vitamin C.
- Acerola is a significant cash crop for farmers in the regions where they will grow.

The student wants to present a likely cause for acerola being an important cash crop. Which choice most effectively uses relevant information from the notes to accomplish this goal?

(A) The high levels of vitamin C in acerola likely accounts for its value as a cash crop.
(B) Acerola's limited growing area makes it rare and valuable.
(C) The tartness of the fruit makes it perfect for sweet-and-sour candies.
(D) Acerola's red color has a holiday effect.

5. While researching a topic, a student has taken the following notes:

- William Bradford wrote an account commonly called *History of Plymouth Settlement.*
- Some Christians in England began to worship based on their own understanding of the Bible.
- They were persecuted, including some being put in prison, for not conforming to the established Church customs, practices, and beliefs.
- They went to Holland between 1607 and 1608 to escape persecution.
- Their decision to leave England meant leaving properties, livelihoods, and friends.
- These farmers did not speak the language of Holland and did not know how to engage in trade, Holland's chief industry.
- The English government closed British ports to them, not allowing them to leave.
- They attempted to escape by bribing ship captains to secrete them out of England.
- They were sometimes betrayed by the captains, who stole their belongings and turned them over to officers to be brought before magistrates and put in prison.

The student wants to summarize the hardships encountered by the religious dissidents in their attempts to escape persecution in England. Which choice most effectively uses relevant information from the notes to accomplish this goal?

(A) The Christians attempting to escape England were tortured and killed by religious zealots.
(B) The established government saw opportunities to acquire properties and lands by restricting the movements and religious freedoms of Christian dissidents.
(C) In seeking freedom, these Christians faced giving up all they had and putting themselves in the hands of ruthless people to escape to an uncertain future in an alien land.
(D) The persecuted Christians lost their homes, monies, friends, rights as British citizens, and dignity as humans.

6. While researching a topic, a student has taken the following notes:

- Acids can be inorganic or organic.
- Inorganic acids are manufactured to use in making such things as explosives or metals.
- Organic acids can be found in different foods.
- Fats and oils contain fatty acids; rhubarb contains oxalic acid; cranberries are a source of benzoic acid.
- Citric acid is in citrus fruit (oranges, lemons, limes), but acetic acid is in vinegar.

The student wants to emphasize the diverse nature of acids. Which choice most effectively uses relevant information from the notes to accomplish this goal?

(A) The only acids found in nature are types of food.
(B) Acids can be organic or inorganic, manufactured or natural, and in a life-giving food or in a deadly explosive.
(C) An overconsumption of organic acids can contribute to health issues.
(D) Both organic and inorganic acids have important roles to play in our lives.

7. While researching a topic, a student has taken the following notes:

- Acoustics is a branch of physics.
- The science of acoustics involves studying how sound is produced and transmitted and then determining the effects of sound.
- Noise or sound is caused by vibrations.
- Acoustical engineers explore ways to control sound, such as using thick walls to quiet noise transmission or installing carpets and acoustical tiles, which absorb the vibrations.
- Echoes come from reflected sound vibrations that are delayed for more than 1/20 of a second from the time the sound is produced until the time it reaches the listener.

The student wants to emphasize how acoustical engineers could use acoustics to make hospital settings quieter for patients. Which choice most effectively uses relevant information from the notes to accomplish this goal?

(A) Poor acoustics can ruin a live music performance.
(B) Echoes are an especially serious issue in emergency rooms.
(C) Engineers could control noise levels in patient rooms by utilizing acoustical tiles in ceilings, walls, and portable screens.
(D) Because of acoustical engineers, sound effects, in conjunction with light shows, have become a mainstay of modern music venues.

8. While researching a topic, a student has taken the following notes:

- The ability of an airplane to fly is determined by many factors.
- Lift is the upward force created by air moving across the wings when a plane moves forward.
- The air moving across the curved upper part of the wing moves faster than the air moving across the flattened bottom of the wind (Bernoulli's principle).
- Air flow increases if the wing is turned at an angle in relation to the approaching airstream (the angle of attack).
- If the angle of attack is about 15 degrees, the lift will stop and the airplane will fall.
- The faster the plan goes (the air speed), the greater the lift.
- Drag is caused by friction fighting against the forward motion of the airplane.

The student wants to present a likely connection between pilot skill and keeping an airplane airborne. Which choice most effectively uses relevant information from the notes to accomplish this goal?

(A) Pilots would have very little control over most contributing factors of lift.
(B) To avoid drag, wings should be coated with high-gloss paint.
(C) To prevent losing lift, the pilot must pay close attention to the angle of attack and air speed.
(D) Air speed is in direct proportion to the angle of attack and drag.

9. While researching a topic, a student has taken the following notes:

- The early residents of the region that became Alaska were mostly Eskimos, Aleuts, and members of several Native American tribes.
- Danish explorer Vitus Bering, a captain in the Russian Navy, was commissioned to explore and chart the lands to the east of Siberia in 1728.
- Russian fur traders established the Three Saints Bay settlement in 1784.
- Europeans began exploring the territory for trade, greatly impacting Russian profits.
- Russia sold its Alaskan claims (called Russian America) to the United States in 1867.
- Prospectors discovered gold in the Yukon Territory in 1896, which began the great Alaskan Gold Rush, ending in 1904.
- Canada made territorial claims that would have left America's Alaska Territory with very little land left.
- An international commission decided in favor of the United States, in 1903, establishing the southeastern boundary where it is today.

The student wants to present a likely cause for the conflict between the United States and Canada over the Alaska Territory. Which choice most effectively uses relevant information from the notes to accomplish this goal?

(A) Russia's sale of its Alaskan holdings to the United States angered Canadians who did not want to be surrounded by American lands.
(B) The discovery of gold in Alaska likely made ownership of the territory very desirable for both the United States and Canada.
(C) The Bering Strait became a significant access point to the Alaska Territory and made the area more desirable for Canadian fur traders.
(D) Russian, European, Canadian, and American interests were likely countered by those of the Native Alaskans.

10. While researching a topic, a student has taken the following notes:

- *Little Women* is a book written by Louisa May Alcott in 1868–1869 (in two parts).
- In the novel, Alcott tells the story of the March family and its heroine Jo March.
- Literary scholars believe that some of the story is based on the Alcott family and Louisa's own life.
    - Louisa's parents were transcendentalists.
    - Her father was a teacher and taught his four daughters at home.
    - He was not able to support his family financially.
    - Louisa started an unsuccessful school but was successful in her writing career, which enabled her to support her family.
- Unlike Jo March, Louisa May Alcott never married.

The student wants to summarize Louisa May Alcott's relationship to her most well-known book, *Little Women*. Which choice most effectively uses relevant information from the notes to accomplish this goal?

(A) Louisa May Alcott wrote a (semi)autobiographical novel called *Little Women*, as well as other works, to help support her family financially.
(B) Louisa followed in her father's footsteps by being unsuccessful as a teacher.
(C) Only on the point of marriage did Louisa May Alcott's life differ from that of Jo March.
(D) Jo March was a transcendental reflection of Louisa May Alcott, as seen in the fact that she never married.

11. While researching a topic, a student has taken the following notes:

- Alfalfa has historically been a major feed crop for livestock in the United States and Canada.
- It is a perennial flowering legume that is called "lucerne" in Europe.
- Alfalfa is also used to increase soil fertility.
- It is well adapted to dry climates because its roots grow deep to find water.
- Alfalfa is among the crops that have been genetically modified (GMO) to survive applications of weed killers.
- Some farmers and consumers worry about safety risks surrounding the consumption of GMO crops by humans and livestock.
- A study in 2013 found that 27% of wild alfalfa has been cross-pollinated with GMO alfalfa plants.

The student wants to emphasize that GMO or genetically engineered crops cannot coexist with organic non-GMO crops. Which choice most effectively uses relevant information from the notes to accomplish this goal?

(A) Some countries ban all imports of GMO products in an effort to protect their organic crops.
(B) Because alfalfa is perennial, risks surround GMO plants surviving for decades.
(C) The deep roots of alfalfa draw water from underground sources where genetically engineered gene splices can be carried to organic fields.
(D) Organic, non-GMO crops are at risk of GMO contamination as seen in stands of feral alfalfa where over one-quarter of the plants are transgenic.

12. While researching a topic, a student has taken the following notes:

    - Algae are water plants that grow around the world.
    - They contain chlorophyll and react to sunlight by manufacturing sugars.
    - Fish and many water animals eat algae.
    - Types of algae include blue-green (found in lakes and pools of water) algae, freshwater green algae, brown algae in salt water, and red algae found in the ocean.
    - The food industry uses algae to produce agar and carrageenan, as well as other types of food additives, to thicken and stabilize foods.
    - Algae is in some sausages, fish products, breads, and daily products.
    - Algae grows quickly and is high in protein.
    - In October, 2022, Charles Green, Professor Emeritus of Earth and Atmospheric Sciences at Cornell University, suggested that algae can supply the world's protein needs.

    The student wants to emphasize that algae is a sustainable human food source. Which choice most effectively uses relevant information from the notes to accomplish this goal?

    (A) Because that fish and other water animals eat algae suggests that algae is a reliable food source for humans, as well.
    (B) Algae can be found in moldy bread, nonorganic sausage, and soured dairy products.
    (C) Algae is sustainable because of its prevalence around the world.
    (D) Algae, which is already being used by the food industry, is commonly found and is a rich source of protein, making it a nutritional superstar.

13. While researching a topic, a student has taken the following notes:

- The alphabet is named after the first two letters in the Greek alphabet: "alpha" and "beta."
- Each letter has a history, often including multicultural contributions. For example:
  - The letter "A" dates back to the Egyptians in about 3,000 B.C.
  - The earliest letter "A" meant "ox" and was shaped like the head of an ox.
  - The Semites borrowed the Egyptian hieroglyphic "ox," and later the Greeks called it "alpha."
  - Our current letter "A" was shaped by the Romans.
- Modern English has distinctive sounds that cannot be represented by the current Roman alphabet, resulting in some letters representing multiple sounds. For example:
  - A = Short sound (bat)
  - A = Long sound (late)
  - A = Broad sound (farm)
  - A = Unstressed sound (around)
- The International Phonetic Alphabet, consisting of over 80 characters, attempts to provide a more accurate representation of spoken language.

The student wants to suggest a rationale explaining why English is a difficult language for some non-English or English as a Second Language (ESL) speakers to learn. Which choice most effectively uses relevant information from the notes to accomplish this goal?

(A) The fact that there are insufficient letters in the Roman alphabet to represent all the sounds in the English language may make written English more difficult for ESL students.

(B) The extensive historical background behind each of the letters in the Roman alphabet makes the language more confusing, particularly for students who are transferring from their native language to English.

(C) Despite evidence to the contrary, the fact that the Roman alphabet has been affected by many different cultures has made it relatively simple for ESL students to learn English.

(D) The letter "A" is perhaps the most difficult letter for ESL students to learn in the Roman alphabet.

14. While researching a topic, a student has taken the following notes:

- Aluminum is nicknamed "the magic metal" because it can be fashioned into almost any shape.
- Aluminum is lightweight, about one-third the weight of iron.
- In its pure state, aluminum is soft.
- Alloys are mixed with aluminum to strengthen it.
- Aluminum can be mined; however, it cannot be mined in pieces like a gold nugget.
- Over 15% of Earth's crust is made of aluminum-containing compounds, but they are difficult to extract.
- Bauxite ore, which that contains 32% aluminum oxide, provides the most inexpensive source for extraction of aluminum.
- Varying amounts of aluminum can be found all around us in unexpected places, such as the air, drinking water, deodorants, cosmetics, appliances, cookware, foods, and some antacids.
- Aluminum can be toxic when absorbed by the human body through the digestive tract, lungs, and skin and can accumulate in the organs and attack the central nervous system.

The student wants to emphasize the unique characteristics of aluminum. Which choice most effectively uses relevant information from the notes to accomplish this goal?

(A) Aluminum is soft and lightweight and can be found everywhere.
(B) Aluminum's malleability, light weight, and ubiquitous presence in Earth's crust makes it an attractive metal for many uses; however, its absorption into the human body can create health issues.
(C) Despite aluminum's more favorable properties, such as it being lightweight and available from common sources, aluminum is too dangerous for its continued use in our environment.
(D) Environmental concerns and human health advocates need to band together to restrain the use of aluminum in its many forms.

15. While researching a topic, a student has taken the following notes:

- The amaranth family of plants includes weeds (such as giant pigweed) and flowers (such as cockscomb).
- Amaranth is beneficial when grown with garden plants as a companion plant because it loosens the soil, makes some nearby plants more resistant to insects, and enables other plants to increase their yields.
- It produces an edible pseudograin (seed) that some people with gluten sensitivities can eat.
- Like quinoa, amaranth is called a "complete grain" because it is high not just in carbohydrates but also in proteins, including the amino acid lysine (usually found in meat).

The student wants to present reasons to suggest that amaranth can be nicknamed a "one-stop shop" for good health. Which choice most effectively uses relevant information from the notes to accomplish this goal?

(A) Amaranth is a "one-stop shop" for good health because it provides healthy carbohydrates and proteins in our diets, plus when planted in the garden, it increases the health and productivity of garden plants around it.
(B) Amaranth is a "one-stop shop" for good health because it is a garden plant that contains both carbohydrates and proteins necessary to produce a healthier garden.
(C) Amaranth is a "one-stop shop" for good health because it is both a weed and a flower, meaning it is high in wild nutrients, plus it provides calming garden flowers.
(D) Amaranth is a "one-stop shop" for good health because, like meat, it contains lysine.

16. While researching a topic, a student has taken the following notes:

- American literature is difficult to define before 1850.
  - Early settlers and pioneers before 1765 were focused more on survival than literary accomplishment.
  - Colonial works were mostly histories aimed at bringing more Europeans into the colonies, poetry (usually on religious themes), and religious works.
  - From 1765 to 1850 the focus of the new American nation's writers shifted to politics and wit, with Benjamin Franklin leading the way.
  - During this period, New York writers, such as Charles Brockden Brown (European-style Gothic novels), Washington Irving (who formed the "Knickerbocker Group"), James Fenimore Cooper (adventure), and William Cullen Bryant (poetry) appeared.
- America's own literature appeared full scale between 1850 and 1900.
  - The list of American literature from this period is punctuated by the works of transcendentalists Emerson and Thoreau, Longfellow and Holmes of New England's upper class, plus many writers such as Poe, Hawthorne, Whitman, and Dickinson, who blazed trails apart from any movements.

The student wants to present a likely cause for the lack of an identifiable American body of literature prior to 1850. Which choice most effectively uses relevant information from the notes to accomplish this goal?

(A) American writing prior to 1850 likely had to compete first with the realities of wilderness survival and then with the growth struggles of becoming a new nation, with what works they did write aimed at pragmatism rather than art.
(B) Due to the works of Benjamin Franklin, the American writing prior to 1850 likely was an instructional exercise in logic and reason.
(C) Once formation of the "Knickerbocker Group" became known, American writing likely became more sophisticated and worldly.
(D) American writing prior to 1850 likely had to get approval from the British royalty; consequently, no truly American works were written until after 1850.

17. While researching a topic, a student has taken the following notes:

- Many people do not know how to determine if an item is antique or just vintage.
- Items imported into the United States are not taxed if they are antiques.
    - The United States government tax law of 1930 stated that to be an antique, the item had to be made before 1830 (one hundred years old).
    - The "one hundred year rule" was made in 1966.
    - A 1996 revision of the law states that if an antique is repaired more than 50 percent or if an antique's essential character is changed, it is no longer an antique and duty tax will be imposed.
- Usually, antique dealers view items as antique if they are over 100 years old.
- Vintage or collectables are items under 100 years old.

The student wants to summarize the key elements that identify an item as an antique. Which choice most effectively uses relevant information from the notes to accomplish this goal?

(A) Unlike vintage collectables that are under 100 years old, an antique is an item over 100 years old.

(B) An antique is an item over 100 years old that has not been repurposed and has not had more than 50% of the item restored or repaired.

(C) Regardless of age, an antique can be very old if it has not been restored or repaired more than 50%.

(D) To be considered an antique, an item must be at least 100 years old and be in its original condition.

18. While researching a topic, a student has taken the following notes:

    - Many southern and western states (including Texas, where it is the official state small mammal) are home to the nine-banded armadillo.
    - These mammals average about 2 feet long and can weigh up to 15 pounds.
    - They have hard bony plates that protect their bodies and long claws to dig holes and tunnels.
    - Armadillos cannot bite.
    - They use their long tongues to lick up insects.
    - Armadillos are considered a nuisance animal in many areas because they dig holes in gardens, lawns, and field crops in their search for insects.
    - They are expanding their range: they entered Georgia in the 1980s and are now as far north as Virginia.
    - Scientists believe that armadillos may be spreading a newly found strain of leprosy (Hansen's disease) to people in southern states, including Florida.
    - The only two species that can carry and contract leprosy are humans and armadillos.
    - People are being advised not to handle the mammals and not to eat armadillo meat.

    The student wants to emphasize the seriousness of armadillos expanding their territory. Which choice most effectively uses relevant information from the notes to accomplish this goal?

    (A) The proliferation of armadillos may herald the beginning of a new pandemic of sorts.
    (B) The increasing numbers and range of armadillos may mean that leprosy may spread to other animals, including domestic pets.
    (C) As armadillos spread deeper into the U.S., what once was considered an interesting and unusual mammal may become a destructive and economic burden and a threat to public health and safety.
    (D) Although armadillos cannot bite, their destructive nature could cause the need for increased legislation in efforts to control their spread.

19. While researching a topic, a student has taken the following notes:

- Allergies are the result of certain substances (allergens) being harmful to individuals who are sensitive to them.
- Large-molecule groups such as carbohydrates and proteins are the most common allergens.
- Small-molecule groups can also be allergens.
- Reactions to allergens can vary greatly, such as hives, digestive issues, and asthma.
- When an allergen combines with an antibody in the allergic person, histamine is released into the bloodstream, causing swelling.
- People are often allergic to animals, such as cats; however, cats can also be allergic to people.

The student wants to summarize the cause of most common allergies. Which choice most effectively uses relevant information from the notes to accomplish this goal?

(A) Carbohydrates, proteins, and small molecules cause allergens to enter the bloodstream and in turn cause allergic reactions.
(B) Allergic cats and allergic people have many things in common, such as the release of histamines into their bloodstreams.
(C) Allergens, the root cause of allergic reactions, appear in the form of hives, digestive issues, and asthma.
(D) Some people have sensitivities to specific substances that combine with antibodies to release histamines and cause allergic swelling.

20. While researching a topic, a student has taken the following notes:

- The first cowboys in North America were the Spanish vaqueros who settled in Mexico.
- Vaqueros were skilled in working with cattle and in the cattle industry.
- They came originally from Spain in the 1500s, populating large ranches with European horses and cattle.
- Wranglers, in contrast to cowboys, work with horses rather than with cattle.
- English-speaking settlers began adopting the vaquero (cowboy) lifestyle in the early 1800s.
- As the railroad began crossing the western plains, groups of cowboys would herd thousands of cattle to be put on trains and sent to sales destinations.

The student wants to emphasize the significance of the Spanish vaqueros to the cattle industry. Which choice most effectively uses relevant information from the notes to accomplish this goal?

(A) The vaqueros were successful cattle ranchers; however, the arrival of the railway ended the era of the vaquero.
(B) Spanish vaqueros (cowboys) established and ran successful cattle ranches for almost three hundred years before eastern settlers came west and adopted the vaquero ways.
(C) Vaqueros, in conjunction with wranglers, established a monopoly in the western cattle industry that lasted into the late 1800s.
(D) The English-speaking settlers adopted the lifestyle of the vaquero to learn the cattle business in anticipation of the arrival of the railroad.

21. While researching a topic, a student has taken the following notes:

- Phineas T. Barnum, showman and promoter, purchased Jumbo, an African elephant of tremendous size, from the London Zoo in 1883 for $10,000.
- Many in Great Britain, including Queen Victoria, attempted to stop the sale.
- The almost 12-foot-tall Jumbo was special to the British people; but Jumbo was sold and transported to New York.
- Jumbo's mate, Alice, remained in the London Zoo.
- In February of 1882, *The London Gazette* printed a song about Alice and Jumbo in protest of the sale.
- In the song, Alice accuses Jumbo of not loving her because he's leaving her behind to go to Yankee Land.
- Barnum put Jumbo on tour, but while in St. Thomas, Ontario, Jumbo was killed when an unscheduled freight train hit him as his keeper was taking him to be loaded in his cage.

The student wants to emphasize the attempts made to stop the sale of Jumbo. Which choice most effectively uses relevant information from the notes to accomplish this goal?

(A) Not only did the famous *London Gazette* anthropomorphize Jumbo and his mate Alice in a song aimed at protesting the sale, but Queen Victoria, herself, attempted to stop Jumbo's sale.

(B) The people of London protested the sale and attempted to keep Jumbo and his mate together.

(C) Jumbo's tragic end was foreshadowed by the intensity of the public reaction to his pending sale and separation from his mate.

(D) There were rumors that Jumbo's great size was a determining factor in his not being able to avoid being hit by the train.

22. While researching a topic, a student has taken the following notes:

- Many ecologists are concerned over the health of bee populations worldwide.
- Some species of bees have now been included on the endangered list under the Endangered Species Act of 1973.
- Threats to bee populations include pesticides, climate change, and decreasing habitats.
- Without bees to function as pollinators, many plant species will fail to survive, causing ecological downturns and food shortages.

The student wants to present likely ways to slow or prevent the decline of bee populations. Which choice most effectively uses relevant information from the notes to accomplish this goal?

(A) The most likely preventative measure to ensure that our bee populations are protected would be to increase the varieties of bees put on the Endangered Species List.

(B) It is reasonable to assume that making sure bees have sufficient plants to pollinate would likely lessen the risk of ecological downturns and food shortages.

(C) Because the decline in bee populations is a global issue, the best response would be an international effort to protect bees.

(D) A reasonable assumption can be made that our response to declining bee populations should be to stop the use of pesticides, lessen our carbon footprint that contributes to global warming, and provide backyard habitats that are bee friendly.

23. While researching a topic, a student has taken the following notes:

- Grades of beef depend on the cattle from which the cuts are taken.
  - Steers/heifers: prime or choice cuts
  - Dairy cows: good, standard, or commercial cuts
  - Calves to 12 weeks: veal
- Determining the grades of beef is controlled by the U.S. Department of Agriculture.
- Beef can be prepared for eating in many ways, including cooking, curing, smoking, and drying.
- Beef can be corned using salt.
- Research in the last few years has stressed that eating beef carries certain health risks and consumption of beef should be limited to three small servings per week.
- Some researchers point to studies that indicate eating red meat should be eliminated altogether.
- Yet other studies claim that beef is healthy to eat if the meat comes from cattle fed on organic grass with no GMO (genetically modified) grains added to their diets.
- A 2019 study concluded that researchers found little evidence of harmful effects of eating red meat.

The student wants to summarize the research results concerning eating beef as the results relate to consumers. Which choice most effectively uses relevant information from the notes to accomplish this goal?

(A) Despite studies to the contrary, research indicates that consumers should avoid red meats, which would include beef.

(B) Consumers can be guided by the grades of beef as determined by the U.S. Department of Agriculture to be sure to get safe cuts of beef.

(C) Conflicting and contradictory research studies make it clear that a consensus on the efficacy of eating beef is not easily reached, leaving consumers no definitive answer.

(D) By looking at guidelines on the proper cooking methods for preparing beef, the consumer can better mitigate any health risks.

24. While researching a topic, a student has taken the following notes:

- Bells probably originated in Asia around the 3rd millennium B.C.
- They were used as musical instruments and for ceremonies in China and Assyria.
- Throughout history, bells have served functional roles, such as warning of danger, gathering worshippers, honoring fallen royalty, and celebrating and announcing special events.
- Ringing bells can be said to symbolize anything that is meaningful in people's lives, whether it's a call to dinner or the ending of a life.
- America's Liberty Bell was rung to announce the signing of the Declaration of Independence.
- England's Big Ben is the Palace of Westminster's clock tower in London.
- Bells can either be "hung dead," which means mounted in a stationary position and struck to produce the sound, or they can be mounted in such a way that they can swing, allowing the internal clapper to strike and produce the sound.
- Most bells are made of cast metal in a process called bell founding.
- The best bells are 80% copper and 20% tin.
- Bells can be used to play songs by using bells "tuned" to produce individual notes.

The student wants to summarize the significance of bells. Which choice most effectively uses relevant information from the notes to accomplish this goal?

(A) Bells are mainly used for religious and political events.
(B) Bells are part of a mysterious and difficult-to-explain part of human history.
(C) Bells are the product of metal castings that produce sound either by being struck or by swinging to allow a clapper to hit the metal internally.
(D) Bells are an ancient form of expression that can produce music and mark significant moments in life as well as serve practical functions.

25. While researching a topic, a student has taken the following notes:

- Several types of cultivated blueberries produce large, sweet fruit, such as the northern highbush blueberry (genus and species *Vaccinium corymbosum*) and the lowbush blueberry (*Vaccinium pennsylvanicum*).
- Researchers have been studying the wild lowbush blueberry (*Vaccinium angustifolium*), native to the northeastern United States and parts of Canada, because despite their small berry size, they contain twice the antioxidant capacity of cultivated varieties.
  - Scientists speculate that wild blueberries produce more phytochemicals (called polyphenols) in response to the harsh growing conditions they encounter in the unprotected areas where they are exposed to extreme cold.
  - Wild blueberries are a very dark blue color, indicative of a host of health benefits.
  - Polyphenols are very potent antioxidants in wild blueberries and are associated with reducing inflammation and oxidative stress in aging adults.
  - Wild blueberries increase beneficial bacteria in the gut microbiome.
  - Wild blueberries are rich in fiber, manganese, and iron.
- A study reported by the University of North Carolina in September 2022 suggests that freeze-dried wild blueberry powder consumption significantly improved the brain function and speed of study participants (older adults with cognitive issues) within six months.
- Earlier studies on wild berries in Alaska showed similar results.

The student wants to emphasize how doctors can use these research findings to help patients improve their daily quality of life. Which choice most effectively uses relevant information from the notes to accomplish this goal?

(A) Doctors could help patients with early-onset cognitive decline make dietary changes to include wild blueberries as part of their daily diet.

(B) Wild blueberries could be especially helpful in encouraging patients who are picky eaters.

(C) Wild fruits and vegetables could be made part of an ongoing study across age groups.

(D) Wild blueberries would be the most effective treatment for patients with hypersensitivity issues.

26. While researching a topic, a student has taken the following notes:

- A 2022 poll found that 27% of Americans do not budget their money because they don't see a need for a budget.
- An earlier survey revealed that of 1,500 people asked, over 900 did not know how much money they had spent the previous month. Reasons:
    - Some people do not want to feel restricted.
    - Inconsistent income or expenses make budgeting difficult.
- The COVID-19 effect:
    - During the quarantine in 2020, the household savings rate jumped to 16.3%, the highest since 1960.
    - Between March and June of 2022, the household savings rate fell to 5.18%.
- A 2023 study found that work-related expenses for employees working remotely from home on average are less than half that of office-based employees.
- For those who are unable to keep a budget, money experts suggest starting an emergency fund that builds to at least 6 weeks of expense money.

The student wants to present the likely reason that the household savings rate increased during 2020. Which choice most effectively uses relevant information from the notes to accomplish this goal?

(A) Employees working remotely from home during the quarantine of 2020 likely lowered work-related expenses, enabling greater savings.
(B) Income volatility was a significant issue in 2020.
(C) Lack of training in budget management is a significant factor in the drop in savings between 2020 and 2022.
(D) Families had no need to prepare an emergency fund during the 2020 quarantine period.

27. While researching a topic, a student has taken the following notes:

- Plant-based or vegan butters are trending right now.
- In the four years prior to 2020, plant-based alternatives to milk rose by 50 million gallons while dairy sales decreased by 300 million gallons.
- In 2020, the worldwide sales of plant-based butter exceeded 2.4 billion dollars, with markets expected to double by 2032.
- Consumers are concerned about environmental issues surrounding animal husbandry.
- Many people advocate vegan/vegetarian diets as being part of a healthier lifestyle.
- Flexitarians are considered a major consumer group by industry leaders.
- Nutritionists warn that vegan butter comes in a block that is solid at room temperature, indicating high levels of saturated fats, usually palm or coconut oil.

The student wants to emphasize the irony present in the popularity of plant-based/vegan butter among health-conscious consumers. Which choice most effectively uses relevant information from the notes to accomplish this goal?

(A) While sales of milk alternatives went up, at the same time, sales of real dairy ironically went down.

(B) Ironically, consumers seeking heathier dietary choices may be replacing the saturated fat in dairy butter with another form of saturated fat in vegan butters that is just as unhealthy.

(C) In a twist of fate, worldwide sales of plant-based butter exceeded 2.4 billion dollars in the shadow of markets expected to double in the next 10 years.

(D) It is ironic that flexitarians, vegetarians who will eat meat from time to time, are willing to give up dairy butter for plant-based substitutes.

Answer Explanations

1. **(B)** Technology (C) and belief systems (D) are not addressed in the notes. Choice (A) is accurate but fails to include the major causes. Choice (D) directly states the cause and effect relationship the student wants to convey.

2. **(B)** Pointing out that the use of abbreviations has continued from the ancient past to the present suggests the scope of its importance.

3. **(D)** This question deals with using suggestive or connotative language. The student wants to present a nonbiased perspective, one that does not use language that might bias the reader. Choice (A) calls Yeti a "legend" and points out that the accounts of witnesses are "claims." Choice (B) includes an unproven statement: "many have seen it." Choice (C) states that "scientists have failed." Only choice (D) uses neutral wording and presents both sides of the issue in an unbiased manner.

4. **(A)** The growing area of acerola is quite large. Although acerola perhaps could be used for making candy, the notes do not include that information. The keynote feature is its high vitamin C content.

5. **(C)** The question asks you to summarize the hardships the people encountered. No mention of torture is made in the notes (A). Although the government may have profited from confiscations, this motive is not included either. Choice (D) is a partial summary; however, it focuses on the hardships encountered while in England. Only choice (C) suggests the uncertainty of the people's lives after they escaped to a foreign country.

6. **(B)** The student wants to emphasize the diversity of acids. The notes do not include the idea that all natural acids are edible. Choice (B) pairs the contrasting elements, producing that emphasis.

7. **(C)** The notes directly state that thick walls and acoustical tiles can absorb vibrations and quiet noise transmission.

8. **(C)** The notes point out that a 15-degree angle of attack can cause the airplane to fall and that higher air speeds increase lift. These both would usually be within the control of the pilot.

9. **(B)** The timing of the Alaskan Gold Rush (1896–1904) corresponds with the conflict between Canada and the United States over Alaska, with the settlement being made in 1903.

10. **(A)** The notes confirm that scholars believe that "some" of the events are biographical (based on her family's life) and autobiographical (based on her own life). The notes also state that she wrote books to support her family.

11. **(D)** The notes state that wild (feral) alfalfa (which would be organic) has cross-pollinated with GMO plants (transgenic).

12. **(D)** The notes point out that algae can be found all around the world and is being used in a wide range of human foods.

13. **(A)** Logically, that single letters can be pronounced multiple ways suggests that English might be difficult to learn for some ESL students.

14. **(B)** The notes include several key points: "It can be fashioned into almost any shape" (malleability), "Aluminum is lightweight," "Over 15% of Earth's crust is make of aluminum-containing compounds" (ubiquitous presence), and "Aluminum can be toxic when absorbed by the human body."

15. **(A)** The student wants to emphasize amaranth's role in good health. The notes point out that it is a "complete grain" in terms of nutrition and that it is healthy for the garden.

16. **(A)** The notes state that Colonial writing included religious works and histories aimed at bringing more people to the colonies prior to 1765 and then shifted to politics. These three topics would be very pragmatic to pioneers and to the people who were forming a new nation.

17. **(B)** The 1966 U.S. tax law established the "one hundred year rule." The 1996 revision dictates the amount of repair/restoration allowed and disallows changing the "essential character" of the item,—in other words, what makes that item what it is in terms of purpose and form.

18. **(C)** The notes suggest that armadillos are expanding their range and that they are digging holes in gardens, lawns, and field crops. Logically, this would have a growing economic impact. Additionally, they carry a disease that could be contracted by humans.

19. **(D)** The reciprocal nature of allergies to cats is not germane to the summary of the cause of allergies. Based on the notes, an allergy is somewhat of a chain reaction: "When an allergen combines with an antibody in the allergic person, histamine is released into the bloodstream, causing swelling.

20. **(B)** The notes establish a timeline that places the vaqueros in successful cattle operations several hundred years before pioneers came west to live. The fact that the pioneers adopted their ways gives credence to the idea that the vaqueros were successful.

21. **(A)** The student wants to emphasize the attempts made to stop Jumbo's sale. Yes, the people did protest (B), but the real emphasis was made with Queen Victoria's involvement in the efforts to stop the sale.

22. **(D)** The notes claim that "pesticides, climate change, and decreasing habitats" are the factors threatening the bee populations. Logically, the likely ways to slow or prevent the decline of bee populations would be to address each of those threats.

23. **(C)** One study says not to eat red meat, another says to eat limited amounts, yet another says to eat only grass-fed meat, and the 2019 study says red meat is not harmful to eat. Clearly, there is no definitive answer for the consumer.

24. **(D)** The student's notes identify bells as originating thousands of years ago. Some produce music, some mark special events, and some serve functions, such as dinner bells.

25. **(A)** The notes specifically identify the remarkable results being manifested in older adults with cognitive issues.

26. **(A)** During the quarantine, the workplace shifted from office to home. "Work-related expenses for employees working remotely from home on average are less than half that of office-based employees."

27. **(B)** The notes point out that "nutritionists warn that vegan butter comes in a block that is solid at room temperature, indicating high levels of saturated fats, usually palm or coconut oil."

Math

Math Practice Questions

Before we begin, note that the SAT Math section will be divided into two modules each containing four sections:

- Algebra
- Advanced Math
- Problem Solving and Data Analysis
- Geometry and Trigonometry

Algebra

The Algebra portion of the digital SAT Math section will require the test taker to be proficient in the following areas:

- Linear equations in one and two variables
- Linear functions
- Systems of equations
- Inequalities in one or two variables

Solving Equations

Drill 1

For multiple-choice questions, solve the problem and pick the correct answer from the provided choices. Each multiple-choice question has only one correct answer. For student-produced response questions, solve each problem and write down your answers separately.

$$2(-3x - 7) = 4 - 2x$$

1. In the equation above, what is the value of x?

   (A) -9

   (B) $\frac{-9}{2}$

   (C) $\frac{2}{9}$

   (D) $\frac{7}{2}$

2. If $\frac{3x}{5} = 12$, what is the value of x?

   (A) 15

   (B) 20

   (C) 30

   (D) 60

TIP

In order to excel in the Algebra section, the test taker should be well-versed in the order of operations. Use the term PEMDAS to remember the sequence of mathematical operations in any math question.

P: Parentheses
E: Exponents
M: Multiplication
D: Division
A: Addition
S: Subtraction

Multiplication and division are to be treated with equal priority, as are addition and subtraction. If a line of mathematical calculation contains solely multiplication and division or solely addition and subtraction, calculate from left to right.

3. If $\frac{x+1}{4} = y$ and $y = 4$, what is the value of x?

(A) 15
(B) 13
(C) 11
(D) 8

$$|m - 3| = 12$$
$$|n + 7| = 22$$

4. In the equations above, $m < 0$ and $n < 0$. What is the value of $m - n$?

(A) 14
(B) 18
(C) 20
(D) 24

$$\frac{1}{4}(12x + 2y) = \frac{27}{4}$$
$$y = 3x$$

5. In the system of equations above, what is the value of x?

$$3x + 6y = 14$$
$$2x + 5y = -11$$

6. If (x, y) is a solution to the system of equations above, what is the value of $x + y$?

(A) 3
(B) 17.5
(C) 24
(D) 25

$$2n + n + n + n - 6 = 4 + n - 2n$$

7. What is the value of n in the equation above?

(A) $\frac{-3}{4}$
(B) $\frac{-2}{3}$
(C) $\frac{5}{4}$
(D) $\frac{5}{3}$

$$n = 3.65 + 0.35x$$
$$m = 4.25 + 0.15x$$

8. In the equations above, m and n represent the heights of bamboo plants, in feet, x weeks after September 15.

   What was the height of the two plants when their heights were equal?

   (A) 1.5
   (B) 3.0
   (C) 4.7
   (D) 4.8

$$4 - 2x \leq 6x - 20$$

9. Which of the following is the solution to the inequality above?

   (A) $x \leq -3$
   (B) $x \leq -8$
   (C) $x \leq 3$
   (D) $x \geq 3$

10. What value(s) of n satisfies $|n + 11| \geq -12$?

    (A) $-1 \leq n \leq 1$
    (B) $n \geq 11$ or $n \leq -23$
    (C) There is no value n
    (D) All real numbers

Answer Explanations

1. **(B)** Simplify to solve for x.

$$2(-3x - 7) = 4 - 2x$$
$$-6x - 14 = 4 - 2x$$
$$-6x + 2x - 14 = 4 - 2x + 2x$$
$$-4x - 14 = 4$$
$$-4x - 14 + 14 = 4 + 14$$
$$\frac{-4x}{-4} = \frac{18}{-4}$$
$$x = -\frac{18}{4} = -\frac{9}{2}$$

2. **(B)** Multiply both sides of the equation by $\frac{5}{3}$ to isolate x.

$$\left(\frac{5}{3}\right)\left(\frac{3x}{5}\right) = (12)\left(\frac{5}{3}\right)$$
$$x = 20$$

3. **(A)** Substitute 4 for y and solve for x.

$$\frac{x+1}{4} = 4$$
$$x + 1 = 16$$
$$x = 15$$

4. **(C)** Solve each absolute value equation.

$$|m-3|=12$$

Therefore:

$$m-3=12 \text{ or } m-3=-12$$
$$m=15 \text{ or } m=-9$$

Therefore:

$$|n+7|=22$$
$$n+7=22 \text{ or } n+7=-22$$
$$n=15 \text{ or } n=-29$$

Since m and n are both less than 0, select -9 and -29 for m and n, respectively.

$$m-n=-9-(-29)=20$$

5. $\mathbf{\frac{3}{2}}$ **or 1.5** Multiply both sides of $\frac{1}{4}(12x+2y)=\frac{27}{4}$ by 4.

$$4\left(\frac{1}{4}(12x+2y)=\frac{27}{4}\right)$$
$$12x+2y=27$$

Substitute $3x$ for y and solve for x.

$$12x+(2)(3x)=27$$
$$18x=27$$
$$x=\frac{3}{2}$$

6. **(D)** Although the system of equations can be solved by using elimination or substitution, it is easier to subtract the equations.

$$\begin{array}{r} 3x+6y=14 \\ \underline{-(2x+5y=-11)} \\ x+y=25 \end{array}$$

7. **(D)** Combine like terms and isolate the variable.

$$2n+n+n+n-6=4+n-2n$$
$$5n-6=4-n$$
$$6n=10$$
$$n=\frac{10}{6}=\frac{5}{3}$$

8. **(C)** Setting $m=n$ will show the number of weeks when the two plants were the same height.

$$n=3.65+0.35x$$
$$m=4.25+0.15x$$
$$3.65+0.35x=4.25+0.15x$$

Solve for x.

$$3.65+0.35x=4.25+0.15x$$
$$0.2x=0.6$$
$$x=3$$

After 3 weeks passed, the two plants were identical heights. Replace x with 3 in either equation to find the height when they were the same.

$$3.65 + 0.35(3) = 4.7$$

The two plants were both 4.7 feet three weeks after September 15.

9. **(D)** Simplify to solve for x.

$$\begin{aligned} 4 - 2x &\leq 6x - 20 \\ 4 - 2x - 6x &\leq 6x - 20 - 6x \\ 4 - 8x &\leq -20 \\ 4 - 4 - 8x &\leq -20 - 4 \\ -8x &\leq -24 \\ \frac{-8x}{-8} &\leq \frac{-24}{-8} \\ x &\geq 3 \end{aligned}$$

TIP

Remember to reverse the direction of the inequality sign when multiplying or dividing an inequality by a negative number.

10. **(D)** The absolute value of a quantity is greater than or equal to 0. Therefore, any value of n satisfies $|n + 11| \geq -12$. The solution set to the inequality, then, is all real numbers.

Drill 2

For multiple-choice questions, solve the problem and pick the correct answer from the provided choices. Each multiple-choice question has only one correct answer. For student-produced response questions, solve each problem and write down your answers separately.

$$7x - 23 = 47$$

1. Solve for x in the equation above.

(A) 10
(B) 8
(C) 6
(D) 4

2. If $3(-2x - 6) + 4(4x - 2) = -30$, what is the value of x?

(A) -0.4
(B) 0.8
(C) 2.4
(D) 3.2

3. If $\frac{m}{n} = 7$, what is the value of $\frac{2n}{m}$?

(A) 14
(B) $\frac{7}{2}$
(C) $\frac{2}{7}$
(D) $\frac{1}{7}$

4. If $\frac{6}{n} = \frac{18}{n + 24}$, what is the value of $\frac{n}{12}$?

(A) 1
(B) 1.5
(C) 2
(D) 4.5

5. If the quotient of n and 8 is 12, what is the value of $2n - 144$?

$$2x - 3y = 24$$
$$x + 4.5y = -12$$

6. In the system of equations above, what is the value of the product of x and y?

(A) 18
(B) 12
(C) −24
(D) −36

7. Which of the following is not a solution of the inequality $-7x + 4 \leq 4x - 5$?

(A) 0
(B) 1
(C) 3
(D) 4

8. Ephraim has two summer jobs. The first, as a delivery person, pays $11.50 per hour. Ephraim's second job, as a math tutor, pays $15.00 per hour. He wants to work no more than 20 hours per week, and he wants to earn at least $270.00 weekly. If x and y represent the hours he works as a delivery person and as a tutor, respectively, which system of inequalities correctly models the situation?

(A) $x + y < 20$
$11.50x + 15y > 270$

(B) $x + y \leq 20$
$11.50x + 15y \geq 270$

(C) $x + y > 20$
$11.50x + 15y \leq 270$

(D) $x + y \geq 270$
$11.50x + 15y \leq 20$

9. If $5x + 3y = 16$ and $4x + 15y = 26$, what is the value of $3x + 6y$?

(A) 15
(B) 14
(C) 11
(D) 7.5

10. If $f(x) = x^2 + 2$ and $g(x) = 2x + 3$, what is the value of $g(3) - f(-2)$?

(A) 15
(B) 9
(C) 3
(D) 4

Answer Explanations

1. **(A)** Simplify to solve for x.

$$7x - 23 = 47$$
$$7x - 23 + 23 = 47 + 23$$
$$7x = 70$$
$$x = 10$$

2. **(A)** Simplify to find the value of x.

$$3(-2x - 6) + 4(4x - 2) = -30$$
$$-6x - 18 + 16x - 8 = -30$$
$$10x - 26 = -30$$
$$10x = -4$$
$$x = -0.4$$

3. **(C)** If $\frac{m}{n} = 7$, then $\frac{n}{m} = \frac{1}{7}$. So $\frac{2n}{m}$ can be interpreted as $(2)\left(\frac{n}{m}\right)$. Since $\frac{n}{m} = \frac{1}{7}$, then double that value, $\frac{2n}{m}$, must equal $\frac{2}{7}$.

4. **(A)** Cross-multiply and solve for n.

$$\frac{6}{n} = \frac{18}{n + 24}$$
$$6(n + 24) = (18)(n)$$
$$6n + 144 = 18n$$
$$144 = 12n$$
$$12 = n$$

Find the value of $\frac{n}{12}$ by substituting 12 for n.

$$\frac{12}{12} = 1$$

5. **48** Solve for n and then insert into $2n - 144$.

$$\frac{n}{8} = 12$$
$$n = 96$$
$$2(96) - 144 = 48$$

6. **(C)** Multiply $x + 4.5y = -12$ by -2 to attain the same coefficient of x but with different signs.

   Solve by elimination.

$$\begin{aligned} 2x - 3y &= 24 \\ -2(x + 4.5y &= -12) \end{aligned}$$

   Solve by eliminating x.

$$\begin{aligned} 2x - 3y &= 24 \\ + -2x - 9y &= 24 \\ \hline -12y &= 48 \\ y &= -4 \end{aligned}$$

   Replace y with -4 in $2x - 3y = 24$.

$$\begin{aligned} 2x - 3(-4) &= 24 \\ 2x + 12 &= 24 \\ 2x &= 12 \\ x &= 6 \end{aligned}$$

   The product of x and y is $(6)(-4) = -24$.

   This problem could also have been solved by using the substitution method.

$$\begin{aligned} x + 4.5y &= -12 \\ x &= -4.5y - 12 \end{aligned}$$

   $(-4.5y - 12)$ would be substituted for x in $2x - 3y = 24$.

7. **(A)** Simplify by subtracting $4x$ from both sides of the inequality.

$$\begin{aligned} -7x + 4 &\leq 4x - 5 \\ -7x + 4 - 4x &\leq 4x - 5 - 4x \\ -11x + 4 &\leq -5 \end{aligned}$$

   Subtract 4 from both sides of the inequality.

$$\begin{aligned} -11x + 4 - 4 &\leq -5 - 4 \\ -11x &\leq -9 \end{aligned}$$

   Divide both sides of the inequality by -11, remembering to reverse the direction of the inequality sign.

$$\frac{-11x}{-11} \leq \frac{-9}{-11}$$

$$x \geq \frac{9}{11}$$

8. **(B)** Ephraim will work as many as 20 hours per week but not more. Thus, $x + y \leq 20$ models the number of hours he wants to work for both jobs. His pay must be at least \$270.00. He'll work x hours at \$11.50 per hour as a delivery person and y hours at \$15.00 per hour as a math tutor. Therefore, $11.50x + 15y \geq 270$ models his weekly earnings. Choice (B) is the only answer that features both of these conditions.

9. **(B)** Although the system of equations can be solved using either the elimination or the substitution method (or even via graphing), a quicker way to calculate the value of $3x + 6y$ is to add the equations together.

$$\begin{array}{r} 5x + 3y = 16 \\ +4x + 15y = 26 \\ \hline 9x + 18y = 42 \end{array}$$

Next, multiply by $\frac{1}{3}$.

$$\frac{1}{3}(9x + 18y = 42)$$
$$3x + 6y = 14$$

10. **(C)** Given that $g(x) = 2x + 3$, calculate $g(3)$.

$$g(3) = 2(3) + 3 = 9$$

Since $f(x) = x^2 + 2$, calculate $f(-2)$.

$$f(-2) = (-2)^2 + 2 = 6$$

Thus, $g(3) - f(-2) = 9 - 6 = 3$.

Choice (A) is incorrect because it is the sum of $g(x)$ and $f(x)$. Choice (B) is incorrect because it is the value of $g(3)$. Choice (D) is incorrect because it is the result of improper calculations.

Drill 3

For multiple-choice questions, solve the problem and pick the correct answer from the provided choices. Each multiple-choice question has only one correct answer. For student-produced response questions, solve each problem and write down your answers separately.

1. If $x - 2 = 0.2x$, what is the value of x?

(A) 2.0
(B) 2.5
(C) 3.0
(D) 3.5

2. If $4(6 - 2x) - 3(4 + 6x) = -2x + 6$, what is the value of x?

(A) $-\frac{1}{4}$
(B) $-\frac{1}{8}$
(C) $\frac{3}{16}$
(D) $\frac{1}{4}$

3. If $2x$ is 12 less than 48, what is the value of $2x - 6$?

(A) 16
(B) 24
(C) 30
(D) 36

$$n + 4m = 7$$

4. If $n = 8$ in the equation above, what is the value of m?

(A) $-\frac{1}{4}$
(B) $-\frac{1}{7}$
(C) 1
(D) $\frac{5}{4}$

5. If $\frac{7}{2a} = \frac{9}{16}$, what is the value of a?

$$y = 4x - 7$$
$$y = 4x - 2b$$

6. If the system of equations above has infinite solutions, what is the value of b?

$$2x + 3y = 4$$
$$5x - y = -7$$

7. At what coordinate pair in the xy-plane will the two equations above intersect?

(A) $(1, -2)$
(B) $(-1, 2)$
(C) $(2, 4)$
(D) $(4, -4)$

$$3x + 2y = 6$$
$$7x + 4y = -12$$

8. Consider the system of equations above. What is the value of $5x + 3y$?

(A) -3
(B) 0
(C) 2
(D) 3

$$|-2x + 6| < 4$$

9. Which value(s) satisfy the inequality above?

(A) $x < 1$ or $x > 5$
(B) $1 < x < 5$
(C) $-5 < x < -1$
(D) There are no values that satisfy this inequality.

10. If $f(x) = x^2 + 2$ and $g(x) = 2x - 1$, what is the value of $f(g(-2))$?

Answer Explanations

1. **(B)** Simplify to find the value of x.

$$x - 2 = 0.2x$$
$$x - 2 - x = 0.2x - x$$
$$-2 = -0.8x$$
$$\frac{-2}{-0.8} = \frac{-0.8x}{-0.8}$$
$$2.5 = x$$

2. **(D)** Find the value of x by simplifying.

$$4(6 - 2x) - 3(4 + 6x) = -2x + 6$$
$$24 - 8x - 12 - 18x = -2x + 6$$
$$12 - 26x = -2x + 6$$
$$6 = 24x$$
$$\frac{1}{4} = x$$

3. **(C)** The question requires the test taker to translate the words into an algebraic equation. "If $2x$ is 12 less than 48, what is the value of $2x - 6$?" becomes the following.

$$\begin{aligned} 2x + 12 &= 48 \\ 2x &= 36 \\ x &= 18 \end{aligned}$$

Plug in 18 for x in $2x - 6$.

$$2(18) - 6 = 30$$

4. **(A)** Substitute 8 for n and solve for m.

$$\begin{aligned} n + 4m &= 7 \\ 8 + 4m &= 7 \\ 4m &= -1 \\ m &= -\frac{1}{4} \end{aligned}$$

5. $\mathbf{\frac{56}{9}}$ **or 6.222**

Cross-multiply and solve for a.

$$\begin{aligned} \frac{7}{2a} &= \frac{9}{16} \\ (7)(16) &= (9)(2a) \\ 112 &= 18a \\ 6\frac{2}{9} &= a \end{aligned}$$

This solution will not fit into the digital test form. Transform the solution into an improper fraction or a decimal.

Improper fraction: Multiply 6 by 9 and add 2. Keep 9 as the denominator.

$$\frac{(6 \times 9 + 2)}{9} = \frac{56}{9}$$

Decimal: Divide 56 by 9 = 6.222...

Fill in 6.222 as your final answer.

6. **3.5 or** $\mathbf{\frac{7}{2}}$ If two equations have an infinite number of solutions, their slopes and y-intercepts are the same. Both equations have the same slope, 4, and must also have the same y-intercept. Thus, set $-2b$ equal to -7 and solve for b.

$$\begin{aligned} -2b &= -7 \\ b &= \frac{7}{2} \end{aligned}$$

The answer can also be expressed as 3.5.

7. **(B)** This system of equations can be solved using either the elimination or the substitution method.

$$\begin{aligned} 2x + 3y &= 4 \\ 5x - y &= -7 \end{aligned}$$

Let's use the elimination method by multiplying the second equation by 3.

$$3(5x - y = -7) \rightarrow 15x - 3y = -21$$

Add the new equation to the top equation.

$$\begin{aligned} 2x + 3y &= 4 \\ 15x - 3x &= -21 \\ \hline 17x &= -17 \\ x &= -1 \end{aligned}$$

You need not solve for y; only selection (B) shows $x = -1$. You can also use a plug-and-check strategy, although it may be overly time-consuming.

8. **(A)** Notice how the question does not ask for the values of x and y. This is a clue that there is a way to bypass the elimination or substitution methods. Add or subtract the equations as presented and see if the result gives a clue to the correct solution. Let's try adding the equations.

$$\begin{aligned} 3x + 2y &= 6 \\ 7x + 4y &= -12 \\ \hline 10x + 6y &= -6 \end{aligned}$$

Divide both sides of $10x + 6y = -6$ by 2.

$$\frac{10x + 6y}{2} = \frac{-6}{2}$$

$$5x + 3y = -3$$

The correct solution to the question is -3.

9. **(B)** The inequality should be divided into two separate inequalities.

$$|-2x + 6| < 4$$

$$\begin{aligned} -2x + 6 &< 4 & -(-2x + 6) &< 4 \\ -2x &< -2 & 2x - 6 &< 4 \\ x &> 1 & 2x &< 10 \\ & & x &< 5 \end{aligned}$$

Remember to reverse the direction of the inequality when you divide or multiply by a negative number. The solution is expressed as a compound inequality.

$$1 < x < 5$$

10. **27** First find $g(-2)$ by replacing x with -2 in $g(x)$.

$$g(x) = 2x - 1$$

$$g(-2) = 2(-2) - 1 = -5$$

Next, find $f(-5)$ by replacing x with -5 in $f(x)$.

$$f(x) = x^2 + 2$$

$$f(-5) = (-5)^2 + 2 = 27$$

Thus, $f(g(-2) = 27$.

Word Problems and Function Interpretation

Drill 1

For multiple-choice questions, solve the problem and pick the correct answer from the provided choices. Each multiple-choice question has only one correct answer. For student-produced response questions, solve each problem and write down your answers separately.

1. A learning therapist has shown that students can increase reading levels by increasing their required summer reading. She models the increase using the formula $y = 1.09x + 0.17$, where x represents the current grade reading level and y represents the improvement after the program. Which of the following represents the meaning of 1.09 in the equation?

   (A) The difference between the students who use the program and those who do not
   (B) The increase in the number of students using the reading program
   (C) The increase in the reading level plus a constant of 0.17
   (D) A 17% increase in reading level

2. After researching the future cost of a four-year college education, Sergio and Maria began saving for their daughter's tuition. After two years, they had accrued $2,870 for their college fund. After five years, the account balance was $7,150. If Sergio and Maria continue to save at the same rate as they have for the past five years, approximately what will their savings be after 78 months?

   (A) $7,846.33
   (B) $8,413.17
   (C) $9,290.02
   (D) $9,417.63

3. Ted needs to purchase shirts and belts for the costumes in his school's play. He can buy s shirts and b belts, but the quantity may not exceed 100 items. Which of the following inequalities represents the conditions of Ted's purchases?

   (A) $s + b > 100$
   (B) $s + b < 100$
   (C) $s + b \leq 100$
   (D) $sb \leq 100$

4. Jerry has joined a gymnasium for which he pays dues of $75 each month plus a daily rate of $10 for each day that he uses the facilities. The function shown below can be used to determine the cost in dollars per month for being a member of this club, where d is the number of days.

   $$f(d) = 75 + 10d$$

   Jerry spent $155 in January, $195 in February, and $225 in March. If he spent a total of $850 for the months of January, February, March, and April, what was the total number of days that he spent at the club for those four months?

5. A small wooden bridge has a maximum carrying capacity of 15,000 pounds. Three cars are currently crossing the bridge, each with a mean weight of 3,250 pounds. What is the greatest weight, in pounds, a fourth car or truck can have and still cross the bridge safely?

6. Two friends are returning home from Vacaville, CA, to Carlsbad, CA, a round trip of 984 miles. They would like to stop over in Bakersfield to go to the Museum of Art, which has free admission on Fridays. They would also like to eat lunch within walking distance of the museum, spending \$8 each. This side trip would add 54 miles to the trip. They have designated a budget of \$90 for the return trip to Carlsbad. Each gallon of gas costs \$3.64, and their car gets 26 miles per gallon. Do they have enough money to take this extra stop?

(A) Yes, they will have \$7.43 extra after the side trip.
(B) Yes, they will have \$4.32 extra after the side trip.
(C) No, they will need an additional \$2.44.
(D) No, they will need an additional \$8.73.

7. Gina runs 28 meters in 4.7 seconds. If she continues to run at this rate, which of the following is the closest to the distance (in meters) she will run in 2.4 minutes?

(A) 269 meters
(B) 542 meters
(C) 653 meters
(D) 858 meters

8. An airline company is calculating its passenger cost for a transatlantic flight. The plane flies approximately 3,000 miles at an average air speed of 500 miles per hour. The cost is given by the following function.

$$C(x) = 100 + \frac{x}{10} + \frac{36{,}000}{x}$$

where x is the ground speed. Ground speed is defined as air speed $\pm$ wind speed. What is the airline's cost if there is no wind during the flight?

(A) \$176
(B) \$222
(C) \$358
(D) \$422

9. A scuba diving instructor charges \$75 per lesson plus an additional fee for the use of her boat. The charge for the use of her boat varies directly with the square root of the time the boat is used. If a lesson plus 25 minutes of boat time costs \$110, what is the total amount charged for a lesson that uses the boat for 36 minutes?

(A) \$117
(B) \$122
(C) \$127
(D) \$133

10. A food stand sells Mexican fare. Tacos cost \$2.00 each, and enchiladas cost \$4.50 each. On a certain day, revenue from tacos and enchiladas was \$198.00, and the number of tacos and enchiladas sold was 54. How many enchiladas were sold?

(A) 54
(B) 36
(C) 27
(D) 18

Answer Explanations

1. **(C)** The learning therapist has demonstrated that her program increases students' reading levels. The coefficient 1.09 in the equation ensures growth. For example, if a student is in the second grade and uses the program, we get the following.

$$x = 2$$
$$y = 1.09(2) + 0.17$$
$$y = 2.35$$

This means a student in second grade would read at a level more than 3 months in advance (assuming a 10-month school year) of students who are not in the reading program.

2. **(C)** The phrase "...at the same rate..." means use the linear model $y = mx + b$. Find the slope by using the ordered pairs (2, \$2,870) and (5, \$7,150).

$$m = \frac{y_2 - y_1}{x_2 - x_1} = \frac{7{,}150 - 2{,}870}{5 - 2} = \frac{4{,}280}{3} = 1{,}426.67$$

Replace m with 1,426.67.

$$y = 1{,}426.67x + b$$

Replace x and y with either point.

$$2{,}870 = 2(1{,}426.67) + b$$
$$16.66 = b$$
$$y = 1{,}426.67x + 16.66$$

Replace x with 78 months, but remember to convert it to years first.

$$78 \text{ months} = 6.5 \text{ years}$$
$$y = 1{,}426.67(6.5) + 16.66$$
$$y = 9{,}290.02$$
$$\$9{,}290.02$$

3. **(C)** The number of shirts (s) and belts (b) cannot exceed 100 items, but they can be equal to that sum. We therefore add the two quantities and ensure that they could not exceed 100 items.

$$s + b \leq 100$$

Choices (A) and (B) can be eliminated at once. The question suggests that the number of items cannot exceed 100 items. That implies the number of items could be equal to 100 but not more. Therefore, the symbol $\leq$ is needed, but using $<$ would be incorrect.

4. **55** The dollar amount in April was $\$850 - \$155 - \$195 - \$225 = \$275$. The number of days for January can be found by solving the equation $155 = 75 + 10d$. Subtract 75 from each side to get $80 = 10d$. Then $d = 8$. In a similar manner, the number of days for each of February, March, and April can be determined by solving the equations $195 = 75 + 10d$, $225 = 75 + 10d$, and $275 = 75 + 10d$, respectively. We find that Jerry spent 12 days in February, 15 days in March, and 20 days in April. Thus, the total number of days spent at the club was $8 + 12 + 15 + 20 = 55$.

5. **5,250** Find the weight of the three cars currently crossing the bridge. Subtract that sum from 15,000, the carrying capacity of the bridge. Since the average weight of the three cars is 3,250 pounds, multiply that value by 3 to find the weight of all three.

$$3 \times 3{,}250 = 9{,}750$$

Subtract 9,750 from 15,000 to find the maximum allowable weight for a fourth car or truck.

$$15{,}000 - 9{,}750 = 5{,}250$$

6. **(C)** The return trip from Vacaville to Carlsbad is 492 miles. Add 54 miles to get a total of 546 miles. Divide this number by 26 miles to the gallon, which comes out to 21 gallons. Multiply 21 by \$3.64, which comes to \$76.44. Add \$16 for the two lunches to \$76.44, which brings the cost to \$92.44. The friends allocated \$90 for the cost of the return trip, so the side trip and the two lunches will exceed their budget by \$2.44.

7. **(D)** Use the proportion $\frac{\text{distance}}{\text{time}} = \frac{\text{distance}}{\text{time}}$ to find how far Gina will run in 2.4 minutes. Since the original ratio is stated in seconds, first convert 2.4 minutes into seconds. Then use the proportion to solve.

$$2.4 \text{ minutes} = 2.4(60) = 144 \text{ seconds}$$
$$\frac{28}{4.7} = \frac{n}{144}$$
$$4.7n = (144)(28)$$
$$4.7n = 4{,}032$$
$$n \approx 858$$

8. **(B)** Ground speed is defined as air speed $\pm$ wind speed. If there is no wind, then the ground speed is the air speed because $500 \pm 0 = 500$.

$$C(500) = 100 + \frac{500}{10} + \frac{36{,}000}{500} = 222$$

9. **(A)** The \$75 fee for the lesson is a fixed cost. Subtract that amount from the \$110.00, which is the total charged for the lesson and 25 minutes of time on the boat.

$$\$110 - \$75 = \$35$$

Create a proportion based solely on the time paid for the boat. The question indicates that the fee varies directly with the square root of the time spent on the boat.

$$\frac{\sqrt{\text{time}}}{\text{fee}} = \frac{\sqrt{\text{time}}}{\text{fee}}$$
$$\frac{\sqrt{25}}{35} = \frac{\sqrt{36}}{x}$$
$$\frac{5}{35} = \frac{6}{x}$$

Cross-multiply and solve for x.

$$5x = 210$$
$$x = 42$$

Add \$42.00, which is the fee for the 36 minutes spent on the boat, to \$75.00, which is the fixed cost of the lesson.

$$\$75 + \$42 = \$117$$

Choices (B), (C), and (D) are incorrect due to erroneous calculations.

10. **(B)** Although a plug-and-check strategy is possible for this problem, using a system of equations is easier.

Let $x =$ tacos sold
Let $y =$ enchiladas sold

There were 54 items sold, so the first equation is $x + y = 54$. Tacos cost \$2.00, and enchiladas cost \$4.50. The revenue generated was \$198.00, giving us $2x + 4.5y = 198$.

Use either elimination or substitution to proceed.

$$x + y = 54$$
$$y = 54 - x$$

Substitute $54 - x$ for y in the equation $2x + 4.5y = 198$.

$$2x + 4.5(54 - x) = 198$$
$$2x + 243 - 4.5x = 198$$
$$-2.5x = -45$$
$$x = 18$$

Substitute 18 into $y = 54 - x$ to find the number of enchiladas sold.

$$y = 54 - 18 = 36$$

Drill 2

For multiple-choice questions, solve the problem and pick the correct answer from the provided choices. Each multiple-choice question has only one correct answer. For student-produced response questions, solve each problem and write down your answers separately.

1. A marathon runner can run m miles at d miles per hour in h hours. The formula for the distance she runs is $hd = m$. If m is a constant, which of the following conclusions is correct?

   (A) When d increases, h increases.
   (B) When d decreases, h decreases.
   (C) As h increases, d decreases.
   (D) d will never increase, but m can increase or decrease.

2. Tina repairs sinks in a large housing development. Each month, the number of sinks she has to repair is represented by the following equation.

   $$B = 360 - 88w$$

   where B is the balance of sinks left to repair and w is the number of weeks she has worked in a certain month. What is the meaning of 360 in the equation $B = 360 - 88w$?

   (A) Tina will repair 360 sinks each week.
   (B) Tina starts each month with 360 sinks to repair.
   (C) Tina repairs 360 sinks a year, almost one per day.
   (D) Tina repairs 360 sinks daily.

3. Flour costs \$1.50 per pound. What is the cost, in dollars, of $(2x + 6)$ pounds of flour? (Ignore the \$ sign.)

   (A) $\frac{2x+6}{1.50}$
   (B) $2x + 7.50$
   (C) $\frac{1.5}{2x+6}$
   (D) $3x + 9$

4. The volume of a certain enclosed gas is shown by the following equation:

   $$V = \frac{0.7T}{P} + 3.77$$

   where:
   V = volume of the gas (in cubic centimeters)
   P = pressure (in kilograms per square centimeter)
   T = temperature (in Kelvin)

   Which of the following expresses temperature in terms of volume and pressure?

   (A) $T = (P - V)(0.7) - 3.77$
   (B) $T = \frac{P}{0.7}(V - 3.77)$
   (C) $T = \frac{(V + 3.77)}{P}$
   (D) $T = \frac{P}{V - 3.77}$

5. The volume of a certain enclosed gas is shown by the following equation:

$$V = \frac{0.7T}{P} + 3.77$$

where:

V = volume of the gas (in cubic centimeters)
P = pressure (in kilograms per square centimeter)
T = temperature (in Kelvin)

Find the temperature (in Kelvin) when the volume of the gas is 8,000 cubic centimeters and the pressure is 1.2 kg/cm^2.

(A) 7,407
(B) 8,176
(C) 13,708
(D) 16,511

6. Belts cost $11, and blouses cost $18. If Kara spends at least $51 but no more than $62 for x belts and one blouse, what is one possible value of x?

7. Ms. Garcia has a jar containing m milliliters of a solution for her chemistry class. If she gives 8 milliliters to each student, she will have 6 milliliters left over. If she provides 10 milliliters to each student, she will need an additional 16 milliliters. How many students are in her class?

(A) 10
(B) 11
(C) 17
(D) 22

8. The formula for the area of a trapezoid is shown by this formula

$$A = \frac{1}{2}(h)(b_1 + b_2)$$

Which of the following expresses b_1 in terms of h, A, and b_2?

(A) $\frac{2A}{h} - b_2$
(B) $\frac{h}{2A} - b_2$
(C) $b_2 + 2Ah$
(D) $\left(\frac{A}{2h}\right) - b_2$

n	1	2	3	4
$r(n)$	−1	1	3	5

9. The table above shows some values of the linear function r. Which of the following defines r?

(A) $r(n) = 2n + 3$
(B) $r(n) = 3n - 5$
(C) $r(n) = n - 3$
(D) $r(n) = 2n - 3$

10. Jamie is considering two different companies to rent him a mobile home trailer for one day. One service charges \$30 per day and \$0.25 per mile. The other service charges \$40 per day and \$0.20 per mile. At what number of miles is the cost for the two services equal?

Answer Explanations

1. **(A)** Use simple values for m, d, and h to find the correct conclusion.
   Let $m = 12$
   $hd = m$

h	d
1	12
2	6
3	4
4	3
6	2
12	1

As h increases, d decreases.

2. **(B)** Tina starts each month with 360 sinks to repair. As each week passes, Tina has 88 fewer sinks to repair within the month.

3. **(D)** Multiply the cost per pound of flour by the number of pounds.

$$(1.50)(2x + 6) = 3x + 9$$

4. **(B)** Isolate T by subtracting 3.77 from each side of $V = \frac{0.7T}{P} + 3.77$.

$$V = \frac{0.7T}{P} + 3.77$$

$$V - 3.77 = \frac{0.7T}{P}$$

Multiply both sides of the equation by $\frac{P}{0.7}$, which is the reciprocal of $\frac{0.7}{P}$.

$$\left(\frac{P}{0.7}\right)(V - 3.77) = \left(\frac{0.7T}{P}\right)\left(\frac{P}{0.7}\right)$$

$$\left(\frac{P}{0.7}\right)(V - 3.77) = T$$

5. **(C)** Use the formula $V = \frac{0.7T}{P} + 3.77$, and input 8,000 for V and 1.2 for P.

$$8{,}000 = \frac{0.7T}{1.2} + 3.77$$

$$7{,}996.23 = \frac{0.7T}{1.2}$$

Multiply each side of the equation by $\frac{1.2}{0.7}$, which is the reciprocal of $\frac{0.7}{1.2}$.

$$\left(\frac{1.2}{0.7}\right)(7{,}996.23) = \left(\frac{0.7T}{1.2}\right)\left(\frac{1.2}{0.7}\right)$$

$$13{,}708 \approx T$$

6. **3 or 4** Subtract \$18 from \$51 and \$62 to find the amount of money Kara may have spent on belts.

$$51 - 18 = 33$$
$$62 - 18 = 44$$

Kara may have spent between \$33 and \$44 for belts. Given that each belt costs \$11, Kara could have purchased 3 or 4 belts.

7. **(B)** Let x equal the number of students in the chemistry class. When providing 8 milliliters per student, we get $m = 8x + 6$. This reflects the fact that 6 milliliters are left over from the jar containing m milliliters. When Ms. Garcia provides 10 milliliters per student, she requires an additional 16 milliliters to ensure each student has the same amount. This situation is represented by the equation $m = 10x - 16$. Since $8x + 6$ and $10x - 16$ both equal m, set the expressions equal to one another and solve for x.

$$10x - 16 = 8x + 6$$
$$2x = 22$$
$$x = 11$$

8. **(A)** Begin to isolate b_1 by multiplying the area formula by 2.

$$A = \frac{1}{2}(h)(b_1 + b_2)$$
$$(2)A = \frac{1}{2}(h)(b_1 + b_2)(2)$$
$$2A = (h)(b_1 + b_2)$$

Divide both sides of the equation by h, the height of the trapezoid.

$$\frac{2A}{h} = \frac{(h)(b_1 + b_2)}{h}$$
$$\frac{2A}{h} = b_1 + b_2$$

Subtract b_2 from both sides of the equation.

$$\frac{2A}{h} - b_2 = b_1$$

9. **(D)** Use the formula $\frac{\text{rise}}{\text{run}}$ to find the slope of the linear function. As n increases by 1, $r(n)$ increases by 2. Thus, $r(n) = 2n + b$, with b representing the y-intercept. Input any of the points to calculate b.

$$(4, 5)$$
$$5 = 2(4) + b$$
$$5 = 8 + b$$
$$-3 = b$$
$$r(n) = 2n - 3$$

10. **200** Let $x =$ the number of miles for the two trailer rental costs to be equal.

$$40 + 0.20x = 30 + 0.25x$$
$$40 + 0.20x - 0.20x = 30 + 0.25x - 0.20x$$
$$40 = 30 + 0.05x$$
$$10 = 0.05x$$
$$200 = x$$

Drill 3

> For multiple-choice questions, solve the problem and pick the correct answer from the provided choices. Each multiple-choice question has only one correct answer. For student-produced response questions, solve each problem and write down your answers separately.

1. The term *light-year* refers to the distance light travels in one year. If light travels 186,000 miles per second, which of the following is closest to the distance from Earth to Sirius, 8 light-years distant?

   (A) 47 billion miles
   (B) 198 billion miles
   (C) 9 trillion miles
   (D) 50 trillion miles

2. The term *light-year* refers to the distance light travels in one year. If light travels 186,000 miles per second, how far does light travel in one-billionth of a second? (Note: 1 mile = 5,280 feet)

   (A) 10 miles
   (B) 1 mile
   (C) 1 foot
   (D) 0.01 feet

x	$g(x)$
0	6
−2	2
−3	0
−4	−2

3. The function g is defined by a certain polynomial. Some of the values of $g(x)$ are shown in the table above. Which of the following must be a factor of $g(x)$?

   (A) $x - 6$
   (B) $x - 3$
   (C) $x + 3$
   (D) $x + 6$

4. The density of an object is found by dividing the object's mass by its volume. If the density of an object is 4 grams per milliliter and its mass is 30 grams, what is the volume in milliliters of the object?

   (A) 4.8
   (B) 6.1
   (C) 7.5
   (D) 9.2

x	$f(x)$
0	5
2	3
4	1
5	0
8	−2

5. The function f is defined by a polynomial. Some values of x and $f(x)$ are shown in the table above. Which of the following must be a factor of $f(x)$?

(A) x
(B) $x - 3$
(C) $x - 5$
(D) $x - 8$

$$F = \frac{9}{5}C + 32$$

6. The equation above shows how a temperature, C, measured in degrees Celsius, relates to a temperature, F, measured in degrees Fahrenheit. Based on the equation, which of the following must be true?

I. An increase in temperature of 1 degree Celsius is equivalent to an increase of 1.8 degrees Fahrenheit.
II. A temperature of 5°F is equivalent to −15°C.
III. A temperature of 20°C is equivalent to 62°F.

(A) I only
(B) I and II
(C) I and III
(D) III only

7. A manufacturer of surgical equipment measures its profit by using the following function, where x is the number of units the company sells in a three-month period.

$$P(x) = 11{,}000x - 6{,}750$$

If the company's profit over a three-month period was \$9,321,250, how many units did it sell?

8. The golden ratio compares dimensions that are appealing to the eye. Sometimes the golden ratio appears in nature but more frequently appears in painting and architecture. The ratio has been found to be $\frac{1+\sqrt{5}}{2}$:1, which corresponds to length:width.

   A new downtown cultural center is being planned for construction in 2027. The city planners hope to construct the main amphitheater using the golden ratio. If the proposed width of the amphitheater is to be 87 meters, what will be its length? (Round your answer to the nearest meter.)

   (A) 211
   (B) 176
   (C) 157
   (D) 141

9. In a homecoming game, a girls' basketball team scored $\frac{1}{3}$ of its points during the first quarter, $\frac{1}{4}$ of its points during the second quarter, $\frac{1}{3}$ of its points in the third quarter, and 8 points in the fourth quarter. How many points did the team score in the game?

   (A) 84
   (B) 90
   (C) 96
   (D) 102

10. Conner needs to plan a production budget for a computer firm. In order to maximize profit, he needs to buy m computer frames at \$18.75 and r keyboards at \$13.25 each. If the cost of this transaction must be less than \$139.00, which of the following inequalities represents Conner's model for profit maximization?

    (A) $18.75m + 13.25r < 139$
    (B) $18.75m + 13.25r \leq 139$
    (C) $18.75r + 13.25m < 139$
    (D) $18.75r + 13.25m \leq 139$

Answer Explanations

1. **(D)** Find the number of seconds in one year.

   $$(365 \text{ days}) \times (24 \text{ hours in a day}) \times (60 \text{ minutes in an hour}) \times (60 \text{ seconds in a minute}) = 31{,}536{,}000 \text{ seconds in one year}$$

   Next, find the product of 31,536,000 and 186,000 to find how many miles light travels in one year.

   $$186{,}000 \times 31{,}536{,}000 = 5{,}860{,}000{,}000{,}000 \text{ (about 6 trillion miles)}$$

   Multiply 5,860,000,000,000 by 8 to find the number of miles to Sirius.

   $$5{,}860{,}000{,}000{,}000 \times 8 = 46.9 \text{ trillion}$$

   Choice (D), 50 trillion miles, is the closest to this figure.

2. **(C)** Divide 186,000 miles by 1 billion. Scientific notation will facilitate this process.

$$\frac{1.86 \times 10^5}{1 \times 10^9} = 1.86 \times 10^{-4} = 0.000186$$

In one-billionth of a second, light travels 0.000186 miles. Multiply 0.000186 by 5,280 feet, which is the number of feet in a mile.

$$0.000186 \times 5{,}280 = 0.98 \text{ foot}$$

The distance 0.98 foot is closest to choice (C), 1 foot.

3. **(C)** Note that when $x = -3$, $y = 0$. When a function intersects the x-axis in the xy-plane, then $y = 0$; that x-value is a root of the function. We therefore conclude that $x = -3$ is a root of the function. Adding 3 to both sides yields $x + 3 = 0$.

4. **(C)** The formula for the density of an object is presented as density $= \frac{\text{mass}}{\text{volume}}$. Input 4 grams per milliliter for the density and 30 grams for mass to find the volume.

$$4 = \frac{30}{V}$$

Multiply both sides of the equation by V.

$$(V)(4) = \left(\frac{30}{V}\right)(V)$$
$$4V = 30$$
$$V = 7.5$$

5. **(C)** A polynomial has a zero x if $f(x) = 0$. The chart indicates (5, 0) satisfies the function, so $f(5) = 0$ and $x = 5$. By subtracting 5 from both sides of the equation, we get $x - 5 = 0$. Therefore, $x - 5$ is a factor of $f(x)$.

6. **(B)** Verify the accuracy of the statements.

I. An increase in temperature of 1 degree Celsius is equivalent to an increase of 1.8 degrees Fahrenheit.
Use $C = 1$ and $C = 2$

$$\frac{9}{5}(1) + 32 = 33.8$$
$$\frac{9}{5}(2) + 32 = 35.6$$
$$35.6 - 33.8 = 1.8$$

Statement I is correct.
II. A temperature of 5°F is equivalent to −15°C.

$$5 = \frac{9}{5}C + 32$$
$$-27 = \frac{9}{5}C$$
$$-15 = C$$

Statement II is correct.
III. A temperature of 20°C is equivalent to 62°F.

$$\frac{9}{5}(20) + 32 = 68$$

Statement III is incorrect. Statements I and II are correct and statement III is incorrect.

7. **848** Replace $P(x)$ with \$9,321,250, which is the company's profit.

$$\begin{aligned} 9{,}321{,}250 &= 11{,}000x - 6{,}750 \\ 9{,}328{,}000 &= 11{,}000x \\ 848 &= x \end{aligned}$$

8. **(D)** Use a proportion to find the length of the proposed amphitheater in the downtown cultural center. This operation can be facilitated by approximating the length in decimal form: $\frac{1+\sqrt{5}}{2}$:1 is approximately equal to 1.62:1. Use this ratio, substituting 87 for the width.

$$\frac{1.62}{1} = \frac{x}{87}$$

Cross-multiply and solve for x.

$$x = (1.62)(87) = 140.94$$

When 140.94 is rounded to the nearest meter, the result is 141.

Choice (A) can be eliminated quickly (and possibly choice (B) as well). Once it is determined that the golden ratio is about 1.62:1, 211 would surely seem more than twice as large as 87.

9. **(C)** Let $x =$ the number of points scored in the game.

$$\begin{aligned} \frac{1}{3}x + \frac{1}{4}x + \frac{1}{3}x + 8 &= x \\ \frac{11}{12}x + 8 &= x \\ 8 &= \frac{1}{12}x \\ 96 &= x \end{aligned}$$

10. **(A)** The cost for m computers at \$18.75 each is \$18.75m. The cost for r keyboards at \$13.25 each is \$13.25r. The cost must be less than \$139, so we arrive at the following inequality.

$$18.75m + 13.25r < 139$$

Choices (B) and (D) can automatically be eliminated because each features $\leq$ (less than or equal to). The problem stipulates the cost must be less than \$139.

Lines and Slopes

Drill 1

For multiple-choice questions, solve the problem and pick the correct answer from the provided choices. Each multiple-choice question has only one correct answer. For student-produced response questions, solve each problem and write down your answers separately.

1. Which of the following is an equation for the line graphed above?

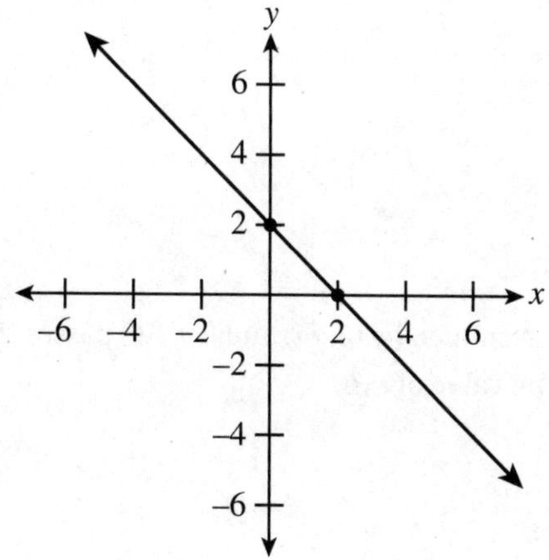

(A) $y = -x + 2$
(B) $y = x + 2$
(C) $y = 2$
(D) $x - y = 2$

$$y = -\frac{5}{8}x + 3$$

2. Which of the following is an equation of a line that is parallel to the equation above?

(A) $5x + 8y = 48$
(B) $5x - 8y = 24$
(C) $6x + 3y = 22$
(D) $3x - 5y = 17$

3. Line A is perpendicular to a line that is parallel to $y = \frac{5}{9}x + 7$. What is the slope of line A?

(A) $\frac{9}{5}$
(B) $\frac{5}{9}$
(C) $-\frac{5}{9}$
(D) $-\frac{9}{5}$

4. Which of the following equations represents a line that is parallel to the line with the equation $y = \frac{3}{2}x - \frac{7}{4}$?

(A) $6x + 4y = 8$
(B) $-6x + 4y = 11$
(C) $x - 2y = -4$
(D) $3x + 2y = 7$

5. A line passes through the points $(x, 6)$ and $(9, 0)$. If the slope of the line connecting the two points is $\frac{2}{3}$, what is the value of x?

6. In a linear function, $f(4) = 6$ and $f(-2) = 14$. What is the value of $f(9)$?

(A) $\frac{20}{3}$
(B) $\frac{2}{3}$
(C) $-\frac{2}{3}$
(D) -3

7. In the xy-plane, the line determined by $(6, m)$ and $(m, 54)$ passes through the origin. Which of the following could be the value of m?

(A) 2
(B) 18
(C) 36
(D) 48

x	$f(x)$
−2	−2.2
0	−3
6	−5.4
7	−5.8

8. Some values of the linear function f are shown in the table. What is the value of $f(8)$?

(A) −0.6
(B) −1.8
(C) −3.2
(D) −6.2

9. Given the equation in the xy-plane $-5x + 6y = -7$, which of the following equations is perpendicular to the graph of the equation above?

(A) $-6x + 10y = 7$
(B) $6x + 5y = 15$
(C) $6x - 20y = 15$
(D) $5x + 6y = -18$

10. Line $\overleftrightarrow{AB}$ has a slope of $\frac{7}{2}$. If the line passes through $(-6, 3)$ and $(x, -3)$, what is the value of x?

(A) $\frac{2}{7}$

(B) $-\frac{37}{57}$

(C) $-\frac{8}{7}$

(D) $-\frac{54}{7}$

Answer Explanations

1. **(A)** The line crosses the y-axis at $(0, 2)$. So b, which is the y-intercept, is 2. Using $\frac{\text{rise}}{\text{run}}$ to identify the slope, we go down 1 unit and move to the right 1 unit. Thus, the slope, m, equals -1. With the slope equaling -1 and the y-intercept at 2, the equation of the line in the graph is $y = -x + 2$.

2. **(A)** Parallel lines have the same slope but different y-intercepts. The slope of $y = -\frac{5}{8}x + 3$ is $-\frac{5}{8}$, and the y-intercept is 3. Transform each of the answer choices into slope-intercept form to assess slopes and y-intercepts. Choice (A) is $5x + 8y = 48$. Begin the transformation by isolating y.

$$5x + 8y = 48$$
$$8y = -5x + 48$$
$$y = -\frac{5}{8}x + 6$$

Rewriting $5x + 8y = 48$ in slope-intercept form yields the same slope, $-\frac{5}{8}$, but a different y-intercept, 6. So, choice (A) is parallel to the given equation.

3. **(D)** Parallel lines have the same slope. Since the slope of $y = \frac{5}{9}x + 7$ is $\frac{5}{9}$, then a line parallel to it will also have a slope that measures $\frac{5}{9}$. Perpendicular lines have slopes that are the opposite reciprocals of one another. Thus, a line perpendicular to a line with slope of $\frac{5}{9}$ will have a slope of $-\frac{9}{5}$.

4. **(B)** Parallel lines have the same slope but distinct y-intercepts. The equation $y = \frac{3}{2}x - \frac{7}{4}$ has slope $\frac{3}{2}$ and y-intercept $-\frac{7}{4}$. Transform each of the equations to slope-intercept form, $y = mx + b$, to compare slopes and y-intercepts. Choice (B) offers the following:

$$-6x + 4y = 11$$

Transform to slope-intercept form by isolating y.

$$-6x + 6x + 4y = 6x + 11$$
$$4y = 6x + 11$$

Divide both sides of the equation by 4.

$$\frac{4}{4}y = \frac{6}{4}x + \frac{11}{4}$$
$$y = \frac{3}{2}x + \frac{11}{4}$$
$$m = \frac{3}{2} \text{ and } b = \frac{11}{4}$$

The equations $y = \frac{3}{2}x + \frac{11}{4}$ and $y = \frac{3}{2}x - \frac{7}{4}$ have the same slope but different y-intercepts, so the two lines are parallel.

5. **18** The slope of a line can be found by using the formula $\frac{\text{rise}}{\text{run}}$ or $\frac{y_2 - y_1}{x_2 - x_1}$. Substitute (9, 0) for x_2 and y_2 and $(x, 6)$ for x_1 and y_1. Set the value of that fraction to $\frac{2}{3}$, which is the slope of the line connecting these two points.

$$\frac{0-6}{9-x} = \frac{2}{3}$$

$$\frac{-6}{9-x} = \frac{2}{3}$$

Cross-multiply and solve for x.

$$2(9-x) = (-3)(6)$$
$$18 - 2x = -18$$
$$-2x = -36$$
$$x = 18$$

6. **(C)** A linear function that contains $f(4) = 6$ and $f(-2) = 14$ indicates that the points (4, 6) and (−2, 14) satisfy the function. Use these points to find the slope of the function.

$$m = \frac{y_2 - y_1}{x_2 - x_1} = \frac{14-6}{-2-4} = \frac{-4}{3}$$

Use the point-slope form of a line to create the linear function.

$$y - y_1 = m(x - x_1)$$

Substitute either point for x and y.

$$y - 6 = \frac{-4}{3}(x - 4)$$

Substitute 9 for x to find $f(9)$.

$$y - 6 = \frac{-4}{3}(9 - 4)$$

$$y - 6 = -\frac{20}{3}$$

$$y = \frac{-2}{3}$$

Therefore, $f(9) = \frac{-2}{3}$.

7. **(B)** In order for the line containing $(6, m)$ and $(m, 54)$ to pass through the origin, each point must share the slope that connects it to the origin. Use the formula $\frac{\text{rise}}{\text{run}}$ for both points, and set the quantities equal.

$$\frac{m}{6} = \frac{54}{m}$$

Cross-multiply and solve for m.

$$m^2 = 324$$

$$m = 18 \text{ or } m = -18$$

Although both 18 and −18 are solutions to the equation, only 18 was provided as an answer choice.

8. **(D)** Find the slope of $f(x)$ by selecting values from the table, such as $(-2, -2.2)$ and $(0, -3)$.

$$m = \frac{-3 - (-2.2)}{0 - (-2)} = -0.4$$

The table shows the coordinates $(0, -3)$, which means that the y-intercept is -3. Thus, the linear function f is defined as $f(x) = -0.4x - 3$.

Substitute 8 for x.

$$f(8) = -0.4(8) - 3$$
$$f(8) = -6.2$$

9. **(B)** The slopes of perpendicular lines are the opposite reciprocal of one another. Transform $-5x + 6y = -7$ to slope-intercept form to determine its slope.

$$-5x + 6y = -7$$
$$6y = 5x - 7$$
$$y = \frac{5}{6}x - \frac{7}{6}$$

The slope of the line $-5x + 6y = -7$ is $\frac{5}{6}$. The slope of a line perpendicular to $-5x + 6y = -7$ is $\frac{-6}{5}$. Only choice (B) has slope $\frac{-6}{5}$.

$$6x + 5y = 15$$
$$5y = -6x + 15$$
$$y = \frac{-6}{5}x + 3$$

When expressed in slope-intercept form, the slope of $6x + 5y = 15$ is $\frac{-6}{5}$. Choices (A), (C), and (D) are incorrect because their slopes are $\frac{3}{5}$, $\frac{3}{10}$, and $\frac{-5}{6}$, respectively.

10. **(D)** Use the slope formula to solve for x.

$$m = \frac{y_2 - y_1}{x_2 - x_1}$$
$$\frac{-3 - 3}{x - (-6)} = \frac{7}{2}$$
$$\frac{-6}{x + 6} = \frac{7}{2}$$

Cross-multiply and solve for x.

$$(2)(-6) = 7(x + 6)$$
$$-12 = 7x + 42$$
$$-54 = 7x$$
$$-\frac{54}{7} = x$$

Drill 2

For multiple-choice questions, solve the problem and pick the correct answer from the provided choices. Each multiple-choice question has only one correct answer. For student-produced response questions, solve each problem and write down your answers separately.

1. What is the slope of a line that passes through (6, −4) and (−12, 2)?

   (A) $-\frac{1}{3}$
   (B) $-\frac{1}{6}$
   (C) $\frac{1}{2}$
   (D) $\frac{2}{3}$

2. What is the slope-intercept form of a line passing through (6, −4) and (−12, 2)?

   (A) $y = -\frac{1}{3}x - 6$
   (B) $y = -\frac{1}{3}x - 4$
   (C) $y = -\frac{1}{3}x - 2$
   (D) $y = -\frac{1}{3}x$

3. The line $6x + 4y = -3$ is written in standard form. What is the slope of a line that is parallel to $6x + 4y = -3$?

   (A) $\frac{3}{2}$
   (B) $\frac{3}{4}$
   (C) $-\frac{2}{3}$
   (D) $-\frac{3}{2}$

4. What is the slope of a line that is perpendicular to $y = -\frac{3}{2}x - \frac{3}{4}$?

   (A) $-\frac{3}{2}$
   (B) $-\frac{2}{3}$
   (C) $\frac{2}{3}$
   (D) $\frac{4}{3}$

5. The lines $y = \frac{5}{8}x - 7$ and $4x - 3y = 7$ intersect at how many points?

   (A) 0
   (B) 1
   (C) Infinitely many points
   (D) There is not enough information to make a conclusion.

6. The lines $4x - 7y = 5$ and $7x + 4y = 3$ intersect at how many points?

   (A) 0
   (B) 1
   (C) Infinitely many points
   (D) There is not enough information to make a conclusion.

7. The lines $y = \frac{5}{3}x - 3$ and $y = \frac{5}{3}x - 5$ intersect at how many points?

   (A) 0
   (B) 1
   (C) Infinitely many points
   (D) There is not enough information to make a conclusion.

8. The lines $3x + 2y = 6$ and $9x + 6y = 18$ intersect at how many points?

   (A) 0
   (B) 1
   (C) Infinitely many points
   (D) There is not enough information to make a conclusion.

9. The slope of $\overleftrightarrow{RS}$ is $-\frac{7}{5}$. If the line passes through $(6, -10)$ and $(4, y)$, what is the value of y?

10. What is the x-intercept of the line $y = -\frac{2}{3}x - 6$?

   (A) $(-9, 0)$
   (B) $(0, -6)$
   (C) $(4, 0)$
   (D) $(8, 0)$

Answer Explanations

1. **(A)** Calculate the slope, m, by using the slope formula and the points $(6, -4)$ and $(-12, 2)$.

$$m = \frac{y_2 - y_1}{x_2 - x_1}$$

$$\frac{2 - (-4)}{-12 - 6} = -\frac{6}{18} = -\frac{1}{3}$$

2. **(C)** Find the slope

$$m = \frac{y_2 - y_1}{x_2 - x_1}$$

$$\frac{2 - (-4)}{-12 - 6} = -\frac{6}{18} = -\frac{1}{3}$$

Use this information to find b, the y-intercept.

$$y = -\frac{1}{3}x + b$$

Use $(6, -4)$ or $(12, -2)$ to calculate b. Let's use $(-12, 2)$. Substitute -12 for x and 2 for y.

$$2 = \left(-\frac{1}{3}\right)(-12) + b$$

$$2 = 4 + b$$

$$-2 = b$$

In slope-intercept form, the equation of a line that passes through (6, −4) and (12, −2) is the following.

$$y = -\frac{1}{3}x - 2$$

3. **(D)** Parallel lines have the same slope. Convert $6x + 4y = -3$ into slope-intercept form to find the slope.

$$6x + 4y = -3$$
$$4y = -6x - 3$$
$$y = -\frac{6}{4}x - \frac{3}{4}$$
$$y = -\frac{3}{2}x - \frac{3}{4}$$

The slope of $6x + 4y = -3$ is $-\frac{3}{2}$. A parallel line would also have a slope of $-\frac{3}{2}$.

4. **(C)** Perpendicular lines have slopes that are the negative (or opposite) reciprocals. The line $y = -\frac{3}{2}x - \frac{3}{4}$ has a slope that equals $-\frac{3}{2}$. The negative reciprocal of $-\frac{3}{2}$ is $\frac{2}{3}$.

5. **(B)** Find the slope of each line.

$$y = \frac{5}{8}x - 7$$
$$m = \frac{5}{8}x$$
$$4x - 3y = 7$$
$$-3y = -4x + 7$$
$$y = \frac{4}{3}x - \frac{7}{3}$$
$$m = \frac{4}{3}$$

Lines that have different slopes intersect at 1 point.

6. **(B)** Transform each line from standard form to slope-intercept form to compare the slopes.

$$4x - 7y = 5$$
$$-7y = -4x + 5$$
$$y = \frac{4}{7}x - \frac{5}{7}$$

$$7x + 4y = 3$$
$$4y = -7x + 3$$
$$y = -\frac{7}{4}x + \frac{3}{4}$$

The slopes of the lines, $\frac{4}{7}$ and $-\frac{7}{4}$, are negative reciprocals of each other, so the lines are perpendicular. Perpendicular lines intersect at 1 point.

7. **(A)** The lines have the same slope but different y-intercepts. Lines with the same slope and different y-intercepts are parallel and thus do not intersect.

8. **(C)** $3x + 2y = 6$ and $9x + 6y = 18$ are the same line.

$$(3)(3x + 2y = 6)$$
$$9x + 6y = 18$$

Since the two equations represent the same line, they intersect at an infinite number of points.

9. $-\frac{36}{5}$ **or** -7.2

Use the slope formula to calculate the value of y.

$$m = \frac{y_2 - y_1}{x_2 - x_1}$$
$$-\frac{7}{5} = \frac{y - (-10)}{4 - 6}$$
$$-\frac{7}{5} = \frac{y + 10}{-2}$$

Cross-multiply and solve for y.

$$(-7)(-2) = 5(y + 10)$$
$$14 = 5y + 50$$
$$-36 = 5y$$
$$-\frac{36}{5} = y$$

The fraction $-\frac{36}{5}$ can be expressed as -7.2.

10. **(A)** You can use a plug-and-check strategy to solve this problem quickly. Plug in (9, 0) for x and y in the equation $y = -\frac{2}{3}x - 6$.

$$0 = \left(-\frac{2}{3}\right)(-9) - 6$$
$$0 = 0$$

Selection (B), (0, −6), is the y-intercept.

TIP

Although some cubic equations may occur on the SAT, the majority of nonlinear functions are quadratic. When graphed, a quadratic equation will be a parabola in the ***xy***-plane. It's important to know how to graph the ***x***- and ***y***-intercepts and the vertex of a parabola. In addition, the test taker must know how to translate a parabola up or down and left or right. These practice questions will help you master those translations.

Advanced Math

The Advanced Math portion of the digital SAT Math section will require the test taker to be proficient in the following areas:

- Equivalent expressions
- Nonlinear equations in one variable
- Systems of equations in two variables
- Nonlinear functions

Polynomials and Factoring

Drill 1

For multiple-choice questions, solve the problem and pick the correct answer from the provided choices. Each multiple-choice question has only one correct answer. For student-produced response questions, solve each problem and write down your answers separately.

1. If $m = 2x^3 + 3x - 11$ and $n = 4x^2 + 5x - 7$, what is $3n - m$ in terms of x?

(A) $-2x^3 - 4x^2 - 2x - 18$
(B) $-(2x^3 + 3x^2 - 5x - 6)$
(C) $2x^3 - 12x^2 - 12x + 10$
(D) $-2x^3 + 12x^2 + 12x - 10$

$$2(2x^2 - 7.5x + 3) - (-4x^2 + 2x - 7)$$

2. If the expression above is written in the form of $ax^2 + bx + c$, what is the value of $a + b + c$?

$$3x^2 + 3x - 36 = 0$$

3. What are all of the values that satisfy the quadratic equation above?

(A) $x = -3$ and $x = 4$
(B) $x = -4$ and $x = 3$
(C) $x = 3$ and $x = 4$
(D) $x = -3$ and $x = -4$

$$-4xy^2 - 2xy + xy - 8mn + mn$$

4. Which of the following is equivalent to the expression above?

(A) $-5x^3y^3 - 8m^2n^2$
(B) $-5x^3y - 7m^2n^2$
(C) $32y - 8$
(D) $-4xy^2 - xy - 7mn$

5. Which of the following is equivalent to $\dfrac{1}{\dfrac{1}{x+4}+\dfrac{1}{x+6}}$?

(A) $x^2 + 10x + 24$

(B) $\dfrac{\frac{1}{1}}{x+12}$

(C) $\dfrac{x^2+10x+24}{2x+10}$

(D) $\dfrac{x+4}{x+6}$

$$f(x) = \frac{1}{2(x-3)^2 + 4(x-3) + 2}$$

6. For what value of x is the function f undefined in the equation above?

7. If $m^2 - 6m + 8 = 0$, what is one possible value of $\frac{1}{m}$?

$$(-4x^3y - xy^3 + 4x) - (7x - 4xy^3 + 2x^2)$$

8. Which of the following is equivalent to the expression above?

(A) $-4x^3y + 3xy^3 - 2x^2 - 3x$

(B) $6x^3y^3 - 3x$

(C) $-4x^3y + 3xy^3 + 2x^2 - 11x$

(D) $-9x^3y^3 + 3x$

9. If $x^2 + y^2 = 12$ and $xy = -13$, what is the value of $2(x-y)^2$?

(A) -26

(B) 1

(C) 38

(D) 76

10. If $\dfrac{m^{x^2}}{m^{y^2}} = m^{36}$, $m > 1$, and $x + y = 9$, what is the value of $x - y$?

(A) 4

(B) 6

(C) 9

(D) 16

Answer Explanations

1. **(D)** Substituting for m and n into $3n - m$ results in the following:

$$3(4x^2 + 5x - 7) - (2x^3 + 3x - 11) =$$
$$12x^2 + 15x - 21 - 2x^3 - 3x + 11$$

Combine like terms by adding and subtracting those terms with variables raised to the same power.

$$-2x^3 + 12x^2 + 12x - 10$$

2. **4** First multiply $2(2x^2 - 7.5x + 3)$. Next multiply each term in the second polynomial by -1. Then combine like terms.

$$2(2x^2 - 7.5x + 3) - (-4x^2 + 2x - 7)$$
$$4x^2 - 15x + 6 + 4x^2 - 2x + 7$$
$$8x^2 - 17x + 13$$

The expression $8x^2 - 17x + 13$ yields $a = 8$, $b = -17$, and $c = 13$.

$$a + b + c = 8 - 17 + 13 = 4$$

3. **(B)** Simplify the equation and factor.

$$\frac{1}{3}(3x^2 + 3x - 36 = 0)$$
$$x^2 + x - 12 = 0$$
$$(x + 4)(x - 3) = 0$$

Set each factor equal to 0 and solve for x.

$$x + 4 = 0 \qquad x - 3 = 0$$
$$x = -4 \qquad x = 3$$

4. **(D)** Combine like terms by adding and subtracting the coefficients. Like terms are those that contain the same variable(s) raised to the same power(s). In this example, the following are the like terms.

$$-2xy,\ xy \text{ and } -8mn,\ mn$$
$$-4xy^2 - 2xy + xy - 8mn + mn = -4xy^2 - xy - 7mn$$

Remember, a term such as mn is understood to have a coefficient of 1.

5. **(C)** Multiply $\frac{1}{x+4}$ by $\frac{x+6}{x+6}$ and $\frac{1}{x+6}$ by $\frac{x+4}{x+4}$.

$$\frac{1}{\frac{1}{x+4} \times \frac{(x+6)}{(x+6)} + \frac{1}{x+6} \times \frac{(x+4)}{(x+4)}} =$$

$$\frac{1}{\frac{x+6+x+4}{(x+4)(x+6)}} =$$

$$\frac{1}{\frac{2x+10}{(x+4)(x+6)}} =$$

$$\frac{x^2 + 10x + 24}{2x + 10}$$

6. **2** Simplify the denominator.

$$f(x) = \frac{1}{2(x-3)^2 + 4(x-3) + 2}$$

$$f(x) = \frac{1}{2x^2 - 12x + 18 + 4x - 12 + 2}$$

$$f(x) = \frac{1}{2x^2 - 8x + 8}$$

$$f(x) = \frac{1}{2(x^2 - 4x^2 + 4)}$$

$$f(x) = \frac{1}{2(x-2)^2}$$

Division by 0 is not allowed. Set $x - 2$ equal to 0 to find the restriction.

$$x - 2 = 0$$
$$x = 2$$

7. $\mathbf{\frac{1}{4}}$ **or** $\mathbf{\frac{1}{2}}$ Solve for m.

$$m^2 - 6m + 8 = 0$$
$$(m-4)(m-2) = 0$$
$$m - 4 = 0 \text{ or } m - 2 = 0$$
$$m = 4 \text{ or } m = 2$$

So $\frac{1}{m}$ equals $\frac{1}{4}$ or $\frac{1}{2}$.

8. **(A)** To find the equivalent of $(-4x^3y - xy^3 + 4x) - (7x - 4xy^3 + 2x^2)$, combine like terms.

$$-xy^3 - (-4xy^3) = 3xy^3$$
$$4x - 7x = -3x$$

There are no other like terms, so arrange the expression as shown in choice (A).

$$-4x^3y + 3xy^3 - 2x^2 - 3x$$

9. **(D)** Expand $(x - y)^2$.

$$(x - y)^2 = x^2 - 2xy + y^2$$

It was given that $x^2 + y^2 = 12$ and $xy = -13$. Therefore, $-2xy = 26$.

$$(x - y)^2 = 12 + 26 = 38$$

Multiply the equation by 2.

$$2(x - y)^2 = (2)(38) = 76$$

10. **(A)** You are given $\frac{m^{x^2}}{m^{y^2}} = m^{36}$. When dividing like terms, subtract the exponents.

$$m^{x^2 - y^2} = m^{36}$$

Since the bases are the same, drop m to get $x^2 - y^2 = 36$. Factor by using the difference of two squares.

$$(x + y)(x - y) = 36$$

It was given in the question that $x + y = 9$, so $x - y$ must equal 4 because $9 \times 4 = 36$.

Drill 2

For multiple-choice questions, solve the problem and pick the correct answer from the provided choices. Each multiple-choice question has only one correct answer. For student-produced response questions, solve each problem and write down your answers separately.

$$\frac{1}{x^2 - 7x - 98}$$

1. What are the restrictions in the fraction above?

(A) $x \neq -12$ and $x \neq 8$
(B) $x \neq 12$ and $x \neq 8$
(C) $x \neq 14$ and $x \neq -7$
(D) $x \neq -14$ and $x \neq 7$

2. If $f(x) = 3(x + 4)^2$, what is the value of $f(-2)$?

(A) 4
(B) 12
(C) 24
(D) 36

$$\frac{1}{x} + \frac{2}{x - 3} = 6$$

3. What are values of x in the equation above?

(A) 7, −2
(B) −7, 2
(C) $\frac{7 \pm \sqrt{41}}{4}$
(D) $\frac{2 \pm \sqrt{33}}{6}$

4. Which of the following completely factors $x^4 - 81$?

(A) $(x^2 - 9)(x^2 + 9)$
(B) $(x + 3)(x - 3)(x^2 - 9)$
(C) $(x + 3)^2(x - 3)^2$
(D) $(x + 3)(x - 3)(x^2 + 9)$

5. Which expression is equivalent to $3x^2 - (5x^2 - 9x^2)$?

(A) $7x^2$
(B) $2x^2$
(C) $-x^2$
(D) $-11x^2$

6. What is the perimeter of a rectangle with a length that measures $7x^2 + 5x - 3$ and a width that measures $2x^2 + 5$?

   (A) $4x^2 + 15x - 9$
   (B) $9x^2 + 5x - 3$
   (C) $x^2 + 2x - 5$
   (D) $18x^2 + 10x + 4$

7. A rectangle has an area that measures 36 in.^{2} and has a length and width that measure $x + 6$ and $x - 3$, respectively. What is the perimeter of the rectangle?

   (A) 24 inches
   (B) 30 inches
   (C) 36 inches
   (D) 42 inches

8. How many real zeros are there in the equation $f(x) = x^2 + 2x + 8$?

   (A) 0
   (B) 1
   (C) 2
   (D) 3

$$\frac{(x^2 - 5x + 6)(x^2 - 9)}{(x^2 - 6x + 8)}$$

9. Which answer choice expresses the fraction above in simplest form?

   (A) $\frac{x^2 - 5x + 6}{x - 4}$
   (B) $\frac{(x + 3)^2(x - 3)}{x - 2}$
   (C) $\frac{(x - 3)^2(x + 3)}{x - 4}$
   (D) 1

10. What polynomial must be subtracted from $5x^2 - 9x + 3$ to get $-2x^2 - 13x + 5$?

   (A) $12x^2 + 12x - 4$
   (B) $12x^2 + 13x + 1$
   (C) $3x^2 - 22x + 8$
   (D) $7x^2 + 4x - 2$

Answer Explanations

1. **(C)** The dominator of a fraction cannot equal 0 because dividing by 0 is undefined. Factor the denominator to find values that make the denominator equal 0.

$$x^2 - 7x - 98 = 0$$
$$(x + 7)(x - 14) = 0$$

Set each pair of parentheses equal to 0 and solve.

$$x + 7 = 0 \qquad x - 14 = 0$$
$$x = -7 \qquad x = 14$$

When $x = -7$ or $x = 14$, the denominator equals 0 and the fraction is undefined.

2. **(B)** Replace x with -2 in $f(x) = 3(x + 4)^2$.

$$f(-2) = 3(-2 + 4)^2 = (3)(4) = 12$$

3. **(C)** The common denominator of $\frac{1}{x} + \frac{2}{x-3} = 6$ is $x(x - 3)$. Multiply both sides of the equation by this value.

$$x(x-3)\left(\frac{1}{x} + \frac{2}{x-3} = 6\right)$$
$$x - 3 + 2x = 6(x)(x - 3)$$
$$3x - 3 = 6x^2 - 18x$$
$$0 = 6x^2 - 21x + 3$$

Simplify the equation by dividing each term by 3.

$$(0 = 6x^2 - 21x + 3) \div 3 =$$
$$0 = 2x^2 - 7x + 1$$

The simplified equation does not factor, so solve by using the quadratic formula.

$$x = \frac{-b \pm \sqrt{b^2 - 4ac}}{2a}$$
$$a = 2 \quad b = -7 \quad c = 1$$
$$\frac{7 \pm \sqrt{(-7)^2 - 4(2)(1)}}{(2)(2)}$$
$$\frac{7 \pm \sqrt{41}}{4}$$

4. **(D)** Use the model for factoring the difference of two squares.

$$a^2 - b^2 = (a + b)(a - b)$$
$$x^4 - 81 = (x^2 - 9)(x^2 + 9)$$

The expression $x^2 + 9$ is the sum of two squares and does not factor. However, $x^2 - 9$ is the difference of two squares and can be factored further.

$$(x^2 + 9)(x^2 - 9) = (x^2 + 9)(x + 3)(x - 3)$$

5. **(A)** Use the order of operations to simplify $3x^2 - (5x^2 - 9x^2)$.

$$3x^2 - (5x^2 - 9x^2)$$
$$3x^2 - (-4x^2)$$
$$3x^2 + 4x^2 = 7x^2$$

6. **(D)** Find the perimeter of the rectangle by using the formula $P = 2l + 2w$ in which P is the perimeter, l is the length, and w is the width.

$$2(7x^2 + 5x - 3) + 2(2x^2 + 5)$$
$$14x^2 + 10x - 6 + 4x^2 + 10$$
$$18x^2 + 10x + 4$$

7. **(B)** The area of a rectangle is found by using the formula $A = lw$ in which A is the area, w is the width, and l is the length.

$$(x + 6)(x - 3) = 36$$
$$x^2 + 3x - 18 = 36$$
$$x^2 + 3x - 54 = 0$$
$$(x + 9)(x - 6) = 0$$
$$x + 9 = 0 \quad x - 6 = 0$$
$$x = -9 \quad x = 6$$

Disregard $x = -9$ because distance cannot be negative. Substitute 6 for x in the perimeter formula.

$$P = 2l + 2w$$
$$P = 2(6 + 6) + 2(6 - 3)$$
$$P = 24 + 6$$
$$P = 30$$

8. **(A)** Use the discriminant to discern the number of real solutions.

If $b^2 - 4ac > 0$, there are 2 real solutions.

If $b^2 - 4ac = 0$, there is 1 real solution.

If $b^2 - 4ac < 0$, there are no real solutions.

$$f(x) = x^2 + 2x + 8$$
$$a = 1 \quad b = 2 \quad c = 8$$
$$(2)^2 - 4(1)(8) = -28$$

Since $-28 < 0$, there are no real solutions.

9. **(C)** Factor the expressions in the numerator and in the denominator.

$$\frac{(x^2 - 5x + 6)(x^2 - 9)}{(x^2 - 6x + 8)} = \frac{(x - 2)(x - 3)(x + 3)(x - 3)}{(x - 4)(x - 2)}$$

Now divide identical factors in the numerator and denominator.

$$\frac{(x - 2)(x - 3)(x + 3)(x - 3)}{(x - 4)(x - 2)} = \frac{(x - 3)^2(x + 3)}{x - 4}$$

10. **(D)** What number must be subtracted from 10 to get 4? You subtract the difference, 4, from 10. Similarly, subtract $-2x^2 - 13x + 5$ from $5x^2 - 9x + 3$.

$$(5x^2 - 9x + 3) - (-2x^2 - 13x + 5) = 7x^2 + 4x - 2$$

Exponents and Roots Drill

For multiple-choice questions, solve the problem and pick the correct answer from the provided choices. Each multiple-choice question has only one correct answer. For student-produced response questions, solve each problem and write down your answers separately.

1. If $a^{\frac{3}{2}} = 64$, what is the value of $\sqrt{a}$?

(A) 2
(B) $2\sqrt{2}$
(C) 4
(D) 8

2. Which of the following is equal to $\left(m^{\frac{1}{3}}\right)^2$?

(A) $\sqrt{m^{\frac{1}{6}}}$
(B) $\sqrt[3]{m^2}$
(C) $\sqrt{3^m}$
(D) $m\sqrt{m}$

$$2x^{\frac{2}{3}} = 6^{\frac{1}{2}}$$

3. In the equation above, what is the value of x?

(A) $\frac{27}{8}$
(B) $\left(\frac{27}{8}\right)^{\frac{1}{4}}$
(C) $\left(\frac{8}{27}\right)^{\frac{1}{4}}$
(D) $\frac{16}{27}$

4. Which of the following is equivalent to $25^{\frac{3}{4}}$?

(A) $\sqrt[3]{25}$
(B) $5\sqrt{5}$
(C) $5\sqrt[3]{25}$
(D) 37.5

5. The square root of x varies inversely with y. When $x = 196$, $y = -\frac{1}{2}$. What is the value of x when $y = -3$?

(A) 3
(B) $\frac{49}{9}$
(C) $\frac{49}{3}$
(D) 49

$$x^3 - 6x^2 + 2x - 12 = 0$$

6. For what real value of x is the equation above true?

7. If $r = 3\sqrt{3}$ and $2r = \sqrt{3x}$, what is the value of x?

8. If $12x - 3y = 5$, what is the value of $\frac{16^{3x}}{8^y}$?

 (A) 4
 (B) 16
 (C) 32
 (D) 64

$$\left(\frac{1}{3}\right)^{x-2} = (27)^{3-x}$$

9. Given the equation above, what is the value of $2x + 11$?

10. If $x^{\frac{y}{4}} = 81$ for positive integers x and y, what is one possible value of y?

Answer Explanations

1. **(C)** Raise each side of the equation to the $\frac{2}{3}$ power to isolate a.

$$\left(a^{\frac{3}{2}}\right)^{\frac{2}{3}} = 64^{\frac{2}{3}}$$
$$a = 16$$
$$\sqrt{16} = 4$$

2. **(B)** When raising an exponent to another, multiply the exponents.

$$\left(m^{\frac{1}{3}}\right)^2 = m^{\frac{2}{3}}$$

Rational exponents can be expressed as radicals: the numerator is the exponent, and the denominator is the root.

$$m^{\frac{2}{3}} = \sqrt[3]{m^2}$$

The root, 3, exceeds the exponent, 2, so $\sqrt[3]{m^2}$ is simplified to its lowest term.

3. **(B)** Begin isolating x by raising both sides of the equation to the sixth power.

$$2x^{\frac{2}{3}} = 6^{\frac{1}{2}}$$
$$\left(2x^{\frac{2}{3}}\right)^6 = \left(6^{\frac{1}{2}}\right)6$$
$$64x^4 = 6^3$$
$$64x^4 = 216$$

Divide both sides of the equation by 64.

$$\frac{64x^4}{64} = \frac{216}{64}$$
$$x^4 = \frac{27}{8}$$

Raise both sides of the equation to the $\frac{1}{4}$th power.

$$(x^4)^{\frac{1}{4}} = \left(\frac{27}{8}\right)^{\frac{1}{4}}$$

$$x = \left(\frac{27}{8}\right)^{\frac{1}{4}}$$

4. **(B)** Transform $25^{\frac{3}{4}}$ to $(5^2)^{\frac{3}{4}}$, which equals $5^{\frac{6}{4}} = 5^{\frac{3}{2}}$. When a number is raised to a rational power, the numerator serves as the power of the number and the denominator as its root. Therefore, raise 5 to the third power and find the square root of that quantity.

$$\sqrt{5^3} = \sqrt{125} = 5\sqrt{5}$$

Choices (A) and (C) are incorrect because $25^{\frac{3}{4}}$ transforms to a square root, not a cube root. Choice (D) is incorrect because it multiplies 25 by $\frac{3}{2}$ rather than raising it to the $\frac{3}{4}$ power.

5. **(B)** Inverse variation uses the model $xy = k$ where k is a constant. Since the question stipulates that the square root of x varies inversely with y, use the model $\sqrt{x}\,y = k$.

$$\sqrt{196} \times -\frac{1}{2} = k$$

$$14 \times -\frac{1}{2} = k$$

$$-7 = k$$

Now input $y = -3$ into the equation.

$$\sqrt{x} \times -3 = -7$$

$$\sqrt{x} = \frac{7}{3}$$

$$(\sqrt{x})^2 = \left(\frac{7}{3}\right)^2$$

$$x = \frac{49}{9}$$

6. **6** Begin factoring $x^3 - 6x^2 + 2x - 12 = 0$ by grouping.

$$(x^3 - 6x^2) + (2x - 12) = 0$$

Extract the greatest common factor from the expressions in the parentheses.

$$x^2(x - 6) + 2(x - 6) = 0$$

Place x^2 and 2 into its own parentheses.

$$(x^2 + 2)(x - 6) = 0$$

Set each of the parentheses equal to 0.

$$x^2 + 2 = 0 \text{ or } x - 6 = 0$$

$$x^2 = -2 \text{ or } x = 6$$

$x^2 = -2$ becomes $x = \pm i\sqrt{2}$, neither of which is a real number. Therefore, the real solution to $x^3 - 6x^2 + 2x - 12 = 0$ is $x = 6$.

7. **36** The question says that $r = 3\sqrt{3}$ and $2r = \sqrt{3x}$. Therefore, $2r$ also equals $(2)(3\sqrt{3})(2)(3\sqrt{3})$ or $6\sqrt{3}$. Set $6\sqrt{3}$ equal to $\sqrt{3x}$ and solve for x.

Remove the radicals by squaring both sides.

$$6\sqrt{3} = \sqrt{3x}$$
$$(6\sqrt{3})^2 = (\sqrt{3x})^2$$
$$108 = 3x$$
$$36 = x$$

8. **(C)** Convert the numerator and the denominator to base 2.

$$\frac{16^{3x}}{8^y} = \frac{(2^4)^{3x}}{(2^3)^y} = \frac{2^{12x}}{2^{3y}}$$

When dividing terms with the same base, subtract the exponents.

$$\frac{2^{12x}}{2^{3y}} = 2^{12x-3y}$$

Since $12x - 3y = 5$, then $2^{12x-3y} = 2^5 = 32$.

9. **18** Solve for x by changing each base to 3.

$$\left(\frac{1}{3}\right)^{x-2} = (27)^{3-x}$$
$$(3^{-1})^{x-2} = (3^3)^{3-x}$$
$$(3)^{-x+2} = (3)^{9-3x}$$
$$-x + 2 = 9 - 3x$$
$$-7 = -2x$$
$$\frac{7}{2} = x$$

or

$$3.5 = x$$

Substitute 3.5 for x in $2x + 11$.

$$(2)(3.5) + 11 = 18$$

10. **1, 2, 4, 8, or 16** The equation $x^{\frac{y}{4}} = 81$, where x and y are positive integers, can be written as follows.

$$3^4 = 81$$
$$9^2 = 81$$
$$81^1 = 81$$
$$(81^2)^{\frac{1}{2}} = 81$$
$$(81^4)^{\frac{1}{4}} = 81$$

If $x^{\frac{y}{4}} = 81$ and if x and y are positive integers, then $\frac{y}{4}$ can equal 4, 2, 1, $\frac{1}{2}$, or $\frac{1}{4}$. Therefore, the value of y can be 16, 8, 4, 2, or 1.

Solving Advanced Equations

Drill 1

For multiple-choice questions, solve the problem and pick the correct answer from the provided choices. Each multiple-choice question has only one correct answer. For student-produced response questions, solve each problem and write down your answers separately.

$$\sqrt{n-b} = n - 2$$

1. If $b = -4$, what is the solution set to the equation above?

(A) $\{-5\}$
(B) $\{0\}$
(C) $\{5\}$
(D) $\{0, 5\}$

2. What are the solutions to $6x^2 + 12x - 15 = 0$?

(A) $2 \pm \sqrt{14}$
(B) $\dfrac{2 \pm \sqrt{14}}{2}$
(C) $\dfrac{-2 \pm \sqrt{14}}{2}$
(D) $-2 \pm 4\sqrt{2}$

3. If $(x + n)^2 = x^2 + 19x + n^2$, what is the value of n^2?

(A) 361
(B) $\dfrac{361}{2}$
(C) $\dfrac{361}{4}$
(D) 38

4. What are the solutions to $2x^2 + 8x - 12 = 0$?

(A) $x = -4 \pm 3\sqrt{10}$
(B) $x = -3 + \dfrac{\sqrt{10}}{10}$
(C) $x = -2 \pm \sqrt{10}$
(D) $x = 2 \pm \sqrt{10}$

$$x - 2 = \frac{4}{x-2}$$

5. Which of the following is the solution to the equation above?

(A) -4
(B) 0
(C) 0, 4
(D) 2, -2

6. The theory of special relativity suggests that an observer moving at great speed experiences the flow of time much more slowly than an observer on Earth. The following formula is used to calculate what is known as time dilation.

$$F(t) = \frac{t}{\sqrt{1 - v^2}}$$

In the formula, t represents some unit of time and v represents velocity as some fraction of light-speed. For example, an observer counts 1 second in a rocket ship traveling at 60% of the speed of light while an observer on Earth measures 1.25 seconds. If an observer traveling at 80% of the speed of light counts off 1 second, how many seconds will be counted by an observer on Earth?

7. The theory of special relativity suggests that an observer moving at great speed experiences the flow of time much more slowly than an observer on Earth. The following formula is used to calculate what is known as time dilation.

$$F(t) = \frac{t}{\sqrt{1 - v^2}}$$

In the formula, t represents some unit of time and v represents velocity as some fraction of light-speed. For example, an observer counts 1 second in a rocket ship traveling at 60% of the speed of light while an observer on Earth measures 1.25 seconds. An observer on Earth measures 2 seconds, while an observer traveling at a fraction of the speed of light measures 1 second. At what fraction of the speed of light was the moving observer traveling?

8. $C(x) = x^3 + 5x^2 + 5x - 2$

In the function above, which of the following can be assumed?

(A) $x + 3$ is a factor
(B) $x + 2$ is a factor
(C) $x - 5$ is a factor
(D) $x + 4$ is a factor

9. $(ax - 7)(bx + 5) = 6x^2 + cx - 35$. If $ab = 6$ and $a - b = -1$, what are two possible values of c?

(A) $c = 2$ or $c = -4$
(B) $c = -11$ or $c = -1$
(C) $c = -2$ or $c = 4$
(D) $c = 12$ or $c = -5$

$$x^3 + x^2 - 210x = 0$$

10. What is the sum of the roots in the equation above?

(A) -14
(B) -1
(C) 1
(D) 15

Answer Explanations

1. **(C)** Square both sides of the equation to get rid of the radical.

$$\sqrt{n-(-4)} = n-2$$
$$\sqrt{n-(-4)}^2 = (n-2)^2$$
$$n+4 = n^2-4n+4$$
$$0 = n^2-5n$$
$$0 = n(n-5)$$
$$n = 0 \text{ or } n-5 = 0$$
$$n = 0 \text{ or } n = 5$$

Check each solution in the original equation to ascertain any extraneous solutions.

Check 5:

$$\sqrt{5-(-4)} = 5-2$$
$$\sqrt{9} = 3$$
$$3 = 3$$

Check 0:

$$\sqrt{0-(-4)} = 0-2$$
$$\sqrt{4} = -2$$
$$2 \neq -2$$

We accept 5 as the solution and reject 0.

2. **(C)** Solve the equation by first dividing all of the terms by 3.

$$(6x^2+12x-15) \div 3 = 0 \div 3$$
$$2x^2+4x-5 = 0$$

The equation cannot be factored, so use the quadratic equation to solve.

$$x = \frac{-b \pm \sqrt{b^2-4ac}}{2a}$$
$$a = 2, \quad b = 4, \quad c = -5$$
$$x = \frac{-4 \pm \sqrt{4^2-4(2)(-5)}}{2(2)}$$
$$x = \frac{-4 \pm \sqrt{16+40}}{4}$$
$$x = \frac{-4 \pm \sqrt{56}}{4} = \frac{-2 \pm \sqrt{14}}{2}$$

3. **(C)** Find the value of n^2 by completing the square in $x^2 + 19x + n^2$. Multiply 19 by $\frac{1}{2}$ and square the product.

$$x^2 + 19x + n^2 = x^2 + 19x + \left(\frac{19}{2}\right)^2 = x^2 + 19x + \frac{361}{4}$$
$$n^2 = \frac{361}{4}$$

4. **(C)** Divide both sides of the equation by 2, which is the greatest common factor of $2x^2 + 8x - 12$.

$$(2x^2 + 8x - 12) \div 2 = 0 \div 2$$
$$x^2 + 4x - 6 = 0$$

The equation does not factor, so solve by using the quadratic equation.

$$x = \frac{-b \pm \sqrt{b^2 - 4ac}}{2a}$$
$$a = 1, \quad b = 4, \quad c = -6$$
$$x = \frac{-4 \pm \sqrt{4^2 - 4(1)(-6)}}{2(1)}$$
$$x = \frac{-4 \pm \sqrt{40}}{2}$$
$$x = \frac{-4 \pm 2\sqrt{10}}{2}$$
$$x = 2 \pm \sqrt{10}$$

5. **(C)** Some test takers may find that a plug-and-check strategy is best for them. If you solve the question correctly and quickly, using that method is fine. Here is the math needed to solve this equation. Multiply both sides of the equation by $x - 2$.

$$(x - 2)(x - 2) = \left(\frac{4}{x - 2}\right)(x - 2)$$
$$(x - 2)^2 = 4$$

Find the square root of both sides of the equation.

$$\sqrt{(x - 2)^2} = \sqrt{4}$$
$$x - 2 = \pm 2$$
$$x = 4 \quad x = 0$$

Check for extraneous solutions.

$$0 - 2 = \frac{4}{0 - 2}$$
$$-2 = -2$$
$$4 - 2 = \frac{4}{4 - 2}$$
$$2 = 2$$

Neither 4 nor 0 is an extraneous solution. So both 4 and 0 are solutions to the equation.

6. **1.66 or 1.67 or $\frac{5}{3}$** Input 80% for v into the formula of special relativity.

$$F(t) = \frac{t}{\sqrt{1 - v^2}}$$
$$F(1) = \frac{1}{\sqrt{1 - (0.8)^2}} = 1.\overline{66}$$

7. **.866** Input 1 and 2 for t and $F(t)$, respectively, into the special relativity formula.

$$F(t) = \frac{t}{\sqrt{1 - v^2}}$$

$$2 = \frac{1}{\sqrt{1 - v^2}}$$

$$2\left(\sqrt{1 - v^2}\right) = 1$$

$$\sqrt{1 - v^2} = 0.5$$

$$\left(\sqrt{1 - v^2}\right)^2 = (0.5)^2$$

$$1 - v^2 = 0.25$$

$$-v^2 = -0.75$$

$$v = 0.866$$

8. **(B)** If $x + 2$ is a factor of $C(x) = x^3 + 5x^2 + 5x - 2$, the remainder, after dividing, is 0.

$$x + 2\overline{\smash{)}x^3 + 5x^2 + 5x - 2}\quad \text{quotient: } x^2 + 3x - 1$$

Since there is no remainder, we know that $x + 2$ is factor of $C(x) = x^3 + 5x^2 + 5x - 2$. An alternate method to answering this question is to substitute -2 for x and assess the results.

$$(-2)^3 + 5(-2)^2 + 5(-2) - 2 = 0$$

The result is 0, which indicates -2 is a root of the function and $x + 2$ is a factor.

9. **(B)**

$$(ax - 7)(bx + 5) = 6x^2 + cx - 35$$

Solve for a or b in $a - b = -1$ and create a system of equations.

$$a - b = -1 \text{ so } a = b - 1$$

Substitute $b - 1$ for a in $ab = 6$.

$$(b - 1)b = 6$$

$$b^2 - b = 6$$

$$b^2 - b - 6 = 0$$

Factor and solve for b.

$$(b + 2)(b - 3) = 0$$

$$b + 2 = 0 \text{ or } b - 3 = 0$$

$$b = -2 \text{ or } b = 3$$

Find a when $b = 3$ or $b = -2$.

$$ab = 6$$

$$3a = 6$$

$$a = 2$$

When $b = 3$, $a = 2$.

$$ab = 6$$

$$-2a = 6$$

$$a = -3$$

When $b = -2$, $a = -3$.

Solve for c when a and b are 2 and 3, respectively.

$$(2x - 7)(3x + 5) = 6x^2 - 11x - 35$$

$$c = -11$$

Solve for c when a and b are -3 and -2, respectively.

$$(-3x - 7)(-2x + 5) = 6x^2 - x - 35$$

$$c = -1$$

You only have to solve for one of the values of c. Choice (B) is the only one that has either of the correct solutions to the question.

10. **(B)** Factor the equation.

$$x^3 + x^2 - 210x = 0$$

$$x(x^2 + x - 210) = 0$$

$$x(x + 15)(x - 14) = 0$$

$$x = 0 \quad x = -15 \quad x = 14$$

$$0 - 15 + 14 = -1$$

Drill 2

For multiple-choice questions, solve the problem and pick the correct answer from the provided choices. Each multiple-choice question has only one correct answer. For student-produced response questions, solve each problem and write down your answers separately.

1. For what value(s) of x is the following expression undefined?

$$\frac{-5x^2y - 4xy}{6x^2 - 13x - 5}$$

(A) $-1, 5$
(B) 5
(C) $-\frac{1}{3}, \frac{5}{2}$
(D) $\frac{1}{3}, \frac{3}{2}$

$$\sqrt{2x} = x - 4$$

2. What value(s) of x satisfy the equation above?

I. 8
II. 2
III. Both 8 and 2

(A) I only
(B) II only
(C) I and II
(D) Neither value satisfies the equation.

3. Which of the following is a step in solving the equation $\sqrt{x-7} = x - 7$?

(A) $x - 7 = x - 7$
(B) $2x = 14$
(C) $(x - 8)(x - 7) = 0$
(D) $(x + 7)(x - 6) = 0$

4. Simplify $-2\left(\frac{x^2 - 8x - 180}{x + 10}\right)$ if $x \neq -10$.

(A) $x - 18$
(B) $-2x + 36$
(C) $-2x^2 + x$
(D) $x + 10$

5. An annuity is a fixed income stream paid out over an agreed upon period of time. A $1,000,000 insurance payment is an annuity if it is paid out over a period of time in fixed installments. The insurance company may offer the payee a lump sum payout called the present value of the annuity. The formula to calculate the present value of an annuity is as follows.

$$P = A\left(1 + \frac{r}{n}\right)^{-nt}$$

where:
$P =$ the present value of the payout
$A =$ the dollars that would have been received over time
$t =$ time in years
$r =$ the interest rate expressed as a decimal
$n =$ compounding periods each year

Jorge and his brothers have inherited a pension plan from their grandfather. The plan will pay each grandchild $10,000 over the course of a 10-year period. Jorge chooses to accept the present value of the inheritance at 8% compounded monthly. How much should he expect his payout to be? (Round your answer to the nearest dollar.)

6. An annuity is a fixed income stream paid out over an agreed upon period of time. A $1,000,000 insurance payment is an annuity if it is paid out over a period of time in fixed installments. The insurance company may offer the payee a lump sum payout called the present value of the annuity. The formula to calculate the present value of an annuity is as follows.

$$P = A\left(1 + \frac{r}{n}\right)^{-nt}$$

where:
$P =$ the present value of the payout
$A =$ the dollars that would have been received over time
$t =$ time in years
$r =$ the interest rate expressed as a decimal
$n =$ compounding periods each year

Samantha received a cash annuity as a gift for college graduation. The annuity would pay an interest rate of 3.5% over a 5-year period compounded quarterly. Samantha elected to receive the present value of the annuity, which totaled $1,621. To the nearest dollar, what would have been the payout of the annuity if she chose to accept the 5-year payout terms?

7. What is the value of x if $x = \dfrac{w^2 + 2w + 1}{\frac{w+1}{3}}$?

(A) $\dfrac{3}{w+1}$

(B) $3(w+1)$

(C) $\dfrac{1}{3w+1}$

(D) $\dfrac{\frac{1}{w}}{3+w}$

8. The points (2, 7) and (−3, 37) lie on the graph of $y = ax^2 - 4x + 7$. What is the value of a?

9. What is the sum of all values of x that satisfy $4x^2 - 2x - 6 = 0$?

(A) $\frac{-\sqrt{2}}{2}$

(B) $-\frac{1}{2}$

(C) $\frac{1}{2}$

(D) $2\sqrt{2}$

$$x^3 - 6x^2 + 2x - 12 = 0$$

10. What real value of x makes the above equation true?

Answer Explanations

1. **(C)** Division by 0 is undefined. Set $6x^2 - 13x - 5$ equal to 0 and solve.

$$6x^2 - 13x - 5 = 0$$

Solve by factoring.

$$(3x + 1)(2x - 5) = 0$$

Set each of the parentheses equal to 0, and solve for the variable.

$$3x + 1 = 0 \text{ or } 2x - 5 = 0$$

$$3x = -1 \text{ or } 2x = 5$$

$$x = -\frac{1}{3} \text{ or } x = \frac{5}{2}$$

The expression $\frac{-5x^2y - 4xy}{6x^2 - 13x - 5}$ is undefined when $x = -\frac{1}{3}$ and when $x = \frac{5}{2}$.

2. **(A)** Square both sides of the equation to eliminate the radical.

$$(\sqrt{2x})^2 = (x - 4)^2$$

$$2x = x^2 - 8x + 16$$

Set the equation equal to 0 and factor.

$$2x = x^2 - 8x + 16$$

$$x^2 - 10x + 16 = 0$$

$$(x - 8)(x - 2) = 0$$

Solve for x.

$$x - 8 = 0 \text{ or } x - 2 = 0$$

$$x = 8 \text{ or } x = 2$$

Check both values to eliminate extraneous answers.

$$\sqrt{2 \times 8} = 8 - 4$$

$$4 = 4$$

$$\sqrt{2 \times 2} = 2 - 4$$

$$2 \neq -2$$

Only 8 is a solution because 2 is an extraneous solution.

3. **(C)** Square both sides of the equation to remove the radical.

$$(x-7)^2 = (x-7)^2$$
$$x - 7 = x^2 - 14x + 49$$
$$x = x^2 - 14x + 56$$
$$x^2 - 15x + 56 = 0$$
$$(x-7)(x-8) = 0$$

This last step reflects answer choice (C).

4. **(B)** Factor and cancel as needed.

$$-2\left(\frac{x^2 - 8x - 180}{x+10}\right) =$$
$$-2\left(\frac{(x+10)(x-18)}{x+10}\right) =$$
$$-2(x-18) = -2x + 36$$

5. **4,505** Use the present value formula and input the known information.

$$P = A\left(1 + \frac{r}{n}\right)^{-nt}$$
$$P = 10{,}000\left(1 + \frac{0.08}{12}\right)^{-(12)(10)} = 4{,}505$$

Jorge can expect to receive \$4,505 as the present value of his \$10,000 ten-year annuity.

6. **1,930** Input the known information into the present value formula and solve for A.

$$P = A\left(1 + \frac{r}{n}\right)^{-nt}$$
$$1{,}621 = A\left(1 + \frac{0.35}{4}\right)^{-(4)(5)}$$
$$1{,}621 = 0.84A$$
$$1{,}930 = A$$

Samantha would have earned \$1,930 if she had elected to receive her gift as an annuity.

7. **(B)** Factor the numerator of the complex fraction.

$$\frac{w^2 + 2w + 1}{\frac{w+1}{3}} = \frac{(w+1)(w+1)}{\frac{w+1}{3}}$$

When dividing a complex fraction, invert the denominator and multiply that quantity with the numerator.

$$\frac{(w+1)(w+1)}{\frac{w+1}{3}} = (w+1)(w+1)\left(\frac{3}{w+1}\right)$$

Cross-divide as needed.

$$= (w+1)(w+1)\left(\frac{3}{w+1}\right) = 3(w+1)$$

8. **2** Substitute either (2, 7) or (−3, 37) for x and y, and solve for a.

$$7 = (a)(2)^2 - (4)(2) + 7$$
$$7 = 4a - 8 + 7$$
$$8 = 4a$$
$$2 = a$$

9. **(C)** This problem can be solved by factoring $4x^2 - 2x - 6 = 0$ or by using the quadratic equation.

$$x = \frac{-b \pm \sqrt{b^2 - 4ac}}{2a}$$

$$a = 4,\ b = -2,\ c = -6$$

$$x = \frac{-(-2) \pm \sqrt{(-2^2) - 4(4)(-6)}}{2(4)}$$

$$x = \frac{2 \pm \sqrt{4 - (-96)}}{8}$$

$$x = \frac{2 \pm 10}{8}$$

$$x = \frac{3}{2},\ x = -1$$

The sum of the roots, -1 and $\frac{3}{2}$, is $\frac{1}{2}$.

10. **6** Factor by grouping.

$$x^3 - 6x^2 + 2x - 12 = 0$$
$$(x^3 - 6x^2) + (2x - 12) = 0$$
$$x^2(x - 6) + 2(x - 6) = 0$$
$$(x^2 + 2)(x - 6) = 0$$
$$x^2 + 2 = 0 \text{ or } x - 6 = 0$$
$$x = \pm i\sqrt{2} \text{ or } x = 6$$

Of the three solutions, only 6 is a real solution to the equation.

Zeros, Parabolas, and Polynomial Graphing Drill

For multiple-choice questions, solve the problem and pick the correct answer from the provided choices. Each multiple-choice question has only one correct answer. For student-produced response questions, solve each problem and write down your answers separately.

1. Which of the following equations has the same x- and y-coordinates for the vertex as does $y = 3(x - 4)(x + 6)$?

   (A) $y = x^2 - 8x + 15$
   (B) $y = 3(x^2 + 4x - 6)$
   (C) $y = 3(x + 1)^2 - 75$
   (D) $y = 3x^2 + 6x - 10$

2. The function g is defined by $g(x) = 2x^2 + 15x - 8$. The x-coordinate of the vertex of the graph is contained within which of the following intervals?

   (A) $-\frac{1}{2} < x < 8$
   (B) $-2 < x < 2$
   (C) $-3.65 < x < -2$
   (D) $-4 < x < 6$

$$y = x^2 + 2x - 24$$

3. The equation above represents a parabola in the xy-plane. Which of the following equations shows the x-intercepts of the parabola as constants or coefficients?

   (A) $y - 24 = x(x + 2)$
   (B) $y = (x + 1)^2 - 25$
   (C) $y = (x + 6)(x - 4)$
   (D) $y = x(x + 2) - 24$

4. Which of the following equations has only one x-intercept in the xy-plane?

   (A) $x^2 + 2x - 48 = y$
   (B) $x^2 + 11x + 30 = y$
   (C) $x^2 - 6x + 8 = y$
   (D) $x^2 + 6x + 9 = y$

5. A furniture manufacturer of office chairs uses the following profit function.

$$P(x) = -0.08x^2 + 23.1x + 500$$

   where x represents the number of chairs that are manufactured and $P(x)$ is profit in dollars. What is the most profitable number of chairs to manufacture? (Round your answer to the nearest whole number.)

6. Which of the following is true about the graph of the equation $y = 4(x - 3)^2 + 13$?

(A) The graph is wider than the graph of $y = (x - 3)^2 + 13$.
(B) It has no real roots.
(C) Its minimum value is -3.
(D) Its roots are $x = 3$ and $x = -13$.

$$h = -4.9t^2 + 32t$$

7. The equation above shows the height of a ball thrown upward from ground level with an initial velocity of 32 meters per second.

After approximately how many seconds will the ball hit the ground?

(A) 5.6
(B) 6.5
(C) 7.4
(D) 8.2

$$h = -4.9t^2 + 32t$$

8. The equation above shows the height of a ball thrown upward from ground level with an initial velocity of 32 meters per second. After how many seconds will the ball be 18 meters in the air?

(A) 2.2
(B) 4.3
(C) 0.6 and 5.9
(D) 0.6 or 6.3

9. Which of the following is an equivalent form of the function h such that the minimum value of h appears as a constant or coefficient?

$$h(x) = (x - 8)(x + 2)$$

(A) $h(x) = x^2 - 6x - 16$
(B) $h(x) = x^2 + 6x - 16$
(C) $h(x) = (x - 3)^2 - 25$
(D) $h(x) = (x + 3)^2 - 25$

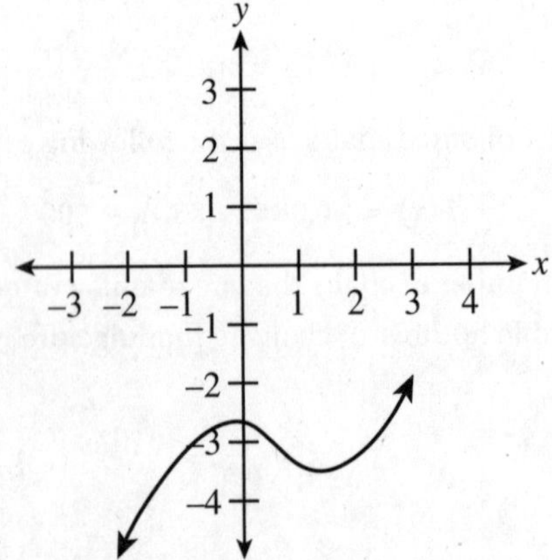

10. Consider the graph of the equation above. How many times would it intersect $f(x) = -3$?

Answer Explanations

1. **(C)** Find the coordinates of the vertex of $3(x - 4)(x + 6)$ by multiplying.

$$y = 3(x - 4)(x + 6)$$
$$y = 3(x^2 + 2x - 24)$$

Begin to transform the equation from standard form to graphing form. First, move -24 to the right of the parentheses, remembering to first multiply it by 3.

$$y = 3(x^2 + 2x) - (24)(3)$$
$$y = 3(x^2 + 2x) - 72$$

Complete the square by squaring $\frac{b}{2}$. Remember to multiply that value by 3.

$$y = 3(x^2 + 2x + 1) - 72 - (3 \times 1)$$
$$y = 3(x^2 + 2x + 1) - 72 - 3$$
$$y = 3(x + 1)^2 - 75$$

The equation is now in graphing form. The vertex is $(-1, -75)$.

2. **(D)** The x-coordinate of the vertex can be found using the formula $x = -\frac{b}{2a}$. Find the values of a and b.

$$g(x) = 2x^2 + 15x - 8$$
$$a = 2, b = 15$$
$$x = -\frac{b}{2a} = -\frac{15}{4} = -3.75$$

Answer choice (D), $-4 < x < 6$, is the only interval among the answer choices that contains $x = -3.75$.

3. **(C)** The factored form of $y = x^2 + 2x - 24$ is $y = (x + 6)(x - 4)$. To find the x-intercepts, let $y = 0$.

$$0 = (x + 6)(x - 4)$$
$$x + 6 = 0 \qquad x - 4 = 0$$
$$x = -6 \qquad x = 4$$

The factored form of $y = x^2 + 2x - 24$ shows the x-intercepts of the parabola as constants.

4. **(D)** Find the x-intercept(s) by letting $y = 0$.

Choice (A):

$$x^2 + 2x - 48 = 0$$
$$(x + 8)(x - 6) = 0$$
$$x = -8 \text{ and } x = 6$$

There are two x-intercepts.

Choice (B):

$$x^2 + 11x + 30 = 0$$
$$(x + 6)(x + 5) = 0$$
$$x = -6 \text{ and } x = -5$$

There are two x-intercepts.

Choice (C):

$$x^2 - 6x + 8 = 0$$
$$(x - 4)(x - 2) = 0$$
$$x = 4 \text{ and } x = 2$$

There are two x-intercepts.

Choice (D):

$$x^2 + 6x + 9 = 0$$
$$(x + 3)^2 = 0$$
$$x = -3$$

There is only one x-intercept.

5. **144** The profit function, $P(x) = -0.08x^2 + 23.1x + 500$, is a parabola that opens down. The vertex is a maximum with the x-coordinate representing the most profitable number of chairs to manufacture. Find the x-coordinate by using the formula for finding the axis of symmetry, $x = \frac{-b}{2a}$.

$$a = -0.08, b = 23.1$$

$$x = \frac{-23.1}{2(-0.08)} = 144.375 \approx 144$$

6. **(B)** One way to solve this problem is to let $y = 0$. Doing so will let us find the roots of the equation.

$$0 = 4(x - 3)^2 + 13$$
$$-13 = 4(x - 3)^2$$
$$-\frac{13}{4} = (x - 3)^2$$
$$\pm\frac{\sqrt{-13}}{4} = x - 3$$
$$3 \pm \frac{i\sqrt{13}}{2} = x$$

7. **(B)** The ball hits the ground when the height is 0 feet. Let h equal 0 and solve for t.

$$0 = -4.9t^2 + 32t$$
$$0 = t(-4.9t + 32)$$
$$t = 0 \text{ or } -4.9t + 32 = 0$$
$$t = 0 \text{ or } t = 6.5$$

The value of $t = 0$ represents the time before the ball was thrown.

8. **(C)** Replace h with 18 as the height the ball attains. Use the formula $h = -4.9t^2 + 32t$.

$$18 = -4.9t^2 + 32t$$

Set the equation equal to 0 and solve for t.

$$-4.9t^2 + 32t - 18 = 0$$

The equation does not factor, so use the quadratic formula $\frac{-b \pm \sqrt{b^2 - 4ac}}{2a}$.

$$a = -4.9, b = 32, c = -18$$

After using the quadratic formula, we arrive at two different answers, 0.6 and 5.9. We get two different answers because after 0.6 seconds the ball attains a height of 18 meters and then rises higher. As the ball returns to Earth, it reaches 18 meters high again, 5.9 seconds after it was thrown into the air.

9. **(C)** Transform $h(x) = (x - 8)(x + 2)$ to graphing form by multiplying the expressions within parentheses.

$$h(x) = (x - 8)(x + 2) = x^2 - 6x - 16$$

Move -16 to the far right of the equation as you complete the square. Remember that as you add a value to complete the square, that same value must be subtracted from -16.

$$h(x) = x^2 - 6x - 16$$
$$h(x) = x^2 - 6x + 9 - 16 - 9$$
$$h(x) = (x - 3)^2 - 25$$

The vertex of the parabola is $(3, -25)$, and the minimum value is -25.

10. **3** Remember that $f(x) = -3$ can be expressed as $y = -3$. Draw the graph of $y = -3$ on the graph of the cubic equation.

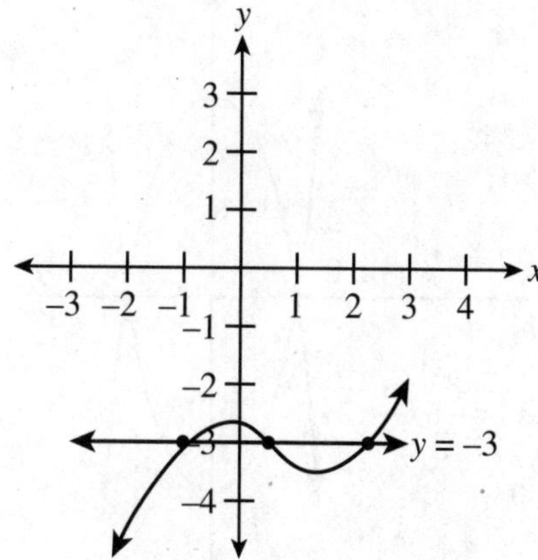

By inspection, the number of intersections is 3.

Function Interpretation and Manipulation

Drill 1

For multiple-choice questions, solve the problem and pick the correct answer from the provided choices. Each multiple-choice question has only one correct answer. For student-produced response questions, solve each problem and write down your answers separately.

1. If $m = 2x^3 + 3x - 11$ and $n = 4x^2 + 5x - 7$, what is $3n - m$ in terms of x?

   (A) $-2x^3 - 4x^2 - 2x - 18$
   (B) $-(2x^3 + 3x^2 - 5x - 6)$
   (C) $2x^3 - 12x^2 - 12x + 10$
   (D) $-2x^3 + 12x^2 + 12x - 10$

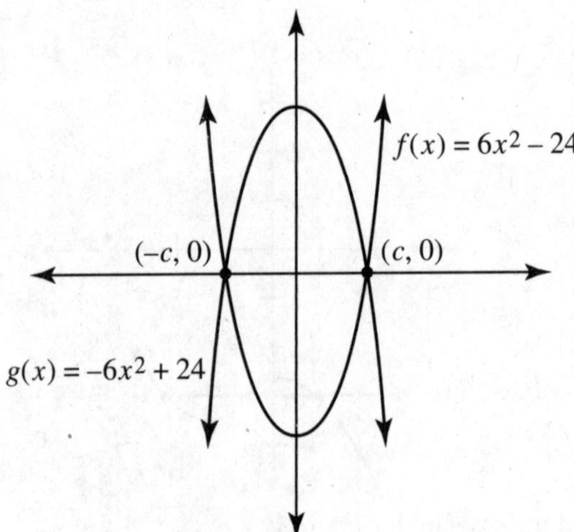

Note: Figure not drawn to scale

2. The functions f and g, defined by $f(x) = 6x^2 - 24$ and $g(x) = -6x^2 + 24$, are graphed in the xy-plane above. The graphs intersect at the points $(c, 0)$ and $(-c, 0)$. What is the value of c?

   (A) -2
   (B) 0
   (C) 2
   (D) 4

3. Conner needs to plan a production budget for a computer firm. In order to maximize profit, he needs to buy m computer frames at \$18.75 and r keyboards at \$13.25 each. If the cost of this transaction must be less than \$139.00, which of the following inequalities represents Conner's model for profit maximization?

   (A) $18.75m + 13.25r < 139$
   (B) $18.75m + 13.25r \leq 139$
   (C) $18.75r + 13.25m < 139$
   (D) $18.75r + 13.25m \leq 139$

4. Californians are very concerned about the continued drought conditions in their state. They are therefore curious about the price and quality of different water plans. A certain popular water plan charges a service fee of $31.50 per month. Each gallon of water used costs $0.17 per gallon plus a local tax of 7.3% (the monthly service charge is tax exempt). Which of the following functions models the monthly cost of the plan?

(A) $f(x) = (0.17x + 0.073)(31.5)$
(B) $f(x) = 31.5 + (0.073x)(0.17)$
(C) $f(x) = 31.5 + (1.073)(0.17 + x)$
(D) $f(x) = 31.5 + (1.073)(0.17x)$

5. Home values in America have increased since the 2008 slump in housing prices. Over the past six years, home prices have increased at an annual rate of 3.72%.

Which of the following functions models the increase in home values?

A = accumulated value of the home over time
P = the purchase price of the home
t = time in years
r = rate expressed as a decimal

(A) $A = P(0.0372)^t$
(B) $A = P(0.9628)^t$
(C) $A = P(1.0372)^t$
(D) $A = P(3.72)^t$

6. Home values in America have increased since the 2008 slump in housing prices. Over the past six years, home prices have increased at an annual rate of 3.72%. A home costing $187,650 purchased in 2010 would be worth how much in 2013?

(A) $194,455
(B) $205,996
(C) $209,380
(D) $217,357

$$h(x) = bx^2 + 30$$

7. For the function h defined above, b is a constant and $h(6) = 138$. What is the value of $h(-4)$?

(A) 24
(B) 64
(C) 78
(D) 86

8. Friendly Car Service charges a flat rate of $1.50 and $0.55 per mile. Mustafa has only $11 to spend on his ride. Write an inequality that represents the maximum distance that Mustafa can travel.

(A) $0.55m - 1.50 \leq 11$
(B) $0.55m + 1.50 \leq 11$
(C) $1.50m + 0.55 \geq 11$
(D) $0.55m + 1.50 \geq 11$

$$S(x) = \frac{3}{5x} + 60$$
$$D(x) = 240 - x$$

9. The quantity of a product supplied to the public and the quantity of a product that is demanded by the public are each functions of the product's price. The functions above model the estimated supply and demand of a particular product. The function $S(x)$ gives the quantity of the product supplied to the market when the price is x dollars, and the function $D(x)$ indicates the quantity of the product demanded when its price is x dollars.

   What will be the effect on the quantity of the product supplied to the market if the price of the product is increased by $15?

   (A) The quantity supplied will increase by 9 units.
   (B) The quantity supplied will decrease by 9 units.
   (C) The quantity supplied will increase by 36 units.
   (D) The quantity supplied will increase by 69 units.

$$S(x) = \frac{3}{5x} + 60$$
$$D(x) = 240 - x$$

10. The quantity of a product supplied to the public and the quantity of a product that is demanded by the public are each functions of the product's price. The functions above model the estimated supply and demand of a particular product. The function $S(x)$ gives the quantity of the product supplied to the market when the price is x dollars, and the function $D(x)$ indicates the quantity of the product demanded when its price is x dollars.

    At what price will the supply of the product be equal to the demand for the product?

    (A) $202.50
    (B) $180.00
    (C) $127.50
    (D) $112.50

Answer Explanations

1. **(D)** Substituting for m and n into $3n - m$ results in the following.

$$3(4x^2 + 5x - 7) - (2x^3 + 3x - 11) =$$
$$12x^2 + 15x - 21 - 2x^3 - 3x + 11$$

Combine like terms by adding and subtracting those terms with variables raised to the same power.

$$-2x^3 + 12x^2 + 12x - 10$$

2. **(C)** The two functions f and g intersect when their x- and y-values are the same. Set the functions equal and solve for x.

$$6x^2 - 24 = -6x^2 + 24$$

Add $6x^2$ and 24 to both sides to isolate x^2.

$$6x^2 - 24 + 6x^2 + 24 = -6x^2 + 24 + 6x^2 + 24$$
$$12x^2 = 48$$
$$x^2 = 4$$

Find the square root of each side of the equation.

$$x^2 = 4$$
$$x = \pm 2$$

Since we are looking for c rather than $-c$, its value is 2.

3. **(A)** The cost for m computers at \$18.75 each is \$18.75m. The cost for r keyboards at \$13.25 each is \$13.25r. The cost must be less than \$139.

$$18.75m + 13.25r < 139$$

4. **(D)** The cost of x gallons of water at \$0.17 per gallon is $0.17x$. The tax applied is found with $0.17x + (0.073)(0.17x)$, which can be rewritten as $(1.073)(0.17x)$. Add the monthly service charge to get

$$f(x) = 31.5 + (1.073)(0.17x)$$

5. **(C)** $A =$ accumulated value of the home over time; $P =$ the purchase price of the home; $t =$ time in years. The formula for the growth of the home over time is the exponential equation $A = P(1.0372)^t$. The addition of 1 and 0.0372 ensures growth in the calculations.

6. **(C)** Input the information provided in the question into the formula $A = P(1.0372)^t$. We substitute 3 for t because three years have elapsed from 2010 to 2013.

$$A = 187{,}650(1.0372)^3 = \$209{,}380$$

7. **(C)** Replace $h(x)$ with 138 and x with 6 to find b.

$$138 = b(6)^2 + 30$$
$$138 = 36b + 30$$
$$108 = 36b$$
$$3 = b$$

Replace b with 3 to find $h(-4)$.

$$h(-4) = 3(-4)^2 + 30$$
$$h(-4) = 78$$

8. **(B)** Let m equal the number of miles. Multiply m by the cost per mile, and add the fixed charge of \$1.50 per transaction.

$$0.55m + 1.50$$

This amount can be no more than \$11 since that is all the money that Mustafa has.

$$0.55m + 1.50 \leq 11$$

Choices (C) and (D) can be immediately eliminated as they express inequalities permitting costs no lower than \$11. Mustafa has only \$11 to spend.

9. **(A)** The quantity of the product supplied to the public is modeled by the function $S(x) = \frac{3}{5}x + 60$. If the price of the product is increased by \$15, the function becomes $S(x + 15) = \frac{3}{5}(x + 15) + 60$. To find the impact of increasing the price of the product by \$15, subtract $S(x)$ from $S(x + 15)$.

$$\begin{aligned} S(x + 15) &= \frac{3}{5}x + 9 + 60 \\ &= \frac{3}{5}x + 69 \\ S(x) &= \frac{3}{5}x + 60 \\ S(x + 15) - S(x) &= \left(\frac{3}{5}x + 69\right) - \left(\frac{3}{5}x + 60\right) = 9 \end{aligned}$$

An increase of \$15 in the price of the product yields an increase of 9 units of the product that is supplied to the public.

10. **(D)** To find the price of the product in which its demand equals supply, set the supply and demand functions equal to one another and solve for x.

$$\begin{aligned} S(x) &= \frac{3}{5}x + 60 \\ D(x) &= 240 - x \\ \frac{3}{5}x + 60 &= 240 - x \\ \frac{8}{5}x &= 180 \\ x &= \$112.50 \end{aligned}$$

Choices (A), (B), and (C) yield prices in which the supply and demand functions are not equal.

Drill 2

For multiple-choice questions, solve the problem and pick the correct answer from the provided choices. Each multiple-choice question has only one correct answer. For student-produced response questions, solve each problem and write down your answers separately.

1. The total area of a right circular cone can be expressed as $TA = \pi rs + \pi r^2$ where TA is the total area, r is the radius of the base, and s is the slant height. Which of the following expresses s in terms of TA and r?

   (A) $s = \frac{TA}{\pi r} - r$
   (B) $s = TA(\pi r - r)$
   (C) $s = (TA - r)^{\pi}$
   (D) $s = \frac{TA}{\pi r - r}$

2. Gina is saving money for a cross-country road trip with two of her friends. She currently has \$240 saved for the excursion and can save \$125 each month in the future. Which of the following expressions represents the amount of money Gina will have saved after m months?

   (A) $365m$
   (B) $125 + 240m$
   (C) $240 + 125m$
   (D) $365m + 240$

$$2{,}500\left[1 + \frac{r}{1{,}200}\right]^{12}$$

3. The expression shown above provides the sum of money, in dollars, that is earned in a year by an initial deposit of \$2,500 in a savings institution that pays an annual rate of r% compounded monthly. Which of the following expressions shows how much additional money is earned at an interest rate of 6% than at an interest rate of 3.2%?

   (A) $2{,}500\left[1 + \frac{6 - 3.2}{1{,}200}\right]^{12}$

   (B) $2{,}500\left[1 + \frac{\frac{6}{3.2}}{1{,}200}\right]^{12}$

   (C) $\dfrac{2{,}500\left[1 + \frac{6}{1{,}200}\right]^{12}}{2{,}500\left[1 + \frac{3.2}{1{,}200}\right]^{12}}$

   (D) $2{,}500\left[1 + \frac{6}{1{,}200}\right]^{12} - 2{,}500\left[1 + \frac{3.2}{1{,}200}\right]^{12}$

4. The standard form of an ellipse with major axis $2a$ in the xy-plane is $\frac{x^2}{a^2} + \frac{y^2}{b^2} = 1$. Which of the following expresses x in terms of y, a, and b?

(A) $x = \frac{(ab)^2}{y - x}$

(B) $x = \pm\sqrt{a^2 + b^2 - y^2}$

(C) $x = a^2 + b^2 - y^2$

(D) $x = \pm\frac{\sqrt{a^2b^2 - a^2y^2}}{b}$

$$P = -1.6x^2 + 2.6xy - 11.4$$

5. The equation above represents a profit function used by an event coordinator at a city museum. In the equation, P represents profit earned, x represents paid admissions ($x > 0$), and y is any rental discount that is offered. Which of the following represents y in terms of x and P?

(A) $y = \frac{1.6xP + 11.4}{2.6x}$

(B) $y = \frac{P + 1.6x^2 + 11.4}{2.6x}$

(C) $y = \frac{1.6x^2 + 11.4}{2.6x}$

(D) $y = \frac{P \pm \sqrt{2.6x}}{11.4}$

6. The density of an object is found by dividing the mass of the object by its volume. What is the volume, in milliliters, of an object with a mass of 48 grams and a density of 4 grams per milliliter?

(A) 12
(B) 14
(C) 16
(D) 24

7. A baseball is thrown into the air with an initial velocity of 64 feet per second. The formula $h(t) = 64t - 16t^2$ provides the height, h, of the baseball after t seconds.

What will be the height of the baseball 2.3 seconds after it was thrown?

(A) 71.43 feet
(B) 62.56 feet
(C) 53.69 feet
(D) 41.37 feet

8. A baseball is thrown into the air with an initial velocity of 64 feet per second. The formula $h(t) = 64t - 16t^2$ provides the height, h, of the baseball after t seconds.

To the nearest tenth of a second, how much time has elapsed when the ball is 41 feet above the ground?

(A) 3.2
(B) 2.1 and 3.6
(C) 0.8
(D) 0.8 and 3.2

$$(4{,}264 + 200m^2) + 6(12m^2 - 125)$$

9. The expression shown above can be written in the form of $am^2 + b$, where a and b are constants. What is the value of $2a + b$?

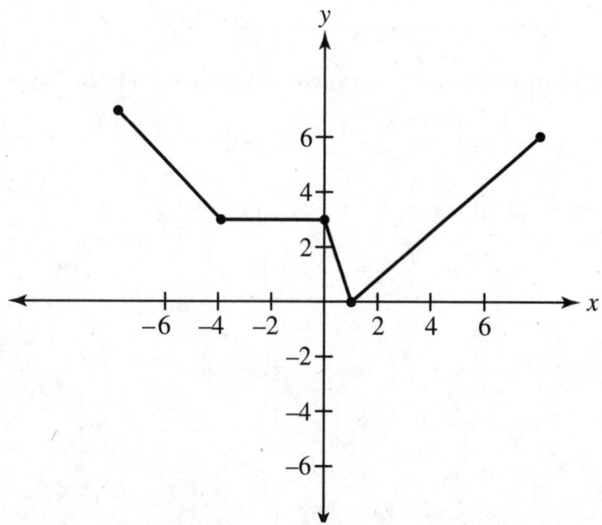

10. The complete graph of the function g is shown in the xy-plane above. What value of x yields the minimum value of $g(x)$?

(A) 0
(B) 1
(C) 2
(D) 5

Answer Explanations

1. **(A)** Begin isolating s by first factoring the greatest common factor.

$$TA = \pi rs + \pi r^2$$
$$TA = \pi r(s + r)$$

Divide both sides of the equation by πr.

$$\frac{TA}{\pi r} = \frac{\pi r(s + r)}{\pi r}$$
$$\frac{TA}{\pi r} = s + r$$

Subtract r from each side of the equation.

$$\frac{TA}{\pi r} - r = s + r - r$$
$$\frac{TA}{\pi r} - r = s$$

2. **(C)** Gina has \$240 saved, so that sum will be part of the answer. Each month, for m months, she will save \$125. Therefore, she will save an additional \$125m after m months. By adding the initial savings and the monthly accumulation of money, we arrive at $240 + 125m$ as the amount saved after m months.

3. **(D)** The formula indicates the amount of money earned at a savings institution on a $2,500 deposit, compounded monthly at r%. To find the additional dollars earned at 6% versus 3.2%, find the difference between the annual earnings at each rate.

$2{,}500\left[1+\frac{6}{1{,}200}\right]^{12}$ represents the amount earned each year at 6%.

$2{,}500\left[1+\frac{3.2}{1{,}200}\right]^{12}$ represents the amount earned at 3.2%.

Find their difference by subtracting the smaller expression from the larger.

$$2{,}500\left[1+\frac{6}{1{,}200}\right]^{12}-2{,}500\left[1+\frac{3.2}{1{,}200}\right]^{12}$$

4. **(D)** Begin isolating x by multiplying the equation by a^2b^2.

$$a^2b^2\left(\frac{x^2}{a^2}+\frac{y^2}{b^2}=1\right)$$
$$b^2x^2+a^2y^2=a^2b^2$$
$$b^2x^2=a^2b^2-a^2y^2$$
$$\frac{b^2x^2}{b^2}=\frac{a^2b^2-a^2y^2}{b^2}$$
$$x^2=\frac{a^2b^2-a^2y^2}{b^2}$$
$$\sqrt{x^2}=\pm\sqrt{\frac{a^2b^2-a^2y^2}{b^2}}$$
$$x=\pm\frac{\sqrt{a^2b^2-a^2y^2}}{b^2}$$

5. **(B)** Use the basic steps of algebra to isolate y.

STEP 1 Add $1.6x^2$ and 11.4 to both sides of the equation.

$$P=-1.6x^2+2.6xy-11.4$$
$$P+1.6x^2+11.4=-1.6x^2+2.6xy-11.4+1.6x^2+11.4$$
$$P+1.6x^2+11.4=2.6xy$$

STEP 2 Divide both sides of the equation by $2.6x$.

$$\frac{P+1.6x^2+11.4}{2.6x}=\frac{2.6xy}{2.6x}$$
$$\frac{P+1.6x^2+11.4}{2.6x}=y$$

6. **(A)** The density of an object is equal to the mass of the object divided by the volume of the object, which can be expressed as density = mass/volume. Thus, if an object has a density of 4 grams per milliliter and a mass of 48 grams, the equation becomes the following.

$$4=\frac{48}{V}$$
$$4V=48$$
$$V=12$$

The volume, then, is 12 milliliters/gram.

7. **(B)** Find $h(2.3)$.

$$h(2.3)=(64)(2.3)-(16)(2.3^2)=62.56\text{ feet}$$

8. **(D)** Replace $h(t)$ with 41.

$$41 = 64t - 16t^2$$

Set the equation equal to 0 and solve.

$$16t^2 - 64t + 41 = 0$$
$$a = 16, b = -64, c = 41$$
$$t = \frac{-b \pm \sqrt{b^2 - 4ac}}{2a}$$
$$t = \frac{-(-64) \pm \sqrt{(-64)^2 - 4(16)(41)}}{2(16)}$$
$$t = 0.8 \text{ and } t = 3.2$$

9. **4,058** Simplify $6(12m^2 - 125)$ and combine like terms.

$$(4{,}264 + 200m^2) + 6(12m^2 - 125)$$
$$4{,}264 + 200m^2 + 72m^2 - 750$$
$$272m^2 + 3{,}514$$

This calculation shows that $a = 272$ and $b = 3{,}514$. Therefore, $2a + b$ equals $2(272) + 3{,}514 = 4{,}058$.

10. **(B)** The minimum value of $g(x)$ occurs at $(1, 0)$ on the graph. The value of x, then, that yields the minimum value of $g(x)$ is 1.

Problem Solving and Data Analysis

The Problem Solving and Data Analysis portion of the SAT Math section will require the test taker to be proficient in the following skills:

- Ratios, rates, and proportional relationships
- Percentages
- One-variable data: distributions and measures of center and spread
- Two-variable data models and scatter plots
- Probability and conditional probability
- Inference from sample statistics and margin of error
- Evaluating statistical claims: observational studies and experiments

TIP

Many of the questions depict surveys conducted in certain environments. The test taker must be certain that survey respondents will be randomly selected and the surveys contain at least 50 respondents. In addition, be careful of biased communities. For example, if a city government surveyed people about the need for additional funds for dog parks, survey all groups. A survey conducted among a group of dog owners would likely be biased.

Measures of Center Drill

For multiple-choice questions, solve the problem and pick the correct answer from the provided choices. Each multiple-choice question has only one correct answer. For student-produced response questions, solve each problem and write down your answers separately.

1. There are nine students in a statistics class. After a recent test, the average (arithmetic mean) score was 79%. What must a tenth student's score be to raise the class average to 81%?

   (A) 87%
   (B) 89%
   (C) 94%
   (D) 99%

2. The average (arithmetic mean) of $2x - 4$, $x + 4$, and $3x - 6$ is $x + 4$. What is the value of $-2x + 3$?

   (A) -9
   (B) -6
   (C) 6
   (D) 12

3. At Santa Fe Elementary School, the 59 students in 4th grade participated in a canned food drive. The table below shows the number of cans contributed by each student.

Number of Cans per Student	Frequency
8	14
9	16
10	7
11	7
12	8
13	5
14	2

Which number of cans contains the median of this data set?

(A) 11
(B) 10
(C) 9
(D) 8

4. A world history class recently took its midterm exam. The following table represents the array of scores.

		x	x	
		x	x	
x		x	x	
x	x	x	x	x
20%	**40%**	**60%**	**80%**	**100%**

If a thirteenth student took the exam the next day, what must that score be to arrive at a class mean score of 60%?

5. Seven students draw numbered cards, each with a value that is a positive integer. The mean of their selections is 14. What is the largest number any student could have drawn?

(A) 92
(B) 70
(C) 28
(D) 14

6. Seven people each select an index card. Every card has a positive integer printed on one side. If the mean value of the cards is 15, what is the greatest value any one card can have?

(A) 69
(B) 79
(C) 89
(D) 99

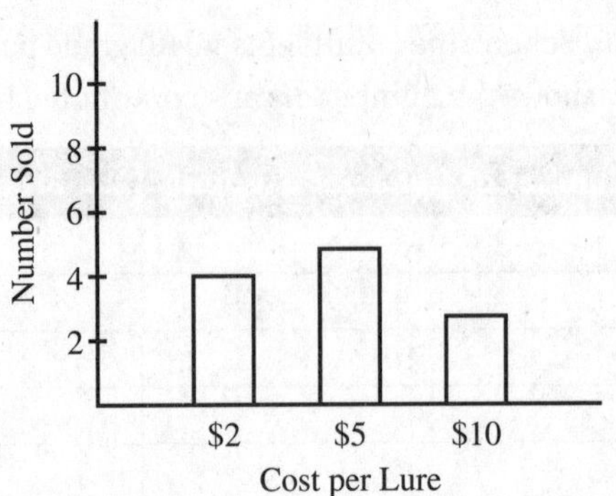

7. The bar graph above represents the fishing lures sold in a sales competition sponsored by the seller. What is the median cost of the lures sold?

8. If x is the average (arithmetic mean) of $2p$ and 12, y is the average of $5p$ and 18, and z is the average of $8p - 6$, what is the average of x, y, and z in terms of p?

(A) $5p + 8$
(B) $3p + 6$
(C) $p + 12$
(D) $p + 6$

Percent of Homeowners Using Solar Power
Fort Myers, Florida

District	Percent of Homeowners Using Solar Power
1	28.1
2	13.6
3	38.3
4	17.9
5	11.6
6	17.4
7	22.0

9. An analysis of all homeowners in Fort Myers, Florida, was conducted to determine the percentage of those who use solar power for their electrical needs. The city has 27 districts, of which 7 are listed in the table above. The median percent of all homeowners who use solar power in Fort Myers is 16.8%. What is the difference between the median of the 7 districts listed above and the median percent of the entire city?

(A) 26.7%
(B) 4.5%
(C) 2.3%
(D) 1.1%

10. If M represents the number of prime numbers less than 25 and r is their range, what is $2M - r$?

 (A) −3
 (B) 3
 (C) 8.9
 (D) 27

Answer Explanations

1. **(D)** If nine students earned an average score of 79%, the class amassed 711 points because $9 \times 79 = 711$. In order for ten students to have an average score of 81, the class must collect 810 points because $10 \times 81 = 810$. By subtracting we get $810 - 711 = 99$. The tenth student must earn a score of 99% to raise the class average to 81%.

2. **(A)** Add the three terms and divide the sum by 3. Set this value equal to $x + 4$, which is the average.

$$\frac{2x - 4 + x + 4 + 3x - 6}{3} = x + 4$$
$$\frac{6x - 6}{3} = x + 4$$
$$6x - 6 = 3x + 12$$
$$3x = 18$$
$$x = 6$$

 Replace x with 6 in $-2x + 3$.

$$-2(6) + 3 = -9$$

3. **(C)** You are told that 59 students participated in the canned food drive. The table arranges the number of cans per student in ascending order. Thus, the median student contribution is the number of cans contributed by the 30th student. Add the frequency of contributions until you arrive at the 30th student.

Number of Cans per Student	Frequency
8	14
9	16

 Adding 14 and 16 yields a total of 30. The 30th student lies in the category of students who contributed 9 cans each.

4. **40** Add the scores of all 12 of the students.

$$(2 \times 20) + (1 \times 40) + (4 \times 60) + (4 \times 80) + (1 \times 100) = 740$$

 In order for 13 students to average 60%, the class must amass 780 points.

$$13 \times 60 = 780$$

 Since the first 12 students accumulated 740 points, the thirteenth student must score a 40% on the test.

$$780 - 740 = 40$$

5. **(A)** Find the sum of the cards by multiplying the mean by the number of cards.

$$7 \times 14 = 98$$

To maximize the value of a single card, minimize the value of the other cards by assigning each a value of 1:

$$1 + 1 + 1 + 1 + 1 + 1 + 92 = 98$$

6. **(D)** Since 7 cards have a mean value of 15, their sum is 105.

$$7 \times 15 = 105$$

If 6 of the cards have the number 1 on them, then 1 card would have 99.

$$105 - (6 \times 1) = 99$$

7. **5** The median of a data set is the middle value when the data are arranged in order. Array the number of lures sold; there are four \$2 lures, five \$5 lures, and three \$10 lures.

2 2 2 2 5 5 5 5 5 10 10 10

The middle numbers are both 5, so find their mean.

$$(5 + 5) \div 2 = 5$$

8. **(A)** Find the average of x, y, and z by calculating their sum and dividing by 3.

$$\frac{(2p + 12) + (5p + 18) + (8p - 6)}{3} = \frac{15p + 24}{3} = 5p + 8$$

9. **(D)** Arrange the percentages in the table in ascending order.

11.6 13.6 17.4 17.9 22.0 28.1 38.3

The median of the data shown is 17.9% because it is the middle term. Subtract 16.8%, the median of all homeowners in Fort Myers, from 17.9%.

$$17.9\% - 16.8\% = 1.1\%$$

10. **(A)** The prime numbers less than 25 are 2, 3, 5, 7, 11, 13, 17, 19, 23. There are nine prime numbers less than 25, so $M = 9$. Find the range of this set of numbers by subtracting the lowest value from the highest.

$$23 - 2 = 21$$

The range of the numbers is 21, so $r = 21$.

$$2M - r = 2(9) - 21 = -3$$

Unit Conversion Drill

For multiple-choice questions, solve the problem and pick the correct answer from the provided choices. Each multiple-choice question has only one correct answer. For student-produced response questions, solve each problem and write down your answers separately.

1. Jenna needs to take a taxicab ride in Chicago to go to an important job interview. The taxi service she has selected provides the following fee schedule.

   First $\frac{1}{4}$ mile: \$2.00

   Each $\frac{1}{4}$ mile after: \$1.25

   Excluding a tip, Jenna's fare was \$15.75. How many miles did she travel?

   (A) 2
   (B) 2.5
   (C) 2.75
   (D) 3

2. Gold has always been coveted for its aesthetic qualities. However, due to its malleability, it also has many industrial and electronic applications. Gold can be stretched so thinly that a single ounce can cover 100 square yards of surface. How many square feet can be covered with 2.5 ounces of gold?

   (A) 2,250 square feet
   (B) 1,125 square feet
   (C) 750 square feet
   (D) 150 square feet

3. The legend on a map shows that 1 inch = 80 miles. The distance on a map shows that Hartford, Connecticut, and Roanoke, Virginia, are 5.05 inches apart. What is the actual distance between the two cities?

   (A) 80 miles
   (B) 205 miles
   (C) 395 miles
   (D) 404 miles

4. Homeowners want to create a circular rock garden that measures 20 feet in diameter. Reference materials state that the space for the garden needs to be 3″ deep. The rocks they wish to buy cost \$80 per cubic yard and must be purchased in whole cubic yards. How much will they have to spend on rocks?

   (A) \$480
   (B) \$400
   (C) \$320
   (D) \$240

	BMI
Underweight	Below 18.5
Normal	18.5–24.9
Overweight	25.0–29.9
Obese	30.0 and above

5. Body mass index (BMI) is a calculation that measures obesity and the potential for serious health risks such as strokes and heart attacks. The BMI can be found by using the following formula.

$$\frac{\text{weight (pounds)}}{\text{height}^2\text{ (inches)}} \times 703$$

What is the category of BMI of a patient who weighs 182 pounds and is 5′10″?

(A) Underweight
(B) Normal
(C) Overweight
(D) Obese

	BMI
Underweight	Below 18.5
Normal	18.5–24.9
Overweight	25.0–29.9
Obese	30.0 and above

6. Body mass index is a calculation that measures obesity and the potential for serious health risks such as strokes and heart attacks. The BMI can be found by using the following formula.

$$\frac{\text{weight (pounds)}}{\text{height}^2\text{ (inches)}} \times 703$$

What is the weight of a patient who is 6 feet tall and has the lowest BMI that is categorized as obese? (Round to the nearest pound.)

(A) 194
(B) 221
(C) 231
(D) 241

1 hectogram = 100 grams
100 centigrams = 1 gram

7. A popular snack is packaged in 2-hectogram containers. If a customer ate $\frac{1}{4}$ of one of these containers, how many centigrams did the customer consume?

(A) 50
(B) 100
(C) 1,000
(D) 5,000

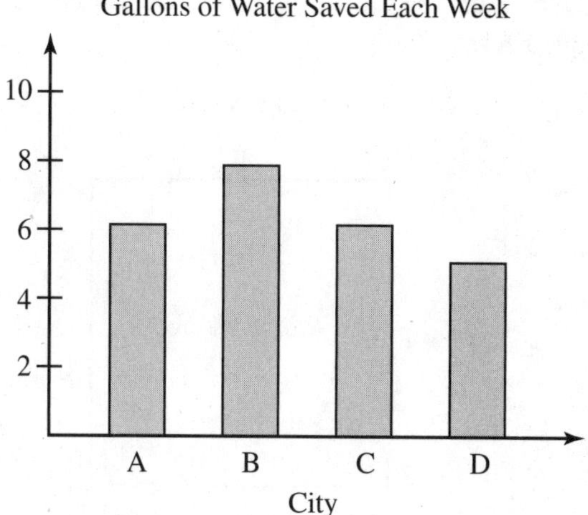

8. Certain cities in the southwestern United States are experimenting with water-saving plumbing. If the total gallons saved as expressed in the graph above equal 25,000 gallons, what is an appropriate label for the vertical axis?

(A) Gallons saved (in tens)
(B) Gallons saved (in hundreds)
(C) Gallons saved (in thousands)
(D) Gallons saved (in hundred thousands)

9. On July 15, 2015, the *New Horizons* planet orbiter transmitted its first pictures of minor planet Pluto. Pluto is approximately 3 billion miles distant from Earth. If the transmission of the photographs traveled at the speed of light, to the nearest hundredth, how many hours did it take for the photographs to reach Earth from Pluto? (Note: light travels 186,000 miles per second)

10. The specific gravity of a substance is the ratio of the weight of the substance compared weight to the volume of an equal weight of water. If water weighs 62.5 pounds per cubic foot, what is the weight in pounds per cubic foot of a liquid that has a specific gravity of 3?

(A) 0.047
(B) 130
(C) 187.5
(D) 260

Answer Explanations

1. **(D)** Subtract \$2.00 from \$15.75 to count the first quarter mile.

$$\$15.75 - \$2.00 = \$13.75$$

Divide \$13.75 by \$1.25 to calculate the remaining quarter miles.

$$\$13.75 \div \$1.25 = 11$$

The taxi traveled a total of 12 quarter miles. Divide 12 by 4 to find the equivalent number of miles.

$$12 \div 4 = 3$$

2. **(A)** An ounce of gold covers 100 square yards of surface, but the question requires the answer to be in square feet.

$$1 \text{ yard} = 3 \text{ feet}$$

30′

30′ Area = 900 feet²

100 square yards is equivalent to 900 square feet, so one ounce of gold covers 900 square feet. Multiply 900 by 2.5 to find the area covered by 2.5 ounces of gold.

$$2.5 \times 900 = 2{,}250 \text{ square feet}$$

3. **(D)** Use the proportion $\frac{\text{map distance}}{\text{actual distance}} = \frac{\text{map distance}}{\text{actual distance}}$ to answer the question.

$$\frac{1}{80} = \frac{5.05}{d}$$

$$1 \times d = 80 \times 5.05$$

$$d = 404$$

The distance between Hartford and Roanoke is 404 miles. Choice (A) can be immediately eliminated; 1 inch = 80 miles and the map shows 5.05 inches.

4. **(D)** Convert everything into yards.

$$3 \text{ inches} = 0.08 \text{ yards}$$

$$10\text{-foot radius} = 3.33 \text{ yards}$$

$$\pi = 3.14$$

Use the formula $V = \pi r^2 h$, the volume of a cylinder, to determine how much rock is needed if 3.33 yards is the radius and 0.08 yards is the height.

$$3.14 \times 3.33^2 \times 0.08 = 3.14 \times 11.09 \times 0.08 = 2.79 \text{ cubic yards}$$

Rounding to the nearest cubic yard, the homeowners must purchase 3 cubic yards of rock.

$$3 \text{ cubic yards} \times \$80 = \$240$$

5. **(C)** Use the BMI formula with the provided data to assess the patient's BMI number. Remember to convert the height to inches: 5 feet 10 inches equals 70 inches.

$$\frac{182}{70^2} \times 703 = 26.11$$

A patient with a BMI of 26.11 is classified as overweight.

6. **(B)** Use the BMI formula with the provided data to assess the patient's BMI weight. Remember to convert the height to inches: 6 feet equals 72 inches. The lowest BMI categorized as obese is 30.0. Let $x =$ the patient's weight.

$$\frac{x}{72^2} \times 703 = 30$$
$$0.136x = 30$$
$$x \approx 221$$

7. **(D)** One hectogram equals 100 grams, so 2 hectograms equal 200 grams. The customer consumed $\frac{1}{4}$ of one container, so 50 grams of the snack was consumed.

$$\frac{1}{4} \times 200 = 50$$

Each gram equals 100 centigrams, so multiply 50 by 100 to find the amount consumed expressed as centigrams.

$$50 \times 100 = 5{,}000$$

8. **(C)** The sum of the measures of the bars in the graph is 25 units. Given that the four cities saved 25,000 gallons of water, the vertical axis should read *Gallons saved (in thousands)* because $25{,}000 \div 25 = 1{,}000$.

9. **4.48** Find the quotient of 3 billion and 186,000 to find the number of seconds elapsed between the transmission and reception of the photos (these are known as "light-seconds").

$$3{,}000{,}000{,}000 \div 186{,}000 = 16{,}129 \text{ seconds}$$

There are 60 seconds in a minute and 60 minutes in an hour, so there are 3,600 seconds in one hour ($60 \times 60 = 3{,}600$). Divide 16,129 by 3,600 to find the number of hours needed to successfully transmit photographs from Pluto to Earth.

$$16{,}129 \div 3{,}600 = 4.48 \text{ hours}$$

10. **(C)** Use the ratio $\frac{62.5 \text{ pounds}}{1 \text{ cubic foot}}$ to find the weight of a liquid that has a specific gravity of 3.

$$\frac{62.5}{1} = \frac{x}{3}$$
$$(3)(62.5) = x$$
$$187.5 = x$$

Percentages

Drill 1

For multiple-choice questions, solve the problem and pick the correct answer from the provided choices. Each multiple-choice question has only one correct answer. For student-produced response questions, solve each problem and write down your answers separately.

1. The Environmental Protection Agency (EPA) has demonstrated that newer automobile emission standards have had a strong positive correlation with cleaner air in large metropolitan areas. Thus, it is the EPA's responsibility to get older cars off the road.

Cars in Operation in 1997

Age of Car	Millions of Cars
<3 years old	21.5
3–5 years old	29.9
6–8 years old	22.2
9–11 years old	16.7
≥12 years old	14.4

What percent of cars in operation in 1997 were between 6 and 11 years old?

(A) 37.2
(B) 41.3
(C) 48.1
(D) 53.2

2. A retailer was unable to sell all of her sofas, so she reduced the price of a sofa by 40%. Once she saw the sofas were beginning to sell, she increased the price by 40%. After the 40% price increase, what percent is the new price of the original price?

(A) 100%
(B) 84%
(C) 75%
(D) 60%

Rank	Country	GDP–per capita (US$)
1	Liechtenstein	141,100
2	Qatar	104,300
3	Luxembourg	81,100
4	Bermuda	69,900
5	Monaco	63,400
6	Singapore	60,500
7	Jersey	57,000
8	Falkland Islands (Islas Malvinas)	55,400
9	Norway	54,200
10	Brunei	50,000

3. The gross domestic product (GDP) is a measure of a country's wealth. The per capita income for a country is found by dividing the sum of all the goods and services that a country produces by the country's population. Which country exceeded the per capita income of Singapore by approximately 4.8%?

(A) Qatar
(B) Monaco
(C) Bermuda
(D) Norway

4. A customer service call center for a credit card company asks 1 in 8 of the callers to take a survey at the conclusion of the call. Approximately 20% of those solicited consent to the survey. If 400 callers were serviced between 2:00 and 3:00 one afternoon and 20% of the callers consented to the survey, how many callers did not consent to the survey?

(A) 20
(B) 30
(C) 35
(D) 40

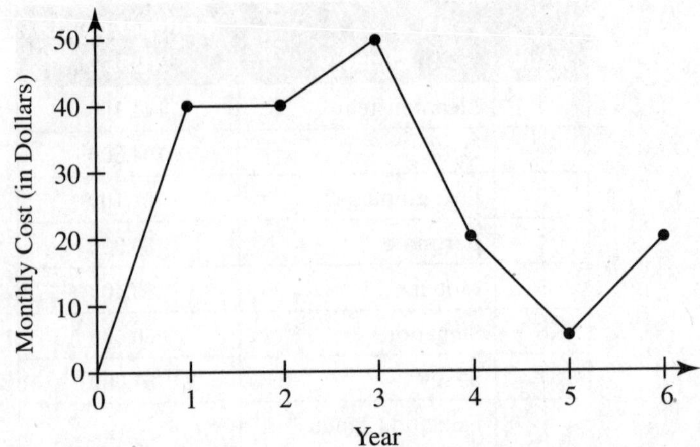

5. The monthly costs of certain internet plans have varied greatly over the six-year period as illustrated in the graph. What was the largest percent drop in price from one year to another?

(A) 25
(B) 50
(C) 75
(D) 85
(E)

6. A recent marathon featured runners of many different ages. The table below shows a listing of the participants as categorized by age and place in the race.

Age	Under 20	20–29	30–39	40–49	50–69	70 and Over	Total
Top 10 finisher	2	6	1	1	0	0	10
Finished in places 11 to 40	11	11	5	3	0	0	30
Finished after 40th place	5	8	23	31	43	12	122
Total	18	25	29	35	43	12	162

What percent of the top forty finishers came from the 30 to 39 age group?

(A) 8%
(B) 10%
(C) 15%
(D) 18%

7. A recent marathon featured runners of many different ages. The table below shows a listing of the participants as categorized by age and place in the race.

Age	Under 20	20–29	30–39	40–49	50–69	70 and Over	Total
Top 10 finisher	2	6	1	1	0	0	10
Finished in places 11 to 40	11	11	5	3	0	0	30
Finished after 40th place	5	8	23	31	43	12	122
Total	18	25	29	35	43	12	162

What is the difference between the percent of runners under 20 years of age who finished in places 11 to 40 and the percent of runners aged 40 to 49 who also finished in places 11 to 40?

(A) 52.5%
(B) 46.4%
(C) 34.2%
(D) 31.1%

AP Tests Taken

Gender	U.S. History	Literature	French	Total
Male	42	31	12	85
Female	33	42	26	101
Total	75	75	38	186

8. The table above shows the number of 11th-grade students at a local high school who took the following AP tests: U.S. History, Literature, and French. Which category accounts for approximately 17.7% of the test takers?

(A) Males taking the U.S. History test
(B) Males taking the French test
(C) Females taking the Literature test
(D) Females taking the U.S. History test

9. Briana bought a pair of running shoes at a 25% discount off the original price. The total she paid the cashier was r dollars, which includes an 8% sales tax on the discounted price. Which of the following represents the original price of the running shoes in terms of r?

(A) $0.81r$
(B) $\frac{r}{0.75}$
(C) $(0.75)(1.08)r$
(D) $\frac{r}{(1.08)(0.75)}$

10. A pair of hiking boots sells for $80.00. After one week, the vendor reduced the cost of the boots by 20%. After two weeks, he raised the current price by 20%. What is the cost of the hiking boots after two weeks? (Ignore the $ sign.)

Answer Explanations

1. **(A)** Use the formula $\frac{\text{part}}{\text{whole}} = \frac{n}{100}$ to find the percent of those operating cars that were 6 to 11 years old.

$$6\text{–}8{:}\ 22.2$$
$$9\text{–}11{:}\ 16.7$$

The number of cars (in millions) that are between 6 and 11 years old is 38.9.

$$22.2 + 16.7 = 38.9$$

Total cars (in millions): 104.7

$$\frac{3.89}{104.7} = \frac{n}{100}$$

Cross-multiply and solve for n.

$$104.7n = 38{,}900$$
$$n = 37.2\%$$

2. **(B)** To facilitate making calculations, assume the original price was \$100. Find the price after the reduction.

$$100 - (0.40)(100) = 60$$

Next, find the price after the increase.

$$60 + (0.40)(60) = 84$$

The new price is $\frac{84}{100}$ of the original price, which is 84%.

3. **(B)** The per-capita income of Singapore is \$60,500. Multiply that value by 0.048 and add it to \$60,500.

$$\$60{,}500 + (0.048)(\$60{,}500) = \$63{,}404$$

At \$63,400, Monaco's per capita income is closest to this value.

4. **(D)** If 1 in 8 callers were solicited for the survey, then one-eighth of the callers were asked to participate. Thus, one-eighth of 400 callers is 50 callers. Since 20% of the callers consented to the survey, then 80% did not want to take part. Find 80% of 50 by multiplying 50 by 0.8.

$$50 \times 0.8 = 40$$

5. **(C)** The greatest drop, as a percentage, occurred between years 4 and 5.

Year 4: \$20

Year 5: \$5

Use the formula $\frac{\text{decrease}}{\text{original}} = \frac{n}{100}$ to find the percent decrease.

$$\frac{15}{20} = \frac{n}{100}$$
$$20n = 1{,}500$$
$$n = 75\%$$

6. **(C)** Of the runners who placed in the top 40, 6 were in the age group of 30 to 39. One runner in that age group finished in the top 10, and 5 others finished somewhere in places between 11 and 40. Divide 6 by 40 to get 0.15, which, when expressed as a percent, is 15%.

7. **(A)** The number of runners under 20 years of age who placed in positions 11 through 40 was 11. Given that the total number of runners in that age group was 18, the percent who finished in places 11 through 40 is 61.1%. The number of runners between the ages of 40 and 49 who also finished in places 11 through 40 was 3. Given that a total of 35 runners were in this category, the percent of those runners who finished in places 11 through 40 was 8.6%. The difference between 61.1% and 8.6% is 52.5%.

8. **(D)** Find 17.7% of 186, which is the total number of students who took the AP tests.

$$(0.177)(186) = 32.92$$

9. **(D)** Let x be the original price of the running shoes, in dollars. The discounted price is 25 percent off the original price, so $x - 0.25x = 0.75x$ is the discounted price, in dollars. The tax is 8 percent of the discounted price, so $0.08(0.75x)$ is the tax on the purchase, in dollars. The price r, in dollars, that Briana paid the cashier is the sum of the discounted price and the tax.

$$r = 0.75x + (0.08)(0.75x)$$

This can be rewritten as $r = 1.08(0.75x)$. Therefore, the original price, x, of the running shoes, in dollars, can be written as $\frac{r}{(1.08)(0.75)}$.

10. **76.8** Find the cost of the boots after one week.

$$\$80.00 - (0.20)(\$80.00) = \$64.00$$

Add 20% to \$64.00 to find the cost after two weeks.

$$\$64.00 + (0.20)(\$64.00) = \$76.80$$

Drill 2

For multiple-choice questions, solve the problem and pick the correct answer from the provided choices. Each multiple-choice question has only one correct answer. For student-produced response questions, solve each problem and write down your answers separately.

1. What number is 175% of 144?

(A) 252
(B) 192
(C) 108
(D) 82.3

2. A high school's 10th, 11th, and 12th grades represent 78% of the student body. What fraction of the student body is the freshman class?

(A) $\frac{39}{50}$
(B) $\frac{67}{100}$
(C) $\frac{11}{50}$
(D) $\frac{1}{50}$

3. Sean owed p dollars for a loan he secured for college expenses. He promised to pay off the debt in monthly installments, with each installment equal to 20% of the existing debt. After two monthly payments, which expression reflects the balance due on his loan?

(A) $0.8p$
(B) $0.64p$
(C) $0.6p$
(D) $0.48p$

4. Connor surveyed a random sample of 80 students in his class regarding the need for additional crosswalks at the school. Only 15.6% of the students felt they were necessary. Of the 320 students in his sophomore class, about how many would favor additional crosswalks?

(A) 50
(B) 58
(C) 71
(D) 74

Year	Hits
2021	2,150
2022	3,230

5. Steve's website statistics page shows the number of hits the website received in 2021 and 2022 as shown in the table above. He believes the percentage increase from 2021 to 2022 will be triple the percentage increase from 2022 to 2023. If Steve is correct, which of the following is closest to the website's projected hits in 2023?

   (A) 1,925
   (B) 2,150
   (C) 3,770
   (D) 4,430

6. Roasted asparagus (134 grams) provides the percentages of minimum daily nutritional requirements shown in the table below.

Nutrient	Percentage of Daily Requirement
Vitamin A	20
Calcium	3
Vitamin D	0
Vitamin B_{12}	0
Vitamin C	12
Iron	16
Vitamin B_6	5
Magnesium	5
Protein	9

   A red bell pepper (92 grams) provides approximately 123% of the daily minimum requirement of vitamin C. Which of the following is closest to the number of grams of roasted asparagus that is equivalent to this amount?

   (A) 1,600
   (B) 1,400
   (C) 1,200
   (D) 1,000

7. Roasted asparagus (134 grams) provides the percentages of minimum daily nutritional requirements shown in the table below.

Nutrient	Percentage of Daily Requirement
Vitamin A	20
Calcium	3
Vitamin D	0
Vitamin B_{12}	0
Vitamin C	12
Iron	16
Vitamin B_6	5
Magnesium	5
Protein	9

Which of the following is closest to the number of grams of roasted asparagus needed to fulfill a person's minimum daily requirement of iron?

(A) 800
(B) 1,000
(C) 1,200
(D) 1,600

8. Nutritionists recommend the daily consumption of 4,700 milligrams of potassium. Men generally consume 3,200 milligrams per day, and women consume about 2,300 milligrams per day. The table below shows a list of potassium-rich foods as recommended by nutrition experts.

Foods with Potassium	Serving Size	Potassium (mg)
Apricots, dried	10 halves	407
Avocados, raw	1 ounce	180
Bananas, raw	1 cup	594
Beets, cooked	1 cup	519
Brussel sprouts, cooked	1 cup	504
Cantaloupe	1 cup	494
Dates, dry	5 dates	271
Figs, dry	2 figs	271
Kiwifruit, raw	1 medium	252
Lima beans	1 cup	955
Melons, honeydew	1 cup	461
Milk, fat free or skim	1 cup	407
Nectarines	1 nectarine	288
Orange juice	1 cup	496
Oranges	1 orange	237
Pears (fresh)	1 pear	208
Peanuts, dry roasted, unsalted	1 ounce	187
Potatoes, baked	1 potato	1,081
Prune juice	1 cup	707
Prunes, dried	1 cup	828
Raisins	1 cup	1,089
Spinach, cooked	1 cup	839
Tomato products, canned sauce	1 cup	909
Winter squash	1 cup	896
Yogurt, plain, skim milk	8 ounces	579

Jake read that the headaches he was enduring after running were caused by potassium depletion. Although he was consuming 3,200 milligrams of potassium daily, he was told he needed at least 10% more potassium than was recommended by nutritionists. To accrue this amount, Jake has decided to consume an extra potato and a cup of lima beans in his daily diet. If he consumes these extra items each day, how much more potassium will he consume than is recommended for his augmented need of this nutrient?

9. A supermarket chain received an average grade (arithmetic mean) of 65% customer satisfaction from 10 recent customer surveys. The chain manager wants to earn at least an 80% rating from its first 20 customer surveys. What is the lowest score the 17th survey can receive and still achieve the 80% satisfaction rate from its first 20 surveys? (Omit the percent sign.)

10. The sum of three numbers is 780. One of the numbers, n, is 50% more than the sum of the other two numbers. What is the value of n?

(A) 144
(B) 312
(C) 424
(D) 468

Answer Explanations

1. **(A)** 175% of a number is greater than 100% of a number. Thus, eliminate choices (C) and (D) as they are less than 144. Let x represent the unknown number. Convert 175% to a calculator friendly 1.75.

$$(1.75)(144) = x$$
$$252 = x$$

2. **(C)** Begin by finding the percent of the class represented by the freshman class.

$$100\% - 78\% = 22\%$$

Convert 22% into a fraction and simplify.

$$22\% = \frac{22}{100} = \frac{11}{50}$$

3. **(B)** After the first month of paying off 20% of his student loan, Sean's remaining balance looks like this.

$$p - 0.2p = 0.8p$$

Sean's loan balance after one month was $0.8p$. He now must pay off 20% of the $0.8p$ that remains as the loan balance.

$$0.8p - (0.2)(.8p) = 0.64p$$

4. **(A)** The survey size of 80 is sizable enough to draw conclusions about the class in general. Since 15.6% of the surveyed students felt that additional crosswalks were necessary, that fraction of the entire class will probably feel the same way.

Find 15.6% of 320.

$$320(0.156) = 49.92$$

Round the answer to 50 students who can be expected to favor additional crosswalks.

5. **(C)** Find the percent increase of hits from 2021 to 2022.

$$\frac{\text{increase}}{\text{original}} = \frac{x}{100}$$

Find the increase from 2021 to 2022.

$$3{,}230 - 2{,}150 = 1{,}080$$
$$\frac{1{,}080}{2{,}150} = \frac{x}{100}$$
$$x = 50.2\%$$

Steve believes the 50.2% increase is triple the projected increase from 2022 to 2023. Thus, divide 50.2% by 3 to get the expected increase from those years.

$$50.2\% \div 3 = 16.7\%$$

Multiply the 2022 figure by 1.167 to find the expected hits on the website in 2023.

$$3{,}230 \times 1.167 = 3{,}769$$

Choice (C), 3,770, is closest to this answer.

6. **(B)** Find the number of servings of roasted asparagus that provide the same nutritional value of vitamin C as one serving of a red bell pepper.

$$123\% \div 12\% = 10.25$$

It takes 10.25 servings of roasted asparagus to equal the amount of vitamin C in one serving of red bell pepper. Multiply the grams in one serving of roasted asparagus, 134, by 10.25.

$$134 \times 10.25 = 1{,}373.5$$

Choice (B), 1,400, is closest to this value.

7. **(A)** Satisfying the minimum daily requirement means 100% of that nutrient has been consumed in a day. Since one serving of roasted asparagus provides 16% of the daily iron requirement, divide 100% by 16% to determine the number of servings needed each day.

$$100 \div 16 = 6.25$$

A person needs 6.25 servings of roasted asparagus to satisfy the minimum daily requirement of iron. Multiply 6.25 by 134 to find the number of grams of roasted asparagus needed to reach this goal.

$$134 \times 6.25 = 837.5$$

Of the selections provided, choice (A), 800, is closest to this value.

8. **66** Although the suggested consumption of potassium for men is 4,700 milligrams, Jake's daily running indicates he needs an additional 10% above the norm. Multiply 4,700 by 1.1 to find the potassium requirement for Jake because of his running.

$$4{,}700 \times 1.1 = 5{,}170$$

Jake currently consumes 3,200 milligrams, so he needs an additional 1,970 milligrams. By adding an extra potato and a cup of lima beans, he will add $1{,}081 + 955 = 2{,}036$ milligrams of potassium. Since he needs 1,970 milligrams, the addition of these new foods will provide $2{,}036 - 1{,}970 = 66$ milligrams more than is necessary.

9. **50** The supermarket chain manager wants to earn an 80% customer service rating from its first 20 customer service surveys. Multiply 20 by 80 to get 1,600, the total number of additional percentage points to be amassed. We found that the first 10 reviews yielded an average score of 65% or $10 \times 65 = 650$ percentage points. By subtracting 650 from 1,600 we get 950, the total number of percentage points to be amassed to earn the overall 80% rating. The question asks what could be the lowest the 17th survey could earn and still achieve the goal of 80% customer satisfaction from the first 20 surveys. Suppose all of the surveys from 11 through 16 and 18 through 20 gave the chain a score of 100%. That would mean those 9 customers added 900 points to the total. Given that we need 950 points from the final 10 customers, the 17th survey could score the chain as low as 50% and the chain would still receive an 80% average from the first 20 surveys.

10. **(D)** If n is the largest of the three numbers, then $780 - n$ is the sum of the other two. Since n is 50% greater than the sum of the smaller numbers, we arrive at the following.

$$n = 1.5(780 - n)$$

$$n = 1{,}170 - 1.5n$$

$$2.5n = 1{,}170$$

$$n = 468$$

$$(0.6)(780) = 468$$

Surveys Drill

For multiple-choice questions, solve the problem and pick the correct answer from the provided choices. Each multiple-choice question has only one correct answer. For student-produced response questions, solve each problem and write down your answers separately.

1. Sammie has done a survey of one hundred 16-year-old Florida students and found that 84% favored including an internship in their schools' curricula. She finds, however, that the margin of error in her survey is 6.9%. What can she do to reduce the margin of error?

   (A) Check similar surveys in other states
   (B) Reduce the survey size
   (C) Increase the survey size
   (D) Survey other age groups as well

2. Pham is interested in starting a 4-H Club at her high school. She randomly sampled a group of 200 students and found that 31.5% of the students in her sample thought that starting a club was a good idea. If her high school has 1,145 students enrolled, approximately how many will consider that starting the 4-H Club was a good idea?

   (A) 360
   (B) 340
   (C) 280
   (D) 225

3. Shameka took a survey of 90 randomly chosen tenth graders to see if they would prefer a year-round school year. The survey results showed that approximately 41.1% of the tenth graders preferred the year-round schedule. If there are 245 tenth graders at the school, how many can be expected to prefer the year-round schedule? (Round your answer to the nearest student.)

   (A) 101
   (B) 100
   (C) 96
   (D) 86

4. A survey of 150 randomly chosen adults in Amarillo, Texas, found that 13.2% prefer electric heat over gas heat. If there are 111,115 adults in Amarillo, how many adults will not prefer electric heat?

   (A) 14,667
   (B) 36,561
   (C) 96,448
   (D) 111,115

5. In a survey of 180 randomly chosen dog owners, 54 preferred Daisy's Dog Treats over another brand. If city A, where the survey was taken, has 4,840 dog owners, approximately how many would likely prefer Daisy's Dog Treats?

(A) 3,388
(B) 2,447
(C) 1,467
(D) 1,452

6. At a busy park, 124 people were surveyed to discern if additional city funds should be provided for additional parks. Of the 124 surveys, 11 chose not to respond. Which factor indicates the survey results will not be reliable?

(A) The weather on the day the survey was given
(B) The percentage of surveys that showed a response
(C) The number of surveys that were returned unanswered
(D) Where the survey was given

7. Maria conducted a survey of people employed in New York's fashion industry. She was disappointed that the margin of error in the results was over 7%. What can Maria do in the next survey to reduce the margin of error by 3%?

(A) Change 40% of the survey questions
(B) Conduct the survey in another city
(C) Increase the number of survey participants
(D) Decrease the number of survey participants

8. Samuel conducted a survey of local Boys Club members regarding the need for a new pool. He was delighted to find that the survey clearly predicted the actual results: 76 of the 171 members did not want a new pool. If Samuel interviewed 50 members, which of the following is closest to the number of respondents who did not prefer a new pool?

(A) 21
(B) 22
(C) 29
(D) 39

9. A manufacturer of hearing aids conducted a study of 200 randomly selected customers. The first group of 100 customers, section A, felt that a new type of hearing aid improved the wearer's hearing by 70%. The second group of 100 customers, section B, used an older style of hearing aid and saw little improvement in their hearing. Which of the following can be concluded about the hearing aid study?

(A) Hearing aids used by section B might not work.
(B) The users in section A and section B will notice similar improvement in their hearing.
(C) Those who use the new style of hearing aid from section A will hear better than those in section B.
(D) No useful conclusions can be drawn from the study.

10. Pollsters predict that Candidate A will be victorious in an upcoming election by garnering 54% of the vote. The margin of error in the survey is $\pm 2.5\%$. What estimate n will the pollsters expect for Candidate A if 150,000 votes are cast?

   (A) $79{,}000 < n < 81{,}000$
   (B) $80{,}100 < n < 81{,}750$
   (C) $118{,}725 < n < 122{,}450$
   (D) $78{,}975 < n < 83{,}025$

Answer Explanations

1. **(C)** If Sammie interviewed every 16-year-old in Florida, she would have no margin of error: she would have all of the data! Thus, the larger the sample size, the smaller the margin of error. Sammie ought to interview additional students to reduce the margin of error in the sample.

2. **(A)** Because Pham surveyed a random sample of the students in her school, her sample was representative of the entire high school. Thus, the percentage of students in the entire high school expected to prefer starting a 4-H Club is appropriately estimated by the percentage of students who preferred it in the sample, 31.5%. Thus, of the 1,145 students in the high school, approximately $1{,}145 \times 0.315 = 360.7$ students would be expected to prefer starting the 4-H Club. Of the choices given, this is closest to 360.

3. **(A)** The survey respondents were randomly chosen, so the results among the tenth graders were unbiased. Therefore, multiply the total class size, 245, by 41.1%.

$$(245)(.411) = 101$$

4. **(C)** If 13.2% of the adults in Amarillo prefer electric heat, then 86.8% do not prefer electric heat.

$$100\% - 13.2\% = 86.8\%$$

   Multiply 111,115, the number of adults living in Amarillo, by 86.8%.

$$(111{,}115)(0.868) \approx 96{,}448$$

   Answer choice (A) refers to the Amarillo adults who prefer electric heat over gas heat.

5. **(D)** The survey respondents were randomly chosen, so the results were unbiased. Multiply 4,840 by $\frac{54}{180}$.

$$\left(\frac{54}{180}\right)(4{,}840) \approx 1{,}452$$

6. **(D)** People who use parks have a bias; they enjoy parks and would likely appreciate additional funds being appropriated for more parks.

7. **(C)** If Maria increased the size of the survey respondents, the margin of error would decrease. Theoretically, if Maria surveyed everyone in the fashion industry in New York, the margin of error would be 0%: she'd have all of the data!

8. **(B)** Construct a proportion to find the number of respondents who did not want a new pool. Use this model.

$$\frac{\text{those who don't want a pool}}{\text{total}} = \frac{\text{those who don't want a pool}}{\text{total}}$$

$$\frac{x}{50} = \frac{76}{171}$$

Cross-multiply and solve for x.

$$(171)(x) = (50)(76)$$

$$171x = 3.800$$

$$x \approx 22.222\ldots$$

Choice (B), 22, is closest to this result.

9. **(C)** Given that users of the new hearing aid heard significantly better, we can conclude that the new hearing aid improves hearing. Although we can also conclude that the older style of hearing aid is less effective than the new style, this fact was not included in the answer choices.

10. **(D)** Find the predicted number of votes earned by Candidate *A*.

$$(150{,}000)(0.54) = 81{,}000$$

The margin of error is $\pm 2.5\%$, so add and subtract 2.5% of 81,000 to and from 81,000.

$$81{,}000 - (0.025)(81{,}000) = 78{,}975$$

$$81{,}000 + (0.025)(81{,}000) = 83{,}025$$

The range of votes collected by Candidate *A* should fall in the following range.

$$78{,}975 < n < 83{,}025$$

Graphs and Data Interpretation

Drill 1

> For multiple-choice questions, solve the problem and pick the correct answer from the provided choices. Each multiple-choice question has only one correct answer. For student-produced response questions, solve each problem and write down your answers separately.

Table of the Seven Lightest Chemical Elements (by atomic mass)

Atomic Mass	Name of Chemical Element	Symbol	Atomic Number
1.0079	Hydrogen	H	1
4.0026	Helium	He	2
6.941	Lithium	Li	3
9.0122	Beryllium	Be	4
10.811	Boron	B	5
12.0107	Carbon	C	6
14.0067	Nitrogen	N	7

1. Based on the table above, the atomic mass of which element is approximately equal to the sum of the atomic masses of helium and lithium?

(A) Nitrogen
(B) Boron
(C) Beryllium
(D) Lithium

Table of the Seven Lightest Chemical Elements (by atomic mass)

Atomic Mass	Name of Chemical Element	Symbol	Atomic Number
1.0079	Hydrogen	H	1
4.0026	Helium	He	2
6.941	Lithium	Li	3
9.0122	Beryllium	Be	4
10.811	Boron	B	5
12.0107	Carbon	C	6
14.0067	Nitrogen	N	7

2. Based on the table above, which element is about 30% more massive than lithium?

(A) Nitrogen
(B) Boron
(C) Beryllium
(D) Hydrogen

3. The graph below shows the number of domestic bee farms in the metropolitan Atlanta area from 2005 to 2010.

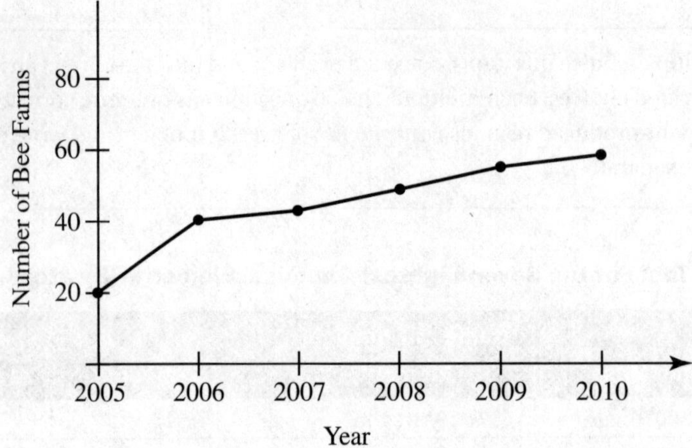

Based on the graph, which of the following describes the trend in the number of domestic bee farms in the Atlanta area?

(A) Exponential growth between 2005 and 2010
(B) Continued but modest growth after 2006
(C) An increase until 2007 followed by a gradual decline after that year
(D) A dramatic decrease after 2008

4. The graph below shows the number of domestic bee farms in the metropolitan Atlanta area from 2005 to 2010.

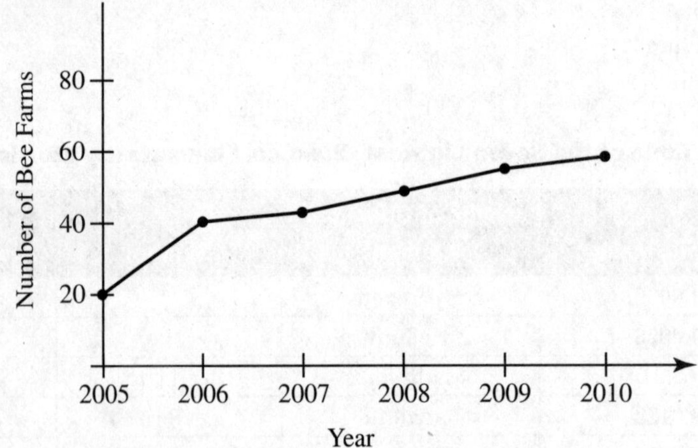

If each bee farm harvests 11,000 gallons of honey annually, which of the following is closest to the number of gallons collected in 2006?

(A) 110,000
(B) 220,000
(C) 440,000
(D) 660,000

5. The following table represents federal spending for NASA for the years 1958 through 1963.

NASA Spending Since 1958

Year	NASA Fed Outlay, $ in Millions	Total U.S. Fed Spending, $ in Millions	NASA as % of U.S. Spending	President	Party
1958	89	71,936	0.1	Dwight D. Eisenhower	Rep
1959	145	80,697	0.2	Dwight D. Eisenhower	Rep
1960	401	76,539	0.5	Dwight D. Eisenhower	Rep
1961	744	81,515	0.9	John F. Kennedy	Dem
1962	1,257	106,821	1.18	John F. Kennedy	Dem
1963	2,552	111,316	2.28	Lyndon B. Johnson	Dem

Which of the following can be concluded about the information portrayed in the table?

(A) From 1958 until 1963, spending on NASA as a percentage of the U.S. budget increased nearly 2,200%.
(B) Between 1962 and 1963, spending on NASA virtually tripled.
(C) In 1963, real spending on NASA exceeded the $1 billion mark for the first time.
(D) The total dollars spent each year from 1958 to 1963 decreased.

6. The following table represents federal spending for NASA for the years 1958 through 1963.

NASA Spending Since 1958

Year	NASA Fed Outlay, $ in Millions	Total U.S. Fed Spending, $ in Millions	NASA as % of U.S. Spending	President	Party
1958	89	71,936	0.1	Dwight D. Eisenhower	Rep
1959	145	80,697	0.2	Dwight D. Eisenhower	Rep
1960	401	76,539	0.5	Dwight D. Eisenhower	Rep
1961	744	81,515	0.9	John F. Kennedy	Dem
1962	1,257	106,821	1.18	John F. Kennedy	Dem
1963	2,552	111,316	2.28	Lyndon B. Johnson	Dem

Total U.S. spending in 1962 was about how many times larger than the NASA budget in 1958?

(A) 77 times
(B) 88 times
(C) 650 times
(D) 1,200 times

7. The table below is a statistics page for an educational website. The visits, files, and other data are shown for the first week of June 2015. The owner of the educational site is wondering how to effectively reach more viewers.

Daily Statistics for June 2015

Day	Hits		Files		Pages		Visits		Sites		KBytes	
1	**327**	6.35%	**274**	6.62%	**250**	7.29%	**85**	7.58%	**60**	8.97%	**2203**	4.87%
2	**432**	8.39%	**383**	9.25%	**349**	10.17%	**64**	5.71%	**57**	8.52%	**2506**	5.54%
3	**283**	5.49%	**235**	5.68%	**181**	5.28%	**56**	5.00%	**50**	7.47%	**2332**	5.15%
4	**249**	4.83%	**208**	5.03%	**143**	4.17%	**47**	4.19%	**56**	8.37%	**2816**	6.22%
5	**265**	5.14%	**164**	3.96%	**134**	3.91%	**39**	3.48%	**44**	6.58%	**1644**	3.63%
6	**165**	3.20%	**142**	3.43%	**114**	3.32%	**45**	4.01%	**42**	6.28%	**1425**	3.15%
7	**250**	4.85%	**155**	3.74%	**134**	3.91%	**50**	4.46%	**51**	7.62%	**1621**	3.58%

Which of the following can be concluded from the table?

(A) The number of visits exceeds the number of sites each day.
(B) On day 7, the ratio of hits to files is greater than the ratio of files to pages.
(C) The ratio of KBytes to sites is greater on day 6 than on day 1.
(D) The ratio of pages to visits is never less than 3:1.

8. The table below is a statistics page for an educational website. The visits, files, and other data are shown for the first week of June 2015. The owner of the educational site is wondering how to effectively reach more viewers.

Daily Statistics for June 2015

Day	Hits		Files		Pages		Visits		Sites		KBytes	
1	**327**	6.35%	**274**	6.62%	**250**	7.29%	**85**	7.58%	**60**	8.97%	**2203**	4.87%
2	**432**	8.39%	**383**	9.25%	**349**	10.17%	**64**	5.71%	**57**	8.52%	**2506**	5.54%
3	**283**	5.49%	**235**	5.68%	**181**	5.28%	**56**	5.00%	**50**	7.47%	**2332**	5.15%
4	**249**	4.83%	**208**	5.03%	**143**	4.17%	**47**	4.19%	**56**	8.37%	**2816**	6.22%
5	**265**	5.14%	**164**	3.96%	**134**	3.91%	**39**	3.48%	**44**	6.58%	**1644**	3.63%
6	**165**	3.20%	**142**	3.43%	**114**	3.32%	**45**	4.01%	**42**	6.28%	**1425**	3.15%
7	**250**	4.85%	**155**	3.74%	**134**	3.91%	**50**	4.46%	**51**	7.62%	**1621**	3.58%

What is the median number of visits in the first seven days of June 2015?

(A) 85
(B) 47
(C) 56
(D) 50

9. The table below is a statistics page for an educational website. The visits, files, and other data are shown for the first week of June 2015. The owner of the educational site is wondering how to effectively reach more viewers.

Daily Statistics for June 2015

Day	Hits		Files		Pages		Visits		Sites		KBytes	
1	**327**	6.35%	**274**	6.62%	**250**	7.29%	**85**	7.58%	**60**	8.97%	**2203**	4.87%
2	**432**	8.39%	**383**	9.25%	**349**	10.17%	**64**	5.71%	**57**	8.52%	**2506**	5.54%
3	**283**	5.49%	**235**	5.68%	**181**	5.28%	**56**	5.00%	**50**	7.47%	**2332**	5.15%
4	**249**	4.83%	**208**	5.03%	**143**	4.17%	**47**	4.19%	**56**	8.37%	**2816**	6.22%
5	**265**	5.14%	**164**	3.96%	**134**	3.91%	**39**	3.48%	**44**	6.58%	**1644**	3.63%
6	**165**	3.20%	**142**	3.43%	**114**	3.32%	**45**	4.01%	**42**	6.28%	**1425**	3.15%
7	**250**	4.85%	**155**	3.74%	**134**	3.91%	**50**	4.46%	**51**	7.62%	**1621**	3.58%

If R is the range of the Files category and r is the range of the KBytes category, what is the value of $2r - R$?

(A) 3,126
(B) 2,541
(C) 254
(D) −249

Age	Target Heart Rate Zone, 50–85%	Average Maximum Heart Rate, 100%
20 years	100–170 beats per minute	200 beats per minute
30 years	95–162 beats per minute	190 beats per minute
35 years	93–157 beats per minute	185 beats per minute
40 years	90–153 beats per minute	180 beats per minute

10. The table above indicates data relating to heartbeat rates for adults between the ages of 20 and 40 as put forth by the American Medical Association. If a woman age 35 has a heart rate that is the mean of the extremes of the target heart rate zone for her age, what percent of the maximum heart rate is that measure? (Round to the nearest tenth of a percent.)

Answer Explanations

1. **(B)** The combined atomic masses of helium and lithium are $4.0026 + 6.941 = 10.9436$. The atomic mass of boron is 10.811. That value is the closest to the combined atomic masses of helium and lithium among the answer choices.

2. **(C)** The atomic mass of lithium is 6.941. Multiply that number by 0.30 and add it to the atomic mass of lithium.

$$6.941 + (0.30)(6.941) = 9.023$$

Of the elements listed in the table, beryllium, with an atomic mass of 9.0122, is approximately 30% more massive than lithium.

3. **(B)** From 2005 to 2006, there was a 100% growth (from 20 to 40). After 2006, however, the graph shows about a 5% increase per year.

4. **(C)** The graph indicates that approximately 40 bee farms were operating in 2006. Multiply 40 by 11,000 to find the 2006 yield of honey.

$$40 \times 11{,}000 = 440{,}000$$

5. **(A)** The percentage of the U.S. budget spent on NASA was 0.1% in 1958. By 1963, the percentage of the U.S. budget spent on NASA was 2.28%. Use the formula $\frac{\text{increase}}{\text{original}} = \frac{n}{100}$ to find the percent increase.

$$\text{Increase} = 2.28 - 0.1 = 2.18$$
$$\frac{2.18}{1} = \frac{n}{100}$$
$$218 = 0.1n$$
$$n = 2{,}180\%$$

Choice (A), 2,200%, is the closest to this figure.

6. **(D)** Total U.S. spending in 1962 was $106,821,000,000. The NASA budget in 1958 was $89,000,000. Divide 106,821,000 by 89,000,000 to calculate how many times larger the 1962 U.S. spending was than the 1958 NASA budget.

$$106{,}821{,}000{,}000 \div 89{,}000{,}000 = 1{,}200.23$$

Choice (D), 1,200 times larger, is the closest.

7. **(B)** On day 7, the ratio of hits to files is greater than the ratio of files to pages. Note the ratio of hits to files.

$$\frac{250}{155} \approx 1.61$$

The ratio of files to pages is $\frac{155}{134} \approx 1.16$.

$$1.61 > 1.16$$

Choices (A), (C), and (D) cannot be supported by the data in the table.

8. **(D)** The median is the middle value when the numbers are arranged in order. The numbers are arranged in order below.

39 45 47 50 56 64 85

The value in the middle, 50, is the median.

9. **(B)** The range of a group of numbers is found by finding the difference between the greatest and least values.

   The range of the Files category is $383 - 142 = 241$.

   $$R = 241$$

   The range of the KBytes category is $2{,}816 - 1{,}425 = 1{,}391$.

   $$r = 1{,}391$$

   Find $2r - R$ by substituting 241 and 1,381 for R and r, respectively.

   $$(2)(1{,}391) - 241 = 2{,}541$$

10. **67.6** A woman age 35 has a target heart rate zone of 93 to 157 beats per minute. Find the mean of that range by adding $93 + 157$ and dividing by 2.

    $$93 + 157 = 250$$

    $$250 \div 2 = 125$$

    Find the percent that 125 is of 185 by dividing 125 by 185.

    $$125 \div 185 = 0.6757$$

    Rounded to the nearest tenth of a percent, 0.6757 is 67.6%. A heart rate of 125 is 67.6% of the maximum heart rate.

Drill 2

For multiple-choice questions, solve the problem and pick the correct answer from the provided choices. Each multiple-choice question has only one correct answer. For student-produced response questions, solve each problem and write down your answers separately.

1. The advent of television, iPhones, and tablets is vying for students' study time. Experts are concerned that the prolonged use of electronic devices adversely affects SAT scores. The graph below demonstrates the correlation between hours spent viewing daily and their effect on SAT scores.

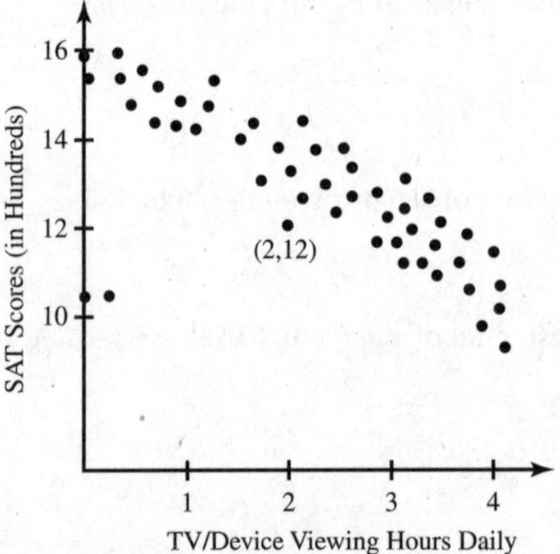

Which of the following can be inferred from the graph?

(A) The impact of viewing 3 versus 4 hours resulted in the same SAT score.
(B) All students who watched 1 hour or less of television/devices daily scored 1200 or higher on the SAT.
(C) SAT scores varied inversely with daily television/device viewing.
(D) SAT scores varied directly with daily television/device viewing.

2. The advent of television, iPhones, and tablets is vying for students' study time. Experts are concerned that the prolonged use of electronic devices adversely affects SAT scores. The graph below demonstrates the correlation between hours spent viewing daily and their effect on SAT scores.

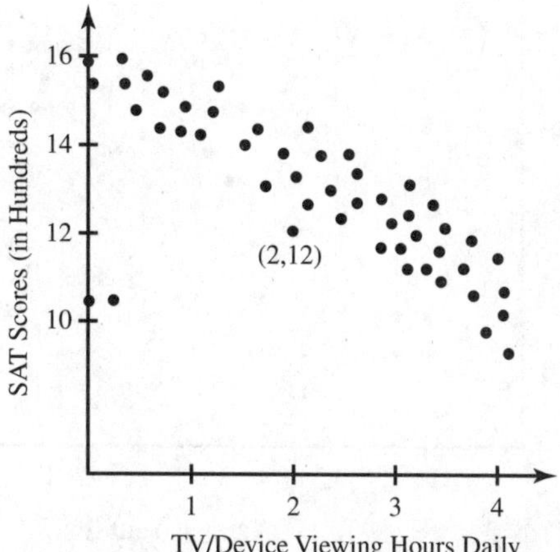

Given the data in the graph, which equation could be the line of best fit?

(A) $y = 2.3x - 4.8$
(B) $y = 0.86x + 0.23$
(C) $y = -6.2x - 5.9$
(D) $y = -2.04x + 15.8$

3. The graph below reflects the average percentage of freshman high school students in America who graduate from high school within four years.

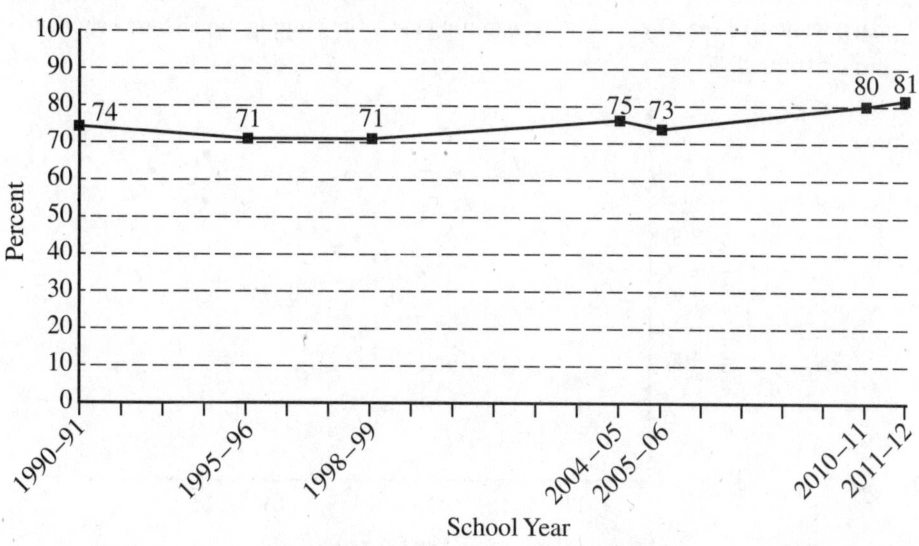

Which of the following can be inferred from the graph above?

(A) From 2006 to 2012 there was approximately an 11% increase in the percentage of high school graduates.
(B) There was a steady increase in the number of high school graduates between 1991 and 2012.
(C) The number of high school graduates decreased from 2006 to 2012.
(D) The state of the national economy had a marked increase on the percentage of high school graduates.

4. A girls' softball coach was recruiting for Behrens High School's spring softball team. The coach wanted to see if age was a determining factor in gauging the distance each girl could throw a softball.

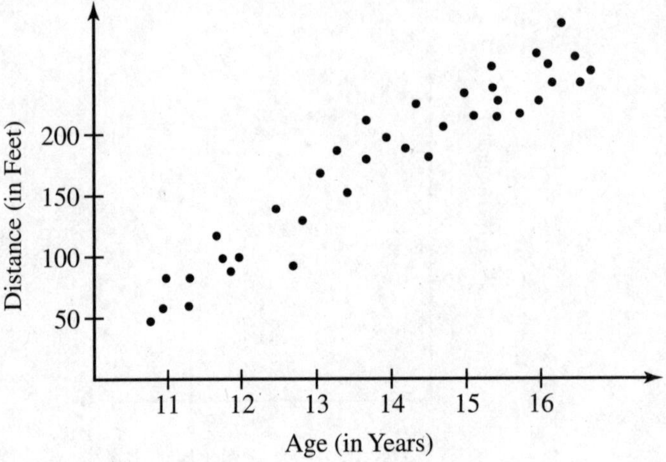

Softball Throws by Age and Distance

Which of the following can be concluded from the graph?

(A) There is a weak negative correlation between age and distance thrown.
(B) There is a strong positive correlation between age and distance thrown.
(C) There is no correlation between age and distance thrown.
(D) There is an inverse relationship between age and distance thrown.

5. A girls' softball coach was recruiting for Behrens High School's spring softball team. The coach wanted to see if age was a determining factor in gauging the distance each girl could throw a softball.

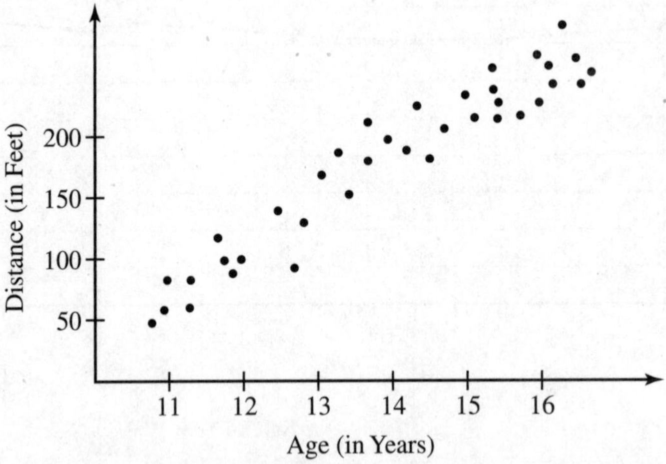

Softball Throws by Age and Distance

Which of the following functions is a line of best fit for the graph?

(A) $y = 5.14x - 123.5$
(B) $y = -43.27x - 231.3$
(C) $y = 33.33x - 299.6$
(D) $y = 14.2 - 2.01x$

6. A botanist was exploring the impact a local red ant population had on local nurseries. An experiment was devised to investigate any correlation between red ant populations and the annual yield of white roses. A scatter plot of the data is shown.

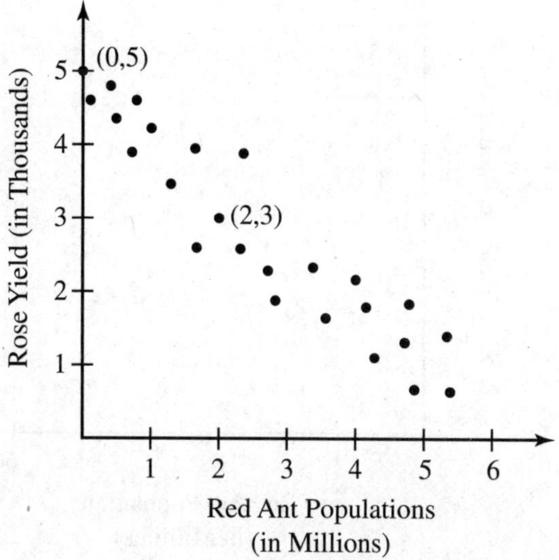

A line of best fit is constructed within the data. Which of the following functions best models the data?

(A) $f(x) = -4.88x + 4.66$
(B) $f(x) = 1.15x + 7.88$
(C) $f(x) = 1.27x + 4.88$
(D) $f(x) = -1.14x + 4.88$

7. A botanist was exploring the impact a local red ant population had on local nurseries. An experiment was devised to investigate any correlation between red ant populations and the annual yield of white roses. A scatter plot of the data is shown.

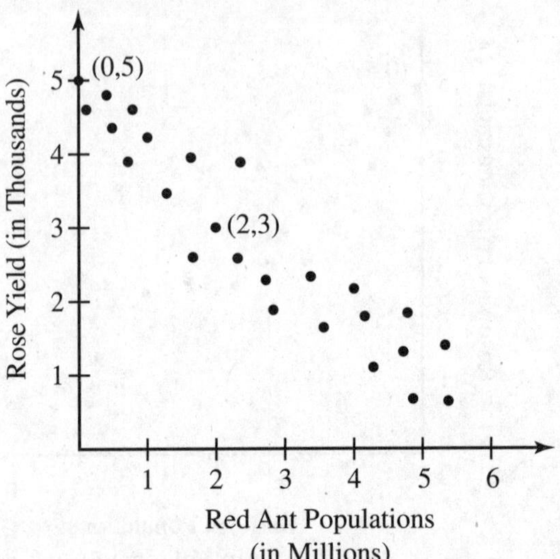

A grower uses a pesticide that will reduce the ant population by 60%. If the grower currently has five million ants, which of the following is the closest to his rose yield after using the pesticide?

(A) 1,000
(B) 1,800
(C) 3,000
(D) 4,200

8. The pie chart below represents the operating costs for Deerfield High School in 2014.

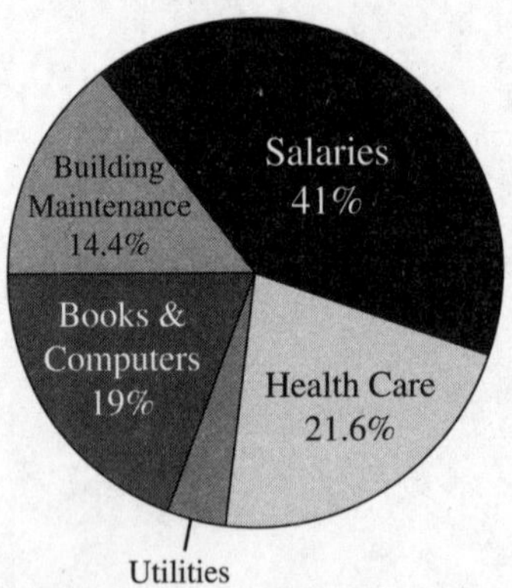

Operating Costs Deerfield HS

The cost for health care benefits in 2014 is $4,100,000. What is the cost for utilities?

(A) $586,113
(B) $637,431
(C) $759,259
(D) $817,437

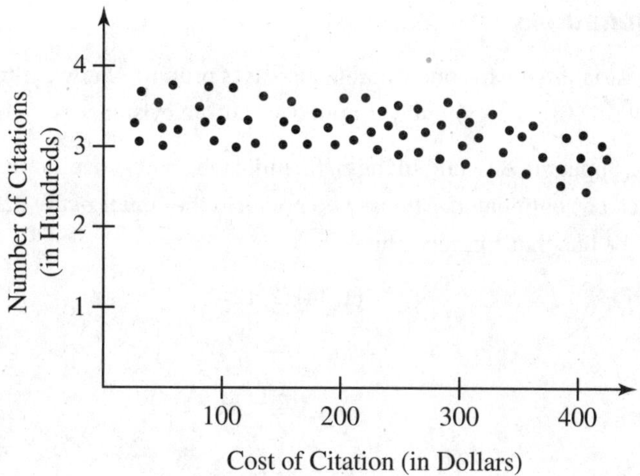

9. The graph shows the number of drivers who have been caught texting while driving and the fines that were levied against them. Which of the following can be concluded from the graph?

(A) There is a strong negative correlation between higher fines and the number of drivers cited for texting while driving.
(B) There is a weak negative correlation between higher fines and the number of drivers cited for texting while driving.
(C) There is a strong positive correlation between higher fines and the number of drivers cited for texting while driving.
(D) There is no correlation between higher fines and the number of drivers cited for texting while driving.

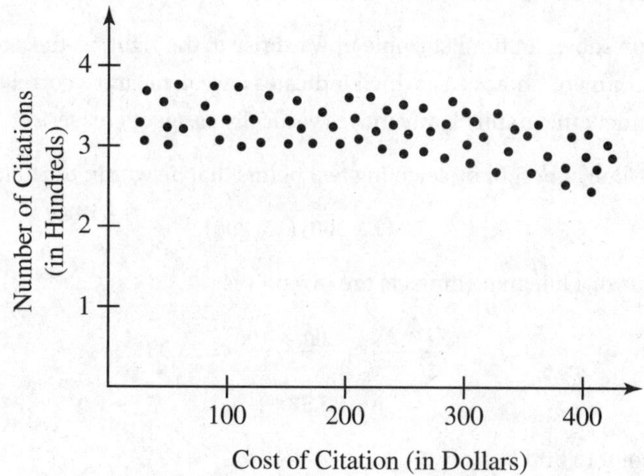

10. If the fine for texting while driving was increased to $800, approximately how many citations could be expected to be issued?

(A) 70
(B) 230
(C) 460
(D) 520

Answer Explanations

1. **(C)** Inverse variation means one variable increases proportionally to the decrease in the other variable. SAT scores generally dropped as daily television/device watching increased.

2. **(D)** The data appear to descend to the right, indicating a negative slope. Therefore, choices (A) and (B) can be eliminated. Choose two points in the center of the data, and derive the equation of the line that connects them.

$$(1, 14)\ (2, 12)$$
$$m = \frac{y_2 - y_1}{x_2 - x_1}$$
$$m = \frac{12 - 14}{2 - 1}$$
$$m = -2$$
$$y = -2x + b$$

Substitute either point for x and y.

$$14 = -2(1) + b$$
$$16 = b$$

The equation of a line of best fit could be $y = -2x + 16$. Choice (D) is the closest to this equation.

3. **(A)** The percentage of high school graduates in 2006 was 73%, and in 2012 the percentage had increased to 81%. Divide 81 by 73 to find the percent increase.

$$81 \div 73 = 1.109$$

The increase was 10.9%; the closest answer to this figure is 11%.

4. **(B)** The graph shows an unmistakable upward rise to the right; as the age increases, so does the distance thrown. Choice (A), which indicates a weak negative correlation in the graph, can be discarded; the graph clearly moves vertically as age increases.

5. **(C)** Find the line of best fit by selecting two points that lie within the data.

$$(12, 100)\ (15, 200)$$

Find the slope of a line that connects the two points.

$$\frac{y_2 - y_1}{x_2 - x_1} = \frac{200 - 100}{15 - 12} \approx 33.33$$
$$y = 33.33x + b$$

Use either point to find b.

$$100 = 33.33(12) + b$$
$$-299.6 = b$$
$$y = 33.33x - 299.6$$

6. **(D)** The data roughly correspond to a line with a negative slope, so only choices (A) and (D) should be considered. By using the points (0, 5) and (2, 3), we can get a sense of the slope:

$$\frac{y_2 - y_1}{x_2 - x_1} = \frac{5 - 3}{0 - 2} = -1$$

Choice (D) is more closely aligned with a slope of -1. Choices (B) and (C) can be eliminated at once. The data appear to descend to the right as the number of ants increases, thus indicating a negative slope. Choices (B) and (C) incorrectly show positive slopes.

7. **(C)** After the grower uses the pesticide, his ant population will be reduced by 60%. Find 60% of 5,000,000 and subtract that amount from 5,000,000.

$$5{,}000{,}000 - (0.60)(5{,}000{,}000) = 2{,}000{,}000$$

The graph indicates the point (2, 3) is on the line of best fit. Thus, when the grower has 2,000,000 ants, he can expect a yield of 3,000 roses.

8. **(C)** Find the percentage of operating costs for utilities in 2015.

$$100\% - (14.4 + 41 + 21.6 + 19) = 4\%$$

Set up a proportion comparing an item's percentage of the budget to its dollar expenditure.

$$\frac{21.6}{4{,}100{,}000} = \frac{4}{x}$$

Cross-multiply and solve for x.

$$(21.6)(x) = (4)(4{,}100{,}000)$$
$$21.6x = 16{,}400{,}000$$
$$x = \$759{,}259$$

9. **(B)** Although the number of drivers cited for texting while driving is reduced slightly as higher fees are levied, a line of best fit would show only a mild negative slope. Thus, there is a weak negative correlation between higher fines and the number of drivers cited for texting while driving.

10. **(B)** The data points in the graph indicate a modest decrease in the number of citations issued as the cost of fines increases. Thus, we expect the number of citations to be fewer than 300. We can eliminate answer choices (C) and (D).

Pick two data points to find a line of best fit, such as (100, 350) and (400, 300).

Start to create an equation for the line of best fit by first finding the slope.

$$m = \frac{300 - 350}{400 - 100} = -\frac{1}{6}$$
$$y = -\frac{1}{6}x + b$$

Select one of the points to calculate b, the y-intercept.

$$300 = -\frac{1}{6}(400) + b$$
$$367 \approx b$$
$$y = -\frac{1}{6}x + 367$$

Replace x with 800 to estimate the number of citations issued when the fine is \$800.

$$y = -\frac{1}{6}(800) + 367$$
$$y = 233$$

Choice (B), 230, is closest to this estimate.

Probability Drill

For multiple-choice questions, solve the problem and pick the correct answer from the provided choices. Each multiple-choice question has only one correct answer. For student-produced response questions, solve each problem and write down your answers separately.

Fish	6–12 inches	13–24 inches	Total
Bullhead	26	18	44
Trout	31	47	78
Mullet	53	44	97
Total	110	109	218

1. A popular fishing site recorded the number of fish caught on a particular day as shown in the table above. If a certain fish caught that day was 11 inches long, what is the probability that the fish was a mullet?

(A) 0.242
(B) 0.316
(C) 0.482
(D) 0.546

2. A game spinner has four colors equally spaced: red, green, blue, and yellow. What is the probability that a single, six-sided die will land on a prime number followed by a spin of yellow or blue?

(A) $\frac{1}{4}$
(B) $\frac{1}{9}$
(C) $\frac{1}{12}$
(D) $\frac{1}{36}$

	10th	11th
Female	17	18
Male	18	20

3. One lucky student at Bristol High School will be selected to attend a College for Kids camp at Johns Hopkins University. The table above represents the number of students in the 10th and 11th grades at the school. If a student is selected at random, what is the probability that the student will be in 10th grade or a male?

(A) 0.753
(B) 0.521
(C) 0.479
(D) 0.472

4. In a 10-question true/false test, what is the probability of guessing correctly on exactly two of the questions from 6 through 8?

(A) $\frac{1}{3}$
(B) $\frac{3}{8}$
(C) $\frac{2}{3}$
(D) $\frac{7}{8}$

	7th Grade	8th Grade	9th Grade
Girls	191	215	174
Boys	162	219	181

5. The data above represent students categorized by gender and grade at a local middle school. If a student is selected at random, what is the probability the student is not an eighth-grade girl? (Round your answer to the nearest hundredth.)

	Boy	Girl	Total
Swim	12	14	26
Water Polo	16	15	31
Total	28	29	57

6. The above chart represents the students who are members of a high school's swim and water polo teams. The water polo and swim teams are having a Spring Banquet. One of the team members will be chosen as athlete of the year. What is the probability the person chosen will be a member of the water polo team or a boy?

(A) $\frac{31}{57}$
(B) $\frac{43}{57}$
(C) $\frac{52}{57}$
(D) $\frac{55}{57}$

7. Swimmers who participate in backstroke races depend on a series of banners strung overhead. The banners warn the swimmer that the wall is 5 yards away. A company sells these banners in long cords that repeat a sequence of colors in the following order:

Red Yellow Blue Green Orange Purple

If a high school bought 40 yards of a banner string that contained 75 banners, what was the color of the 59th banner?

(A) Yellow
(B) Green
(C) Orange
(D) Purple

8. In William's dresser are three pairs of white socks, five pairs of blue socks, and two pairs of brown socks. What is the probability of William selecting a brown pair, replacing it in the drawer, and then selecting a blue pair of socks?

(A) $\frac{1}{10}$
(B) $\frac{2}{19}$
(C) $\frac{3}{10}$
(D) $\frac{7}{10}$

9. Cindy has three pairs of white socks, five pairs of blue socks, and two pairs of brown socks in her dresser drawer. What is the probability of Cindy withdrawing a blue pair of socks and, without replacing it, drawing a pair of white socks? (Round your answer to the nearest thousandth.)

10. There is a 40% chance of rain on Thursday. If it does not rain, a high school baseball team has a 70% chance that it will play its scheduled game. What is the probability that there will not be any rain on Thursday but the game will not be played?

(A) 14%
(B) 18%
(C) 28%
(D) 42%

Answer Explanations

1. **(C)** According to the table, 110 fish were caught that were 6–12 inches long. Of that amount, 53 were mullets. Divide 53 by 110 to find the probability that a particular fish caught that measured 6–12 inches was a mullet.

$$\frac{53}{100} \approx 0.482$$

2. **(A)** Find the probability that a single, six-sided die will land on a prime number. Remember that 1 is not a prime number.

$$p\,(\text{prime number}) = \frac{2{,}3{,}5}{1{,}2{,}3{,}4{,}5{,}6} = \frac{1}{2}$$

Find the probability that the spinner will land on yellow or blue.

$$\frac{\text{yellow, blue}}{\text{red, green, blue, yellow}} = \frac{1}{2}$$

The two events, landing on a prime number and spinning yellow or blue, are independent. So multiply the probabilities.

$$\frac{1}{2} \times \frac{1}{2} = \frac{1}{4}$$

3. **(A)** Use the probability formula.

$$P(x) = \frac{\text{desired outcomes}}{\text{all outcomes}}$$

There are 35 tenth graders and 38 boys. However, some of the tenth graders are boys and should not be counted twice. Thus:

$$P(\text{10th grader or boy}) = [(\text{number of 10th graders}) + (\text{number of boys}) - (\text{number of 10th-grade boys})] \div (\text{total number of students})$$

$$P(\text{10th grader or boy}) = (35 + 38 - 18) \div 73$$

$$P(\text{10th grader or boy}) = 55 \div 73 = 0.753$$

4. **(B)** A total of 8 outcomes are possible when guessing among 3 questions.

Let C = the answers guessed correctly

Let I = the answers guessed incorrectly

CCC, CCI, CIC, CII, ICC, ICI, IIC, III

Of the 8 possible outcomes, 3 contain exactly two correct guesses (and therefore one incorrect guess). Therefore, the probability of guessing correctly on exactly two of the three questions among questions 6 through 8 is $\frac{3}{8}$.

5. **.81** Find the probability that the student selected is an eighth-grade girl and subtract that value from 1.0.

$$\frac{\text{eighth-grade girl}}{\text{all students}} = \frac{245}{1{,}142} = 0.188$$

Subtract 0.188 from 1.0 to find the probability that the student selected is not an eighth-grade girl.

$$1.0 - 0.188 = 0.812$$

The answer, 0.812, rounds to 0.81.

6. **(B)** Find the probability that the athlete will be a boy or a water polo member. Avoid double counting by subtracting the boys who are on the water polo team.

$$\text{boys: } \frac{28}{57} \qquad \text{water polo members: } \frac{31}{57}$$

$$\text{boys on the water polo team: } \frac{16}{57}$$

$$\frac{28}{57} + \frac{31}{57} - \frac{16}{57} = \frac{43}{57}$$

7. **(C)** The banners are sold in the same sequence of repeating colors:

Red Yellow Blue Green Orange Purple

There are 6 banners in each sequence, so divide 59 by 6 the same way you did in 4th grade.

$$59 \div 6 = 9 \text{ remainder } 5$$

The quotient is not important, but the remainder is. The quotient suggests that we have completed 9 full sequences and are now 5 deep into the 10th sequence of colors. Count 5 banners into the series to arrive at orange as the 59th banner.

8. **(A)** The probability of selecting a pair of brown socks is $\frac{2}{10}$. After replacing the pair, the probability of selecting a blue pair is $\frac{5}{10}$. Multiply the two fractions to find the probability of these two probabilities occurring sequentially.

$$\frac{2}{10} \times \frac{5}{10} = \frac{10}{100} = \frac{1}{10}$$

9. **.167 or .166** The probability of Cindy selecting a blue pair of socks is $\frac{5}{10}$ or 0.5. The pair she selected is not replaced, so now there are nine pairs of socks in the drawer. The probability of Cindy selecting a white pair is $\frac{3}{9}$ or 0.333. Multiply 0.5 by 0.333.

$$0.5 \times 0.333 \approx 0.167$$

10. **(B)** There is a 100% chance that rain will or will not occur on Thursday. Subtract 40% from 100% to find the probability of no rain.

$$100\% - 40\% = 60\%$$

There is a 100% chance that the game will or will not be played on Thursday if it does not rain. Subtract 70% from 100% to find the probability that the game will not be played, even if it does not rain.

$$100\% - 70\% = 30\%$$

Multiply the two percentages to find the probability of no rain on Thursday and the game not being played.

$$60\% \times 30\% = 18\%$$

Geometry and Trigonometry

The Geometry and Trigonometry portion of the exam will require the test taker to be proficient in the following topics:

- Area and volume
- Lines, angles, and triangles
- Right triangles and trigonometry
- Circles

The test taker needs to know the relationships of the sine, cosine, and tangent of a right triangle. The trigonometric ratios are as follows:

$$\text{sine} = \frac{\text{opposite side}}{\text{hypotenuse}}$$

$$\text{cosine} = \frac{\text{adjacent side}}{\text{hypotenuse}}$$

$$\text{tangent} = \frac{\text{opposite side}}{\text{adjacent side}}$$

The practice questions in this section will help you strengthen your skills in trigonometry.

TIP

A majority of the geometry formulas will be provided in the reference section of each Math section. The savvy test taker should review these formulas before test day. However, the trigonometry formulas will not appear in this section, so we will show them here.

Area, Perimeter, and Volume Drill

For multiple-choice questions, solve the problem and pick the correct answer from the provided choices. Each multiple-choice question has only one correct answer. For student-produced response questions, solve each problem and write down your answers separately.

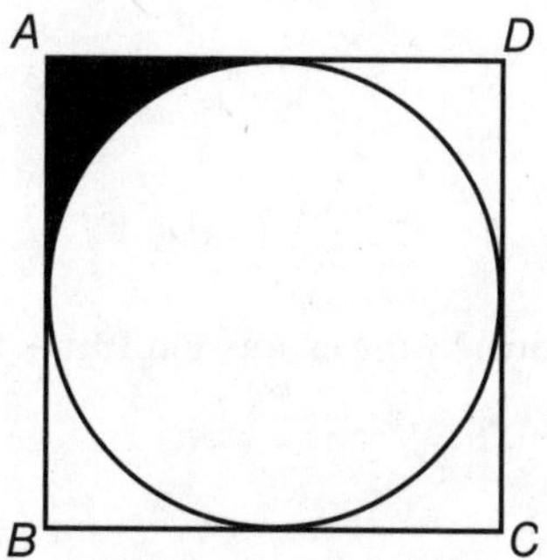

1. A coin toss board is shown above. If square *ABCD* has perimeter 64, what is the probability of a coin landing on the shaded portion of the board?

 (A) 0.363
 (B) 0.182
 (C) 0.098
 (D) 0.053

2. An aquarium is in the shape of a right rectangular prism. The glass container has the following dimensions:

   length: 3 feet
   width: 2 feet

   The water in the tank rises to a height of 1 foot. The water is poured into another aquarium that has the following dimensions:

   length: 4 feet
   width: 1 foot

   If the water rises to a height of x feet in the second aquarium, what is the value of x?

   (A) 1 foot
   (B) 1.5 feet
   (C) 2 feet
   (D) 2.5 feet

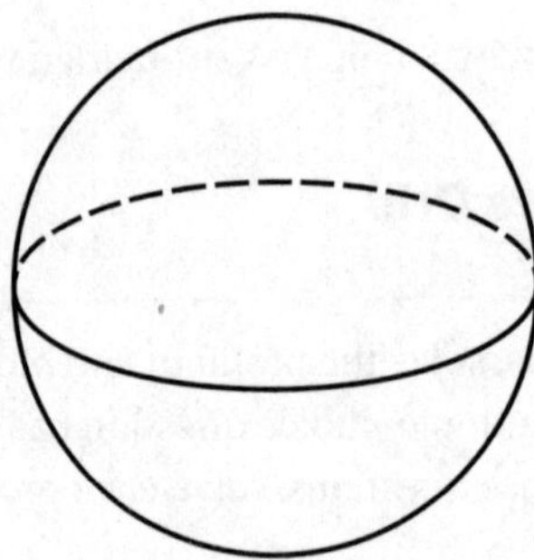

3. A great circle of a sphere contains the sphere's center. If the volume of a sphere is 374 cubic inches, what is the circumference of a great circle on that sphere? (Use $\pi = 3.14$)

   (A) 4.47
   (B) 28.07
   (C) 56.14
   (D) 62.74

4. If the area of a rectangle is shown by the expression $16x^2 - 9y^2$ and the width is $4x - 3y$, what is the perimeter of the rectangle?

   (A) $4(x + y)$
   (B) $16x$
   (C) $64x^2 - 36y^2$
   (D) $2(x + y)$

5. A large snowball is in the shape of a sphere. At 10:00 A.M., the radius of the snowball is 2 feet. The radius grows 6 inches every 10 minutes it is rolled in the snow. If the snowball is continuously rolled, how much greater, in cubic feet, is the snowball at 11:30 A.M. than it is at 10:00 A.M.? (Round your answer to the nearest cubic foot.)

   (A) 1,150
   (B) 1,117
   (C) 167
   (D) 34

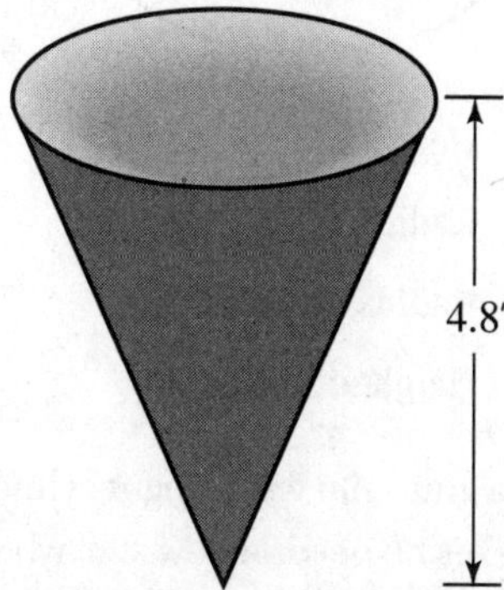

6. A waffle-flavored ice cream cone is pictured above. If the volume of the cone is 14.4π cubic inches, what is the diameter of the cone (in inches)?

7. If the area of a square is doubled, how many times longer is a side of the larger square than is the length of the smaller square?

   (A) 4
   (B) 2
   (C) $\sqrt{3}$
   (D) $\sqrt{2}$

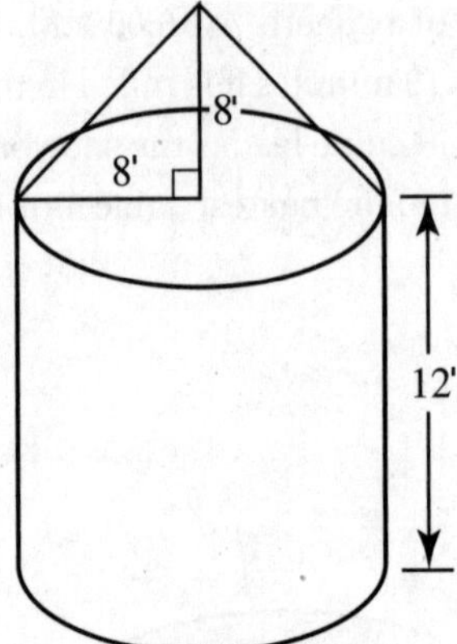

Height of Cylinder: 12′

Radius of Cylinder: 8′

Radius of Cone: 8′

Height of Cone: 8′

8. The diagram above represents a grain silo with a right cylindrical base and a top in the shape of a right cone. The owner believes he needs a new silo, which will store 10% more grain than his existing silo. Which of the following represents the volume of the new silo (in cubic feet)?

(A) 2,123
(B) 2,678
(C) 2,948
(D) 3,243

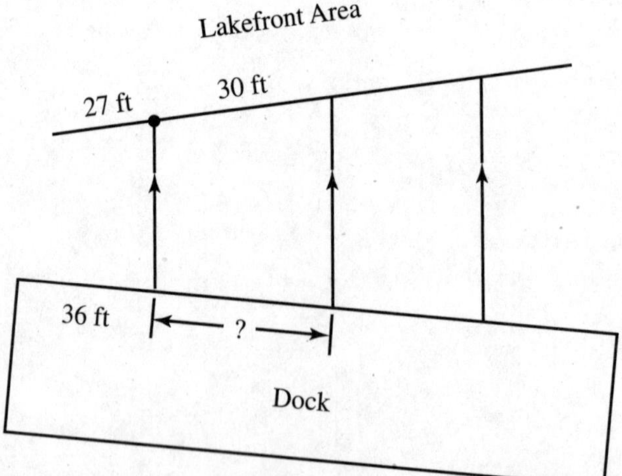

9. The diagram above shows a lakefront area divided into small parcels for boat owners. Each area is marked by a rope to a dock where each owner secures his or her boat. The ropes between the parcels are parallel to one another. What is the length of the docking area in feet for the boat owner who has a 30-foot lakefront border illustrated above?

10. Oscar wants to place molding surrounding the floor in his study room that is in the shape of a rectangle. He remembers that the area of the room is 180 square feet and that the width of the room is 12 feet. However, he does not know the measure of the length of the room. His tape measure is out in the car, but Oscar thinks he can solve the problem with simple algebra. Assuming no waste, how many linear feet of floor molding should Oscar purchase?

Answer Explanations

1. **(D)** Subtract the area of the circle from the area of the square.

$$\text{Area of a square} = \text{side} \times \text{side} = s^2$$

Divide the perimeter by 4 and square that value.

$$\left(\frac{64}{4}\right)^2 = 16^2 = 256$$

The area of the square is 256 square units.

$$\text{Area of a circle} = \pi r^2$$

The diameter of the circle is equal to the length of one of the sides of the square. Each side is 16, so the radius is 8 because the radius of a circle is one-half of the diameter.

$$\pi(8)^2 \approx 201.1$$

Subtract the area of the circle from the area of the square.

$$256 - 201.1 = 54.9$$

Divide the remaining area by 4 to find the shaded area.

$$54.9 \div 4 = 13.73$$

Divide the measure of the shaded area by the area of the square to find the probability of a coin landing in the shaded area.

$$13.73 \div 256 = 0.053$$

The diagram is assumed to be drawn to scale, so choice (A), 0.363, would appear to be much too large.

2. **(B)** The volume of the water in the first aquarium is 6 cubic feet because the volume, length $\times$ width $\times$ height, is $3 \times 2 \times 1 = 6$. The same volume of water is then poured into another aquarium that has dimensions 4 feet by 1 foot and that rises to a height of x feet. Calculate the height.

$$(4)(1)(x) = 6$$
$$4x = 6$$
$$x = 1.5$$

3. **(B)** Find the radius of the sphere by using the formula $V = \frac{4}{3}\pi r^3$.

$$374 = \frac{4}{3}(3.14)r^3$$
$$374 = 4.19r^3$$
$$89.26 = r^3$$
$$4.47 = r$$

The circumference of a circle is found by using the formula $C = 2\pi r$.

$$C = (2)(4.47)(3.14) = 28.07$$

Once you have calculated the length of the radius of the sphere, choice (A) can be eliminated since 4.47 is the radius of the great circle, not its circumference.

4. **(B)** Factoring $16x^2 - 9y^2$ gives $(4x + 3y)(4x - 3y)$. The area of a rectangle is given by the formula Area = (length)(width) or $A = lw$. Since $4x - 3y$ is the width, $4x + 3y$ is the length. The perimeter of a rectangle is found by using the formula $P = 2l + 2w$.

$$2(4x + 3y) + 2(4x - 3y) = 8x + 6y + 8x - 6y = 16x$$

5. **(B)** Find the difference between the volume of the snowball at 10:00 A.M. and at 11:30 A.M. At 10:00 A.M., the radius of the snowball is 2 feet, so input that value into the volume formula of a sphere.

$$V = \frac{4}{3}\pi r^3 = \frac{4}{3}\pi(2)^3 \approx 33.5 \text{ ft}^3$$

Every 10 minutes, the radius of the snowball grows 6 inches, which is 0.5 feet. There are nine 10-minute intervals between 10:00 A.M. and 11:30 A.M., so multiply 9 by 0.5 to find how much the snowball's radius increased.

$$(9)(0.5) = 4.5$$

Add 4.5 feet to 2 feet to get a final radius of 6.5 feet. Replace r with 6.5 in the volume formula of a sphere.

$$V = \frac{4}{3}\pi(6.5)^3 \approx 1{,}150.3 \text{ ft}^3$$

Subtract 33.5 from 1,150.3 to find the increase in the snowball's volume.

$$1{,}150.3 - 33.5 \approx 1{,}117$$

6. **6** The volume of a cone is found by using the formula $V = \frac{1}{3}\pi r^2 h$, where r is the radius of the circular base and h is the height. Input the known data and solve for r.

$$14.4\pi = \frac{1}{3}\pi r^2(4.8)$$
$$14.4 = 1.6r^2$$
$$9 = r^2$$
$$3 = r$$

The question asks for the diameter, so multiply the radius, 3, by 2.

$$2 \times 3 = 6$$

7. **(D)** Imagine a square that has an area of 4 square units. Since the area of a square is found by using the formula, $A = s^2$ (where s is the length of a side), then each side of the square is 2 because $\sqrt{4} = 2$. If the area of the larger square is double the area of the smaller square, the area of the larger square must be 8. Find the square root of 8 to find the length of a side.

$$\sqrt{8} = 2\sqrt{2}$$

When the area of a square is doubled, each side length increases by a factor of $\sqrt{2}$.

8. **(D)** Find the volume of the cylinder and the cone, and then add 10% to that sum.

The volume of a cylinder is $\pi r^2 h$.

$$\pi(8^2)(12) = 2{,}412$$

The volume of a cone is $\frac{1}{3}\pi r^2 h$.

$$\frac{1}{3}\pi(8^2)(8) = 536$$

Add the two quantities to find the volume of the silo.

$$2{,}412 + 536 = 2{,}948$$

The farmer needs 10% more space, so find 10% of 2,948 and add it to 2,948.

$$2{,}948 + (0.10)(2{,}948) = 3{,}243$$

Once the volume of the silo has been determined to be 2,948, you don't need to finish the calculation. Only choice (D), 3,243, is larger than 2,948.

9. **40** If three parallel lines intersect two transversals, they divide the transversals proportionally. The lakefront length that is 27 feet corresponds to a dock length of 36. The lakefront length that is 30 feet should have a docking length that is proportional to the 27:36 ratio. Set up a proportion to find the docking length of the wider dock. You will find it useful to simplify $\frac{27}{36}$ to $\frac{3}{4}$.

$$\frac{3}{4} = \frac{30}{x}$$

$$3x = 120$$

$$x = 40$$

10. **54** The molding, which surrounds the floor, is equal to the rectangle's perimeter. We are missing the length, but we know the area and width. The area of a rectangle can be found by using the formula Area = length × width.

Input the known information to solve for l.

$$180 = l \times 12$$

$$15 = l$$

We now know the rectangular floor has the following dimensions:

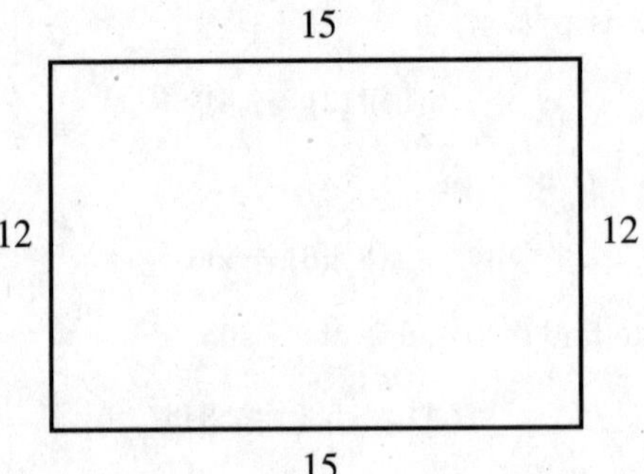

We can use the formula Perimeter = $(2 \times l) + (2 \times w)$ to find the number of feet of molding Oscar needs to surround the floor.

$$(2 \times 15) + (2 \times 12) = 54$$

Oscar needs 54 feet of molding to surround the floor of his study.

Lines, Angles, and Triangles Drill

> For multiple-choice questions, solve the problem and pick the correct answer from the provided choices. Each multiple-choice question has only one correct answer. For student-produced response questions, solve each problem and write down your answers separately.

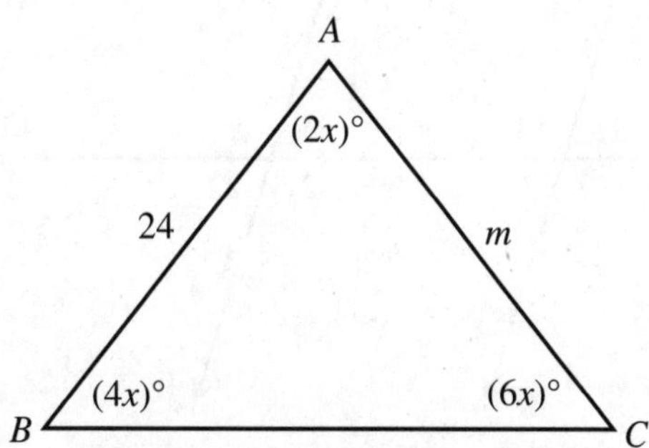

Note: Figure not drawn to scale

1. In ΔABC, what is the value of m?

(A) $12\sqrt{3}$
(B) $12\sqrt{2}$
(C) 12
(D) $3\sqrt{6}$

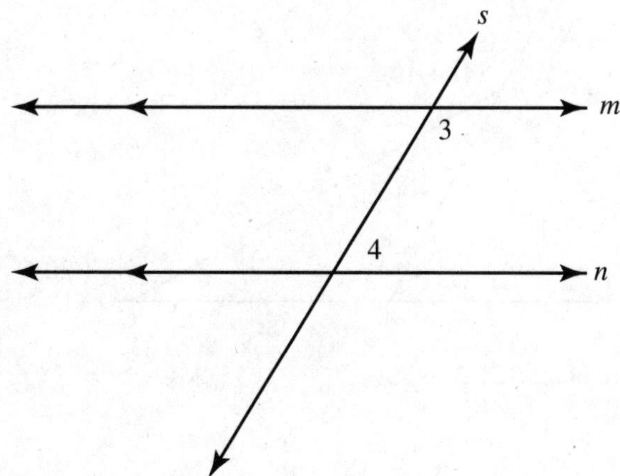

2. In the figure above, lines m and n are parallel. If $m\angle 3 = (3x)^\circ$ and $m\angle 4 = (2x)^\circ$, what is $m\angle 4$?

(A) 36°
(B) 48°
(C) 72°
(D) 108°

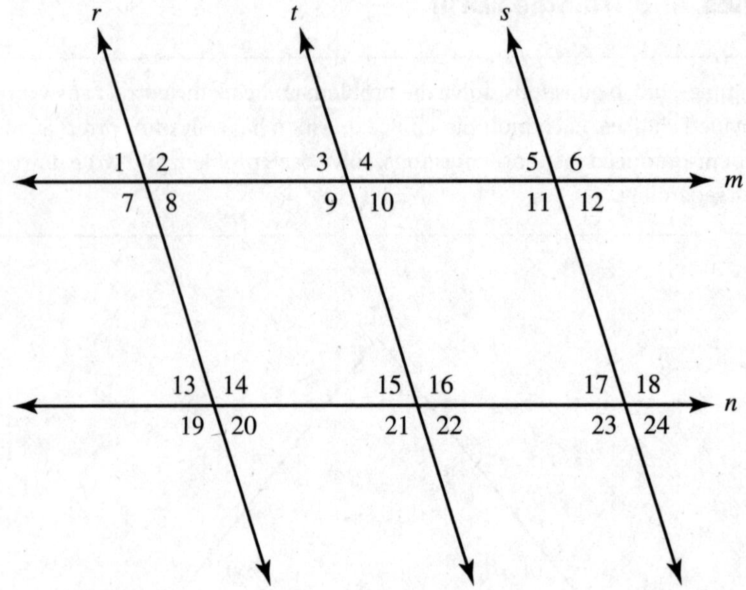

3. In the diagram above, $r \parallel t \parallel s$ and $m \parallel n$. If the measure of $\angle 3 = (2m + 18)°$ and the measure of $\angle 2 = (4m + 42)°$, what is the measure of $\angle 18$?

(A) 122°
(B) 61°
(C) 58°
(D) 20°

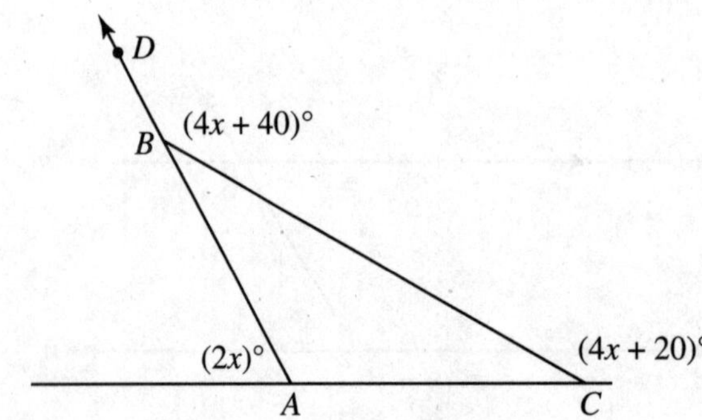

4. What is the measure of $\angle ABC$?

(A) 20°
(B) 40°
(C) 65°
(D) 70°

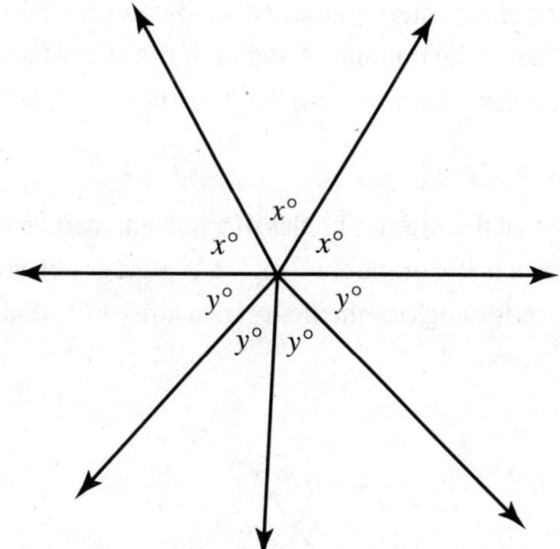

5. In the figure above, what is the value of $(x + y) \div 2(x - y)$?

(A) 3
(B) 3.5
(C) 4
(D) 5.5

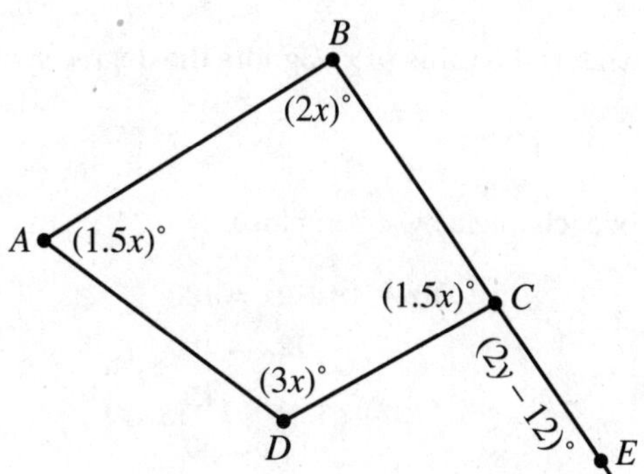

Note: Figure not drawn to scale

6. In the diagram above, what is the measure of y?

(A) 112.5°
(B) 90°
(C) 62.25°
(D) 45°

7. Two sides of a triangle are 7 and 11 inches. If a third side of the triangle is also an integer, what is the product of the smallest and largest values that the side could be?

8. The sum of the measures of the interior angles of a polygon can be found by using the formula $(n-2)(180)$ where n is the number of angles. If the sum of the measures of a regular polygon is 1,260°, what is the degree measure of one interior angle? (Note: Ignore the degree symbol.)

9. The sum of the measures of the interior angles of a polygon can be found by using the formula $(n-2)(180)$ where n is the number of angles. A regular polygon has a side that measures 11 inches. If an exterior angle of the figure measures 45°, what is the measure in inches of the perimeter of the polygon?

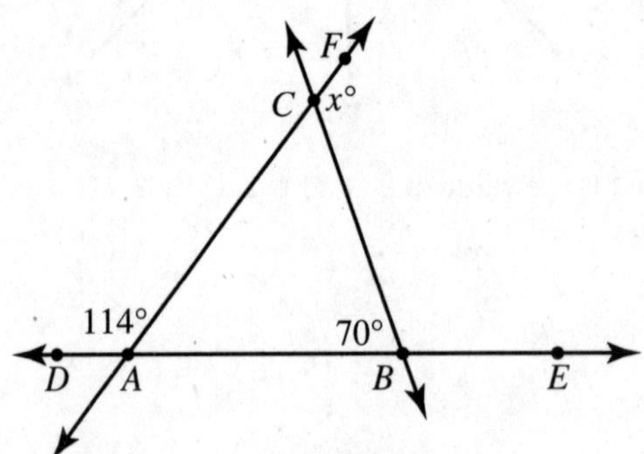

Note: Figure not drawn to scale

10. In the diagram above, what is the value of x? (Ignore the degree symbol.)

Answer Explanations

1. **(A)** Find the measure of each angle by solving for x.

$$6x + 4x + 2x = 180$$
$$12x = 180$$
$$x = 15$$
$$2x = 30$$
$$4x = 60$$
$$6x = 90$$

ΔABC is a 30-60-90 triangle. The hypotenuse measures 24, so m measures $12\sqrt{3}$ because it is opposite the 60° angle.

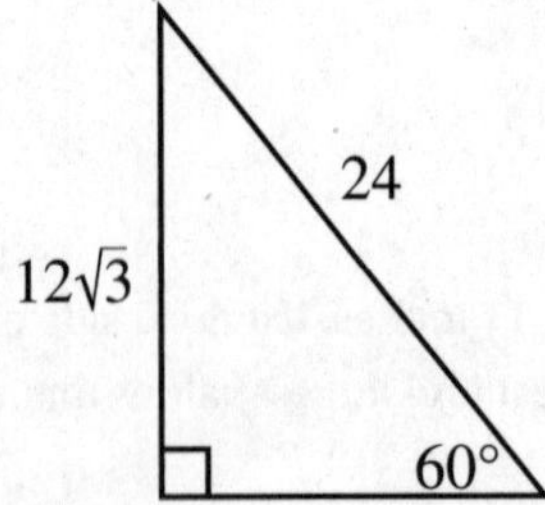

2. **(C)** $\angle 3$ and $\angle 4$ are consecutive interior angles. When lines are parallel, consecutive interior angles are supplementary. Find their sum, and set that value equal to 180°.

$$\begin{aligned} 3x + 2x &= 180 \\ 5x &= 180 \\ x &= 36 \end{aligned}$$

The measure of $\angle 4$ is $(2x)°$, so replace x with 36 and solve.

$$(2)(36) = 72$$

The figure is drawn to scale and angle 4 seems to be acute, so choice (D), 108°, can be eliminated at once.

3. **(A)** Both $\angle 2$ and $\angle 3$ are consecutive interior angles, so their sum is 180°. Solve for m by setting their sum equal to 180.

$$\begin{aligned} (2m + 18) + (4m + 42) &= 180 \\ 6m + 60 &= 180 \\ 6m &= 120 \\ m &= 20 \end{aligned}$$

Substitute 20 for m and find the measure of $\angle 2$.

$$(4)(20) + 42 = 122$$

Since $\angle 2$ and $\angle 6$ are corresponding angles, their measures are equal. Since $\angle 6$ and $\angle 18$ are corresponding angles, their measures are also the same. Using the transitive property, we find that the measure of $\angle 2$ equals the measure of $\angle 6$, which equals the measure of $\angle 18$, which all equal 122°. There are several alternate ways to solve this problem, but the easiest way is visually. The diagram is drawn to scale, and $\angle 18$ appears to be obtuse. Solely choice (A), 122°, appears to have a measure greater than 90°.

4. **(A)** The sum of the measurements of the exterior angles of a polygon is 360°. Add the exterior angles of ΔABC and set them equal to 360 to find x.

$$\begin{aligned} (4x + 40) + (4x + 20) + 2x &= 360 \\ 10x + 60 &= 360 \\ 10x &= 300 \\ x &= 30 \end{aligned}$$

$\angle DBC$ and $\angle ABC$ are supplementary angles; their sum is 180°.

$$\angle DBC = 4x + 40 = 4(30) + 40 = 160$$

Therefore, $m\angle ABC + 160 = 180$ and $m\angle ABC = 20$. The measure of $\angle ABC$ is 20°.

5. **(B)** The sum of the angles above and below the horizontal line are each 180°

$$3x = 180$$
$$x = 60$$
$$4y = 180$$
$$y = 45$$

Inputting 60 and 45 for x and y, respectively, into the expression yields the following.

$$(x + y) \div 2(x - y)$$
$$(60 + 45) \div 2(60 - 45)$$
$$105 \div 30 = 3.5$$

6. **(C)** The sum of the measures of the angles in a quadrilateral is 360°. Solve for x by adding the angle measures and setting that value equal to 360.

$$1.5x + 3x + 1.5x + 2x = 360$$
$$8x = 360$$
$$x = 45$$

$m\angle BCD + m\angle ECD = 180$ because they form a linear pair. $m\angle BCD$ equals 67.5 because $1.5 \times 45 = 67.5$. Therefore, $2y - 12$ is 112.5 because it is supplementary to $\angle BCD$. Set $2y - 12$ equal to 112.5 and solve for y.

$$112.5 = 2y - 12$$
$$124.5 = 2y$$
$$y = 62.25$$

The measure of y is 62.25°.

7. **85** The sum of two sides of a triangle is always larger than the length of the third side. Suppose that 11 is the measure of the longest side. Then $7 + x > 11$ and $x > 4$. The smallest integer that satisfies this inequality is 5.

Suppose the largest side is unknown. Then $7 + 11 > x$ and $18 > x$. The largest value that satisfies this inequality is 17.

The product of the smallest value, 5, and the largest value, 17, is $5 \times 17 = 85$.

8. **140** Use the formula $(n - 2)(180)$ to find the number of angles included in the regular polygon.

$$(n - 2)(180) = 1{,}260$$
$$n - 2 = 7$$
$$n = 9$$

The regular polygon has 9 congruent interior angles. Divide 1,260 by 9 to find the measure of one of the angles.

$$1{,}260 \div 9 = 140$$

9. **88** An exterior angle and an interior angle of a polygon form a linear pair; the sum of their measures is 180°. Thus, one interior angle of the polygon measures 135° because $180° - 45° = 135°$.

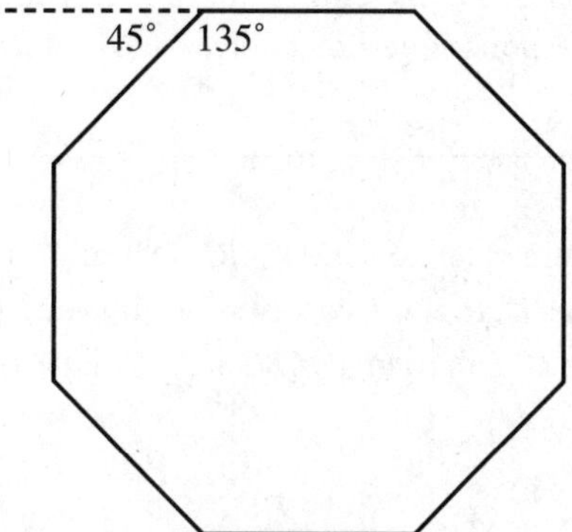

The formula $(n - 2)(180)$ is used to calculate the sum of the measures of all of the interior angles of a polygon. Since n represents the number of congruent angles and congruent sides in a regular polygon, we can use $\frac{(n-2)(180)}{n}$ to find the measure of a single angle.

$$\frac{(n-2)(180)}{n} = 135$$

Solve for n.

$$\frac{(n-2)(180)}{n} = 135$$
$$(n-2)(180) = 135n$$
$$180n - 360 = 135n$$
$$-360 = -45n$$
$$n = 8$$

The polygon has 8 congruent sides and angles (an octagon). Since each side measures 11 inches, the perimeter is $8 \times 11 = 88$ inches.

10. **136** Since $m\angle DAC = 114°$, then $m\angle CAB = 66°$ because the two angles are supplementary. The sum of the measures of the angles in a triangle equals 180°. Therefore, $m\angle ACB = 44°$.

$$66° + 70° + 44° = 180°$$

$\angle ACB$ and $\angle FCB$ are supplementary angles, so their sum is 180°.

$$m\angle ACB + m\angle FCB = 180°$$

Subtract 44° from 180° to find the value of x.

$$180° - 44° = 136°$$

There is a theorem in geometry that states the measure of an exterior angle of a triangle is equal to the sum of the measures of the two remote interior angles. We could have quickly found $m\angle ACB$ by subtracting 70° from 114°.

$$114° - 70° = 44°$$

That step would have reduced your time solving for x.

Right Triangles and Trigonometry Drill

For multiple-choice questions, solve the problem and pick the correct answer from the provided choices. Each multiple-choice question has only one correct answer. For student-produced response questions, solve each problem and write down your answers separately.

1. In triangle ABC, the measure of angle B is $90°$, $BC = 80$, and $AC = 100$. Triangle DEF is like triangle ABC where vertices D, E, and F correspond with vertices A, B, and C, respectively. The scale factor of triangle DEF to triangle ABC is $\frac{1}{10}$. What is the value of $\cos D$?

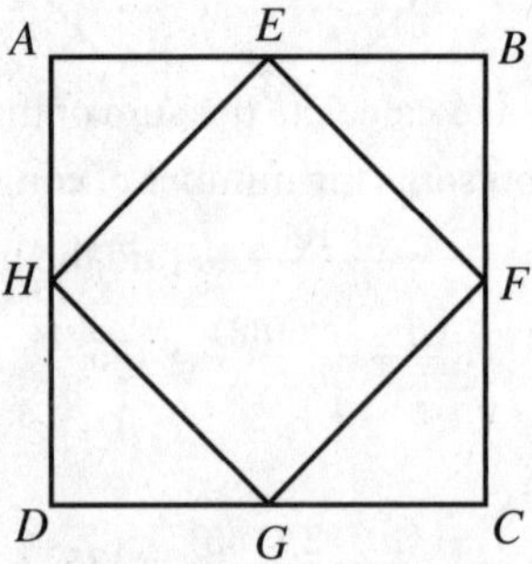

2. Square $EHGF$ lies within square $ABCD$ with E, F, G, and H all being midpoints. If the area of square $EHGF$ is 64 units squared, what is the area of square $ABCD$ (in square units)?

(A) 36
(B) 64
(C) $96\sqrt{2}$
(D) 128

3. In a right triangle. one of the acute angles measures $x°$ where $\sin x° = \frac{5}{8}$. What is the value of $\cos(90° - x°)$?

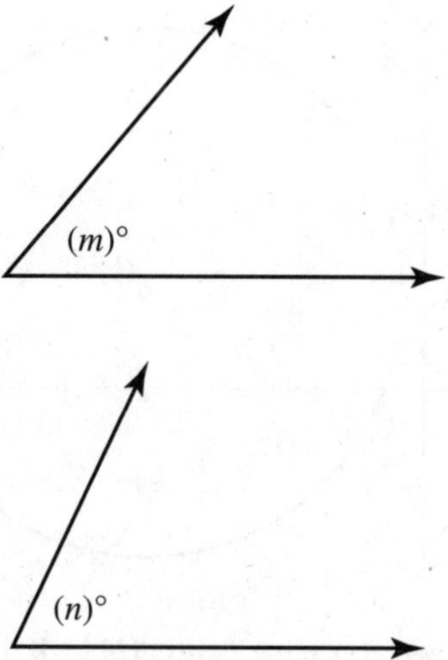

Note: Figures not drawn to scale

4. The angles shown above are complementary, and $\sin (m°) = \cos (n°)$. If $m = (3x - 12)°$ and $n = (6x - 18)°$, what is the value of x?

(A) $13.\overline{3}$
(B) 20.6
(C) 30.25
(D) 40.3

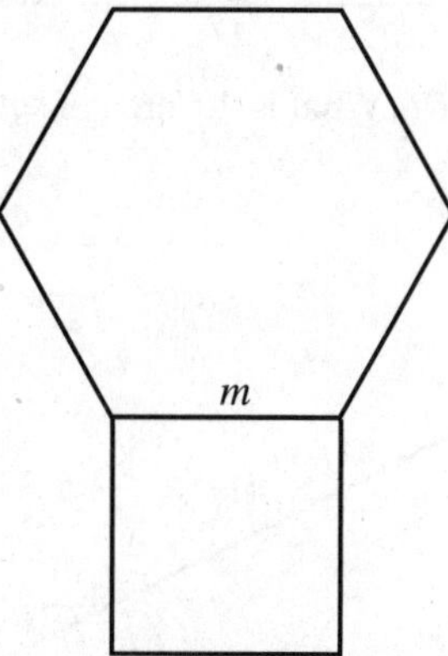

5. The figure above is a regular hexagon with sides of length m and a square with sides of length m as well. If the area of the hexagon is $324\sqrt{3}$ inches, what is the area of the square in square inches?

(A) 108
(B) 216
(C) 256
(D) 324

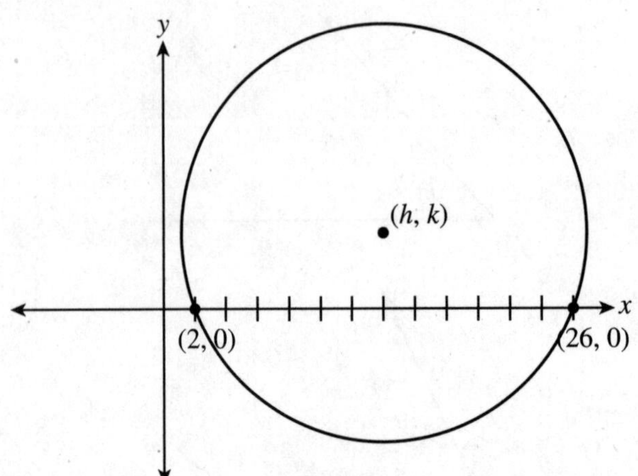

6. In the xy-plane, the circle shown above has center (h, k). If the radius of the circle is 13, what is the value of k?

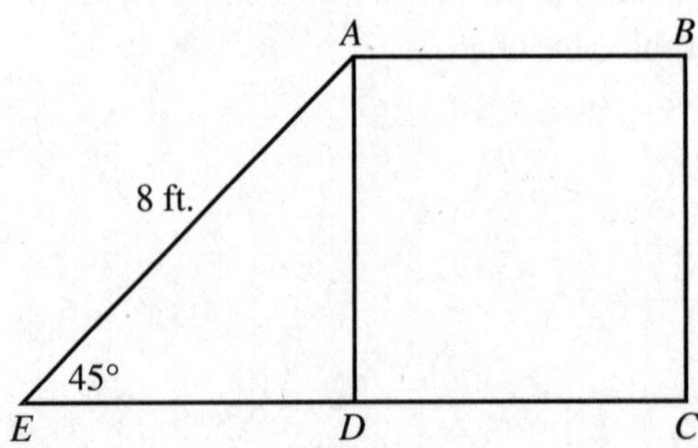

7. Square $ABCD$ is adjacent to $\triangle ADE$. What is the area of square $ABCD$? (Ignore square units in your answer.)

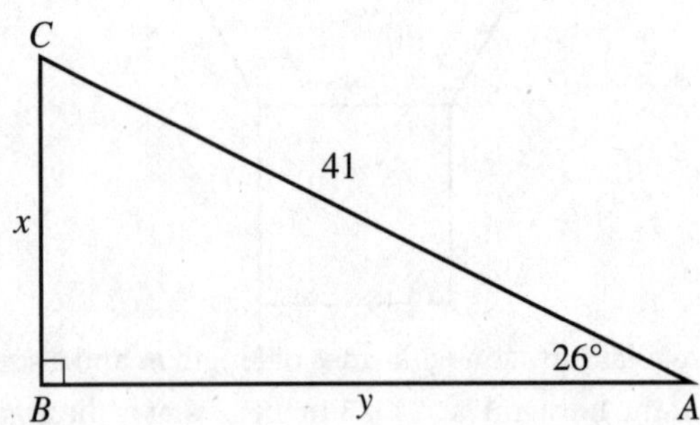

8. In $\triangle CBA$ above, which equation will help find the measure of $\overline{AB}$?

(A) $\tan 64° = \frac{y}{41}$

(B) $\sin 64° = \frac{y}{41}$

(C) $\tan 64° = \frac{41}{y}$

(D) $\sin 26° = \frac{x}{41}$

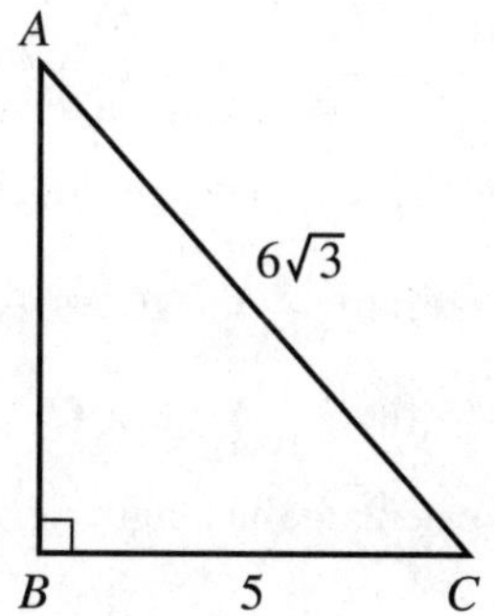

9. What is the perimeter of ΔABC shown above?

(A) $6\sqrt{3} + \sqrt{83}$
(B) $12 + 6\sqrt{3}$
(C) $5 + 6\sqrt{3} + \sqrt{83}$
(D) $3\sqrt{2} + 9\sqrt{3}$

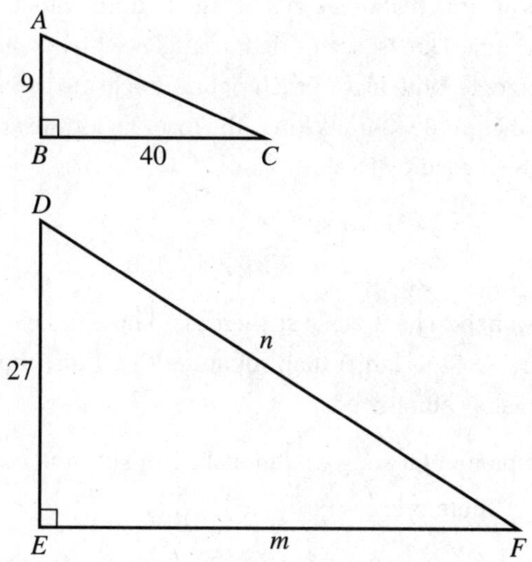

10. ΔABC and ΔDEF are similar triangles. What is the measure of $\overline{DF}$?

(A) 123
(B) 132
(C) 144
(D) 216

Answer Explanations

1. **$\frac{3}{5}$ or .6** The scale factor of triangle *DEF* to triangle *ABC* is $\frac{1}{10}$. So multiply the length of the sides of triangle *ABC* by $\frac{1}{10}$ to find the length of the sides of triangle *DEF*.

$$(100)\left(\frac{1}{10}\right) = 10 = DF$$
$$(80)\left(\frac{1}{10}\right) = 8 = EF$$

Use the Pythagorean theorem to calculate the length of *DE*.

$$a^2 + 8^2 = 10^2$$
$$a^2 = 36$$
$$a = 6$$

The cosine function is found by using the ratio $\cos x = \frac{\text{adjacent side}}{\text{hypotenuse}}$. The side adjacent to angle *D* is 6 and the hypotenuse is 10.

$$\cos D = \frac{\text{adjacent side}}{\text{hypotenuse}} = \frac{3}{5} = 0.6$$

2. **(D)** Square *EFGH* has an area that measures 64 square units, which means each side is 8 units. All four of the triangles are isosceles right triangles with hypotenuse 8. Using the formula for a 45-45-90 triangle, both legs of each right triangle are therefore $4\sqrt{2}$ units. Each side of square *ABCD*, then, is $8\sqrt{2}$ units long. The formula for the area of a square is Area $= s^2$, where *s* is the measure of a side.

$$\text{Area} = s^2$$
$$\text{Area} = (8\sqrt{2})^2 = 128$$

The figures can be assumed to be to scale as there is no note indicating otherwise. We therefore can deduce square *ABCD* is larger than square *EFGH*. Thus, choice (A), 36, and choice (B), 64, can be immediately eliminated.

3. **$\frac{5}{8}$ or .625** By the complementary angle relationship for sine and cosine, $\sin(x°) = \cos(90° - x°)$. Therefore, $\cos(90° - x°) = \frac{5}{8}$.

You can enter your answer as $\frac{5}{8}$ or 0.625 (or just .625) into your digital test form.

4. **(A)** Since the angles are complementary and $\sin(m°) = \cos(n°)$, it follows from the complementary angle property of sines and cosines that $m + n = 90$. Substituting $3x - 12$ for *m* and $6x - 18$ for *n* gives $(3x - 12) + (6x - 18) = 90$, which simplifies to $9x - 30 = 90$. Therefore, $9x = 120$, and $x = 13.\overline{3}$.

5. **(B)** A regular hexagon can be divided into six equilateral triangles. Divide $324\sqrt{3}$ by 6 to find the area of one of the equilateral triangles.

$$324\sqrt{3} \div 6 = 54\sqrt{3}$$

An equilateral triangle can be divided into two 30-60-90 triangles.

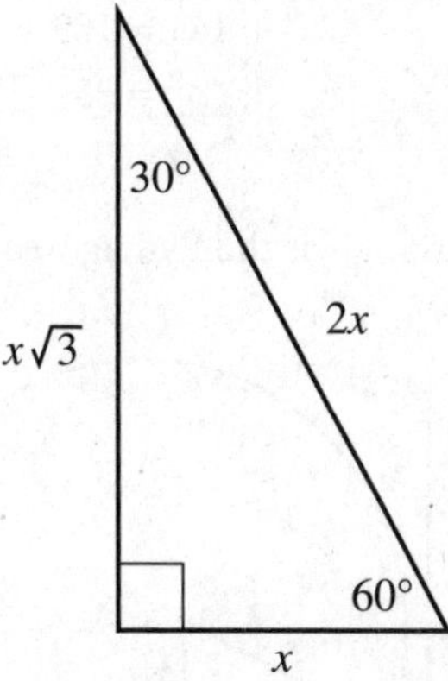

Multiply the base, x, by the height, $\sqrt{3}$, and by $\frac{1}{2}$. Then set that product equal to $27\sqrt{3}$, which is one-half of $54\sqrt{3}$.

$$\left(\frac{1}{2}\right)(x)(x\sqrt{3}) = 27\sqrt{3}$$
$$\frac{1}{2}x^2 = 27$$
$$x^2 = 54$$
$$x = 3\sqrt{6}$$

Multiply $3\sqrt{6}$ by 2 to find one side of the hexagon.

$$3\sqrt{6} \times 2 = 6\sqrt{6}$$

The side length of the hexagon is also the side length of the square. Square $6\sqrt{6}$ to calculate the area of the square.

$$(6\sqrt{6})^2 = 216$$

6. **5** The length of the segment connecting (2, 0) and (26, 0) is 24 because $26 - 2 = 24$. Extend (h, k) to this segment to create an altitude. From $(h, 0)$ to $(2, 0)$ is 12 units because a segment drawn from the center and perpendicular to a segment bisects the segment. Given that the radius of the circle is 13, use the Pythagorean theorem to calculate the height, k, of the circle.

$$a^2 + 12^2 = 13^2$$
$$a^2 + 144 = 169$$
$$a^2 = 25$$
$$a = 5$$

The reader may realize that the triangle is the Pythagorean triple 5-12-13.

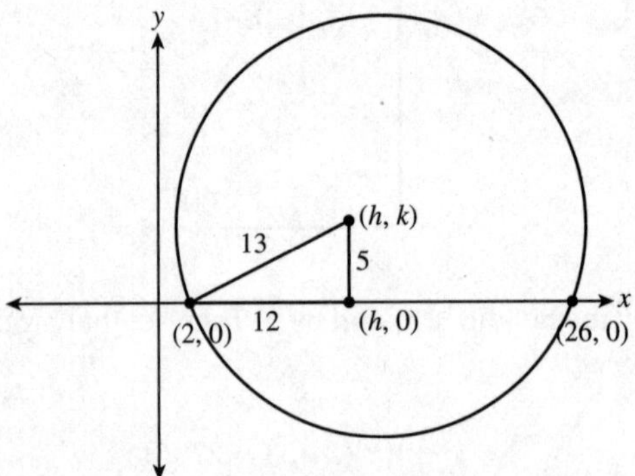

The value of k is 5.

7. **32** A square has four right angles, so the measure of $\angle ADE$ is 90°. Therefore, ΔADE is a 45-45-90 triangle.

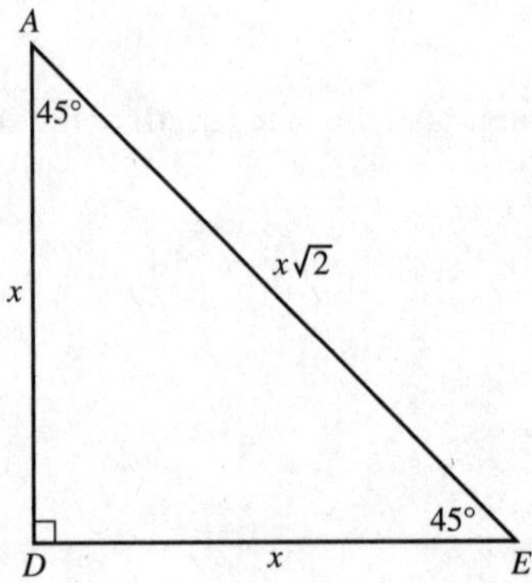

Set 8 equal to $x\sqrt{2}$ and solve for x.

$$x\sqrt{2} = 8$$
$$x = \frac{8}{\sqrt{2}}$$
$$x = \frac{8}{\sqrt{2}} \times \frac{\sqrt{2}}{\sqrt{2}}$$
$$x = \frac{8\sqrt{2}}{\sqrt{2}} = 4\sqrt{2}$$

Each side of the square is $4\sqrt{2}$. The formula for the area of a square is $A = s^2$, where s represents the length of one side. Replace s with $4\sqrt{2}$ and solve.

$$A = (4\sqrt{2})^2$$
$$A = 32$$

8. **(B)** The acute angles of a right triangle are complementary, so m$\angle C = 64°$. The length of $\overline{BA}$, y, is opposite $\angle C$. So use the formula $\sin = \frac{\text{opposite side}}{\text{hypotenuse}}$ to find the length of $\overline{BA}$.

$$\sin 64° = \frac{y}{41}$$

This equation reflects choice (B).

9. **(C)** Use the Pythagorean theorem to calculate the length of $\overline{AB}$.

$$a^2 + 5^2 = (6\sqrt{3})^2$$
$$a^2 + 25 = 108$$
$$a^2 = 83$$
$$a = \sqrt{83}$$

Add the measures of the sides of ΔABC.

$$5 + \sqrt{83} + 6\sqrt{3}$$

None of the quantities above are like terms, so $5 + \sqrt{83} + 6\sqrt{3}$ is the perimeter.

10. **(A)** Find the value of $\overline{AC}$ by using the Pythagorean theorem.

$$9^2 + 40^2 = c^2$$
$$1{,}681 = c^2$$
$$41 = c$$

The two triangles are similar, so the sides are proportional.

$$\frac{AB}{AC} = \frac{DE}{DF}$$
$$\frac{9}{41} = \frac{27}{x}$$

Cross-multiply and solve for x.

$$(9)(x) = (27)(41)$$
$$9x = 1{,}107$$
$$x = 123$$

The measure of $\overline{DF}$ is 123 units.

Circles Drill

For multiple-choice questions, solve the problem and pick the correct answer from the provided choices. Each multiple-choice question has only one correct answer. For student-produced response questions, solve each problem and write down your answers separately.

1. What is the area of a circle that has a circumference that measures 38π ?

(A) 144π
(B) 225π
(C) 361π
(D) 400π

2. What are the coordinates of the center of a circle with the standard form $x^2 + y^2 - 2x + 4y = 4$?

(A) $(1, -2)$
(B) $(-1, 2)$
(C) $(4, 1)$
(D) $(-1, 4)$

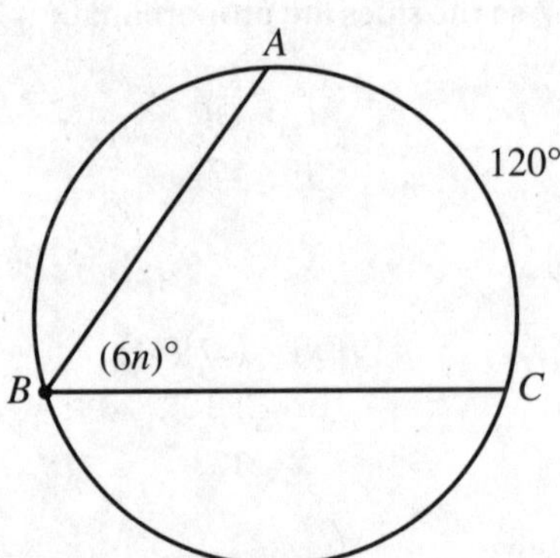

3. What is the value of n in the diagram above?

(A) 5
(B) 10
(C) 20
(D) No conclusion can be drawn from the diagram.

$$x^2 + y^2 + 6x - 8y = 12$$

4. The equation of a circle in the xy-plane is provided above. What is the radius of the circle?

(A) 5
(B) $3\sqrt{3}$
(C) 6
(D) $\sqrt{37}$

5. In a circle with center P, central angle MPN has a measure of $\frac{3\pi}{4}$ radians. The area of the sector formed by the central angle MPN is what fraction of the circle?

6. In the xy-plane, the graph of a circle is $2x^2 + 8x + 2y^2 + 12y = 36$. What is the diameter of the circle?

   (A) $\sqrt{31}$
   (B) $\sqrt{62}$
   (C) $2\sqrt{31}$
   (D) $2\sqrt{62}$

$$x^2 + y^2 - 12x + 3y = -7$$

7. The equation above models a circle in the xy-plane. What is the measure of the diameter of the circle?

   (A) $\frac{5\sqrt{5}}{2}$
   (B) $5\sqrt{5}$
   (C) $10\sqrt{5}$
   (D) $10\sqrt{10}$

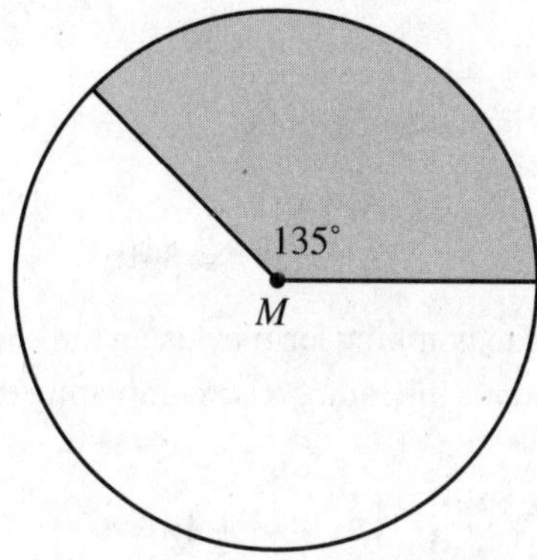

8. Point M is the center of the circle shown above. The shaded area is what fraction of the area of the circle?

9. A central angle in a circle has a measure of 34.4°, and the measure of its sector is 139.6 square units. To the nearest tenth of a unit, what is the measure of the circle's radius? (Use $\pi = 3.14$)

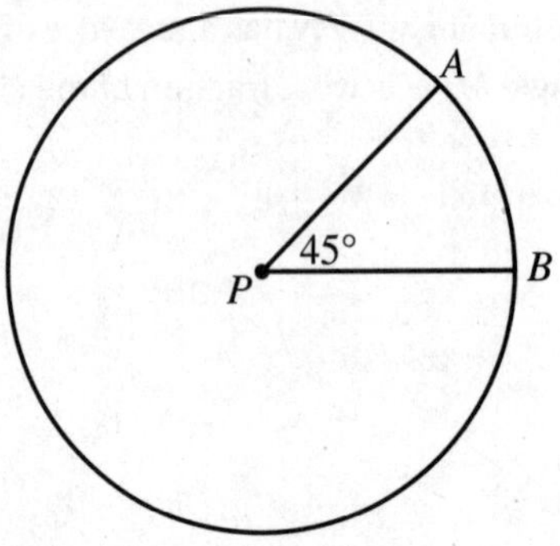

10. Circle P has a central angle that measures 45° and a circumference that measures 88 inches. What is the measure of $\widehat{AB}$?

(A) 44 inches
(B) 22 inches
(C) 11 inches
(D) 5.5 inches

Answer Explanations

1. **(C)** Find the radius of a circle with a circumference measuring 38π.

$$2\pi r = 38\pi$$
$$r = 19$$

Substitute $r = 19$ in the area formula of a circle.

$$A = \pi r^2$$
$$A = \pi(19)^2 = 361\pi$$

2. **(A)** Transform the equation to graphing form by using the equation $(x - h)^2 + (y - k)^2 = r^2$ where (h, k) is the center and r is the radius. Use completing the square method to transform the equation.

$$x^2 - 2x + y^2 + 4y = 4$$

Divide both -2 (the coefficient of x) and 4 (the coefficient of y) by 2, and square each result.

$$\frac{-2}{2} = -1$$
$$(-1)^2 = 1$$
$$\frac{4}{2} = 2$$
$$(2)^2 = 4$$

Add -1 and 4 to both sides of the equation.

$$x^2 - 2x + 1 + y^2 + 4y + 4 = 4 + 1 + 4$$

Factor the trinomials, and simplify the left side of the equation.

$$(x - 1)^2 + (y + 2)^2 = 9$$

By inspection, the center is $(1, -2)$. There will be questions that ask for the radius, which is 3 in this question.

3. **(B)** $\angle ABC$ is an inscribed angle because its vertex is on the circle. An inscribed angle measures one-half of the measure of the intercepted arc.

$$6n = \frac{1}{2}(120)$$
$$6n = 60$$
$$n = 10$$

4. **(D)** The graphing form of a circle is $y = (x - h)^2 + (y - k)^2 = r^2$, where (h, k) is the center of the circle and r is the radius. Convert the equation to graphing form by completing the square.

$$x^2 + y^2 + 6x - 8y = 12$$
$$x^2 + 6x + 9 + y^2 - 8y + 16 = 12 + 9 + 16$$
$$(x + 3)^2 + (y - 4)^2 = 37$$

The radius squared is 37, so find its square root to calculate the length of the radius.

$$r^2 = 37$$
$$r = \sqrt{37}$$

5. $\mathbf{\frac{3}{8}}$ **or .375** The area of a circle is surrounded by an angle of measure 2π radians. Find the ratio of the central angle, $\frac{3\pi}{4}$, to the entire circle.

$$\frac{\frac{3\pi}{4}}{\frac{2\pi}{1}} = \frac{3\pi}{4} \times \frac{1}{2\pi} = \frac{3}{8} \text{ or } .375$$

6. **(C)** The graphing form of a circle is $(x - h)^2 + (y - k)^2 = r^2$ where (h, k) is the center of the circle and r is the radius of the circle.

Divide by 2 to simplify the equation.

$$(2x^2 + 8x + 2y^2 + 12y) \div 2 = 36 \div 2$$
$$x^2 + 4x + y^2 + 6y = 18$$

Next, complete the square for both the x and y components of the equation.

$$x^2 + 4x + 4 + y^2 + 6y + 9 = 18 + 4 + 9$$

Factor the left side of the equation and simplify the right side.

$$(x + 2)^2 + (y + 3)^2 = 31$$

In this circle, $r^2 = 31$. So $r = \sqrt{31}$. The question requires the diameter of the circle, so multiply the radius by 2.

$$2 \times \sqrt{31} = 2\sqrt{31}$$

7. **(B)** Calculate the length of the diameter by first finding the radius. Use completing the square to transform the equation from standard form to graphing form.

$$x^2 + y^2 - 12x + 3y = -7$$
$$x^2 - 12x + y^2 + 3y = -7$$
$$x^2 - 12x + 36 + y^2 + 3y + \frac{9}{4} = -7 + 36 + \frac{9}{4}$$
$$(x - 6)^2 + \left(y + \frac{3}{2}\right)^2 = \frac{125}{4}$$

The graphing form of a circle is $(x - h)^2 + (y - k)^2 = r^2$ in which (h, k) are the coordinates of the center and r is the length of the radius. Find r.

$$r^2 = \frac{125}{4}$$
$$r = \frac{5\sqrt{5}}{2}$$

Multiply the radius by 2 to find the measure of the diameter.

$$d = (2)\left(\frac{5\sqrt{5}}{2}\right) = 5\sqrt{5}$$

8. $\mathbf{\frac{3}{8}}$ **or .375** The shaded area has a central angle that measures 135°. Therefore, the shaded area is $\frac{135}{360}$ of the circle. Reduce $\frac{135}{360}$ to $\frac{3}{8}$ or express it as the decimal .375.

9. **21.6** The area of a sector is found by using the following formula.

$$A = \frac{m}{360}\pi r^2$$

where m = measure of the central angle and r = length of the radius. Input the known data and solve for r.

$$139.6 = \frac{34.4}{360}\pi r^2$$
$$465.33 \approx r^2$$
$$21.6 \approx r$$

10. **(C)** Find the length of $\widehat{AB}$ by using the formula $\left(\frac{m}{360}\right)$(circumference) in which m is the measure of the central angle.

$$\left(\frac{45}{360}\right)(88) = 11$$

The length of $\widehat{AB}$ is 11 inches.

Levels of Difficulty

When taking the SAT, test takers will notice that the level of difficulty increases the further they progress through the test. This final section simulates that aspect of the exam. The reader will now practice questions grouped by levels of difficulty: easy/medium/difficult.

Questions by Level of Difficulty

Easy Questions

> For multiple-choice questions, solve the problem and pick the correct answer from the provided choices. Each multiple-choice question has only one correct answer. For student-produced response questions, solve each problem and write down your answers separately.

1. What is the value of x in the equation $7x + 4 = 95$?

   (A) 12
   (B) 13
   (C) 14
   (D) 15

2. What number is 84% of 17?

3. If $2x - 6 = 18$, what is the value of $x - 3$?

4. If $\frac{r-2}{6} = n$ and $n = 5$, what is the value of r?

   (A) 28
   (B) 30
   (C) 32
   (D) 42

5. Shelley is a salesperson for a local furniture store. She receives a \$24.00 commission for every recliner she sells and \$63.00 for every dinette set. If Shelley sells r dinette sets and d recliners during a work shift, which expression represents her pay for that day?

   (A) $63r + 24d$
   (B) $24r + 63d$
   (C) $24r - 63d$
   (D) $63r - 24d$

6. Cindy owns a candy store and sells individual candies as well as mixes. Her most popular mix is the chocolate and mint collection. The ratio of chocolates to mints in this candy mix is 3 to 5. If she is mixing 7 pounds of the mix, how many pounds are chocolates?

7. Warren has a streaming video account with an online movie channel. The cost for each movie he rents is \$2.25, and his monthly membership fee is \$4.00. If his invoice for the past month was \$24.25, how many movies did Warren rent?

(A) 6
(B) 7
(C) 8
(D) 9

8. The product of an integer, n, and 5, increased by 12, is -13. What is the value of n?

(A) 25
(B) 5
(C) $\frac{1}{5}$
(D) -5

9. Kareem has purchased a hybrid automobile that has an average fuel efficiency of 40 miles per gallon. He filled his 12-gallon tank yesterday, but it now registers $\frac{3}{4}$ full. How many miles did Kareem drive if his mileage reflected his average fuel efficiency?

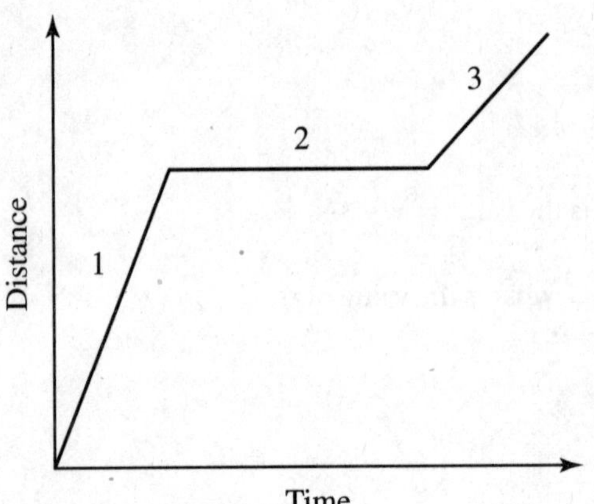

10. Thomas rides his bike to the park and then sits down on a bench to rest. After his rest, he jogs several miles. Which part(s) of the graph represent(s) the time he spent sitting on the bench?

(A) 1 and 2
(B) 2 only
(C) 2 and 3
(D) 3 only

Answer Explanations

1. **(B)** Solve for x.

$$7x+4=95$$
$$7x+4-4=95-4$$
$$7x=91$$
$$\frac{7x}{7}=\frac{91}{7}$$
$$x=13$$

2. **14.28** Set up an equation to solve the problem.

$$x=(0.84)(17)$$
$$x=14.28$$

3. **9** Solve for x.

$$2x-6=18$$
$$2x=24$$
$$x=12$$

Substitute $x=12$ into $x-3$.

$$x-3=9$$

There is a faster way to solve this problem. Divide $2x-6=18$ by 2.

$$(2x-6)\div 2=18\div 2$$
$$x-3=9$$

4. **(C)** Substitute 5 for n as provided in the original equation.

$$\frac{r-2}{6}=5$$

Next, multiply both sides of the equation by 6 to isolate $r-2$.

$$(6)\left(\frac{r-2}{6}\right)=5(6)$$
$$r-2=30$$

Add 2 to both sides of the equation.

$$r-2+2=30+2$$
$$r=32$$

5. **(A)** If Shelley sells 10 recliners and 10 dinette sets, her commission would be $10(24)+10(63)=870$. In other words, multiply each commission by the number of units she sells of a particular item. If she sells r dinette sets and d recliners, her commission would be $63r+24d$.

6. **$\frac{21}{8}$ or 2.62 or 2.63** Since the ratio of chocolates to mints is 3 to 5, the ratio of chocolates to the mix is $\frac{3}{3+5}=\frac{3}{8}$. Remember, there are 8 parts to the mix: 3 parts chocolate and 5 parts mints. Multiply 7 pounds by $\frac{3}{8}$ to find the number of pounds of chocolates in a 7-pound mix.

$$\frac{3}{8}\times 7=\frac{21}{8}\text{ or }2.62\text{ or }2.63$$

7. **(D)** Let x equal the number of movies rented by Warren in the past month.

$$2.25x + 4 = 24.25$$
$$2.25x = 20.25$$

Divide both sides of the equation by 2.25.

$$\frac{2.25x}{2.25} = \frac{20.25}{2.25}$$
$$x = 9$$

8. **(D)** The product of two values is the result of multiplying them. "Increased by" means use addition. We therefore arrive at the following equation.

$$5n + 12 = -13$$

Begin isolating the variable by subtracting 12 from both sides of the equation.

$$5n + 12 - 12 = -13 - 12$$
$$5n = -25$$

Complete the problem by dividing both sides of the equation by 5.

$$\frac{5n}{15} = -\frac{25}{5}$$
$$n = -5$$

Check your solution by replacing n with -5 in the original equation.

$$5(-5) + 12 = -13$$
$$-25 + 12 = -13$$
$$-13 = -13$$

9. **120** Kareem's gas tank registered $\frac{3}{4}$ full, which means he has used $\frac{1}{4}$ of his full tank, which has a capacity of 12 gallons. Multiply $\frac{1}{4}$ by 12 to find how many gallons Kareem used.

$$\frac{1}{4} \times 12 = 3$$

Kareem used 3 gallons of gas. Each gallon lets him drive 40 miles, so he drove a total of $3 \times 40 = 120$ miles.

10. **(B)** Part 2 of the graph is flat, indicating that time passed but no additional distance was covered. Parts 1 and 3 show that both time and distance were covered as evidenced by the upward behavior of the graph.

Medium Questions

For multiple-choice questions, solve the problem and pick the correct answer from the provided choices. Each multiple-choice question has only one correct answer. For student-produced response questions, solve each problem and write down your answers separately.

$$\frac{2}{3}x - \frac{5}{9}y = -7$$
$$bx - \frac{10}{3}y = 17$$

1. In the system of equations above, b is a constant. If the system has no solution, what is the value of b?

(A) -3.75
(B) 3.75
(C) 4
(D) 4.4

Day	Thursday	Friday	Saturday
Chance of rain	65%	74%	31%

2. The coach of the Denver High School baseball team will have to cancel an upcoming tournament if the weather conditions forecast rain. The table presents the probability of rain for the next three days. If it doesn't rain on Friday or Saturday, the coach can plan on holding the tournament at his high school. What is the probability that it will rain on Thursday but not Friday or Saturday?

(A) 18.7%
(B) 16.3%
(C) 14.9%
(D) 11.7%

3. If $2x + 3y = 17$ and $5x - 7y = 31$, what is the value of $\frac{7x - 4y}{8}$?

(A) 6
(B) 7
(C) 8
(D) 12

$$ax + by = 8$$
$$4x + 6y = 48$$

4. The system of equations above has infinite solutions. If a and b are constants, what is the value of $\frac{b}{a}$?

x	1	2	3
$g(x)$	3	5	7

x	3	4	5
$h(x)$	8	16	24

5. Values for $g(x)$ and $h(x)$ are listed above. What is the value for $h(g(2))$?

(A) 24
(B) 36
(C) 48
(D) 72

6. Students at a local art school wish to create a Styrofoam pyramid. The pyramid will have a rectangular base that measures 6 feet by 8 feet and will have a height that measures 12 feet. If each cubic foot weighs 4 ounces and the cost per pound of Styrofoam is \$0.50 per pound, what will be the cost to create the pyramid? (Note: 16 ounces = 1 pound) (Ignore the \$ sign.)

7. A circle in the xy-plane has the equation $(x+2)^2+(y-3)^2=25$. Which of the following coordinate pairs lies in the interior of the circle?

(A) $(-3, 2)$
(B) $(7, -4)$
(C) $(3, -6)$
(D) $(0, -11)$

8. The expression $\frac{4n+6}{n-4}$ is equivalent to which of the following?

(A) $-\frac{4+6}{4}$
(B) $4-\frac{6}{4}$
(C) $4+\frac{6}{n-4}$
(D) $4+\frac{22}{n-4}$

$$g(x)=(x+4)(x-8)$$

9. Which of the following shows an equivalent form of the function g so that a minimum value of $g(x)$ appears as a constant or coefficient?

(A) $g(x)=x^2-32$
(B) $g(x)=x^2-4x-32$
(C) $g(x)=(x-2)^2-36$
(D) $g(x)=(x-4)^2-32$

10. The distance between the points $(7, 5)$ and $(x, 4)$ is 8. What is/are the coordinate(s) of x?

(A) $7+3\sqrt{7}$
(B) $7-3\sqrt{7}$
(C) $3\pm\sqrt{7}$
(D) $7\pm3\sqrt{7}$

Answer Explanations

1. **(C)** If the system of equations has no solution, each equation has the same slope and a different y-intercept, thus making the lines parallel. In this system of equations, the x's and y's must be multiples of one another.

   Find the multiple by dividing $-\frac{10}{3}y$ by $\frac{-5}{9}y$.

   $$-\frac{10}{3}y \div \frac{-5}{9}y = 6$$

   Multiply $\frac{2}{3}$ by 6 to find the value of b.

   $$\frac{2}{3} \times 6 = 4$$

   Make sure the constants are different to ensure the lines are parallel. Since $-7(6)$ equals 42 and does not equal 17, the constants are different.

2. **(D)** The probability of rain on Thursday is 65%. Since the probability of rain on Friday and Saturday are 74% and 31%, respectively, subtract each from 100% to find the probability of no rain on both days.

   No rain on Friday: $100\% - 74\% = 26\%$

   No rain on Saturday: $100\% - 31\% = 69\%$

   Each day's forecast is independent of the others, so multiply the three probabilities.

   $$(0.65)(0.26)(0.69) = 0.1166 \approx 11.7\%$$

3. **(A)** Although this system of equations can be solved via the substitution or elimination method, it is much easier to add the two equations together.

   $$\begin{array}{r} 2x + 3y = 17 \\ +\ 5x - 7y = 31 \\ \hline 7x - 4y = 48 \end{array}$$

   $$\frac{7x - 4y}{8} = \frac{48}{8} = 6$$

4. **$\frac{3}{2}$ or 1.5** If the system of equations has infinite solutions, they are equations that represent the same line. Multiply the top equation by 6 to ensure that the constant terms are the same in both equations.

$$6(ax + by = 8) = 6ax + 6by = 48$$

The system of equations now appears as follows:

$$6ax + 6by = 48$$
$$4x + 6y = 48$$

We can now conclude that $6ax = 4x$ and $6by = 6y$.

$$\frac{6ax}{6x} = \frac{4x}{6x}$$
$$a = \frac{2}{3}$$
$$\frac{6by}{6y} = \frac{6y}{6y}$$
$$b = 1$$

Now find $\frac{b}{a}$.

$$\frac{b}{a} = \frac{1}{\frac{2}{3}} = \frac{3}{2}$$

The correct answer can also be entered as 1.5.

5. **(A)** Using the values chart, note that when $x = 2$, $g(2) = 5$. Now check the $h(x)$ values chart for $x = 5$. We find $h(5) = 24$. Therefore, $h(g(2)) = 24$.

6. **24.0 or 24** Find the volume of the pyramid using the formula $V = \frac{1}{3}Bh$, where B is the base area of the pyramid and h is its height.

Use the formula Area = (length)(width) to find the base area.

$$\text{Area} = 6 \times 8 = 48 \text{ square feet}$$

Replace B with 48 in the volume formula.

$$V = \left(\frac{1}{3}\right)(48)(12) = 192$$

The pyramid has a volume that measures 192 cubic feet. Since each cubic foot weighs 4 ounces, multiply 192 by 4 to find its weight in ounces.

$$192 \times 4 = 768$$

Divide 768 by 16, the number of ounces in a pound, to find the weight of the pyramid in pounds.

$$768 \div 16 = 48$$

Multiply 48 by \$0.50 to find the cost for the Styrofoam to make the pyramid.

$$48 \times \$0.50 = \$24.00$$

7. **(A)** In order for a point to lie in the interior of $(x + 2)^2 + (y - 3)^2 = 25$, its coordinates must satisfy $(x + 2)^2 + (y - 3)^2 < 25$. Substitute choice (A), $(-3, 2)$, into the inequality.

$$(-3 + 2)^2 + (2 - 3)^2 < 25$$
$$2 < 25$$

An alternate way to answer the question is by sketching a graph.

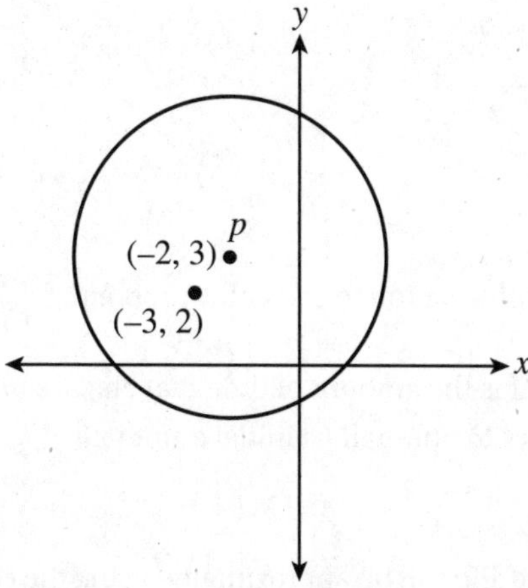

8. **(D)** Use long division to assess the equivalent statement.

$$n - 4 \overline{)\,4n + 6} \quad \text{quotient: } 4 + \frac{22}{n-4}$$
$$\underline{4n - 16}$$
$$22$$

$4 + \dfrac{22}{n - 4}$ is equivalent to $\dfrac{4n + 6}{n - 4}$.

9. **(C)** The vertex, or graphing, form of a parabola shows the vertex. Because the leading coefficient of $g(x) = (x + 4)(x - 8)$ is positive, the parabola opens up and its vertex is a minimum.

Follow these steps to transform the equation from factored form to vertex form.

$$g(x) = (x + 4)(x - 8)$$
$$g(x) = x^2 - 4x - 32$$
$$g(x) = x^2 - 4x - 32$$
$$g(x) = x^2 - 4x + 4 - 32 - 4$$
$$g(x) = (x - 2)^2 - 36$$

The vertex of $g(x) = (x + 4)(x - 8)$ is $(2, -36)$.

10. **(D)** Use the distance formula to find the missing coordinates of x.

$$\sqrt{(x_1 - x_2)^2 + (y_1 - y_2)^2}$$
$$\sqrt{(x_1 - 7)^2 + (4 - 5)^2} = 8$$
$$(x_1 - 7)^2 + 1 = 64$$
$$(x_1 - 7)^2 = 63$$
$$x - 7 = \pm\sqrt{63}$$
$$x = 7 \pm \sqrt{63}$$
$$x = 7 \pm 3\sqrt{7}$$

Difficult Questions

For multiple-choice questions, solve the problem and pick the correct answer from the provided choices. Each multiple-choice question has only one correct answer. For student-produced response questions, solve each problem and write down your answers separately.

1. If $n > 0$, then n^2 is

   (A) greater than n.
   (B) equal to n.
   (C) less than n.
   (D) there is not enough information to solve this problem.

2. The half-life of an element is the amount of time that elapses until a certain mass of an element or compound decays to one-half its initial amount.

   $$A = R_0\left(\frac{1}{2}\right)^x$$

   A certain compound's half-life can be approximated using the equation above where

   R_0 = the initial amount of the compound

   A = the amount remaining after x years

   x = the time elapsed in years

   If 125 grams of the compound is left to decay over 2.3 years, how many grams will remain?

   (A) 16.7
   (B) 25.4
   (C) 29.6
   (D) 41.1

3. Twenty-one students entered into a foul shooting contest in basketball. Each student was given five foul shots to attempt. The table below lists the number of foul shots made and the number of students who made that many foul shots.

Successful Foul Shots	Frequency
0	2
1	4
2	4
3	7
4	3
5	1

If a student who successfully shot at least 2 foul shots was chosen at random, what is the probability that the student successfully shot exactly 4 foul shots?

(A) $\frac{1}{7}$
(B) $\frac{1}{5}$
(C) $\frac{2}{5}$
(D) $\frac{3}{5}$

4. The number of students in an elementary class, *s*, decided to spend *D* dollars for a present for their favorite teacher, Mrs. Konopka. Each student was to contribute an equal amount. Because 15 students refused to contribute, each of those remaining agreed to contribute an additional, equal amount. What was the additional amount each had to contribute, in dollars?

(A) $(s - 15) \div D$
(B) $(s^2 - 15) \div D$
(C) $\frac{15D}{s^2 - 15s}$
(D) $\frac{s^2 - 15s}{15D}$

$$4a + n = 2a - 3$$
$$4b + m = 2b - 3$$

5. If *n* is *m* plus 1, which of the following is true?

(A) *a* is *b* minus $\frac{1}{2}$
(B) *a* is *b* plus $\frac{1}{2}$
(C) *a* is *b* plus 1
(D) *a* is *b* minus 2

6. Which of the following is equal to $\left(\frac{m}{2}+n\right)^2$?

(A) $\frac{m^2}{2}+n^2$
(B) $\frac{m^2}{4}+mn+n^2$
(C) $\frac{m^2}{2}+mn+\frac{n^2}{4}$
(D) $m+\frac{mn}{2}+n$

$$y=m(x+3)(x-5)$$

7. In the quadratic function above, m is a nonzero constant. The graph of the equation in the xy-plane has the vertex (e, f). Which of the following is the value of f?

(A) $16m$
(B) $4m$
(C) $-4m$
(D) $-16m$

$$y=x^2+5x+8$$
$$y+7x+28=0$$

8. The system of equations above has how many solutions?

(A) Exactly 3 solutions
(B) Exactly 2 solutions
(C) Exactly 1 solution
(D) No solutions

9. If $f(x)=2x+3$ and $f(2x+3)=5x$, what is the value of $3x^2$?

$$f(x)=\frac{1}{(x-3)^2+6(x-3)+9}$$

10. For what value of x is the above function f undefined?

Answer Explanations

1. **(D)** Consider the three conditions that each satisfy $n>0$:

(a) Let $n=2$, then $n^2=4$

$$n^2>n$$

(b) Let $n=1$, then $n^2=1$

$$n^2=n$$

(c) Let $n=\frac{1}{2}$, then $n^2=\frac{1}{4}$

$$n^2<n$$

Without more information about n, we cannot make a conclusion about n^2.

2. **(B)** Input 2.3 for the number of years, x, and input 125 for R_0, the initial amount of the compound.

$$A = R_0\left(\frac{1}{2}\right)^x$$
$$A = 125\left(\frac{1}{2}\right)^{2.3}$$
$$A = 25.4$$

After 2.3 years, 125 grams of the compound will be reduced to 25.4 grams.

3. **(B)** Find the probability of selecting a student who successfully shot 4 foul shots by using the formula $\frac{\text{favored outcomes}}{\text{all outcomes}}$.

There are a total of 15 students who successfully shot 2 or more foul shots. Of those 15 students, 3 made exactly 4 baskets. Therefore, $\frac{3}{15}$, or $\frac{1}{5}$, of the students in the sample made exactly 4 baskets.

4. **(C)** If the entire class contributed equally, the cost per student, in terms of s and D, would be $\frac{D}{s}$. However, 15 of the students do not contribute this sum, so $15\frac{D}{s}$ needs to be split among the remaining $s - 15$ students. $\frac{15\frac{D}{s}}{s-15}$ can be rewritten as $\left(15\frac{D}{s}\right)\left(\frac{1}{s-15}\right)$. By multiplying the numerators and denominators, we arrive at $\frac{15D}{s^2 - 15s}$.

5. **(A)** Subtract the two equations and combine like terms.

$$\begin{aligned} 4a + n &= 2a - 3 \\ -(4b + m &= 2b - 3) \\ \hline 4a - 4b + n - m &= 2a - 2b \\ 2a - 2b + n - m &= 0 \end{aligned}$$

Substitute $m + 1$ for n.

$$\begin{aligned} 2a - 2b + m + 1 - m &= 0 \\ 2a - 2b + 1 &= 0 \\ 2a - 2b &= -1 \\ a - b &= -\frac{1}{2} \\ a &= b - \frac{1}{2} \end{aligned}$$

6. **(B)** Use the model $(a + b)^2 = a^2 + 2ab + b^2$ to expand the trinomial $\left(\frac{m}{2} + n\right)^2$.

$$\left(\frac{m}{2}\right)^2 + 2\left(\frac{m}{2}n\right) + (n)^2 = \frac{m^2}{4} + mn + n^2$$

The correct answer could also be found using the FOIL method of multiplication.

$$\begin{aligned} \left(\frac{m}{2} + n\right)^2 &= \left(\frac{m}{2} + n\right) + \left(\frac{m}{2} + n\right) \\ &= \frac{m^2}{4} + \frac{mn}{2} + \frac{mn}{2} + n^2 \\ &= \frac{m^2}{4} + mn + n^2 \end{aligned}$$

Choices (A), (C), and (D) are the results of improperly expanding the trinomial $\left(\frac{m}{2} + n\right)^2$.

7. **(D)** Use FOIL to expand the quantities in the parentheses.

$$y = m(x + 3)(x - 5) = m(x^2 - 2x - 15)$$

Multiply each term in the parentheses by m.

$$m(x^2 - 2x - 15) = mx^2 - 2xm - 15m$$

Find the value of e by using the formula $e = -\frac{b}{2a}$. (This is also the formula for finding the axis of symmetry of a parabola.)

$$e = -\frac{b}{2a} = -\frac{(-2m)}{2m} = 1$$

Find f by replacing x with 1 in $mx^2 - 2xm - 15m$.

$$m(1)^2 - 2(1)m - 15m = -16m$$

The value of f in the vertex is $-16m$.

8. **(C)** Set the second (linear) equation equal to y.

$$y + 7x + 28 = 0$$
$$y = -7x - 28$$

Use the substitution principle to solve for x.

$$x^2 + 5x + 8 = -7x - 28$$

Set the equation equal to 0 and solve for x.

$$x^2 + 5x + 8 = -7x - 28$$
$$x^2 + 12x + 36 = 0$$
$$(x + 6)^2 = 0$$
$$x + 6 = 0$$

Substitute $x = -6$ into the equation $y = x^2 + 5x + 8$ to find the value of y.

$$y = (-6)^2 + 5(-6) + 8$$
$$y = 14$$

There is exactly one solution, $(-6, 14)$, to the system of equations.

9. **243** Use $f(x) = 2x + 3$ and $f(2x + 3)$ together to find the value of x. Since $f(x) = 2x + 3$, then $f(2x + 3)$ must equal $2(2x + 3) + 3$. Set that expression equal to $5x$ and solve for x.

$$\begin{aligned} 2(2x + 3) + 3 &= 5x \\ 4x + 6 + 3 &= 5x \\ 9 &= x \end{aligned}$$

Substitute 9 for x in $3x^2$.

$$3(9^2) = 243$$

10. **0**

$$f(x) = \frac{1}{(x - 3)^2 + 6(x - 3) + 9}$$

Division by 0 is undefined so set the denominator of the function equal to 0.

$$\begin{aligned} (x - 3)^2 + 6(x - 3) + 9 &= 0 \\ x^2 - 6x + 9 + 6x - 18 + 9 &= 0 \\ x^2 &= 0 \\ x &= 0 \end{aligned}$$

When $x = 0$, the function f is undefined.

Acknowledgments

Page 52: from *Indian Country* by Peter Matthiessen, copyright © 1979, 1980, 1981, 1984 by Peter Matthiessen. Used by permission of Viking Penguin, a division of Penguin Group (USA) Inc.

Page 12: from *Flappers and Philosophers* by F. Scott Fitzgerald, 1920.

Page 12: from "Hiroshima: A Soldier's View" by Paul Fussell. Reprinted by permission of *The New Republic*, copyright © 1981.

Page 23: from "The Professionalization of Poetry" in *Heavy Lifting* by David Alpaugh. Copyright © 2007 Alehouse Press. Reprinted by permission of the author.

Page 24: from "Coasts in Crisis, Coastal Change," Jeffress Williams, Kurt Dodd, and Kathleen Krafft Gohn, in *U.S. Geological Survey Circular 1075*, 1990.

Page 149: from "Highlights of Women's Earnings in 2011," U.S. Department of Labor, U.S. Bureau of Labor Statistics, October 2012, Report 1038.

Page 150: from "United States Arctic Science Policy," Alaska Council of Science and Technology, January 1983.

Page 135: from *Museum of Antiquity: A Description of Ancient Life* by L. W. Yaggy, M.S., and T. L. Haines, A.M., published by J. B. Furman & Co., Western Publishing House, Chicago, IL, 1884.

Page 105: from *History of Woman Suffrage, Volume 1*, by Susan B. Anthony, 1887.

Page 25: from *Balzac and the Little Chinese Seamstress* by Dai Sijie. Published by Alfred A. Knopf, 2001. English translation copyright © 2001 by Ina Rilke.

Page 13: from *Reflections of a Neoconservative* by Irving Kristol. Copyright © 1983 Irving Kristol. Reprinted by permission of Basic Books, a member of the Perseus Books Group.

Page 39: from "The Clash of Civilizations?" by Samuel P. Huntington. Reprinted by permission of *Foreign Affairs*, Summer 1993. Copyright © 1993 by the Council on Foreign Relations, Inc., *www.foreignaffairs.com.*

Page 39: from "Do Civilizations Hold?" by Albert L. Weeks in *The Clash of Civilizations: The Debate* published by the Council on Foreign Relations, 2010. Copyright © 1993 by Albert L. Weeks. Reprinted by permission of the author.

Page 13: from Milton Friend, 2014, "Why Bother About Wildlife Disease?" *U.S. Geological Survey Circular* 1401, 76, *p* ., *http://dx.doi.org/10.3133/cir1401.*

Page 13: from Alexis de Tocqueville, *Democracy in America*, originally published in 1835; translated from French into English by Henry Reeve.

Page 74: from Eagles-Smith, C. A., Willacker, J. J., and Flanagan Pritz, C. M., 2014, "Mercury in Fishes from 21 National Parks in the Western United States—Inter- and Intra-Park Variation in Concentrations and Ecological Risk," U.S. Geological Survey Open-File Report 2014–1051, 54 *p.*, *http://dx.doi.org/10.3133/ofr20141051.*

Page 135: from "You're a What? Ornithologist," Bureau of Labor Statistics, Occupational Outlook Quarterly, Summer 2013.

Pages 135,142: from *History of Human Society* by Frank W. Blackmar, Charles Scribner's Sons, 1926.

Page 16: from *The Great Boer War* by Arthur Conan Doyle, 1900.

Page 68: from *Fermat's Enigma* by Simon Singh. Published by Doubleday, a division of Bantam Doubleday Dell Publishing Group, Inc., 1998. Copyright © 1997 by Simon Singh.

Page 14: from "Sustainability and Renewable Resources" by Steven Hayward, Ph.D., Elizabeth Fowler, and Laura Steadman. Copyright © 2000 by the Mackinac Center for Public Policy, Midland, Michigan.

Page 14: from OECD/Nuclear Energy Agency (2000), "Nuclear Energy in a Sustainable Development Perspective," *www.oecd-nea.org/sd.*

Page 29: from "What Poets Can Learn from Songwriters" by David Alpaugh in the October 2011 issue of *Scene4 Magazine*. Copyright © 2011 by David Alpaugh, copyright © 2011 *Scene4 Magazine.* Reprinted by permission of the author.

Page 30: from "*Cassini* Catches Titan Naked in the Solar Wind," NASA News and Features, January 28, 2015, Preston Dyches, *http://www.nasa.gov/jpl/cassini-catches-titan-naked-in-the-solar-wind/#.VNHkMiwpqQ8.*

Page 142: from "You're a What? Acupuncturist," Bureau of Labor Statistics, Occupational Outlook Quarterly, Summer 2002.

Page 136: from *Stained Glass of the Middle Ages in England and France*, Saint Lawrence, B., 1913.

Page 75: from "Adult and Youth Literacy: National, Regional and Global Trends, 1985–2015," UNESCO, 2013.

Page 31: from *No-No Boy* by John Okada. Published by the University of Washington Press, copyright © 2001. Reprinted by permission of the University of Washington Press.

Page 14: from *Disturbing the Universe* by Freeman Dyson. Published by Basic Books, 1981. Copyright © 1979 by Freeman J. Dyson. Reprinted by permission of Basic Books, a member of the Perseus Books Group.

Page 32: from "Medical Lessons from History," from *The Medusa and the Snail* by Lewis Thomas, copyright © 1974, 1975, 1976, 1977, 1978, 1979 by Lewis Thomas. Used by permission of Viking Penguin, a division of Penguin Group (USA) Inc.

Page 15: from "NASA Finds Friction from Tides Could Help Distant Earths Survive, and Thrive" Elizabeth Zubritsky, NASA's Goddard Space Flight Center, *http://www.nasa.gov/content/goddard/friction-from-tides-could-help-distant-earths-survive-and-thrive/#.VNL3bywpqQ8.*

Page 15: from John L. O'Sullivan, "The Great Nation of Futurity." It was originally published in 1839.

Page 76: from "Toxoplasmosis" by Hill, D. E., and Dubey, J. P., 2014, *U.S. Geological Survey Circular 1389, http://dx.doi.org/10.3133/cir1389.*

Page 77: from "Beyond Supply and Demand: Assessing the Ph.D. Job Market," Bureau of Labor Statistics, Occupational Outlook Quarterly, Winter 2002–2003.

Page 143: from "On the Art of Fiction" by Willa Cather, Knopf, The Borzoi, 1920.

Page 19: from *The Americanism of Washington* by Henry Van Dyke, 1906.

Page 65: from Suparna Choudhury, "Culturing the Adolescent Brain: What Can Neuroscience Learn from Anthropology?" *Social Cognitive and Affective Neuroscience*, 2010, 5(2–3), 159–167, by permission of Oxford University Press.

Page 17: from *The Art of Teaching* by Gilbert Highet, copyright © 1950, copyright renewed 1977 by Gilbert Highet. Used by permission of Alfred A. Knopf, a division of Random House, Inc.

Page 78: from "Healthcare: Millions of Jobs," Bureau of Labor Statistics, Occupational Outlook Quarterly, Spring 2014.

Page 18: from *The Indian Today: The Past and Future of the First American* by Charles A. Eastman (Ohiyesa), published by Doubleday, Page & Company, 1915.

Page 137: from *The History of Cuba*, Volume I, by Willis Fletcher Johnson, 1920.

Page 143: from Hiwasaki, L., Luna, E., Syamsidik, Shaw, R. "Local & Indigenous Knowledge for Community Resilience: Hydro-Meteorological Disaster Risk Reduction and Climate Change Adaptation in Coastal and Small Island Communities." Jakarta, UNESCO, 2014.

Page 45: from "Hotspots: Mantle Thermal Plumes" in *This Dynamic Earth: The Story of Plate Tectonics* by Jacquelyne Kious and Robert I. Tilling, U.S. Geological Survey, 1996.

Page 16: from *The Souls of Black Folk* by W. E. B. Du Bois, 1903.

Page 17: from *Lord Jim* by Joseph Conrad, 1917.

Page 11: from *Ex Libris: Confessions of a Common Reader* by Anne Fadiman. Copyright © 1998 by Anne Fadiman. Reprinted by permission of Farrar, Straus and Giroux, LLC.

Page 79: from Centers for Disease Control and Prevention, "Malaria Surveillance—United States, 2010," *MMWR* 2012; 61, pages 4–6.

Page 80: from "Wanted: Trained Teachers to Ensure Every Child's Right to Primary Education 2014," UNESCO, 2014, Policy Paper 15, Factsheet 30.

Page 138: from President Franklin Delano Roosevelt's Message to Congress on the State of the Union, January 11, 1944.

Page 139: from *An Artist's Letters from Japan* by John La Farge, published by The Century Company, New York, 1897.